HOW I BROKE INTO

HOLLYWOOD

ReganBooks

An Imprint of HarperCollins*Publishers*

HOW I BROKE INTO
HOLLYWOOD

★ SUCCESS STORIES FROM THE TRENCHES ★
PABLO F. FENJVES & ROCKY LANG

Photography Credits

Pages 4 and 290 by J. D. Rocks; page 12 by Gary Moss; page 22 by Michael Schmelling; page 28 by Richard Cartwright, courtesy of Spyglass Entertainment; page 38 by Michael Muller; page 58 by Marina Rice Bader; page 64 by Craig Motlong; page 76, *The Devil Wears Prada* © 2005 Twentieth Century Fox. All rights reserved. Page 82 by Jasin Boland; page 90 by John Russo; page 102 by Issa Sharp; page 112 by Chuck Gardner; page 122 by Peter McCabe; page 130 by Michael Yarish; page 136 by Bonnie Greenberg; page 146 by Barry King Hope; page 156 by Anthony Moore; page 166 by Claudette Barius; page 176 by Bob D'Amico; page 198 by Allan Mercer; page 214 by Scott Pasfield, 2002. Courtesy of IFC. Page 224 by Lynn London; page 232 courtesy of *The Bernie Mac Show* © 2002 Regency Television Productions, Inc. All rights reserved. Page 238 by Paul Ruscani; page 244 by Alexandra Penney; page 264 by Mika Manninen; page 270 by S. Tymer; page 298 by David James; page 308 by Jay Lawrence Goldman; page 318 by Lisa Flores; page 324 by Gene Page; page 336 by Linda Shamest; page 346 by Cyrille Schiff; page 362 by Victor Jih; page 370 by Pam Schwartz; page 380, *How Stella Got Her Groove Back* © 1998, Twentieth Century Fox. All rights reserved. Page 392 by Cliff Watts; all other photos courtesy of the contributors.

HarperCollins books may be purchased for educational, business, or sales promotional use. For information please write: Special Markets Department, HarperCollins Publishers Inc., 10 East 53rd Street, New York, NY 10022.

FIRST EDITION

Designed by Kris Tobiassen

Printed on acid-free paper
Library of Congress Cataloging-in-Publication Data

Fenjves, Pablo F.
    How I broke into Hollwood : success stories from the trenches / Pablo F. Fenjves and
Rocky Lang.—1st ed.
        p. cm.
    Includes index.
    ISBN-13: 978-0-06-078964-0 (alk. paper)
    ISBN-10: 0-06-078964-6 (alk. paper)
        1. Motion pictures—California—Los Angeles—Biography.   I. Lang, Rocky.   II. Title.

PN1998.2.F45 2006
791.4302'93—dc22
[B]

                                                                                    2006042536

06 07 08 09 10 RRD 10 9 8 7 6 5 4 3 2 1

For my son, Nick.

—PABLO

**For my dad, Jennings Lang,
who broke me into Hollywood.**

—ROCKY

CONTENTS

INTRODUCTION

If you want to break into Hollywood, if you *really, truly* want to break into Hollywood, you're already a little damaged. But don't worry. That helps. The odds of making it in this town are so slim that you can't think about them. In fact, you *shouldn't* think about them. Among the legions of people who arrive in Los Angeles every day, desperately hoping to find jobs in the entertainment industry, a few actually succeed. So why not you?

The men and women you are about to meet in these pages—actors, writers, editors, technicians, directors, producers, designers, executives—were once outsiders themselves. Some of them arrived knowing absolutely nothing about the business. Others came out of film school. Still others were self-taught, or *thought* they were self-taught, and showed up brandishing screenplays and low-budget movies—or what they *described* as movies.

Still, all of them made it.

Some of them will be familiar to you, notably the actors, but most of the others work behind the scenes, and—unless you're in the business already—you probably won't recognize their names. On the other hand, you *will* know their work. The men and women in this book lent their talents to some of the most successful feature films ever made, from *Star Wars* and *The Terminator* to *My Best Friend's Wedding* and *Out of Africa*. They have also left their mark on television: *The Cosby Show, Two and a Half Men, The*

O.C., Sex and the City, Curb Your Enthusiasm, Scrubs, and *Desperate Housewives,* to name just a few.

Now, in their own words, they're going to tell you how they did it.

You'll meet the kid who was answering phones on the set of *X-Men,* and ended up with sole screenwriting credit on a film that grossed more than $300 million.

You'll hear from a director who started as a production assistant on *Apocalypse Now* and whose first job was to hike into the mountains, locate a tribe of headhunters, and convince them to play extras in the movie.

There's the talent agent-turned-producer who applied for a job with the Central Intelligence Agency, certain he'd be happier in Langley, Virginia, than he was in Hollywood, only to be informed that he had *none* of the qualifications they were looking for. And there's the eleven-year-old girl who was told by her music teacher that she was tone deaf and wholly without talent, only to become the most successful songwriter of her generation.

You'll go back a few years to learn how Marlon Brando literally changed the life of an agent-trainee by tapping him as his representative. And you'll read about the young man who was dissuaded from trying to make it as an actor and went on to win two Academy Awards—as a director.

There's the producer whose very first job out of college involved getting lunch for the divine Robert Redford, and whose second job revolved around the needs of the less-divine Divine, a 300-pound transvestite. And there's the firefighter-turned-sound-mixer who has been nominated for an Academy Award an astonishing seventeen times, and is *still* polishing his acceptance speech.

You'll meet an athlete who gave up a successful career as a professional tennis player to make the kinds of movies he fell in love with as a child, in his native India, and a producer who had to choose between the William Morris mail room and the Harvard Business School, opting for the latter only because the agency had no openings.

You'll hear from an actor who spent seven years behind bars for manslaughter, discovered theater in prison, and went on to the Yale School of Drama and a brilliant career—on both stage and screen; from an Academy Award-winning producer who got his start by sneaking onto studio lots, pretending to be a messenger; and from a wide-eyed, fresh-faced college coed who parlayed her first job—getting beer for the guys in the truck—into a partnership at one of the most successful TV production companies in entertainment history.

You'll also hear from plenty of people you'll recognize, including Sydney Pollack, Bernie Mac, Peter Gallagher, Greg Germann, and David Paymer, and you'll find out how they paid their dues. Waiting tables. Cleaning apartments. Frying fish.

Beyond the personal stories, there is plenty of advice. Making it in Hollywood is about passion and originality and hard work. And it's about not quitting. If you really want to break in, monomania and self-delusion are a good start.

Yes, we know and you know: Hollywood is a fiercely competitive town. There are almost as many film schools and acting classes in Los Angeles as there are restaurants, and the local colleges and universities have turned film-related courses into a cottage industry. But some of those students are going to succeed: Statistically, it couldn't be otherwise.

And as long as we're talking statistics, here's a daunting one: The Writers Guild of America registers more than sixty thousand screenplays *every year*. That's more than a thousand a week; two hundred *every single day*. Very few will ever become movies, but those that do have the power to transform the lives of the men and women who wrote them. That's why they wrote them.

Yes, it's tough. People who make it in Hollywood are the ones who are almost pathologically impervious to defeat—the ones who believe in themselves to the point of madness. If that doesn't seem like too high a price, we have one word for you: *Believe*.

PABLO F. FENJVES
& ROCKY LANG
LOS ANGELES, FEBRUARY 2006

ASHOK AMRITRAJ

PRODUCER

"Even when you're at your lowest, you keep fighting. Even when you think you have nothing left, you keep swinging."

Ashok Amritraj, a native of India, began his career as a tennis pro, playing in every major tournament from Wimbledon to the U.S. Open. He eventually found his way to Los Angeles, where in 1978, after winning the World Team Tennis Championship, he decided to try his luck in Hollywood.

The business was a lot tougher than he imagined. After a number of lean years, convinced that the studio system was virtually impenetrable, he chose the independent route, an environment he felt better able to control.

The gamble paid off, eventually bringing him full circle. Today, as chairman and CEO of Hyde Park Entertainment, a company he founded, Mr. Amritraj is among the most successful producers in Hollywood. Some of his credits include *Bandits*, *Moonlight Mile*, *Bringing Down the House*, *Walking Tall*, and *Raising Helen*.

Mr. Amritraj was interviewed on June 3, 2005, at his Santa Monica office.

I was born and raised in Madras, India, which is now called Chennai, and attended Loyola College, a classic Jesuit school. When I was very young, I started playing tennis, and I represented India in the Junior Davis Cup. Before long, I was on the international tennis circuit. At age fifteen, I was in the Juniors at Wimbledon, and by age seventeen I had made it to the finals. Two years later, I was invited to play tennis in Los Angeles, with World Team Tennis.

I became part of the Los Angeles Strings, along with my brother, Vijay, and we played with some of the greats: Chris Evert, Ilie Nastase, Björn Borg, Martina Navratilova. This was at a time when tennis was becoming a hugely popular sport. I remember seeing many of the big studio heads in the stands, watching us play, and after the games I'd find myself socializing with all manner of celebrities, people like Sydney Poitier, Charlton Heston, and Sean Connery.

These were people I had seen in the big American movies, growing up in India, and while I'd seen plenty of Indian movies, too, I was partial to Hollywood films. I still remember sitting through the credits and seeing the tag-line at the very end of the some of the films: *When You're in Southern California, Visit Universal Studios.*

Well, here I was in Southern California, and from the very first day, I fell in love with the motion picture industry. I decided I was going to get into the movie business; it was only a question of when and how. I thought tennis was my way in, and I imagined that my friendships with these powerful people in the industry would give me a leg up. I was hanging out with these guys. *How difficult could it be to break in?*

In 1978, the Los Angeles Strings won the World Team Tennis Championship. It was a big year, with lots of television coverage, and I was voted Most Valuable Player. I was handed the keys to a brand-new Jaguar, and in some ways that helped make up my mind. I was definitely going to get into the movie business.

Unfortunately, I had seriously underestimated what it was going to take. For the next five years, I optioned the rights to various plays and screenplays, but very little happened. I would send a script to the studio, and I would wait two weeks before calling the executive. They generally took my calls right away, and for the next fifteen or twenty minutes, they would ask me for pointers on their backhand, or on ways to get more spin into their serve. Then I would get around to the business at hand.

"I sent you a script two weeks ago," I'd say.

"Oh, yeah," they'd reply. "We already passed on that."

After five years of developing screenplays, I decided I should try my luck with independent movies. I wanted to be on a set, making movies, and controlling which movies got made. If nothing else, I had taste, and I had opinions, and I could make my own decisions about what I wanted to see on the screen. This was in the mid-1980s, and it was a real boom-time for the video market. HBO and USA were making first-run movies, and they were hungry for material, and I thought I could capitalize on that.

I ended up raising a little money, and risking some of my own, and I made a few small movies in the $1 million- to $3 million range. Some of the money had come from foreign distributors, and many of the films were profitable, so they continued to invest. I loved every minute of it. Before long, I was making eight or nine of these small movies a year. I remember standing in the Arizona desert in the 120-degree heat and absolutely loving it. It was fabulous. I was running from pillar to post, feeling young and energetic and ready to do it all. This was genuine moviemaking. I had wasted five years trying to develop scripts and sitting in on endless studio meetings, and nothing had come of it, but now I was making movies and becoming an actual producer.

There's a real art to low-budget movies, by the way, and it's worth learning. In the Hollywood studio business, when people get into trouble, they just throw more money at the picture and the problem goes away. Or not. But in the low-budget world, you are forced to make do with what you have. It's a great training ground.

In 1990, during my annual pilgrimage to Cannes, where I was busy raising money for my next batch of movies, a good-looking young man spotted me and hurried over.

"Ashok!" he exclaimed. "Do you remember me?"

I did remember him. Five or six years earlier, when I was an out-of-work producer, sitting in my little office in Los Angeles, going through my mail, I opened a manila envelope and found myself looking at a photograph of this same young man. He seemed like a nice enough person, even in the photograph, so I invited him in for a chat, and he came over. He couldn't speak English very well, but we managed.

"What do you do?" I asked him.

"I act."

"And what do you do for a living?"

"I drive limousines."

Now here he was in Cannes, these many years later, shaking my hand and smiling. "Do you know that I sent copies of that photograph to 800 producers in Los Angeles," he said, "and that I only got one response—from you."

"No," I replied. "I didn't know that."

"Well," he said. " "You and I are going to make a movie together."

That young man's name was Jean-Claude Van Damme. In 1990, we made *Double Impact* together. It was my first big break and his first big break. The film cost $11 million to make and grossed over a $100 million worldwide. That movie catapulted me into the mainstream action-movie business. For the next five or six years, I started making movies in the $10- to $15-million range, with stars like Cuba Gooding Jr., Alec Baldwin, and Antonio Banderas. Most of them, while released domestically, were oriented toward the foreign market, with which I was already quite familiar, and which was very vibrant in the mid-1990s.

In the years that followed, I formed Hyde Park Entertainment and began to cofinance major studio movies. By putting up a significant portion of the budget, I was able to hold on to the foreign rights—a mainstay of my business. In fact, on many of my projects, the studio only functions as a distribution partner in the United States and Canada, and they leave most of the decisions to me.

It had always been my dream to make movies in Hollywood. Today, the reality has far exceeded the dream. At this point in my career, I've made about ninety movies, and I believe I've had the pleasure of working with most of the studios. I've also worked with some of the most talented actors in the business, including Dustin Hoffman, Susan Sarandon, Steve Martin, Antonio Banderas, Bruce Willis, Cate Blanchett, and Angelina Jolie. This year, I have two films opening on the same day in October, and both of them premiered at the Toronto Film Festival. One is *Shopgirl*, with Steve Martin and Claire Danes, which is based on Martin's own novella, a comedy/drama about a girl who works at Saks Fifth Avenue in Los Angeles. The other is *Dreamer*, with Kurt Russell and Dakota Fanning. It's a wonderful, touching story about a horse trainer, his daughter, and the injured horse they hope to race.

I love the movie business, but if I knew then what I know now, I must admit that I probably would have remained in tennis. The first five or six years were incredibly difficult. I was leaving a fairly successful and lucrative career in sports, and going into a business I assumed would be fairly easy to break into. I knew a lot of people in the business, some of them famous and powerful, and I thought they would pave the way.

But the truth is, this town really grinds you pretty good. You have to pay your dues. And there's more to it than just knowing people and working hard. Hard work is a given. You'll work harder than you can imagine. What you need is passion. I know the word is overused, but it's overused for a reason. Only passion is going to give you the staying power to succeed. Passion. Discipline. Hard work. Focus. Persistence. But passion above all. You really have to want it to make it.

If I were to compare the movie business to tennis, I would tell you that it's a five-setter every day. You think you have nothing left to give, but you reach inside and find what you need to get you through the next point.

But even that comparison doesn't do it justice. Sport has a certain purity to it. If you play better than the other guy, you're going to win. If he plays better, he wins. It's that simple: The result can be directly attributed to your talent and performance and hard work. The movie business, on the other hand, is elusive and full of gray areas, and only now, more than two decades later, am I beginning to figure out certain aspects of it. Still, I honestly believe that one of the things that got me through the early days was the discipline I learned on the tennis court. You keep your eye on the ball. You keep practicing that swing until it's flawless. You never waver. Even when you're at your lowest, you keep fighting. Even when you think you have nothing left, you keep swinging.

I used to train with Pancho Gonzalez, and he taught me that I had to honestly believe that all the hard work would eventually pay off. That was immensely helpful to me in the film business in the early years, when absolutely nothing was happening. I told myself that it would eventually pay off, and I believed it.

Now, these many years later, my career and my life are much more balanced. I went though an arranged marriage, and it just so happens that my wife and I fell in love *after* we were married. We have two kids now, ages eleven and seven, and my family means everything to me. If you're part of a close family, it makes the business easier to handle. When I get home to my wife and kids, I can let go of the business. And I need that distance. This business is mentally exhausting. If you don't get away from time to time, it will drive you insane.

If you're trying to break in, the best advice I can give you is this: You have to be monomaniacal to succeed, but you have to take a break from it once in a while. Success comes to those who find balance.

SUSAN BEAVERS
WRITER/PRODUCER

"If you're really serious about breaking in, start at the bottom."

Susan Beavers began her writing career by answering phones for the producer of *Barney Miller*, and subsequently worked on a number of sitcoms before the sitcom was declared dead. Her credits include *Gimme a Break!*, *Newhart*, *Golden Girls*, *Growing Pains*, *My Sister Sam*, *Hudson Street*, *Dharma & Greg*, and—more recently—the runaway hit *Two and a Half Men*, on which she is both writer and executive producer.

Ms. Beavers had a tenuous connection to the business, through her father, and fell into television production almost by accident. But once she discovered the thrill of hearing someone say something in front of the cameras, *something she had written*, she was hooked.

Ms. Beavers lives in Santa Monica, California, with her son, Jackson, and more dogs than she can count. She was interviewed on May 14, 2005, at her home, while her son and his friend, Nick, played video games in the next room.

I was born right here in Santa Monica, not far from where I live now. My father used to work for Chevrolet, and he was in charge of looking for television shows for them to sponsor. He would spend a great deal of time

watching pilots and making recommendations to the company, and months later the shows would appear on TV, accompanied by those magic words: "Brought to you by Chevrolet!" Some of the shows he picked included *Bonanza*, *Bewitched*, and *My Three Sons*, so he had a pretty good track record.

I guess you could say that television has always been part of my life, even peripherally. My father became friendly with one of the writer-producers on *Bewitched*, a man named Danny Arnold, and Danny and his wife, Donna, would often come over to our house with their two sons, David and Dannel. Danny's company was called 4-D Productions, for reasons that are fairly obvious.

In any event, whenever they came over, my five younger brothers and sisters and I would all perform for Danny, to show him that we were star material. I remember marching around my parents' living room, singing and dancing and twirling my baton and grinning to beat the band. I also remember riding around in Danny's Rolls Royce when I was sixteen years old. I thought he probably should have been driving a Chevy, to show his allegiance to the company that supported his show, but one day he let me take the car for a spin around the block and I didn't think so anymore. I thought the Rolls Royce had been a magnificent choice.

I ended up going to college at Cal State, in Northridge, and living at home. I was an English major, and I was sitting in the living room reading *The Norton Anthology of English Literature*, when I paused to answer the ringing phone. "Susan Beavers, please," a woman said. "Danny Arnold calling."

"This is Susan Beavers," I said. I thought this was ridiculous. Why couldn't Danny dial his own phone?

"Hold on for Mr. Arnold please."

A moment later, there he was. "Hey kid," Danny said. "You want to make a couple of bucks?"

"Sure," I said.

"Great," he said. "Be in my office Monday morning."

I don't think he knew I was in college, and I'm not sure he cared. I showed up at his office on Monday, early. He was at CBS at the time, on the Radford lot, and I didn't know what was expected of me—whether I was going to get his lunch, wash his car, or toss my baton around for a roomful of executives. I walked into the office and found him and a fellow writer, Jerry Davis, trying to figure out how to make coffee using a paper towel instead of a filter. The secretary had quit, and apparently she hadn't bothered telling them where she kept the coffee filters.

"Kid," Danny said. "That's your desk and these are your filing cabinets and that's your typewriter."

And I said, "You've made a terrible mistake. I can't type and I don't know anything about filing. I can wait tables and I can tell you more than you want to know about junior miss clothing, but that's the extent of my job skills—so far."

"That's okay," he said. "We just finished shooting the pilot for *Barney Miller* and we're waiting to see if it gets picked up. I can't afford a real secretary."

"What do I do?" I asked worriedly.

"Well, it's not that hard," he said. "When the phone rings, pick it up and say, '4-D Productions.' And if they ask for me, say, 'No, I'm sorry. Danny's at the race track.' Then take a message."

With that, he left, trailing cigar smoke, and he took Jerry with him.

That was my first job in show business. I had to reschedule all my classes—I took a couple very early in the morning, and the rest late in the day, after I was done at work—but it was worth it: I was making seventy-five dollars a week.

I was usually the only person in the office; Danny actually *was* always at the race track, but he'd call in from time to time—he had one of the earliest car phones, a prototype for all I know—to see what was going on. I didn't know what was going on. I was busy teaching myself to type on the IBM Selectric. I had bought a record album that came with plastic flip-up keys that showed you the letters as you typed, and I was struggling along. I also read absolutely everything in the office, including the scripts that arrived every day, day after day.

One morning, big surprise, Danny actually showed up at the office. "Kid," he said. "Can you type?"

"Yes," I lied.

"Good," he said. "This is a treatment for a new show. I'm going to need it first thing tomorrow morning."

He had a Dictaphone—I'm dating myself here—and he handed me a tape. I got to work at around noon. At ten thirty that night I was still on the first page. I didn't know how to erase. Every time I made a mistake, I had to start over. At one point I found myself literally crying, and some woman from down the hall popped her head in to find out what was wrong. She worked for Dino De Laurentiis, the famous producer, and they had only recently moved in, and they were busy setting up well into the night.

"I can't type," I said, drying my tears. "I'm supposed to have this ready by morning, and I always make a mistake just as I'm getting near the bottom of the first page."

"Don't you have Ko-Rec-Type?" she asked.

No, I did not have Ko-Rec-Type. I had never heard of Ko-Rec-Type. But it sure sounded like that's what I needed.

It still took me six hours to finish the treatment. I left it on Danny's desk at 4:30 in the morning, went home, got some sleep, and I was back in the office before ten. When I walked in, I could smell the cigar smoke, so I knew he was there. I went into his office and he was reading it, and all I could think was, *Dear God, I hope he didn't find any mistakes.* Still, now that I'd had a little sleep, I could see how genuinely terrible the pages looked. Ko-Rec-Type helped cover the mistakes, but when every other stroke is a mistake, it's still a long way from perfect.

Danny finished reading and looked up at me, slowly, and I could see he felt badly for me. "Kid," he said, "What time did you leave here?"

"Oh, not a bad time," I said. "A regular time."

"What time?" he repeated gently.

"Eight-thirty. Maybe nine o'clock."

He took a long beat. "Well, you did a good job, kid."

Clearly, the man was blind.

The treatment I'd typed up for Danny was about some guy who got hit by lightning and could make things happen, and it didn't go anywhere. But *Barney Miller* got picked up. It was a comedy about cops, for those of you who weren't around then, and it starred Hal Linden, Barbara Barrie, Abe Vigoda, Max Gail, Ron Glass, and Jack Soo.

Suddenly I was part of a show, and I was actually being paid to be part of a show, so I started paying attention. It was absolutely astonishing. Danny would think of something, put it down on paper, fiddle with it a little, and the next thing I knew the actors were rehearsing and everyone was laughing.

This was my first awareness of the craft of writing, of dialogue, and one of the lessons I took from watching Danny work was that you always had to be true to the character. The character couldn't just say something to move the plot along. The character had to say something because that's who he or she *was*.

There were other writers on the show, of course: Chris Hayward, who later worked on *Alice*; Tony Sheehan, who graduated to *Mr. Belvedere*; and Reinhold Weege, who created *Park Place* but had much more success with *Night Court*. At the beginning of the week, they would sit around and try to come up with stories, and they'd rustle up six or seven pages, which I dutifully went off and typed. But by the end of the week, they'd have a finished script—a full sixty or seventy pages. I'd have to type the entire script on mimeograph paper, and pump copies out on the roller. It was exhausting, but it was also exhilarating: I was watching a television show come to life.

One Friday, they were working on an episode called "Community Relationships," and they didn't have an ending. Danny got up and put on his jacket and said, "I'm going to the track. Somebody come up with an ending for this." He was talking to Tony and Reinie, of course, but I took it as a personal challenge and got to work. I wrote a three-page ending and left it on his desk.

When Danny got back from the track, I was on stage, working on the set, and he called down and asked the associate producer if they'd started rehearsing the ending yet. And the producer said, "Which ending?" And Danny said, "The one where they make the bet."

Well, that was *my* ending. "You mean Susan's ending?" the producer said. There was a long pause—it was obvious Danny hadn't known—and then he said, "Yeah. Susan's ending."

I don't know what Danny was thinking at that moment, but he was probably wondering if he should stop going to the track: It obviously wasn't safe to leave us alone in the office.

He had Tony and Reinie rewrite my three pages, but some of my words actually survived. There was something miraculous about it. I had just been given a taste of something unlike anything I'd ever experienced, and I was hooked.

I worked on *Barney Miller* for two years, but not as a writer. I was basically there to learn, and that's what I did: I devoured every script that crossed my desk. When we were in rehearsal, I was able to watch the transition from printed word to spoken word, and I began to figure out what worked and what didn't. Sometimes something looked great on paper, but it didn't translate. And sometimes the opposite was true: A line that looked dull on the page got the biggest laugh.

When I left *Barney Miller*, I went to work on *Fish*, as a script supervisor, which was a step up for me. Later, I did more of the same on a few specials, some short-lived sitcoms, and then on *Soap*.

When *Soap* got cancelled, I still wasn't a writer, and I wasn't sure I was ever going to become one, so I ended up taking a job in Northern California, helping a multimillionaire turn one of his properties into a resort. I wasn't happy there, however—that was the real world, where people went to work in suits and skirts and kept normal hours and tried to be politically correct—and before long I was back in Los Angeles.

I ended up sleeping on a futon in a friend's laundry room, until I got a job on *Night Court* as a script supervisor, thanks to my old friend Reinhold Weege. One day, while watching rehearsals, I decided to write a spec script, to show people I could write, but *Night Court* wasn't really my thing. I ended up writing a spec script based on *It's a Living*, a show that had been cancelled two years earlier. That was pretty naïve. If you're going to write a spec script, it's best to base it on the current hot show, not on something that got flushed down the toilet a few seasons back.

As luck would have it, however, and unbeknownst to me, *It's a Living* was in the process of being picked up for first-run syndication, and one of the associate producers on *Night Court* was friendly with the people at Witt-Thomas, the company that owned the show. She sent it over and they bought it. It was the strangest thing. I had sold a sample script, based on a cancelled show. This was unheard of. Clearly somebody up there was trying to tell me something: I was going to become a writer.

Now I needed an agent. I didn't know much about this part of the business, either. I looked at the lists of agents and at the names of agents on the phone logs, trying to find a popular one—an agent whose name was always popping up. There was a man named Stu Robinson at a company called Robinson-Weintraub, and I called him cold. "Stu Robinson, please," I barked at the secretary, trying to bluff my way past her. "Susan Beavers calling."

"What can we do for you?" she asked.

"I'd like to hire him as my agent," I said.

"I'm sorry. Have you been produced? We only take writers who've been produced."

"Well, I think I have. Or I'm about to be. Witt-Thomas just bought my spec."

There was a beat. "Hold on," she said.

A moment later, Stu Robinson got on the phone and agreed to meet with me, and two days later I walked into his office. Before I even sat down, he said, "Let's get this out of the way first: Do you know Jim Beavers?"

"Yes," I said. "He's my dad."

Stu was floored. "You know something," he said, "back in the day when your father worked in development, he was the only guy who was nice to me. I was a young agent then, and he was the only one who bothered listening to me."

And that's how Stu Robinson became my agent.

I wrote an episode of *Golden Girls* and another for *Newhart*. Warner Brothers put me on the staff of *Growing Pains*, which I was already familiar with: I had been the script supervisor on the pilot, and now I was back as a writer. I couldn't believe it. They were paying me to write!

While I was still coming to terms with this, somebody at Warner Brothers asked if I could write a pilot in nine days. They had the concept and the story, but the original writer, Stephen Fischer, had to go home to tend to his dying father.

Nine days later, I turned in a finished pilot, based completely on Stephen's original idea. Of course I was new at this, and the nine days turned into nine drafts, but that script became the pilot for *My Sister Sam*, a comedy about a woman photographer whose sister comes to live with her. It was Stephen's show, but he was kind enough to petition the Writers Guild to give me credit. As a result of his generosity, I got a check on every single episode.

After *Growing Pains*, I worked on *Empty Nest*, *Nurses*, and *Dudley*, a show I created with Dudley Moore. I also did several episodes of *The Office*, starring Valerie Harper. This was in the old days, when the half-hour sitcom was king.

I also worked briefly on *Hudson Street*, a cop show with Tony Danza, and at one point they asked me to run the show. I wasn't crazy about the idea—what did I know about cops?—but I did it. When we first aired, they put us up against a show starring John Lithgow as an alien. We were ecstatic. That was about the most ridiculous idea we'd ever heard, so we knew they didn't have a chance. We were wrong. That show turned out to be *3rd Rock from the Sun*, and it killed us. *Hudson Street* got very dead very fast. Tony was crushed. He loved his show.

In 1996, I stopped working to have a baby. Looking around, I noticed I didn't have a husband, so I decided to do it on my own, through artificial insemination. The result was my wonderful son, Jackson. The whole experience was and continues to be a miracle, but having taken a year off to raise my baby, I realized I had to write something new. I had just lived through an experience that was full of comedic potential. The process was incredibly Byzantine—the insemination, the doctors, the friends who support you, the ones who think you simply got knocked up—and I knew there was something there.

But here's the thing: I was only writing the script to show people what I was capable of doing. It was a spec pilot, and it was never going to get produced, so I could get as crazy as I wanted to. And that's what I did: I wrote a pilot with a staggering forty-six scenes, which included film within film, and all sorts of crazy flashbacks, and my agent sent it around to show people that Susan Beavers still had the touch.

Within days, I got a call from the Lifetime network. "We want to make this," they said.

"Excuse me?"

"We want to make this."

I tried to talk them out of it, but they wouldn't listen. The show was called *Oh Baby*. I executive produced it for two years. It was my favorite job ever and a true labor of love.

These days, with the sitcom in trouble, I feel very lucky to be working on one of the few surviving shows, *Two and a Half Men*. No one really knows why this show works where others have failed, but I think it's because it is emotionally honest; because it has heart.

If you're a writer, and you're trying to get into the business, my advice would be to write the best spec script you can. But write from the heart. Write something because you truly understand it and feel it. That's when you do your best work.

Of course, that's no guarantee of anything, either. If you're on the outside, it's hard to get anyone to read your script. So if you're *really* serious about breaking in, start at the bottom. If you're in the production office making coffee, and you write a script, you can actually, physically hand it to them, and—take my word for it—they will actually, physically read it. (They'll also tell you what's wrong with it, so don't let them see it unless you can take it.)

"Hey, Bob, nice job washing my car today. How are you doing?"

"I wrote a script."

"Really?"

"Yes."

"Let me read it."

You might still be washing cars a year or two from now, but maybe not. If the script is as good as you think it is, your car washing days are over.

BRUCE BERMAN

CEO, VILLAGE ROADSHOW

"It really boils down to a combination of things: a good resume, some contacts, the willingness to do the work, and qualities that set you apart from the pack."

Bruce Berman was born in New York but came west with his family when he was twelve. He dabbled in photography in high school, and later on gave serious thought to becoming a movie director. But after two years of film school, he decided he was better suited for the life of a studio executive, and he went off to study law.

Berman returned to Hollywood with a law degree and parlayed it into a series of jobs that paved the way to the position he holds today: chairman and CEO of Village Roadshow Pictures.

As a young film executive, he worked on such hits at *Fast Times at Ridgemont High*, *The Breakfast Club*, and *Sixteen Candles*. As an executive at Warner Brothers, he was involved in the production of dozens of movies, including *Presumed Innocent*, *Goodfellas*, *Robin Hood*, *The Bodyguard*, and *The Fugitive*. And as top man at Village Roadshow, he has overseen the production of more than forty films, including *The Martrix*, *Three Kings*, *Training Day*, *Ocean's Eleven*, *Mystic River*, *Charlie and the Chocolate Factory*, and *The Dukes of Hazzard*.

Berman was interviewed at his Burbank office on July 25, 2005.

I was born in Manhattan and grew up in Great Neck, New York. When I was twelve, the family moved to Santa Monica, California. My father had a heart condition, and he moved us here for his health. When I was in high school, we moved again—this time to Palm Springs.

I went to Palm Springs High, and I was interested in photography. I still am, but I'm a collector now, not a shooter. I was also interested in film. I loved the movies of the 1930s and 1940s: *Out of the Past, The Postman Always Rings Twice, Double Indemnity*. I also loved Hitchcock.

I went to Bennington College, in Vermont, and I wasn't sure what I was going to do with my life, so I majored in history. At the end of the first year, however, I transferred to California Institute of the Arts, in Valencia. I decided I was going to become a film director. I spent two years there, and I actually started a feature-length documentary on people who believed in UFOs—these sort of UFO cultists. I didn't have the money to finish it, but I still think it would have made a good film.

I met a number of people at Cal Arts who would later play significant roles in my career, including Sean Daniel and Thom Mount, but after two years I decided that I needed to find a career in which I could make a living. Directing seemed like a long shot to me.

I was curious about the people who ran the studios, so I began to look into who they were. When I discovered that many of them had law degrees, I set my sights on law school. Up until that point, I had taken a lot of artsy classes, so I went to UCLA for two years to get more academic credits, and in 1975 I went off to Georgetown Law School, in Washington, D.C.

While I was there, I was introduced to Jack Valenti, who at the time was chairman and chief executive officer of the Motion Picture Association of America. I offered to work for him free, saying I'd do anything, and he gave me a small job at the MPAA, with an equally small salary. I worked for him part-time during the academic year, and full-time during the summers.

Meanwhile, I had to think about what I was going to do when I got out of law school. I wanted to go to work for one of the Hollywood studios, but it was very difficult to get a studio gig in those days. I didn't want to end up unemployed, however, so I interviewed with several law firms, too.

At around that time, back in 1976, Universal and Disney were suing Sony over the Betamax Case. Sony had introduced this then-revolutionary recording device, and the Hollywood studios felt that the machine's ability to copy programming off the air was an infringement of copyright. They wanted nothing less than to halt the sale of the devices. I found the case so interesting that I decided to write an article about it for the *Law Review*. I spent all of my free time working on the article, and in the end I wasn't able to get it published, but Jack Valenti read it and liked it and submitted it to all the studios as a reference tool. It got me a lot of attention, and I got interviews at all the studios. I hoped it would lead to a job, but no job materialized.

Then I got a call from Peter Guber, the producer. He had read my unpublished article and was himself very interested in the new technology. He offered me a job, on a week-to-week basis, and I took it. I was basically a gofer, doing anything Peter wanted me to do. I would fill his car with gas (this was 1978, and there were gas lines that year); I took his wife's clothes to the cleaners; I went to Santa Ynez to look at property for him. But I also helped write a prospectus when he decided to sell part of his company, and that worked out very well.

About a year into the job, Guber was getting ready to hire two creative executives, and it became clear that I wasn't one of them. He had offered me a job at business affairs, and I was either going to take that or leave. So I left. The handwriting was on the wall. There was no reason for me to stick around.

I called Sean Daniel, whom I knew from Cal Arts, and who was over at Universal with Thom Mount, another Cal Arts graduate, and I asked him if they could use me there. Sean told me that they had just hired a creative executive, but that I should come over and meet Joel Silver, one of the other guys they were working with. I went over and met with Sean and Joel, and a week later they hired me as a creative executive. I believe they told my unfortunate predecessor that things weren't working out with him.

They found a desk for me in the steno pool, a room that no longer exists. It was where the scripts where transcribed, and all I heard all day was the clacking of fifty typewriters. It made telephone conversation next to impossible.

For the next year, I worked exclusively with Sean and Joel, and then Joel left Universal. At that point, I became Sean's right-hand man, and I eventually worked my way up to vice president of production. In those days, Universal could be a very bureaucratic place, and there were essentially three things that filmmakers cared about: office space, parking, and setting up screenings. I made sure I was connected with the people in charge—nothing was beneath me—and I had those three elements wired. This was very helpful to everyone involved, and Sean was impressed enough that he let me supervise my first movie, *Fast Times at Ridgemont High*. Other movies followed in quick succession: *The Incredible Shrinking Woman, Xanadu, Where the Buffalo Roam, The Breakfast Club,* and *Sixteen Candles*.

I enjoyed everything about the movie business. It was my life. I would get to work early and stay on the lot till ten at night, and then a few of us would go get dinner somewhere and talk about movies. That's what we did and it seemed as if it was *all* we did: worked on movies. I became close with a number of directors, including Joel Schumacher, Cameron Crowe, and John Hughes.

One night, during a test screening for *Fast Times*, I was sitting with Amy Heckerling, the director, and Cameron Crowe, who had written both the book and the screenplay, and the three of us were absolutely thrilled at the way people were responding to Jeff Spicoli, Sean Penn's character. And we sat down after the screening and invented a whole new scene for Sean, a dream sequence where he's surfing.

There was lots of craziness in those days. I remember being asked to go find some hookers for Andy Kaufman, but I didn't do it. I guess *some* jobs were beneath me. Somebody did it, though.

I also remember the way Sean Daniel and Joel Silver would walk around the near-empty lot, late at night, saying, "One day we're going to run this place!"

I also met my wife, Nancy, during this period. She was in creative advertising, and she used to come in to show me the ad campaigns. Sean and Joel had hired her away from Warner Brothers, and before I met her they told me, "You're going to fall in love with her." And it was true: It really *was* love at first sight. But I didn't ask her out until many months later, when Peter Guber hired her away at double her salary. At that point, I thought it was okay to ask her out, since we weren't working together, and it was a very short courtship: six months.

Then something very bad happened: A guy named Frank Price came to the studio. Frank had his own way of doing things, and he had the right to do them his way, but it wasn't the way I'd been doing them. I got an offer from Mark Rosenberg, at Warner Brothers, and even though it was a lateral move, I decided I wanted to take the job. Universal wouldn't let me out of my contract, though. They gave me a raise and told me to go back to work.

Two months later, still unhappy, the raise notwithstanding, I called Rosenberg and asked him if the offer was still good. He said it was, so I went in to see Frank Price to take another stab at getting out of my contract. I told him I wasn't happy, and that I could hardly face the elevator to get to my office. A few days later, I found myself standing in front of the dreaded elevator, next to Marvin Antonowsky, Frank Price's right-hand man. "I suggest you talk to an independent third party," he said.

"Who would that be?" I asked. "My wife?"

"No," he said. "A psychiatrist."

Eventually, they let me out my contract, and in 1984 I went to work for Mark Rosenberg and Mark Canton, at Warner Brothers. Canton was made head of production a short time later, and in the months ahead I got offers to run production at four different studios. Every time I got an offer, I went to see Bob Daly, who ran Warners with Terry Semel, and I would ask him if I could leave. "No," he'd say. "You're under contract. Go back to work."

Bob kept telling me I had a future at Warners, though he never promoted me, and I kept getting offers I was unable to accept. Finally, in 1989, Bob made good on his promise and made me head of production.

That lasted until 1996, when I started getting restless. I wrote up one of those Jerry McGuire–type mission statements, in which I suggested to Bob and Terry that they should form a new position at the studio—Head of the Motion Picture Group, that type of thing. After reading it, Bob and Terry suggested that I might want to be an independent producer, which was their way of firing me, and I started a company called Plan B.

The production deal was really part of a settlement, and it was very generous, but if you're on the lot and you're not being supported by the people who run the studio, you're really not going to accomplish anything. In order to succeed, they have to take an active interest in your success, and that wasn't happening.

Also, I realized I was more of a buyer than a seller. As a seller, you are expected to focus on two or three projects and work on them extensively to get them produced, and I wasn't all that comfortable in that position. I was more of a buyer. People would bring me things—a script, a book, a pitch—and I could choose the projects I responded to. That was my talent. I've always been very comfortable picking projects in order to create a menu.

It was obvious that I needed a change, that I needed to get back to what I enjoyed doing. So I set about trying to figure out how to work at one of those companies that were cofinancing movies, places like New Regency and Morgan Creek, and I happened to hear that Warners was talking to Village Roadshow about just such a deal.

I knew Graham Burke, the CEO of Village Roadshow Ltd., the parent company, and I also knew David Puttnam, who was on the board. So I discretely asked a few people to recommend me for the job, and two of the people who helped me get it, ironically enough, were Bob and Terry—the guys who had fired me only eighteen months earlier.

That was in 1997, and I am still here.

It is tough for me to give advice to people trying to break into the business. I broke in so long ago that I don't know if what I did then would be a good strategy today. But one of the reasons I wrote that article for the *Law Review*—the one that never got published—was because I knew people would notice it. I was interested in the subject, of course, and I knew something about it, and I also knew it would set me apart from the rest of the pack.

There are so many people trying to get entry-level jobs at the studios that that's what you need: something that differentiates you, something that makes people remember. In my case, I had worked for Jack Valenti, I had some real knowledge of the coming technology, and I had a legal background—all of which added up to a certain type of candidate. I also had relationships from film school, which served me well.

So it really boils down to a combination of things: a good resume, some contacts, the willingness to do the work, and qualities that set you apart from the pack. That's what gets you through the door. And that's when the real work starts.

ROGER BIRNBAUM

CEO, SPYGLASS ENTERTAINMENT

"If you have a point of view, and you have the ability to articulate that point of view, you have a good chance of breaking in."

Roger Birnbaum is cochairman and CEO of Spyglass Entertainment Group, which he runs with his partner, Gary Barber. Their films include *The Sixth Sense*, *Seabiscuit*, *The Insider*, *Bruce Almighty*, and *The Pacifier*.

Before that, Birnbaum cofounded Caravan Pictures, where he was responsible for such box-office hits as *Rush Hour*, *Grosse Pointe Blank*, and *While You Were Sleeping*, and earlier in his career he was president of Worldwide Production and executive vice president of Twentieth Century Fox, where he oversaw production of *Home Alone*, *Sleeping with the Enemy*, *Edward Scissorhands*, and many other hits.

In a previous role, as president of production for United Artists, he developed *Rain Man*, which was nominated for eight Academy Awards and went home with four: Best Picture, Best Director (Barry Levinson), Best Actor (Dustin Hoffman) and Best Screenplay (Ronald Bass and Barry Morrow).

At the time of the interview, which took place on August 15, 2005, at Birnbaum's Westwood office, the company was awaiting the release of two films: *Memoirs of a*

(*From left*) Roger Birnbaum, Owen Wilson, and Jackie Chan on the set of *Shanghai Knights*

Geisha, directed by Rob Marshall, and *The Legend of Zorro*, which reunites Catherine Zeta-Jones and Antonio Banderas for director Martin Campbell.

I was born in Teaneck, New Jersey, and—like every kid growing up in the late 1950s and early 1960s—I spent a lot of time going to the movies, especially the Saturday afternoon double-features. I never thought about the movies as a business, though; I just really liked movies.

When I was in high school, I saw a movie called *Putney Swope*. The movie was directed by Robert Downey Sr., and it was a send-up of the advertising business, where a black guy accidentally becomes head of an ad agency. Early in the film, he calls a board meeting to allay everyone's worst fears. "Don't worry," he says, "I'm not going to rock this boat. I'm going to *sink* it."

There was another character in the film who always wore fatigues, and by the time I got to the University of Denver—where I thought, briefly, about going into the Foreign Service—I sometimes dressed in fatigues as an homage to that character.

One afternoon, while wearing my customary fatigues, I invited a college friend to go to the movies with me. "Fine," he said. "But I'm on the Board of Governors for the school, and we're meeting to nominate a new president, so we have to make a quick stop."

I went to the meeting with him, which was filled with mostly fraternity and sorority people, a very straitlaced crowd that reminded me of the *Putney Swope* boardroom scene. I sat back and watched, waiting for the meeting to be over so we could go to the movies. Someone nominated a preppy girl for the Board of Governors, and somebody else seconded it, and then my friend looked over at me—in fatigues, unshaven, with longish hair—and said, "I nominate Roger Birnbaum." A moment later, a guy with a sense of humor seconded the nomination, and the next thing I knew I was president of the Board of Governors. We were rocking our own boat.

I was barely nineteen years old and suddenly it was my responsibility to bring speakers and entertainers to the school. I invited William Kunstler, the radical lawyer, and also Ralph Nader. I booked James Taylor. Suddenly I was in show business, bringing all sorts of entertainers to the school. I didn't necessarily "rock the boat" or even "sink it," but I certainly had fun.

One day, I was on the phone with my brother in California. He was studying film and sharing a place with a guy who was managing a band called The Persuasions—five African American guys singing a cappella. The guy was hoping I could do him a favor and book the band for a show at the school.

They arrived in Denver with nowhere to stay—no one had thought it through—and I told them they could crash in my apartment. Five African American guys and me, in a one-room, studio apartment. The next day, they did their show and got a great reception and then thanked me and went on their way.

At the end of that first year, college didn't hold my interest anymore, and I left without graduating, much to my father's chagrin. One evening, over dinner, he asked me what I intended to do for the rest of my life, though not in such polite terms, and I told him not to worry—that I could get a job. The next day I was driving a taxi, running people between New Jersey and Manhattan, and at the end of the first week, I was robbed. I thought, *This job is not for me.*

My mother stepped in. She knew someone who worked for NBC radio, Ben Grauer, a fairly well-known broadcaster, and she sent me to see him. "Maybe there's a job for you there," she said.

I went to see Grauer, who didn't know what to do with me, but he suggested I fill out an application to become a page, and to try to work my way up from there. I wasn't particularly interested in the job, but staying out of my father's way was a great motivator, so I filled out an application.

A few weeks later, I got a call from NBC: "You're hired."

I went to work as a page. I had to wear a suit and take people on tours of the NBC radio and TV studios, which I found pretty humiliating. I knew right from the very first day that the job wasn't for me, so I asked around and heard about this thing called The Job Board. It was basically a bulletin board where they listed all the jobs that were available within the organization, and I went over and had a look and saw an opening in something called Broadcast Control. The word "control" appealed to me. I didn't bother to look at the fine print, which included the word "technical."

I applied for the job. A week later, I got a call and went to see someone to discuss it and they hired me on the spot. The other pages were amazed. Some of them had been there forever, and they had never heard of anyone moving so quickly to another position. I really thought I was on my way. This sounded big.

On my first day, I was ushered into a room the size of a closet—I kid you not. My job was to sit in that room, in front of a TV set, and keep a log, manually, of every single commercial that aired—from Charmin toilet paper to Hershey's chocolates. I was basically creating a log for the FCC (Federal Communications Commission), and my entire job consisted of sitting in that room watching soap operas and waiting with my pen poised for the commercials to kick in.

Five weeks into the job, I found myself thinking incessantly about soap operas. I was beginning to understand their appeal. It worried me. I was scared by what was happening to me. I also knew all the commercials by heart. Plus I had radiation burns on my eyes from sitting so close to the TV.

One afternoon, I was walking down the street and I ran into my brother's old roommate, the guy who used to manage The Persuasions.

"What are you doing?" he asked me.

"I'm going to lunch," I said. I didn't think he meant with my *life;* I thought he meant at that very moment.

We went to lunch together. He told me he was an A&R executive at Capitol Records, and explained that "A&R" stood for Artists and Repertoire, which was the division of the label responsible for scouting and developing talent. "I'm looking for a secretary," he said.

"How much are you paying?" I asked.

"A hundred and ten a week," he said.

That was a lot more than I was getting at NBC, so I took the job. I became his secretary at Capitol Records in New York. He was still managing The Persuasions, along with a lot of other acts, and he was often away from the office for several days at a time. Whenever he left town, I would listen to some of the tapes that people submitted, and one day I came across a tape I kind of liked. I called the contact number on the tape, and I told the guy on the phone to come in to see me. The next day, these three guys came in. I didn't even know what I was supposed to do. They said they were looking for a record deal and had no manager, but they gave me the name of their attorney, Freddie Gershon. After they left, I called Gershon and told him I liked the guys. We made a date to meet at the office the following week.

The very next day, my boss left the company and I was out of a job. I called Gershon and told him what had happened, and he said that the guys had liked me, too, and that I should come in and talk to him. It turned out that Gershon was a big-time entertainment attorney, and we hit it off.

"Why don't you manage the guys?" he said.

"I wouldn't know what I was doing," I said.

So he suggested we find an established manager and that as part of the deal, I would go to work for the new manager and learn the business. He made a deal with Jerry Weintraub, at Management Three, and I went to work.

I had a ball. That first band came and went, but before long I was working with plenty of talented musicians and beginning to understand the management business. Within a few months, I even got my own apartment in New York City, which had been one of my dreams as a kid. When I lived in New Jersey, I would look across the river at the Empire State Building, and I would tell myself that someday I would live in New York. And there I was, living the dream for $280 a month.

Less than three weeks after I'd moved into my dream apartment, I ran into Kip Cohen. I had met him when he was head of A&R at Columbia Records, where he had worked for Clive Davis, and he appeared happy to see me. "I want you to know that I've left Columbia, and that I've been offered a job at A&M Records in Los Angeles, as head of A&R." he said. "I've always liked you. If you ever want a job in California, you've got it."

"I'll take it!" I said. I don't know what came over me. I was just a kid, and moving across the country sounded almost too big for me, but I felt I was ready for something new and I really wanted the job. I heard opportunity knocking.

"I'm not even there yet," he replied. "I'll call you in a few months."

I figured it would never happen and went back to my job at Management Three. Forty-eight hours later, I got a telegram from Kip—this was in the days before e-mail—in which he said, "Come immediately. I have a job waiting for you."

A few days later, I packed my one suitcase and left my dream apartment with my life savings, sixty dollars. I flew out to Los Angeles and moved into an apartment with my brother and his roommates, and I went off to work for Kip Cohen at A&R. Before long, I was touring the country, looking for bands to sign. I felt good about my life. I had a job and I had direction, and I did my job faithfully and passionately. This was the 1970s, and a lot of guys in my position got a little wild and crazy, but I didn't do any of that. I knew this was serious work and I treated it as such. I felt someone had dealt me a wonderful hand, and I appreciated it.

Two and a half years into the job, Clive Davis formed Arista Records and called me to ask if I'd be interested in heading up his West Coast A&R operation. I was thrilled. This was *Clive Davis*. He said he wanted to see me on his next visit to town, and he suggested I prepare a tape of ten unknown songs that I believed had the potential to become hits. Two weeks later, I was sitting in a bungalow at the Beverly Hills Hotel, meeting with Clive and his CEO, Elliot Goldman. At one point, we were interrupted by some other business, and Clive asked me to stick around so we could talk some more. A short time later he was back, and after about an hour of conversation, he asked me to play the tape I had brought—one of those reel-to-reel tapes. As I knelt on the ground, threading it, I stopped myself. With my finger poised over the play button, I turned to Clive and said, "I don't think I can play you this tape." He looked at me, surprised. "Why not?" he asked. And I said, "If I play you this tape, I'm giving away my gold. I can't play it unless I know I have the job."

Clive turned to Elliot, then excused himself and the two men disappeared into another part of the bungalow. Five minutes later, they were back, "Okay," Clive said. "You've got the job. Let's listen to some music." I gladly obliged, and the results were good: Several of my choices went on to become hits, including Barry Manilow's *Weekend in New England* and *Can't Smile Without You*, and *Right Time of the Night*, performed by Jennifer Warnes.

Before long, Clive became my mentor, and whenever he was in Los Angeles, I was with him around the clock. We would work during the day, go out at night, then work some more.

A lot of times, we would be joined by Alan Hirschfield, the chairman of Columbia Pictures, which owned Arista Records. On one such occasion, Alan suggested that I go over to the studio and play some of our new music for the producers and executives. In those days, movies were scored as movies and—with a few exceptions, such *Easy Rider* and *The Graduate*— rarely used songs.

So I went over and played some music for the folks at Columbia, and they were unimpressed. They were really rude about it, too. I was telling them I had a lot of great music they could use in their films, but they were clearly not interested.

One day, however, one of the executives invited me to watch some dailies of *Casey's Shadow*, a Martin Ritt movie. This was a new experience to me. I didn't even know what dailies were. No one had told me that we were watching rough footage of the movie, or that Martin Ritt was still shooting and still putting the film together. I was sitting in the back, listening to these big-shot executives talk about the movie, and about what was wrong with it, what they liked and didn't like, and I thought to myself, *I can do that*. I was young and I was a dreamer. I knew a little something about music, and this business of critiquing what you saw on the screen didn't seem all that difficult or mysterious to me, especially if you spoke from the gut.

It was right at that time that I got a call from Freddie Gershon, the entertainment attorney who had helped me out back in New York. He was now president of the Robert Stigwood Organization. They had just made *Saturday Night Fever*, with John Travolta, and they were working with people like Eric Clapton, in music, and Andrew Lloyd Weber, in theater. "I want to talk to you," Gershon said. "Come see me."

I went to see him. He told me that Robert Stigwood was looking for someone to be his right-hand man, and that he was coming to Los Angeles and wanted to meet me. I met with Stigwood, and he offered me the job. I took it. I saw it as an opportunity to keep my hand in music, which I was already familiar with, and to try to get into film and maybe even theater. It turned out that they were in the early stages of mounting the musical *Evita*, in the West End of London, so it was a very exciting time to be there.

Before long, I found myself traveling the world with Robert Stigwood, learning a little something about both film and theater. I liked it, and much of it was very interesting, but I began to feel like I was out of the loop. Stigwood seemed to spend most of his time abroad and I wanted to be in Hollywood. So I told him I didn't think I could do this anymore. He said I should go back to New York and produce two TV specials that he had sold to NBC TV with David Frost, the British television personality. The first was a 90-minute special on the Bee Gees. The second was a live concert at the United

Nations, starring the top musical acts of the day, and all of the proceeds were going to go to UNICEF.

I felt like I was a big part of putting the show together, and when I was done I decided it was time for me to return to Hollywood to become a movie producer. No one cared. Then I got a call from Henry Winkler, whom I'd met back when he was first making a name for himself as The Fonz, on *Happy Days*. He told me he had a producing deal at Paramount and needed my help. "I'm an actor," he said. "I don't know how to do this. I need you."

"I don't know how to do it either," I said.

"Well," he said. "You're smart and I trust you and you're my friend."

And that's how it started. Suddenly I was a film producer and my partner was Henry Winkler. We heard a pitch from a writer and fell in love with it and took it around town to all the studios, but everyone turned it down. Then we tried our luck with Embassy Pictures, which was the last place you took a project before you shot yourself. Amazingly, they bought it, and we developed and produced the movie, which was released in 1985 as *The Sure Thing*. It was directed by Rob Reiner and starred John Cusack and Daphe Zuniga.

As soon as the movie came out, I got a call from Jeffrey Katzenberg. "You know, Roger, you pitched me that movie and I passed on it and I was wrong," he said. "I should have bought that movie. It was great. Do you have any other movies you want me to look at?"

And I said, "Well, I've got this other movie that this kid Chris Columbus is writing. It's called *Young Sherlock Holmes*, and it's very good."

And Katzenberg said, "Send me the script."

I sent him the script and he called me a few days later. "Michael Eisner and I have read the script and we both think it's the best script we've read in two years," he said. "We want to make the movie."

And they did. And that's how I broke into Hollywood.

So here's my advice: If you really want to be in show business, and you really want to be a producer, you have to have a point of view. And you have to be able to articulate that point of view. If you don't have a point of view, forget it.

Executives in Hollywood are sitting at their desks waiting for people like you to come in and tell them stories. They're like bankers. Banks need you to borrow money from them to stay in business. They *want* to lend you money. Similarly, studios are desperate for good ideas. They need to make movies. They depend on producers to come up with ideas and develop them.

So if you have a point of view, and you have the ability to articulate that point of view, you have a good chance of breaking in.

When I was a kid, driving a cab, I didn't have a plan. This was not my dream, but I'm here, and I did it. Do I still enjoy it? There are parts of the process of I enjoy, yes. Someone walks in with a wonderful pitch, or you read a great script and you know you really want to make that movie. Or listening to a composer conduct a score for a film, which is still my favorite part of making movies, given my background in music. And of course there's nothing quite like sitting in a dark theater and watching people enjoy a movie that you helped bring to life.

But the business of making movies—that part I don't enjoy as much. It's a crazy business. It's not fun, honestly. And it's getting less fun.

There's an old story about director Fred Zinnemann, a great filmmaker (*High Noon, From Here to Eternity, A Man for All Seasons*, etc.). He was getting on in years and he went to meet with a young executive at one of the studios. The executive kept him waiting and waiting and waiting, and finally Zinnemann was shown into his office.

"So, Fred," the executive said. "What have you been up to?"

And Fred said, "You go first."

That, for me, is the nightmare: that a man of Zinnemann's stature could find himself pitching to a clueless twenty-five-year-old. But in this town that happens every day, and it's tough when you're selling. That's why I like being a buyer. I prefer being on *this* side of the desk.

ERIKA CHRISTENSEN

ACTOR

"[She] taught me one thing I've never forgotten:
'If they tell you you're no good, don't believe them.' "

By the time she was six years old, with several television appearances to her credit, Erika Christensen decided she'd had it with show business. For the next five years, she didn't even think about acting, but when she was eleven she got involved in amateur theater and rediscovered the craft.

Ms. Christensen got back into the business with a vengeance, and before long she was booking guest spots on TV. *Nothing Sacred*, *The Practice*, *Frasier*, *3rd Rock from the Sun*, *Touched by an Angel*, *The Pretender*, to name just a few.

Before long, she made the move to features, landing a supporting role in *Leave It to Beaver*, and she hasn't stopped since. You may remember her as Michael Douglas's drug-addicted daughter in *Traffic*, for which she won a Screen Actors Guild Award, or as the troubled young woman in *Swimfan*. She was also in *The Banger Sisters*, *The Perfect Score*, *The Upside of Anger*, and *Flightplan*.

Ms. Christensen was interviewed in a Hollywood restaurant on May 25, 2005.

I was born in Seattle, Washington, and I still have a lot of family there, but my parents moved to Los Angeles when I was three. I have one older brother and identical twin brothers, four years younger than me.

My mother worked as a construction manager and my father worked for an insurance company. Being in Los Angeles, people kept saying to my parents, "Your kids are really cute. You should get them into show business."

So my mother decided it might be fun and she started making the rounds with me and my little brothers. I was five and the twins were just a year old. Before I knew it, I was getting bit parts on TV shows, and then I got a commercial for McDonald's. One day, however, we were on the set and I refused to say my line. I had a little bit of a sore throat, see, but I didn't tell anyone that that was my reason, so my mother felt awful. She thought she was turning into "one of those parents" who push their kids into doing things they don't want to do, and right then we stopped auditioning and got on with our non–show business lives.

At age eleven, however, I joined a performing group with some school friends. We sang and danced and put on skits, and it turned out to be a life-changing experience. I watched members of the audience laughing and crying at all the right places, and it was a great feeling. When I looked them in the eyes from the stage, they would look right back at me; they were so happy to have me singing directly to them. They would come up to me after the show and tell me how much they enjoyed it. We were up there *entertaining* people, and it felt wonderful.

After about a year of stage performances, my parents asked me where this was going, and it just hit me: *This is what I want to do with my life. I want to be an actor.*

My mom and dad were awesome. They saw that I was completely honest and serious about it, even at that age, and they took it just as seriously as I did. My mother signed up for a seminar on how to help your kid get into show business, and I ended up auditioning for one of the people who ran the seminar. That woman helped me get an agent, and almost immediately I booked three commercials, including another one for McDonald's.

I put a lot of work into it. I was taking dance classes, acting classes, and voice lessons, and I was performing with four different groups. All the time on stage really helped me get over my stage fright. When you step onto the stage there's this mad rush of adrenaline—the audience fuels you—but you have to learn to get over the significance of any one performance. Put everything you've got into it and don't worry: there will always be a next time.

I started booking spots on TV shows, including an episode of *The Practice* during its very first season, and episodes of *Frasier* and *3rd Rock from the Sun*. This was very different from stage work. If you messed up, there was another take right away; you didn't have to wait for the following week. Sometimes *lots* of other takes. You did it again and again until the director was happy and you were happy and everyone felt it worked. In film, you get the chance to take risks and try things, and you can really take advantage of that. I've also learned by watching other actors—fantastic actors—take risks of their own, which is an exciting part of the craft.

My first feature role was in *Leave It to Beaver*, released in 1997. I had three callbacks before I landed the role. It was between me and one other girl. We were acquaintances and almost friends, but somehow I didn't doubt that I was going to get the part. That's another thing: You have to believe in yourself.

The movie was fun and such a learning experience. You learn the film vernacular. *First team out, second team in*—stuff like that. At first I didn't know what any of those things meant and I really had to pay attention and find my way. But I wasn't really nervous. My stage experience had helped me develop my abilities, but even more importantly, my self-confidence. I can't stress how important that is: You have to believe that you can do it.

One of the ways to get to that point is to prepare. Even if it's a small role in an acting class, you need to do your homework. Get as much information as you can about the character. Figure out who you're dealing with. If it's a period movie, find out as much as you can about the period, down to the types of clothes you'd be wearing and the music you'd be listening to and the books that were popular back then.

Also, if it's a contemporary piece, or a contemporary screenplay, talk to the writer. He has lived with these characters for a long time. And talk to the director to see what he wants and how he interprets the story and the characters.

One of the things I do is to look for the parts of the character that are like me. It's a search to understand the person and to get to know them.

There's always something about every character, as there is about every person you meet, that you can connect to—and, in terms of acting, that's what's helps make the character come alive.

It's funny, because when people talk to me about my performances, they often say something like, "That's crazy! You're so *not* like that character!" And I think, *Well, we definitely don't do the same things, but I do understand her (the character).*

In *Traffic*, I played a drug-addict. I was young and wholesome looking and I had curly blonde hair. The character was described as, "Sixteen. But really sixteen—she looks twelve." The girl-next-door look worked because I was the type of girl you wouldn't think could become addicted to drugs. I was the girl who could be anyone's daughter—the kid you weren't worried about but perhaps should have paid more attention to.

When I heard I got the part, I practically hyperventilated! What an important film! What an intense role! The character represented the most personal part of drugs, the user. The set was calm and full of talented people, and despite the dark story I had a real fun time working on that film.

I feel very lucky to be an actor. I've been lucky to be around so many people who have taken the time to help me and teach me, beginning with my parents.

Professionally, I think I was lucky right out of the gate, with my first manager, Gay Ribisi. She'd say that it was okay to go on auditions and not book anything, but that I wasn't allowed to be upset or think less of myself even if I went to fifty auditions and still booked nothing. And if you truly believe in yourself, you *will* book something. Gay also taught me one thing I've never forgotten. "If they tell you you're no good, don't believe them."

A casting director once told Burt Reynolds he couldn't act, and he told Clint Eastwood that he was ugly! You can't believe it. If they tell you you're not good enough, fine; tell yourself you can do better. But don't take it personally. And *don't believe them.*

I think one of the most important things you can do for yourself, as an actor and as a person, is to make up your own mind about who and what you are. Don't let anyone interfere with that. You can make mistakes along the way, but you'll get through them.

And you can't worry about the past. It's about moving on. Every day is a new day, full of new opportunities. Every experience, good and bad, is a learning experience. And every day, even every minute of the day, you get a chance to start fresh.

I feel very good about my career. This year, I was in *The Upside of Anger*, a terrific movie. And I just finished shooting *Flightplan*, with Jodie Foster. Jodie plays a woman whose daughter is kidnapped on a plane, and I play one of the flight attendants. It was the first time I've gotten to wear a uniform in a movie! The costume itself had a whole attitude that came with it.

I still think back to the way my life began to change, at age eleven, when I was performing with my friends from school. I was really into it, and my parents were constantly driving me from one place to the next. They said, "Erika, what are you thinking about here? Are you just having fun or is this going someplace?" I think maybe they saw where I was going before I did. I loved what I was doing and they could see how much I loved it.

I think loving what you do is a big part of success. In film, you don't get the instant gratification that you get on stage—you don't instantly see the way your performance affects the audience—but it's a very powerful and far-reaching medium.

If you ask a ballerina, "Why did you become a dancer?", nine out of ten times she'll tell you, "Because I saw *The Red Shoes* when I was a little girl."

One film can change a person's life. And look at the result: Art begets art.

It doesn't get much better than that.

PETER LYONS COLLISTER

CINEMATOGRAPHER

"You can't make it in Hollywood without giving it everything you've got."

A native of Cleveland, Ohio, Peter Lyons Collister first fell in love with photography, and dreamed of traveling the world for *National Geographic*. But when he got to high school, a friend with a passion for movies enlisted his help on a small film. That film went on to win a local award, and the experience changed Collister's life.

A graduate of the USC School of Cinema-Television, Collister has been gainfully employed as a cinematographer for more than two decades, an accomplishment in and of itself. He has shot more than two dozen films, including *The Amityville Horror*, *Win a Date with Tad Hamilton!*, *The Replacement Killers*, and *Poetic Justice*.

Mr. Collister was interviewed at a restaurant in Westwood, California, on April 9, 2005.

I started making short, 8-millimeter movies in Cleveland, when I was in the eighth and ninth grade, with my friend Dwight Little. He's the one that got me interested in movies, but not because he thought I had talent. My father had a station wagon and a stepladder, and Dwight knew that they would come in handy.

The first film we made was a Civil War movie called *The Last Soldier*. It was a sixteen minute, Super 8, black-and-white movie about a Union soldier in the Civil War who saves and befriends a wounded, southern rebel. It won second prize in a PBS affiliates contest, and right away I knew I was going to go to Hollywood.

Before that fateful day, I briefly considered becoming a photographer for *National Geographic*, until I found out that just about every other kid with a camera wanted to work for *National Geographic*. I loved nature, but I didn't think I loved it enough to survive such intense competition. I also entertained the idea of becoming a fashion photographer, but I was far more intrigued by film, so I decided to try to turn my evolving interest in movies into a career.

I ended up at USC, with my friend Dwight, who went on to become a director. I was more interested in cinematography, however. My dream was to shoot at least one major motion picture before I died. I thought, *If I can make one movie I'm really proud of, that will be enough.*

While I was still in film school, I met Randal Kleiser, the director. This was years before he made a name for himself with *Grease*, *The Blue Lagoon*, *White Fang*, and more than a dozen other features. When we met, he had just finished working on a short film called *Peege*. It starred Bruce Davison, Barbara Rush, and Jeanette Nolan. Jeanette played the title character, a grandmother struggling with Alzheimer's. My own grandmother had just been diagnosed with Alzheimer's, and when I saw the film, I was so overcome that I decided I would follow Randal anywhere.

I went to work for him as a production assistant for seventy-five dollars a week, which was big money at the time, at least for me. I worked on an ABC After-School Special called *Portrait of Grandpa Doc*, which was a companion piece to *Peege*. Then I worked as an intern on *Grease*, learning as much as I could from cinematographer Bill Butler.

Months later, when Kleiser was asked to direct *The Blue Lagoon*, he sent me off to Fiji during preproduction to shoot some second unit stuff. There was a hurricane scene in the script, and I was supposed to sit there and wait for a hurricane. I lived on a deserted island for a couple of weeks, but the hurricane didn't come, so the scene was written out of the script and I went home. Randall told me that at one point he had considered sending me a football helmet for protection, but he never got around to it.

I stayed on *Grease* as the camera assistant, working with Nestor Almendros, one of the great European cinematographers. He won the Academy Award for *Days of Heaven*, and he had just done *Kramer vs. Kramer*. After *The Blue Lagoon* he worked on *Still of the Night*, *The Last Metro*, *Sophie's Choice*, and countless other movies. I really admired him. Nestor knew more about composition than anyone I'd ever met, and he was especially gifted when it came to working with natural light.

Ever since that experience with Nestor, one of my goals has been to shoot a film that would make him proud of me, and I am still trying to make that movie. The only one that even comes close, in my opinion, is *The Replacement Killers*. Nestor passed away in 1992, and he never saw it.

After *The Blue Lagoon*, I returned to USC to finish film school. I remember other students pointing me out and saying, "That's Peter Collister. He's really lucky. He was just working on a big feature with Brooke Shields." It struck me that luck is what you make it. Luck is about seeing opportunities and pursuing them. The flipside is *not* seeing opportunities. That's what makes you unlucky. So my advice is: Look for the opportunities and seize them.

After film school, in 1984, my friend Dwight and I met Sandy Howard, a producer who had made something of a name for himself with low-budget movies. He was trying to get a little movie off the ground, *KGB: The Secret War*, and we signed on—Dwight to direct and me to shoot it. We helped design a poster to make it look exciting, and Sandy went off to the various overseas film markets and managed to raise $800,000 in foreign sales. We were still $300,000 short, though, and Dwight and I knew that the only way we were going to get to shoot this movie was to raise the money ourselves. And that's exactly what we did. We talked to everyone we knew and told them we were making a movie, and we said that anything they could do to help us would be greatly appreciated. It took a while, but we raised the money—even getting some help from a shady little bank in Australia.

It was an amazing experience. Here we were, Dwight and I, two kids from suburban Cleveland, and we were actually shooting a 35-millimeter film in Los Angeles.

Alas, it was not a great movie, and just about everyone lost their investment. But it got made. And, more importantly, it helped launch our careers. People were able to look beyond the finished product to see that Dwight actually had some directing talent, and that I knew how to shoot a low-budget feature and make it look good.

Of course, it's not as if our lives changed all of a sudden. People didn't simply hand you a movie. For a long time, while I waited for my big break, I did a lot of second-unit photography. The studios had seen what I could do on *KGB*, and from time to time they would call and offer me little jobs. I never turned anything down. I enjoyed it, too. Second unit is a great way to learn technique. You have to shoot films without fuss and without waste, and without anyone looking over your shoulder and second-guessing you. So you figure it out yourself. And you hope the result impresses the people who write the checks.

I did some second unit on *Summer Lovers*, another Randal Kleiser movie, which we shot in Greece. And after that I did second unit on *Blame it on Rio*, for director Stanley Donen. I was getting paid to see the world, and I was learning how to shoot and frame and light a movie, and I was very happy. On the other hand, I was eager to make the leap to cinematographer. I wanted to shoot a movie from start to finish, to be part of the storytelling machinery, not just the guy who shot the odd bits and pieces that the real cinematographer didn't have time to shoot.

I got my big break in 1989, on the movie *Problem Child*, my first union job. This made me a bona fide cinematographer. The producer, Robert Simonds, had heard good things about me from Dennis Dugan, the director, and when I went in to meet with them, I was completely prepared. I had read the script several times, and I had plenty of ideas about how it might look, and how I might light it, and the hard work paid off.

I did *Livin' Large* the next year, and *Poetic Justice*, the year after that. I especially remember *Poetic Justice*. Jon Singleton was the director, and the movie starred Janet Jackson and Tupac Shakur. A reporter from *Premiere* magazine had been following us around, looking for a story, and one afternoon, when we were up near Oakland, he approached and asked me a few questions. Singleton came over later, wondering what I'd shared with the guy, and I said, "Oh, I told him wonderful things about you and Janet Jackson."

"Is that it?" he said.

"No," I said. "I told him that there was a little tension between Tupac's people and the rest of the crew."

Singleton shook his head and smiled. "That's what they're going to run with," he said.

Sure enough, when the story appeared a few weeks later, that was the angle: racial tension on the set of *Poetic Justice*.

At this point in my career, I am proudest of *The Replacement Killers*. It is the story of a troubled hit man, and it was directed by Antoine Fuqua, who had made a name for himself as a commercial director (and went on to direct *Training Day*, which got Denzel Washington his Academy Award).

Neither of us thought the script was particularly strong, but the movie'd been greenlit, and we were on our way. Still, Antoine was worried. It was a fairly tight budget, and we couldn't afford to make mistakes. "We can't screw up," he said. "We can't go too dark or too light, so why don't we give each character a color and go for broke. It's going to be about a look and a style."

I knew we could pull it off. If we locked in, if we committed to the look, we'd be safe. And I knew how to play it safe. In the low-budget world, if you don't like the way something is lit, you can't just start over. You have to live with what you shot because you can't afford to shoot it again. That's it. That's all you get.

So that's what we did. Each character got his or her own color. I remember Mira Sorvino was green. We made her room green, and we used green glass to amp it up.

The day after we shot that first green scene, one of the producers came on set and said, "I'm not sure I like this green. Is there anything you can do about it?"

"No," I said. "Not now. That's the way it's been shot, and it can't be fixed."

I was worried about how the studio would respond, and I dreaded that call, and when the phone finally rang, I felt my stomach lurch. "Hey, that green," the executive said, and Antoine and I braced ourselves, because this was the opinion that counted. "It's really cool. I love it."

If Nestor Almendros were alive today, I would show him *The Replacement Killers* with pride. I put a lot of myself into that movie.

People often ask me why I don't want to direct, as if to suggest that cinematography is a step in that direction. I'm sure it is for a lot of people, but not for me. I love being a cinematographer. I love lighting and camera work. I love the process of telling a story with film.

From time to time, I *am* asked to direct a movie, but I love shooting. That's my job—to shoot the movie, and to shoot it as beautifully as possible—and that's more than enough for me.

I also love directing second unit. I worked on Antoine Fuqua's *Bait*, which was an exhilarating experience, and I worked on *Bad Boys* and *The Rock* for Michael Bay, doing some of the most visual work I've ever done.

There are times—not many, mind you, but they exist—when everything actually comes together. The script. The acting. The directing. You find yourself looking through the lens, and it's magical. You feel like you're part of something truly phenomenal, and it's a wonderful feeling.

Whenever I start a new project, that's what I hope for. That feeling; that kind of magic. As a result, I never find my work boring. I always look for something to like, even in the most mediocre script, and I go into it determined to learn something new from the experience—and hoping, despite the odds, for that touch of magic.

If you want to get into this business, you've got to want it—really, truly want it. I know I'm not the first person to say it, but you can't make it in Hollywood without giving it everything you've got. It's very hard work, harder than you can imagine. It's tough on your relationships and on your body, and on your psyche. So if you don't really want it, if you aren't prepared to make the necessary sacrifices, you really shouldn't pursue it.

The film business is outrageously competitive. When I was starting out, there were a couple of dozen so-called film schools around the country. Now there are about six hundred. But we aren't turning out any more great scripts or great movies, so it makes you wonder.

That reminds me of a story. I was invited to host a film class at USC, and I decided to screen *Eye of the Tiger*, a film I had just shot. It was directed by Richard Sarafian, who had done such a terrific job on *Vanishing Point*, and it starred Gary Busey as a Vietnam veteran who had just been released from prison. Yaphet Kotto was also in the film, and when I was offered the job, I jumped at the chance. It was a very attractive package.

Months later, I decided to screen that picture for that class at USC, and I sent it to Leon Roth, the teacher, so he could take a look at it first. When I showed up on campus, he seemed very grim. "They're going to crucify you," he said, not mincing words. "This is a poor man's *Walking Tall*. I can't believe you did this movie."

Well, he was right—the class didn't like it. After the lights came back up, it was time for questions, and the very first question was, "How could you do this movie?"

I decided to play a little game with them. "Well," I said. "My agent called and offered me three different pictures. The first one was called *The Color Purple*. It was going to be directed by Steven Spielberg, and I had heard that Spielberg was really hard on his cinematographers, so I passed. The second one was *Out of Africa*, and it sounded pretty good. Sydney Pollack was directing and Meryl Streep was attached to star, but I didn't feel like going to Africa. My wife and I were trying to have a baby at the time, and I thought that was more important. And the third film was this film, *Eye of the Tiger*. I had really liked *Vanishing Point*, and I thought Yaphet Kotto was a great actor. So this was the film I took."

The kids were sitting there, their mouths hanging open, and that was the point of my little story. I *hadn't* been offered those two other films. We don't always get the films we'd like to get. But life goes on. We have mortgages to pay and bills coming in and lives to lead. Sometimes, we take what we can get. And every time, we do the absolute best we can.

The fact is, I'm happy with my career. I am a cinematographer. I shoot movies. Sometimes I pick the wrong script, or I pick the right script, and it doesn't turn out exactly as I had hoped. But that's life. I make my choices and I do the best job I can, and I try not to look back.

I may not always get the A-pictures, but I take the pictures I like, and I behave as if each one is a masterpiece. To do otherwise, to do less than that, would be a disservice, both to myself and to the picture. That's my reality, and I'm happy with it. I'm doing something I love, and I'm making a living at it. And how can I complain about that?

ROGER CORMAN
PRODUCER/DIRECTOR

"Hollywood is always looking for people who aren't afraid of twenty-hour days. If you're one of those people, you'll make it."

Roger Corman arrived in Hollywood during World War II, seemingly destined to become an engineer, like his father before him. While he was off in college, however, pursuing that engineering degree, he began to review movies for the college newspaper, and he fell hopelessly in love with the medium.

Less than a decade later, Corman was well on his way to establishing himself as the most prolific producer and director of low-budget movies in the history of filmmaking. To date, through his various companies—New World Pictures, Concorde Entertainment, and New Horizons—he has produced more than 400 films.

Some early favorites included *Bucket of Blood*, which was one of the first movies to combine horror with comedy, and *Little Shop of Horrors*, starring Jack Nicholson—which he shot in two days. Other notable titles include *The Fall of the House of Usher*, based on the story by Edgar Allan Poe; *The Intruder*, a racially charged film about segregation; *Wild Angels*, with Peter Fonda; and *Bloody Mamma*, starring Robert De Niro.

Corman knew how to make movies fast and cheap, and he knew how to make them profitable, and that talent eventually earned him the moniker "King of the Bs."

But Corman wasn't only in it for the fast buck. He genuinely loved movies, he loved entertaining people, and he had an eye for talent. And in fact his films were so inexpensive to shoot that he was able to take risks on people who would never have been given the same opportunities at the studios. He helped launch the careers of some of the country's notable directors, including Martin Scorsese, James Cameron, Francis Ford Coppola, Ron Howard, and Peter Bogdanovich, and he took chances on then-unknown actors, such as Jack Nicholson, Robert De Niro, Sylvester Stallone, and Sandra Bullock.

Now in his late seventies, Corman is still making movies.

He was interviewed on July 7, 2005, in his Los Angeles office.

I came to Hollywood in 1941, during the war. My father had been an engineer in Detroit, and when he retired he moved the family to Beverly Hills. I went to Beverly Hills High School, where I immediately met all sorts of kids whose parents were in the film industry. I can't remember any of their names, but I certainly remember June Haver, who went on to have a wonderful career as an actress.

I came from a long line of engineers, and I was on track to become an engineer myself, and I had never really given much thought to the movie business. I don't even remember much about the movies I saw as a kid, except for one 1937 English film that has stayed with me to this day. It was called *Things to Come*, and it was based on an H. G. Wells science-fiction story. The visuals were incredibly striking, and I was impressed by the imagination of the filmmakers and the way they portrayed the future. In some ways, the film was prophetic. It was released just before World War II, and it predicted the partial collapse of civilization. At the time, however, it meant nothing to me beyond interesting entertainment; I was going off to Stanford University, to become an engineer, like my father.

When I got to Stanford, I found out that I could get into movies for free if I wrote reviews for *The Stanford Daily*. This seemed like a good deal to a college kid looking for cheap entertainment, and I wrote a sample review for the editors and got the job. That's how I got seriously interested in film, and that's when I began to think about the business of making movies. After all, as a reviewer, I was no longer a passive spectator; I was really thinking about the movie and noticing everything and taking notes and analyzing the entire process.

By the time I graduated from college, I knew I didn't want to be an engineer, and I returned to Los Angeles and looked for work at the studios. The best job I could find was as a messenger at 20th Century Fox, and I took it. I can't say I was thrilled, but I was in the door and on the lot, and—given my writing background—I felt it was only a matter of time before I moved up in the world.

In fact, while I was still a messenger, I found out about these people called "story analysts," who took the scripts that had been submitted to the studio and basically reviewed them. I began reading scripts for the studio, on my own time, and submitting my written reports to the story department. Based on those reports, I was hired as a story analyst. Most of the scripts I was given to read were pretty bad, but I came across one that really impressed me. It was a western called *The Big Gun*, and it just so happened that the studio was actively looking for a western for Gregory Peck. I carefully reread the script and went so far as to make some suggestions on how it might be improved, and I submitted it to the story department with a recommendation that they pursue it. That was the first script I read for the studio that I actually thought was worth making. As luck would have it, the studio agreed with me, bought the script, incorporated a few of my ideas, and went on to turn it into *The Gunfighter*, a classic.

Eventually, I left Fox to become a literary agent at the Dick Hyland Agency. While there, I wrote a script and submitted it under a pseudonym, and I sold my own script, as both writer and agent, to Allied Artists. This was in 1954, and that was my first big break. The script was called *The House in the Sea*, and it was a noir thriller with a big chase at the end that took place in a half-flooded house. It was later released as *Highway Dragnet* because the TV show *Dragnet* was very popular at the time.

Before the film went into production, I told the producer, Bill Broidy, that I would work for nothing if I could get a coproducer credit. Bill agreed, which made me a writer-producer, and I left the literary agency. Dick Hyland wasn't too happy about it, but he got his 10 percent commission and we parted on good terms.

Now that I was a producer, I set myself up in a little office in Hollywood and went off to raise money to make my first movie, a little something called *It Stalked the Ocean Floor*. I managed to scrounge up $12,000 from my friends and family, and I got a film lab to give me a deferment on their fees, then I went out and made the picture in one week. I sold it to Lippert Releasing, who didn't like my arty title and changed it to *Monster from the Ocean Floor*. The movie was a success and I immediately took my profit and made another movie, *The Fast and the Furious*, about a man who gets into a long-distance car race to escape the law. It was the first movie ever released by American International Pictures, and the owners, Jim Nicholson and Sam Arkoff, liked the result enough to reward me with a two-picture deal. I ended up directing one of those two pictures, *Five Guns West*, with Mike Connors, who went on to play the lead in *Mannix*. That movie also did well, and suddenly I was the go-to guy for inexpensive movies.

I kept making movies. I was making pictures on two-week schedules, in black and white, and studios would put them together as double features: two horror movies, two westerns, two action movies, etc., etc.

In 1959, I made a movie called *Bucket of Blood* which was my first attempt at combining comedy with horror. Whenever I went to a sneak-preview or a screening, I noticed that a good part of the audience would scream exactly when I wanted them to scream, and that they generally followed it up with nervous laughter. From this I learned that audiences are always looking for release. If you build tension, you have to smash the tension, too. And this applies equally to horror films, thrillers, and comedies.

One day, A.I.P. offered me a budget of $150,000 to make two more horror pictures, back to back, but I balked. I told them we'd be better off making one color picture for $200,000, and they liked the idea—they were just as interested in polishing A.I.P.'s image as I was in polishing mine. When they asked me what I might want to make at that budget, I suggested *The Fall of the House of Usher*, based on the Edgar Allan Poe story, which I had read as a child. Arkoff was familiar with the story, but he was concerned. "There's no monster," he said. "There needs to be a monster in it." And I said, "The *house* is the monster. The house is *alive*."

He liked the idea, so I sat down and wrote a line for the movie to drive home the point: "The house lives! The house lives!" When we got to that part in the film, Vincent Price, our lead actor, told me, "I can't say that line! I don't know what it means." So I took him aside and whispered, "Just say it. That's how we got the movie financed." Price looked at me and smiled. "I *can* say that line," he said.

The Fall of the House of Usher went on to be a big success for A.I.P., and it also got great reviews. The studio got the kind of attention it had been looking for, and it helped cement my reputation as a director.

In 1962, I made *The Intruder*, which to this day remains one of the most memorable films of my career. I thought it was a wonderful story about racial prejudice and integration, and this was back in the days when the Civil Rights movement was beginning to pick up steam, but no one would back me. So I put my own money into the film and put William Shatner in it, then an unknown young actor.

When the movie was released, the reviews were terrific, and I can still quote one of them from memory: "This motion picture is a credit to the entire American film industry." Despite the positive reviews, *The Intruder* was the only film I ever made that didn't make money. Forty years later, I rereleased it on home video, with a new soundtrack, and it finally turned a small profit.

In terms of advice, I think that in order to succeed in this business you should really try to learn every aspect of the business. In my day, there weren't a lot of film schools around, and—from what I've seen—you can learn a lot in film school. But if you can't get into a good film school, take the first job that'll get you through the door. Once you're on the lot, other doors will open—if you have the drive and the intelligence to make them open.

One of the most surprising things about this business, and, for all I know, about any other business, is the number of people who *aren't* committed to their jobs. They just do enough to get by, and no more. Well, people who work hard get noticed, especially in the movie business. If you do more than is expected of you, it'll pay off. Hollywood is always looking for people who aren't afraid of twenty-hour days. If you're one of those people, you'll make it.

CHARLES DUTTON
ACTOR/DIRECTOR/PRODUCER

"Do everything in your power to make it happen, but be realistic."

Charles Dutton made his Broadway debut in a 1984 production of *Ma Rainey's Black Bottom*, for which he earned a Tony nomination, then went on to a spectacular career in film and television, on both sides of the camera.

As a film actor, you may have seen him in, *Q&A*, *Alien 3*, *Rudy*, *A Time to Kill*, *Get on the Bus*, *Mimic*, *Cookie's Fortune*, *Random Hearts*, *Secret Window*, and *Gothika*—just a few of the dozens of movies he's made over the past two decades. On television, you may remember him from *Roc*, the series on which he also served as executive producer, from his Emmy-nominated role on *Without a Trace*, or from more TV movies than we have room to list.

His directing credits include *Against the Ropes*, with Meg Ryan; *The Corner*, a miniseries; and *First Time Felon*, a 1997 TV movie.

Dutton discovered acting in prison, where—in another life—he did time for manslaughter. We spoke to him in Los Angeles, on September 19, 2005.

I was born in 1951, in Baltimore, Maryland, and grew up in and around several housing projects. I had an older brother and a younger sister, and our parents split up when I was five. My mom pretty much raised the three of us, but my dad came around from time to time, though he died young, at age forty, of a heart attack.

When I was a kid, I was into boxing. It was sort of an everyday thing in our household—my dad, my uncles, my cousins, everyone was into it. Other families played baseball, we boxed. I was in about fifteen or sixteen amateur bouts, but by the time I was thirteen, I was mostly into street fighting and hell-raising, and I paid for it: Between 1964 and 1967, I spent most of my time in and out of juvenile facilities. Finally, in 1968, I got into a fist fight that turned into a knife fight. The guy stabbed me, and I stabbed him back. I lived, he died.

I should have beat the charge on self-defense, but I went into court with an unremorseful attitude—even my lawyer asked me to at least *act* like I was sorry—and I got sent to prison. The judge said he felt compelled to sentence me, based partly on my juvenile record, and partly on my attitude.

I wound up doing twenty-two months, but shortly after I was released, I got arrested for armed robbery and possession of a deadly weapon. I was acquitted on the armed robbery charge, but I was given a three-year sentence on the weapons charge (eighteen months for each pistol).

About two years into my sentence, I got into a fight with a prison guard, but nothing much came of it. They let me finish my sentence, and on the day they released me, when I was literally at the gate, on my way out of the prison, they handed me an indictment, charging me with assaulting the prison guard. They could have done it a year earlier, when it had actually happened, but they wanted to mess with my head, and they succeeded. I was held over, appeared in court, and was sentenced to another eight years.

When I went back inside, I fancied myself a revolutionary and joined the Black Panthers. I honestly believed there was going to be an armed overthrow of the American government, and I really wanted to be a part of it. I did a lot of hell-raising in prison. Whenever there was a riot, I was in the thick of it.

One day, a girlfriend sent me a book called *New Black Playwrights: An Anthology*. It had all these black writers I'd never heard of—Douglas Turner Ward, Adrienne Kennedy, Lonne Elder, William Wellington Mackey, Ed Bullins—and I just set it on the shelf, with my other books.

A short time later, I got in trouble for refusing to clean toilets, and I was told I'd be spending six days in isolation. When the guards came to get me, I was reaching for the book I'd been reading, *The Wretched of the Earth*, by Frantz Fanon, but picked up the anthology by mistake.

Isolation was a pretty common punishment back then. They put you in a cell that was maybe five feet by seven feet, with no toilet and no bed, and with only a little hole in the floor with a metal grate to do your business. There was an old sink in there, too, for drinking water, and every seventy-two hours they'd come by with food.

I had been in isolation before, and it takes a good twenty-four to thirty-six hours to adjust. The cement floor is bitterly cold, you're hungry as hell, and you can't get away from the smell of urine and feces. But you adapt, and as soon as I adapted, I reached for my book and realized I'd reached for the wrong book. But I began reading the anthology—it was all I had—and I was immediately hooked.

The one play that struck me above all the others, however, was *Day of Absence*, by Douglas Turner Ward. It was a hilarious, political satire, and I read it over and over again. I told myself, *When I get out of this hole, I am going to round up the craziest guys in this prison and put on the play.*

As soon as I got out, I went to see one of the women who taught at the prison, and she helped me get a dozen guys together, and we ended up staging the play for the prison talent show. I not only directed the play, I acted in it.

I found my calling during that performance, more than thirty years ago now. My character was in the middle of one of his speeches, and I looked up and realized I had this captive audience, pun intended: Every one of those guys was in the palm of my hand. I was in complete control. I could make them pensive or reflective. I could make them sit up in their seats and take note. Or I could make them lean back and relax. And at that moment it dawned on me that I had just discovered what I was born to do. It was an incredibly powerful feeling. Somehow I knew that when I got out of prison, I would have to pursue this to the fullest of my abilities, and that if I failed I would probably spend the rest of my life in a penitentiary. It just didn't seem as if there was a middle ground. It was either this or back to crime.

At that point, I dropped all the negative karma I had around me. I told my fellow prisoners that I was retiring from all the stupidity. My days as a hell-raising revolutionary were over. They thought I was kidding, or scheming up a plot to start a riot or some other shit, but I surprised them all. I even began studying for a college degree, and I took my studies very seriously.

In 1976, after serving four and a half years, I made parole, and I immediately went over to Towson State University, in Baltimore, with two years of credits to my name, and enrolled in their fine arts program. I graduated in 1978 and began doing local theater in and around Baltimore, along with a little sketch comedy.

My theater acting got me some good reviews, especially from one local critic, a woman. She wrote a particularly glowing review after I appeared in *Equus*, the Peter Shaffer play, and I still remember the last line: "Great as it is, Charles Dutton's performance has one tragic flaw—and that flaw is that he's still in Baltimore, doing plays."

I remember running around the city, trying to collect as many copies of the newspaper as I could find, and dumping them in the trash. I didn't want anyone to read that review, because I didn't realize that the reviewer was actually giving me the highest of compliments. She was basically telling me to take my talent and move on to bigger and better things.

I went to see Paul Berman, the chairman of the theater department at Towson, and asked him what I should do. The thing is, I didn't know how to be an actor. After seven and a half years in prison, I was pretty institutionalized. Everything had been done for me. My meals were brought to my cell. I was told when to shower, when to leave my cell, when to take a walk in the yard, and when to put my book down. I didn't know how to make things happen for myself. I asked Paul, "Should I go to New York and try to become a professional actor?"

"No," he said. "You don't want to wait on tables and all that stuff. Why don't you go to Yale?"

I thought he was kidding. "Come on, Paul! An ex-con! I'd never get accepted at Yale!"

And he said, "Give it a shot. You never know. Those guys up there, they're a bunch of bleeding hearts."

So I applied, and in 1980 I was accepted into the Yale Drama School on a full scholarship. By the time I graduated, in May of 1983, I had an agent, and not long after that, in April of 1984, I was in a Broadway production of *Ma Rainey's Black Bottom*, the August Wilson play. I played Levee, the volatile, self-destructive trumpet player at the heart of the story, and I was nominated for a Tony.

I was living in New York at the time, and my agent began sending me out on auditions. My very first film role was in a movie called *Cat's Eye*, a trilogy based on a number of Stephen King stories. In the film, I hit a guy and knocked him into a car and delivered my one line: "Let's go!"

The following year, I was in *No Mercy*, a slightly more significant role, and finally in 1991 I decided it was time to move to Los Angeles, where I have lived ever since.

Hollywood is a tough nut to crack. The three main unions in this town—the Screen Actors Guild, the Writers Guild, and the Directors' Guild—have an unemployment rate of about 85 percent. It is important for outsiders to be aware of this. If you're chasing the dream and it's not happening, don't waste your life. Set some limits, and do everything in your power to make it happen, but be realistic.

When I got out of prison, after seven and a half years, I gave myself that same amount of time to make it as an actor. I guess in some ways it was a self-imposed sentence: I either made it, or I looked for something else. Well, I sort of made it: Seven years and *eight* months after walking out of prison, I was on Broadway, doing *Ma Rainey's Black Bottom*.

I think, for an actor, you really should train on stage. TV and the movies will make you a star, but theater will make you an artist. And as an artist you're better equipped to handle the lean times. After all, if you got into the business as an artist, and not simply to get rich and famous, you'll have a better sense of who you are, and of your own humanity, and those strengths are going to help you survive.

JACK EPPS JR.

WRITER

"Good luck is when you get an opportunity and you've done all the hard work and everything comes together."

Jack Epps Jr. grew up in Detroit and fell in love with movies early on. When he was a little boy, his father converted a side porch into an elaborate, 16-millimeter projection booth, and the game room became an early version of a home entertainment center, complete with an eighteen-foot screen. Epps was hooked right from the very start.

He went off to Michigan State to study medicine, looking for a career, but quickly discovered he was more attracted to writing, and his friendship with Jim Cash—a professor at Michigan State—ended up changing the course of both men's lives. After Epps graduated, with a B.A. in English, the two men decided to try to write together, and they began a long-distance collaboration that lasted over two decades.

Their credits include *Legal Eagles*, starring Robert Redford and Debra Winger; *Top Gun*, starring Tom Cruise and Kelly McGillis; *The Secret of My Success*, with Michael J. Fox; *Turner & Hooch*, with Tom Hanks; *Dick Tracy*, starring Warren Beatty and Madonna; *Anaconda*, with Jennifer Lopez, Eric Stoltz, and Jon Voight; and *The Flintstones in Viva Rock Vegas* (2000).

Cash died in March of 2000, before their last film was released. Today, Epps continues to write on his own, for both film and television, and also teaches screenwriting at the USC film school, where he is a tenured professor.

He was interviewed on June 1, 2005, in Santa Monica, California, where he lives with his wife and children.

I was born in Detroit, Michigan, and I'm definitely one of those kids who always had fantasies about making movies. It started with my father, who had a 16-millimeter film camera and a projector and enjoyed showing home movies. By the time I was twelve, I was running the projector myself, which meant I could screen movies for my buddies. Occasionally, we'd get a feature length film from one of my parents' friends, a local distributor for Columbia Pictures. I still remember watching *The Forbidden Planet*, and this was light years before video, so it was a pretty big deal.

I also wanted to be a professional hockey player, like every other kid in the state, and I was a walk-on member of the freshman hockey team at Michigan State. I beat out the scholarship player to become the top goaltender on the team, but I didn't make varsity. In retrospect, that was probably a lucky break. If I had made the team, I wouldn't have discovered film, and I'd probably be tending bar in Saskatchewan.

One night on campus, I went to a local MSU student film festival and had the classic response: "I can do better than that." At that time, MSU had one of the leading Television and Radio departments in the nation, so I took a film class. It wasn't much of a class. They just gave you equipment and told you to go off and make a film. I made a little film about a college kid who is confronting the Vietnam War, and the way he is affected by the pressure. It was just a class assignment, but I put a lot into it, and I got a great response. I realized that my life had changed. I had found something I was passionate about, and I haven't looked back since.

One of my professors at MSU was Jim Cash, who years later became my writing partner. He worked at the local PBS station, mostly on documentaries and on the occasional talk show, and he was also an unpublished novelist. Since I was interested in making movies, I thought that I should learn to write them, too. So I tried to enroll for the only screenwriting class on campus and found it filled. I begged Jim to let me in. Jim was a soft touch, and that probably was one of the luckiest doors to ever open in my life. I'd like to think it was fate.

At about the same time, I became a film reviewer for the campus newspaper, and I began making small movies of my own. One of them was a documentary called *The Pigs vs. The Freaks*. It was an annual event at MSU: The police and the hippies played a football game to raise money for charity. Years later, my little film became the basis for an NBC Movie of the Week, which I also coproduced.

I also tried my hand at a couple of short, dramatic films, honing my skills as a cameraman and a storyteller, and won a few awards on the film circuit. The films were fairly pretentious, which was a good thing: By the time I got to Hollywood, I had that element out of my system.

Right after I graduated, I moved to Los Angeles and began to work as a cameraman. I had a good eye, and I loved composing pictures. This was well outside the Hollywood system—documentaries and such—but I was making a living with a camera.

By this point, I think my values were in the right place, in terms of movies, anyway. I come from the Midwest and I had already gone through my pretentious phase. Now I was interested in entertaining. I related to Preston Sturges, who had been criticized for being too "light," and who responded by making *Sullivan's Travels*. The message there was that one of the most important things that you can do as a filmmaker is to entertain people, and I agreed with him. In college, I was thinking about Bergman and Fellini; in Hollywood, I was more influenced by Wilder and Hitchcock.

Given my background, I managed to get an internship at the American Film Institute, working for Tony Bill on *Hearts of the West*. It starred Jeff Bridges as a writer of Wild West novels who dreams of becoming an actual cowboy, and it was directed by Howard Zieff.

I spent six months on that film, Xeroxing and running errands and basically doing everything I was told to do, and I learned how a feature film got made, from the ground up. Tony was a very good guy, and a great mentor. He let me in on everything. I lived on the set; went to dailies; talked to the writer, Rob Thompson; and hung out with Jeff Bridges. The time I spent with the actors left an indelible impression on me; specifically, that *you have to write for actors*. That doesn't seem like much of an epiphany, but until you're there—until you see it and feel it and smell it—you don't really understand what that means. Everything—the sets, the crew, the director, the script—is geared to the scene, to the moment. Movies are shot one set-up at a time, and unless the actors have something to play—something dramatic—there's nothing to shoot. It's about performance, and that performance has to be on the page.

It basically comes down to this: There's the real world, and there's the movie world, and the movie world is hyperreality. It's our world on steroids. Everything in a movie has to be amplified. We don't go to a movie to be bored. We go to movies to see something that's larger than life. That's what a film has to be. It was one of the earliest lessons I learned as a writer, and to this day I still think it was one of the most important. It boils down to what I call *momentum writing*; if you have enough momentum, the story will carry you through the bumps that defy logic, and everyone will be glad they went along for the ride.

Tony also let me work for him as a reader, and I began to read screenplays voraciously, and to begin to understand how they were put together. My wife, Cynthia, worked for Paramount at the time, and she would bring scripts home from the studio for me to read: *The Godfather, Chinatown, Day of the Locust.* I remember reading *The Sting*, by David Ward, and thinking it was absolutely phenomenal. More than anything else, I admired the way that movie was structured. The entire script is beautifully constructed and expertly woven together. There was not a wasted word on the page. Every line, every word, had a purpose.

At around this time, I looked up a guy I had met briefly at Michigan State. His name was Anderson House, and we decided to write a spec treatment for *Hawaii Five-O*. Andy's father knew one of the producers of *Hawaii Five-O*, so we put together every cliché we could think of and sent it to them. They loved it. They said, "Hey! You guys really know our show!" They ended up hiring us to write an episode, and we later sold another episode to *Kojak*, but eventually we went our separate ways. As writing partners, our talents were too similar, so—in a way—we were cancelling each other out.

We had scored a major coup by getting that first show on the air, though, and Jim Cash called from Michigan to congratulate me. We talked about perhaps writing together, but Jim seemed a million miles away, and nothing came of it. When I went back to Michigan to visit my family, however, I went to see him. We met at the campus's Union Grill and came up with ten ideas. None of these clicked, but on my way back to Los Angeles, somewhere in Kansas, I understood what Jim had been getting at. One of the ideas focused on two prohibition agents, Izzy and Moe, and it had elements of *The Sting*, with all the requisite twists and turns. I called him and told him we should work on it.

I knew the script had to be exceptional to get noticed. It had to be flawless, a page-turner that grabbed you from the very start, with solid, well-drawn characters. I had read enough scripts to know that this was the level of writing they were looking for in Hollywood, and we kept hammering at it until we both felt it was perfect.

We were working long-distance, in the pre-Internet days, so we relied on mail. We didn't even talk too often by phone, because AT&T was a monopoly in those days and long-distance calls cost a fortune. Neither of us minded the hard work. We were writing and not getting paid, but each successive draft was getting better, and that kept us going. It took us two years and five or six drafts, but I knew we only had one chance, so we put everything into it. In the meantime, I was getting work as a cameraman, and Jim had his regular job back in Michigan.

When Jim and I felt the script was ready, a friend introduced me to Sam Adams, an agent. He read it and liked it and called and said, "Well, now that you've got me, what do you want to do with me?"

Hollywood was a much smaller town in those days, without all of the independents there are now, and we sent the script to everyone we felt might respond, knowing that this was our one and only chance. They all loved the writing, but there was no bidding war. A few days later, when it was clear there would be no big sale, Bud Yorkin, an established director/producer, decided to option it. He paid us a hundred thousand dollars for the rights.

That was, like—*Wow!* To an established writer, that might not have meant much, but to us—well, we had succeeded. That was all the encouragement we needed, and we sat down to try again.

We went back to our original list of ten ideas and began to sift through them, but both of us kept our day jobs. I liked life on the set and I liked camera work. I was good at it, but I didn't have the education or background to become a serious director of photography. That was probably for the best. If I had, that's what I might be doing today.

The idea we both responded to was called *Old Gold*. It was about an archeologist who is always a day late and a dollar short, and has an opportunity to redeem himself when he discovers a mystery about some missing gold. This was in the pre-*Indiana Jones* days, so you might say we were on the right track.

At the time, Peter Guber was at a company called Casablanca, and he paid $250,000 for the script. We came within six weeks of getting it made, then the whole thing fell apart. It's probably just as well. We hadn't been part of the rewrites, and from what we'd heard, it wasn't getting any better.

That script got us a lot of attention, though. It was better than our first effort. It was more contemporary; it had better characters, and a more compelling story. At this point, our agency told us that we should begin considering assignments. We were in the game now, so I quit camera work and started making the rounds of the studios.

One of the first producers I met with was Joe Wizan, who pitched us an idea about two people in New York who find each other halfway through the movie, only to discover that they are being accused of murder. Jim and I tossed it around for a while and I went back with another version of the same thing. It had a lot of what we used to call "Charm & Chase": two opposites bantering at each other from start to finish. Wizan loved it. We took it to the studio and pitched it and sold it. Now we were under contract to write a script, which was suddenly a little daunting. Here's the thing: Jim and I were very independent. We had written two spec scripts and sold both of them, and we had our own way of doing things, and we didn't want people to get in our way.

We said, "Leave us alone, and we'll deliver a script. We're not coming in with progress reports every couple of weeks, and we're not delivering pages."

They agreed, a bit reluctantly, but even so it was harder than we thought. We were writing on assignment, and getting paid for it, and we felt the pressure. We had never done this before. In the end, though, it turned out to be the best thing we had ever written, and that script—*Whereabouts*—

took us to the highest possible levels. It was read by every studio executive in town, and they all wanted to be in business with us. We were offered a ton of jobs, but we turned them all down. We were independent. We didn't give a shit. We preferred writing specs.

As for the script, over the next few years, it was set up seven or eight times, but it never got made. Joe Wizan made a fortune off that script. Every time a studio passed, he bought it back with his own money, and resold it over and over again. I think there's about $10 million against it.

At one point, early on, *Whereabouts* was set up with director John Landis. He offered us *Dick Tracy*, which he was going to direct. I wasn't all that enthused about the job, but Jim wanted to do it, so we agreed. As with all of our projects, I came to love it very quickly. Also, we were working with the director, and we knew this vastly improved our chances of getting the movie made. Landis never directed it, though. It went through four directors before Warren Beatty signed on.

Then Jeffrey Katzenberg called. He was an executive at Paramount at the time, and he brought us in and pitched us eight ideas. "Take your pick," he said. He had something called *Top Guns*, with an "s," and I liked that one best. I had been a member of the Spartan Flying Club, at Michigan State, and had my private pilot's license. Once again, fate played a huge role in my life. I had a license. I loved flying. If nothing else, I figured I'd get to ride in a jet fighter. Jim, on the other hand, was deathly afraid of flying. He wasn't interested in the film, but he knew I really wanted to do it, and he agreed. That's always the way we worked. If one of us was passionate about a project, we would go with it. Passion always played a huge role in the work. We didn't just write scripts; we lived them.

Also, at this point, Jim and I were rethinking our independence. We had written all these scripts and none of them were getting made. We didn't realize how hard it was to get a movie off the ground. Our agents told us that the best way to get a movie made was to get into business with some hot producers, and a pair of hot producers were attached to the *Top Guns* project. They had just done *Flashdance* and were working on *Beverly Hills Cop*. Their names were Don Simpson and Jerry Bruckheimer.

Still, I wasn't convinced this was the right movie for us. I had read the article in *California* magazine, which had inspired the idea, and I thought it might be too similar to *The Right Stuff*, which was about to come out. But after reading the script for that movie, I realized that they were completely different stories, so we went ahead and made the deal to write it.

The article was very inspiring, but what really struck me was the photograph that accompanied it. It showed a fighter pilot in his headgear, with two planes on either side of him, and it was such a striking image that I felt I knew exactly what the movie was about. These guys were modern-day warriors, battling in the clouds at 28,000 feet. The visual imagery was unbeatable; that was the movie Jim and I wanted to make.

When I went down to the Naval Air Station, in Miramar, however, and sat with these guys, the story began to change. I did more than forty hours of interviews with them, and then I took a ride in the jet. At that point, I realized that this was not at all the story we thought it was. Flying those planes was one of the most grueling, rigorous, physically demanding events one could experience. The G-forces alone were almost unbearable. I called Jim after the flight, still reeling, and I told him, "This is not what we thought it was. These guys are *athletes*."

The concept changed. It became a movie about a group of highly competitive athletes who just happen to be competing with fighter jets. *Top Gun* was really a sports movie, and that's the script we set out to write. And we brought personal experience to it: Jim had been a high school quarterback and I'd played a little hockey at Michigan State.

We went back to Simpson and Bruckheimer and made our deal: "You guys leave us alone. We won't tell you what the movie is or give you pages. We'll come back when we're done and deliver a finished script."

They hated being in the dark, but we had enough power to pull it off. Still, it wasn't easy. While we had no trouble nailing the characters, we couldn't seem to crack the story. Then Jim suggested we open with a landing on a night carrier, and the movie literally wrote itself. When I went over to hand in the script, before they even sat down to read it, I told them, "Think Tom Cruise." I had seen Tom in *All the Right Moves*, and we had written the script with him in mind. The character, Maverick, is cocky, immature, and in your face. He had to be played by someone very likeable. If

Sean Penn had taken the role, it would have been a completely different movie.

Don read it right away. He called me and said the words every writer wants to hear: "I will kill to get this movie made."

Jim and I were elated. "We're getting a movie made!"

But Paramount didn't like it. They said there were too many planes in the sky. "Who wants to see all those planes?" They said they wanted to make a movie about an unflyable plane. Simpson and Bruckheimer stood firm, though. "That's not the movie we want to make. *This* is the movie we want to make."

It was a stalemate. We were devastated. We had written the slickest, most commercial movie we could think of, and it wasn't going to get made. What had we done wrong? We had written the perfect Saturday night movie. We were desperate to see something on the big screen. We wanted to be in the audience, listening to the response of the crowd, and it didn't look like it was going to happen.

Then our agent, Rand Holston, called to tell us that he was going to marry us to the hottest director in the country: Ivan Reitman. Ivan had just finished *Ghostbusters*, and he pitched us an idea called *Legal Eagles*. It was supposed to be a comedy with Dustin Hoffman and Bill Murray, but Dustin went off to do *Ishtar* and Bill Murray said he wouldn't do it because he hated attorneys. So Ivan said, "Let's turn it into a romantic comedy." And that's what we did. He got Robert Redford and Debra Winger on board, and suddenly we were getting a movie made.

The movie got greenlit before we had finished the script. So there we were, writing and delivering pages and cutting and pasting—not the way we like to work at all. And while we were in the middle of this, there was a change of administration at Paramount, and the new guys responded to *Top Gun*. Suddenly, that got greenlit, too. So we went from not being able to get a movie made to having two movies going at once.

Then Frank Price hired us to write *The Secret of My Success*, for Michael J. Fox, and that also got greenlit. In the space of a year, we had three movies released. I guess at that point you might say we'd pretty much broken in.

We did *Turner & Hooch* in 1989. *Dick Tracy* moved ahead the following year. And we worked on *Anaconda* and *The Flintstones in Viva Rock Vegas*.

With the advent of computers, the writing was easier and communication was much faster. But it was always long distance. In all the years we worked together, we only worked in the same room twice—and that was only because I was back visiting my family.

Then one day in late March, 2000, Jim collapsed and was rushed to the hospital with a blockage in his intestine. He flatlined, and the doctors brought him back, but he didn't make it.

It was a huge loss for me. When you work with someone for as long as I worked with Jim, it was like a marriage. And in fact we used to say that there were really three of us. There was Jim; there was me; and there was this third person, Cash & Epps, who was actually a combination of the two of us—a separate entity with his own personality. So for me, when Jim died, I really lost two of my closest friends.

In terms of advice, I think the most important thing is to know exactly what you want to do. Do you want to be a writer or a director?

The other thing important element is to keep learning, to keep practicing your trade. The learning never ends. You have to keep writing script after script after script until you live and breathe your craft.

One of the problems nowadays is that you have a generation of kids who have been raised on movies, and don't really understand storytelling. The stories are homogenized, and the movies aren't compelling because the characters aren't compelling.

If you want to be a writer, make sure you're writing stories about people who are struggling to overcome some kind of personal problem. It's not only *what* happens, but *who* it happens to. And, even more important, make sure you're writing stories that will appeal to name actors. Movies get made for one reason: *because actors want to play those roles*. It all boils down to casting. Our movies got made because Tom Cruise and Robert Redford and Warren Beatty and Tom Hanks and Michael J. Fox wanted to be in them; because they responded to the characters we created.

And part of the reason they responded is because the characters are larger than life. It goes back to what I said earlier: there's the real world, and there's the movie world, and the movie world is hyperreality. It's our world on steroids. Everything in a movie has to be amplified. Remember that.

Even then, it's going to be tough. You have to be persistent, you have to believe in yourself, and you have to be prepared.

Bad luck is when you get an opportunity and you're not prepared for it. Good luck is when you get an opportunity and you've done all the hard work and everything comes together.

At some point, that opportunity will present itself, and you have to be ready to grab it. And that only comes from years of preparation. So don't sit back and wait for it: start getting ready now.

DAVID FRANKEL

WRITER/DIRECTOR

"If there's one thing you need to understand about show business, it's that it is mostly about rejection, and that you're going to need a great deal of stamina to survive."

David Frankel grew up in New York City, the son of the *New York Times* executive editor Max Frankel, and knew early on that he wanted to become a writer. He attended Harvard College, where he was a reporter and movie critic for *The Crimson*, and studied political science and filmmaking.

Frankel has directed episodes of *From the Earth to the Moon*, *Sex and the City*, and *Band of Brothers*, along with a number of television pilots and a movie of the week. His feature credits include *Miami Rhapsody*, *Funny About Love*, and *Nervous Ticks*, and at the time of this interview he was in preproduction on *The Devil Wears Prada*, a film based on the bestselling book, starring Meryl Streep.

He was interviewed on May 15, 2005, by phone from Miami, Florida, where he resides.

The summer after my sophomore year, I went to Los Angeles with a friend who had a job teaching tennis to Alan Alda. We got a room at a boarding house near UCLA, and I was determined to find work—any kind of work—

on a movie set. My father knew someone who knew someone who knew Robert Evans, and he managed to arrange a meeting for me. I remember going over to Evans's majestic office on the Paramount lot, and Evans asked me, "What do you want to do?"

"I want to be a writer," I said.

So he said, "Why don't you go home and write? I could get you a job on a set but all you'd be doing is getting coffee for assholes."

So that's what I did: I went home to write. It was good advice and it's the same advice I'd give anyone who's trying to write or direct. People think Hollywood is incredibly glamorous, and parts of Hollywood *are* glamorous, but mostly it's hard work and drudgery. If you want to be creative, be creative. If you want to be a writer, write. Unlike an actor, you have the freedom to do so.

I was also deeply inspired by Alan Alda. I spent a lot of time at his place while my friend was helping him improve his tennis game. Alda had just finished starring in *The Seduction of Joe Tynan*, which he had also written, and there was always a lot going on around him. He had great barbecues, and some of his guests were well-known people from the industry. I got a taste of what Hollywood's inner sanctum was like, and it made for a weird dichotomy: I was living in a boarding house in Westwood, and then I'd drive into Bel Air and spend time with people who were at the top of Hollywood's food chain. I found it pretty seductive. Before the summer was over, I vowed that I would return to Hollywood as a writer, and, with some luck, as a director.

One of my first breaks occurred after I got back to college, while I was writing for *The Harvard Crimson*. The president of a TV syndication company called Telepictures came to *The Crimson*, looking to hire an intern for the following summer. They were working on a few low-budget originals, and they were taking old television shows and redistributing them. It sounded like I could learn something from that. It wasn't the Hollywood I had imagined coming back to, but it was a step in the right direction, so I applied for the job and got it.

The day I arrived for work, they were previewing their very first show. I thought it was horrible. The set was wobbly, the host was awkward, and the proceedings weren't all that interesting. I didn't think anyone would ever watch it. The show was *People's Court* and it went on to make millions of dollars for the company.

One of my responsibilities at Telepictures was to cut trailers for those old television shows, the ones they were trying to sell. It taught me a lot about how film worked, or didn't work. In the evening, and on weekends, I wrote screenplays, some of them not very good. But I wrote.

At the time, there were two producers who had a deal at Telepictures, Frank Konigsberg and Larry Sanitsky, and they took me under their wing and made me a development executive. Frank and Larry went out of their way to teach me everything they could about television movies: how to sell ideas, how to work with writers, how to launch a production. I spent a lot of time listening to ideas and trying to help them figure out which of them could be turned into network movies. While I was at Telepictures, Frank and Larry produced *The Glitter Dome*, starring James Garner and Margot Kidder, and I spent months in the editing room, reworking the film. I wrote narration to make it easier to follow, supervised the scoring and sound mixing, and even directed some second-unit sequences. It was better than any film school.

I spent a number of years at Telepictures, and it was a great experience, but it also included one of the low points of my career. I had been steadily climbing the ladder, and at one point I was a development executive on *Meet Your Neighbor*, a game show not unlike *The Newlywed Game*, but with neighbors instead of couples. The day we were supposed to pitch the pilot to NBC, I was sent to represent Telepictures. I was feeling like a big shot, but our only production assistant was called away on an emergency, so—instead of sitting with the network executives—I ended up lying on the floor behind the cardboard set, with an air horn and a bell, ringing and blasting every time one of the contestants got the wrong answer.

I got my first real break when I sold an idea to Warner Brothers called *Hotter Than July*. It was a love story, along the lines of *Casablanca*, set in Cuba shortly after Castro swept to power. That became my first professional writing assignment. I didn't quit Telepictures, though. I continued to write at night and on weekends. I knew Hollywood was fickle, so I kept my day job.

At the time, I was dating a woman who knew an agent, and she gave him one of my scripts. He liked it enough to pass it on to a producer, who gave it to another agent, who gave it to Norman Steinberg, who had cowritten *Blazing Saddles* and *Mr. Mom*. Norman responded to the script and we met and hit if off. At the time, Norman had a lot going on, and he asked me to help him write a pilot that had been commissioned by ABC, for Ellen Burstyn. The pilot got picked up, so I quit my job at Telepictures and moved to New York to produce *The Ellen Burstyn Show* with Norman. It was part of my ongoing education. I began soaking up everything I could about writing comedy.

Working in New York, it occurred to me that I might be able to have a Hollywood career without actually living in California. I didn't dislike Hollywood, or the people in it, but the town tends to be a little one-dimensional—it's all about showbiz—and I wanted some distance from that, some perspective. Coincidentally, I started seeing my college sweetheart again, and I fell in love with her for a second time. She was talking about moving back home, to Miami, and the idea appealed to me.

Norman and I later did another show called *Doctor Doctor*, and after that I did a short-lived show of my own, *Grapevine*, in Miami. It got noticed by Disney executives, including Jeffrey Katzenberg, who encouraged me to write a film for him. That became *Miami Rhapsody*, starring Sarah Jessica Parker and Antonio Banderas.

After that, I wrote *Dear Diary*, a spec TV pilot. It was the story of a complicated day in the life of a New York woman. I sold it to Katzenberg, who by then was a partner at DreamWorks, and he in turn sold it to ABC. We got Bebe Neuwirth to star, and the show turned out well, but the network found it a little too avant-garde and passed.

But *Dear Diary* wasn't dead. My producing partner, Barry Jossen, was also head of TV production for DreamWorks. He asked Teri Press, who was handling advertising and marketing for DreamWorks, if she thought she could enter *Dear Diary* in some film festivals. She had a better idea: why not enter it in the Short Film category of the Academy Awards?

At the time, DreamWorks was a new studio, and they didn't have any movies in the pipeline. So the marketing department put substantial muscle into promoting *Dear Diary*. We ended up winning the Academy Award (the first TV pilot to ever win an Oscar, and the *last*, thanks to a change in Academy rules), and I thanked ABC—in front of several hundred million people—for *not* having ordered the show.

I would be understating the case if I said I've been very, very lucky. I work hard, certainly, and that hard work has led to meetings with people who have reached out and helped me.

If there's one thing you need to understand about show business, it's that it is mostly about rejection, and that you're going to need a great deal of stamina to survive. I think that's one of the reasons people get paid such outrageous sums of money in this business: Talented, creative people who can produce consistently good work under extreme pressure and ferocious deadlines are as rare as big-league ballplayers. Like professional sports, it's hard to break in, it's hard to succeed after you've broken in, and it's almost impossible to maintain success for any extended length of time. Fortunately, the daunting odds don't scare everyone away.

Larry Kasdan, the writer-director, once said, "Any modestly talented person can write one spec script. And lots of ambitious people can write two. But if someone can shrug off the rejection of those first two and write a third one, on his or her own time, for no money, that person will probably make it in Hollywood because they've got what it takes to keep writing scripts until they finally sell one."

By that he meant, simply, that you have to keep at it. If you really want it, you can't give up. I think that's great advice. You learn by *doing*. You can take all the classes and seminars in the world, and some of them are doubtlessly fascinating, maybe even illuminating, but none of them are going to turn you into a successful writer. Writing makes you a writer. That's what Robert Evans taught me twenty-five years ago.

And Hollywood is always hungry for new material. No matter how hard it seems to break in, write something that gets people's attention, and you'll be on your way.

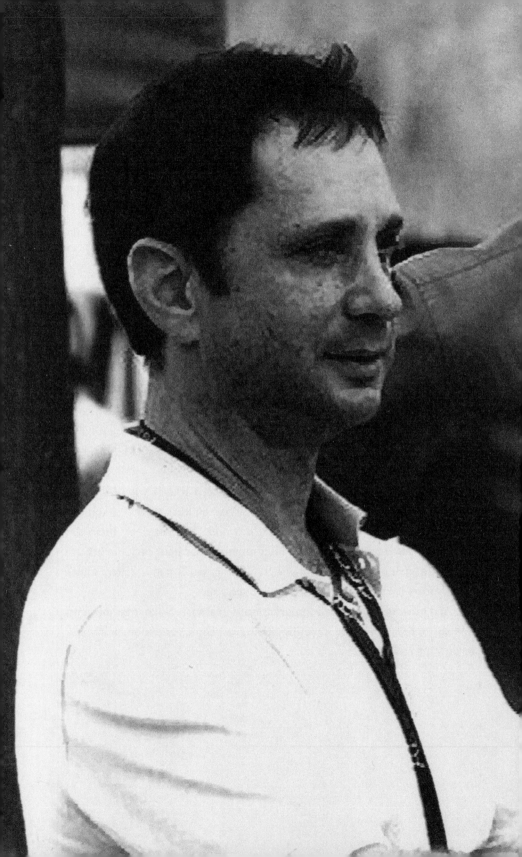

DAVID GALE

EXECUTIVE VICE PRESIDENT, MTV FILMS

"Always ask yourself, Is it worth it? If it is, you're on the right track."

David Gale was already a successful young lawyer in New York City when he decided to do something he was truly passionate about: make movies. Unlike many people, however, who would have immediately packed their bags and moved to Hollywood, Gale's approach was slow and methodical. He switched from business law to entertainment law, worked his way up the ranks, and finally ended up in the business affairs department of International Creative Management, the Los Angeles–based talent agency. The contacts he made at ICM opened doors in the creative end of the business, and Gale eventually left the company to try his luck as a producer.

Today, he is executive vice president of MTV Films, the man who decides which films get made or released under the MTV banner. Some of those films have included *Election*, *The Wood*, *Beavis and Butthead Do America*, *Coach Carter*, *The Longest Yard*, *Napoleon Dynamite*, *Varsity Blues*, and *Hustle & Flow*.

Gale was interviewed on May 23, 2005, at his office on the Paramount lot.

I was born in Miami, in one of those middle- to upper-middle-class families that seemed to be downwardly mobile. My father was a real estate executive who developed properties around the country, usually the right properties at the wrong time, and in the space of twelve years, I attended ten different schools. We moved from Miami to Maryland to northern Florida to Long Island to New York [City] to Connecticut and back to New York [City].

As a kid, I really wanted to be a doctor. I was diagnosed with Crohn's Disease early on, an ailment characterized by the inflammation of the small intestine, and I had to learn to deal with it. It was fairly serious, but I wasn't going to let the illness bring me down. As a result, I became something of an overachiever. I was involved in all the school clubs and in various extracurricular activities, even the most obscure ones, like the Save the Seals Club.

When I graduated from high school, I decided I was going to get as far away from home as possible. I think my illness drove me to assert my independence and show my family, and myself, that I had no fear of being on my own.

Luckily, I got into Stanford University—three thousand miles away. The day I got accepted felt like the best day of my life. I had never been to California, but from what I'd seen and heard, it was going to be a dream come true.

When I got to Stanford, it was even better than I had imagined. It was an idyllic place that gave you plenty of options and plenty of freedom, and of course the weather made it feel like utopia. I knew right away that someday I would settle in California.

By this point, I had lost interest in medical school—too much chemistry and biology—so I majored in international relations. Four years later, I went off to study law at New York University. I thought I would practice international law or maybe even become a diplomat.

Back then, I really didn't have any interest in the actual business of making movies. I loved going to movies and staying up late at night to watch old films on TV. I was just a regular moviegoer—but that's probably the best way to know what an audience wants.

When I graduated from law school, in 1982, I got an offer from Shearman & Sterling, a big banking firm on Wall Street where I had interned one summer. It was an outrageous amount of money for someone right out of school, and I took the job without much thought. The firm had a branch office in Paris, and I hoped to go there to work at some point. Six months into the job, I realized I couldn't spend my life in the world of international banking and securities. It was boring and disconnected from the real world, even in Paris.

I remember when I decided to change my career. I was on a train, coming back into the city from Long Island, where I shared a summer house with some friends, when I realized I could be passionate about being a movie producer.

Since I'm a fairly cautious person, I didn't just quit my job. I decided to try to switch to entertainment law, and I sent 150 resumes to every studio and to every law firm that was even remotely connected to the entertainment industry. I got rejected by all of them except one, a small firm called Beldock, Levine & Hoffman.

One of the partners, Elliot Hoffman, was a major force in the music business in New York, going back to the 1960s. He represented Talking Heads, Eurythmics, Judas Priest, Dizzy Gillespie, The Who, and Jimi Hendrix, among others. He also represented authors and playwrights, and a number of producers, people like Lorne Michaels, of *Saturday Night Live* fame, and Chris Blackwell, of Island Records, who was beginning to get into film production.

I had the good fortune of becoming Elliot's protégé. He was a lawyer who loved what he did. At age sixty, he used to ride to meetings and concerts on his Harley Davidson. He had a big, handlebar mustache, wore three-piece suits, and played an electric piano that he kept under his desk. People who were watching TV in the 1980s videos will recognize him as the tall guy in Cindy Lauper's music video, "Girls Just Want to Have Fun." Elliot's mustache was impossible to miss.

From my very first day with the firm, I found myself excited to be part of the entertainment business—despite the fact that I had taken a big pay cut. At first I didn't even have my own office, but Elliot gave me a front-row seat to his negotiations and his remarkable style of doing business.

Elliot also showed me that you can be most successful in business by always being honest, thoughtful, and direct. To me, he was the epitome of integrity.

Working with Elliot was my first real experience in the movie business. One of the first movie deals I negotiated was a role for Cindy Lauper in *Vibes*, not realizing that it would eventually change the course of my life.

In 1987, after three years with Elliot and his law firm, I decided to move on. It was a difficult decision. I was comfortable there, and I had been working with a man who was a true mentor and whom I adore to this day. But I knew it was time to get closer to my goal of being a movie producer. I also knew that I probably should move to Los Angeles, where movies were made, even if it meant leaving everything and everyone I knew in New York.

As I started to make inquiries into jobs in L.A., I was contacted by Charles Melniker, the head of ICM's feature business affairs department. He was the man with whom I negotiated the Cyndi Lauper deal, and he must have liked the way I handled the negotiations because he asked me to come to work with him at ICM.

Charles handled most of the accounts for Jeff Berg, chairman and COO of ICM, and six months later, when Charles left the company, I became Jeff Berg's guy in business affairs. Berg was pretty intimidating to a young lawyer, but I needed that kind of push. To avoid having to face him too often, I learned to solve problems before he even knew a problem existed.

I worked at ICM for three years. I was involved in deal making with some of the top clients of the agency, people like Jim Cameron, Gale Anne Hurd, Adrian Lyne, and Joe Eszterhas. I got to know many of our clients personally, and I really enjoyed developing those relationships. I learned the world of the agency deal making, and at the same time I was learning about the creative process.

One of the agency's clients was Ridley Scott, who had directed *Blade Runner*, among other movies, and who at the time was working on *Thelma and Louise*. I handled the bulk of his deals, and I had great respect for him. He was an amazing filmmaker.

At the time, Ridley was partnered with a woman named Mimi Polk, and one day they approached me to join their company. I was flattered, and also a little skeptical. But I was being offered a job that showed some confidence in my abilities beyond my knowledge of business affairs, and it was hard to resist. Maybe this was the chance I was looking for to continue pursuing my goal of becoming a movie producer. That would eventually happen, but there was some rough road ahead.

I really liked Ridley, who was always nice to me, but Mimi and I did not see eye to eye on anything. An understatement would be to say that the job turned out to be a lot less than I had hoped for.

Even so, I learned a lot about the entertainment business during my short time with the company—some of which was pretty discouraging.

I began to have doubts about the business. I wondered if I would have to compromise my integrity to get ahead, and whether I had what it takes to make it in Hollywood.

At that moment, I decided to get out of the business. I kept my job, but I took the California bar exam and dreamed of moving to Carmel or Monterrey, hanging up my law shingle, and living a simpler life. Before I had the chance to set those plans in motion, however, I lost my job. It was the first time in my life I was unemployed, and I found it wasn't that bad. I had a lot of time to think and relax and to try to figure out what I really wanted to do with my life, and to focus on what was important to me. I had a lot of friends in the business—people who were looking out for me—and one of them was Lawrence Rose, a lawyer who represented Gale Anne Hurd. Gale was an A-list producer—some of her films included *The Terminator*, *Aliens*, and *The Abyss*—and I had met her in passing over the years. Lawrence told me that Gale was looking for someone to run her company, Pacific Western Productions, and to my surprise I turned out to be that guy. I decided to put off that move to Carmel.

Although Gale could be a very demanding boss, I also found that she is one of the fairest and most honest people in the business. If someone [was] loyal, trustworthy, and smart, she [gave] them tremendous responsibility. She had no trouble sharing success, unlike a lot of people in the business. Gale also had an incredibly great creative team, and I learned a great deal from them.

Over the course of the next four years, working with Gale, I really learned how to be a manager, how to develop a script, how to handle problems on the set, and how to deal with some of the tougher personalities that are attracted to the movie business.

I think more than anything else in this business you have to learn to be agile. You have to be able to shift from topic to topic, problem to problem, and person to person, and you have to learn to do it as quickly as possible, without getting thrown off course.

One of the things that helped me out in that regard was the fact that I had to prepare written updates *every single day*, one of Gale's rules. I would document everything—phone calls, conversations, contracts, scripts—and I would leave a typed report on her desk. (This was before e-mail.) The practice was tough, but it helped clarify what I was doing and why. I now have my own staff do the same for me, but I'm a little more lenient and only ask for updates twice a week.

In 1995, my contract with Gale was coming up, and I found out that MTV was looking for someone to run their new movie division. They were about to release *Joe's Apartment*, and they felt that there was an opportunity to begin developing and producing more movies in-house. After a pretty painless interview process, I was hired.

My official title is executive vice president, MTV Films. I'm responsible for overseeing our staff, for finding projects, for developing scripts, and for producing and acquiring movies. I report to Van Toffler, president of MTV Networks, a great boss, and together we decide what we think are the best projects. All our movies are released through Paramount, which usually finances them, and we work hand in hand with the studio and their executives. My job is a unique one. I work for MTV, under the MTV Films brand, but I'm also a hands-on producer. I've been involved in producing, acquiring, or helping to release many films, including *The Original Kings of Comedy, Tupac: Resurrection, Beavis and Butthead Do America, Jackass: The Movie, Napoleon Dynamite*, and *The Longest Yard*.

Among the movies we've produced, one of my favorites is *Election*. Reese Witherspoon plays an obnoxious, overachieving high school girl who is running for president of the student body. Matthew Broderick plays her troubled, vindictive teacher. It was a unique movie, completely outside the box. The book was brought to me by Albert Berger and Ron Yerxa, and we got Alexander Payne and Jim Taylor to adapt it. Payne recently got a lot of attention with *Sideways*, but prior to *Election* he directed an original little movie called *Citizen Ruth*.

Election didn't do great at the box office, but it got our company's first Academy Award nomination, for Best Adapted Screenplay, and it helped us attract other great filmmakers.

In terms of advice, I think it's good to have both long-term and immediate goals. If you're happy with what you're doing now—if you like the day-to-day aspects of your job, if you're still learning, if you're still finding the work satisfying—that's fine; keep doing what you're doing. But don't lose sight of the long-term goals. Look for those opportunities that will help you move closer to those goals.

In order to succeed, you have to have goals, and you have to take risks. But in the process you can't compromise yourself, or your integrity, and you can't sacrifice the things that are important to you. Fame, success, and money are fine, but not at the expense of happiness.

Always ask yourself, *Is it worth it?* If it is, you're on the right track.

Sometimes, of course, the greater goals are not worth the sacrifices. That's an individual matter. But sometimes they are very much worth the sacrifices. And that, too, is an individual matter.

I think, for me, the most important thing—far more important than fame or money or success—is balance. Outside of my professional life, I am always looking for ways to do the things I really want to do. I have my family, and I have my friends, and beyond that I am involved with a number of charitable organizations that are close to my heart. I have tried to leverage my success into doing things that really matter to me, things that make a difference in my life, and, one hopes, in the life of others, and I'm always looking for opportunities to do better.

I still ask myself, *Is it worth it?* And I'm still saying *Yes*, resoundingly. So, for the moment, anyway, I know I'm on the right track.

PETER GALLAGHER

ACTOR

"You may not end up where you want to be, but wherever you end up is where you need to be."

Peter Gallagher likes to say he feels like the luckiest guy in the world, and he means it from the bottom of his heart. Fresh out of college, he went off to New York to try to make it as an actor, and within three months he was the lead in *Grease*. He hasn't looked back since.

A noted stage actor, Gallagher has appeared in a number of critically acclaimed productions, including *Guys and Dolls*, *Long Day's Journey into Night* (with Jack Lemmon), *The Real Thing*, and *Noises Off*.

In 1980, he made his film debut in *The Idolmaker*, and in the years since has appeared in nearly three dozen movies, including *Sex, Lies, and Videotape*, *The Player*, *Short Cuts*, *The Hudsucker Proxy*, *While You Were Sleeping*, and *American Beauty*. He is currently on the cast of *The O.C.*, the hit television series on Fox.

We spoke to him on June 7, 2005, at his home in Los Angeles.

I was born in New York City and grew up in Armonk, New York, just thirty-five miles from Manhattan. My mother was a first-generation American whose parents had come over from Ireland. During World War II, she worked with a team of doctors and scientists on the development of penicillin. My father was the son of a coal miner from Freeland, Pennsylvania, and seemed destined for a life in the mines, but the local nuns arranged for him and his two brothers to go to school at Notre Dame. At the time, they were the only boys in the county who went off to college.

My background was all about survival and salvation through education, and there was no time, money, or energy left over for entertainment. I didn't see a Broadway show until I was in my teens, and I didn't see many movies growing up. But we had a TV, and I was a big fan of *The Dean Martin Show*. I think part of the reason I loved it [was] because it seemed so unrehearsed. Dean had a spontaneity and a kind of "cool" about him that made everything seem right with the world.

I was constantly doing Dean Martin impressions, for anyone who could tolerate them—though there weren't many people who could tolerate a sixth grader singing "Everybody Loves Somebody Sometime."

Those impersonations were my first brush with showbiz. My next brush came at Byram Hills High School, right there in Armonk, when I was fifteen. They were having auditions for *The Fantasticks*, and they needed someone who could do a cockney accent for the part of Mortimer, the Indian. I had the strongest feeling that I could do a cockney accent, just from watching old movies on TV. I had never actually *done* one, so I didn't really have the nerve to go in and audition for the role, and I was literally pacing up and down the corridor, outside where the auditions were being held, when my French teacher, Mr. Mostica, walked over. "What are you doing, Peter?" he asked.

"I'm trying to get up the nerve to go in and audition for *The Fantasticks*," I said.

"Just go in there and do it," he said, then turned and sauntered off.

I didn't go in and do it, of course. I waited and kept pacing until I saw Mr. Bissell starting to leave. The auditions were over. I began to approach him, timidly, and I managed to half-stammer something about the fact that I was sort of thinking about maybe auditioning, but that I knew it was too late, and I tried to slink off. But he told me to come in and audition, and I ended up getting the part. It had taken me literally four hours of pacing to get the part. And now that I think about it, it took me about four hours of pacing to pick up the phone to call the woman who would later become my wife, but that wasn't until many years later. I never made that connection until now! I got the part of Mortimer, and, much later, I got the part of the husband.

Anyway, being on stage was a wonderful experience. I immediately felt I had a freedom that I did not have in regular, civilian life. And that's where it started. I began doing plays. I distinctly remember the time Mr. Bissel was about to produce his first musical, *110 in the Shade*, and I remember it because I wasn't asked to be in it. I guess I was a bit of a cutup, always looking for attention in the wrong ways, and I was horsing around again while everyone else was dutifully trying to learn one of the songs. Mr. Bissell got very angry. I was always getting sent to the back of the class, but this time he seemed to feel a more severe reprimand was in order. And he said, "Okay, Peter, stand up and sing it for us." And I remember thinking, *A solo? Me?!* And feeling like I wanted to die.

But at the same time I was thinking, *I'll be damned if I'm going to screw this up!* So I stood up and sang it, and I did okay.

I had always suspected I could sing a little, but except for those Dean Martin impressions, I never sang in front of anyone. Years later, ironically enough, I ended up doing a Dean Martin impression on *The Hudsucker Proxy*, but back in high school, even after that marvelous little solo, I still wasn't asked to be in *110 in the Shade*.

My first singing part was in *The Pajama Game*. I was a member of the chorus, and the girl in the part of Babe was played by Laura Branigan, who years later went on to have a hit single, *Gloria*. She was a couple of years older than me and she was unbelievable beautiful and sexy, and she was standing right next to me. And I was asked to do *one* solo line, but I was so overwhelmed by her proximity, and my heart was beating so fast, that I couldn't get it out. So I blew my first solo.

For a while, I did nonsinging roles, with very few lines, and I learned to relax a little, then I went back to musicals and got the part of Snoopy in *You're a Good Man, Charlie Brown*. On the night of the opening performance, Mr. Bisssell took me aside and tried to get me to do a fairly complicated tap routine while I was singing. I couldn't get it right. I was just too tied up in knots to tap dance and sing the song at the same time. And he looked at me and shook his head with disgust and said, "Peter, you couldn't walk and chew gum at the same time!"

I thought very seriously about running away and becoming a hobo. It was preferable to facing the very public humiliation that was only hours away. It was just an awful feeling, and even now, as I think about it, I can feel it all over again. But then I thought to myself, *I know what I'm going to do. I'm just going walk out on that stage and move so fast and smile so hard that nobody's going to be able to tell what my feet are doing.* I just hoped nobody would notice how desperate I was.

Well, whatever I did, it was like Snoopy had taken six tabs of acid and drunk a lot of coffee or something, because I was out there doing my number like a whirling dervish and I literally stopped the show.

> *'Cause it's supper*
> *Supper-*
> *Super duper suppertime!*

The audience just rose to its feet and started hooting and hollering and clapping, and I was very confused. I didn't know what was happening. I had just been trying to survive. I wanted to be the hungriest dog they'd ever seen. The possibility that I might do the number successfully, that wasn't even in the realm of possibility. But the next day I was all over the local press. They were going on and on about Snoopy's performance, and for years afterward I kept running into people around town who'd come over and shake my hand and say, "I remember when you were Snoopy!"

The performance also came as a surprise to Mr. Bissell, of course, but he wasn't particularly effusive about it. I have fond memories of him because he taught me a lot about stagecraft, but he was very tough. He'd had experience in New York, and he told us that he had never personally known anyone who succeeded in showbiz. He was constantly painting a terrifying picture of the life of an actor. There were no rosy predictions about anyone's chances of success. "Forget it! That path is paved with broken hearts and shattered dreams!" He was very convincing, too. It never occurred to me to pursue acting as a profession. But I still loved the escapist element. I loved that for those two hours I was exactly where I should be, doing exactly what I should be doing, and that the rest of my life didn't exist.

Then I went off to college, to Tufts University, where on the very first week of freshman year, I met my wife. I had no intention of pursuing theater, knowing it wasn't a viable profession, so I majored in economics and took a minor in art history. They had a theater department at Tufts but it felt a little precious to me. Or maybe I was just a little intimidated by it, and I *told myself* it was precious. But I was curious and ended up taking a class from Tommy Thompson, a wonderful teacher. I went into it with every intention of being the cutup, as I'd been in high school. One day we were told to bring a poem to class or a bit of writing and act it out for the others in a meaningful way. I found a ridiculous poem in a book of shaggy-dog stories that belonged my brother: *I'm So Lonesome in the Saddle Since My Horse Died.* That was the whole poem; honestly. I thought I'd just lay the class out with how funny and clever I was, and I did my shtick, and I got a few laughs, but immediately afterwards Tommy Thompson turned to me and said, "Okay, Peter. There's a fence there. Imagine you're sitting on the fence. Now do it like you mean it."

And I did it again, and I don't know what came over, but I was in tears. I played this broken-hearted cowboy who was missing his horse, and I wept. And after I pulled myself together, I realized I'd just learned a valuable lesson.

I tried out for a few shows at Tufts, and academically I did enough to get by. Then I auditioned with the Boston Shakespeare Company, because I'd met some of the people there, and I did three seasons with them. I later did *Macbeth*, playing Malcolm, and a couple of papers in Boston singled me out in their reviews and said nice things about my acting. It meant a lot to me.

I kept working with BoShakes, as we called the company, then I did some summer stock at Whitehorse Beach, in Cape Cod, at the Priscilla Beach Theater. It was one of the oldest theaters on the straw-hat circuit. Some guys from Tufts raised a little money, chased the raccoons away, swept the stage, and began to put on musicals. People loved it. We filled the place every night.

I also spent part of each summer at home, seeing my family and making money painting houses. I was a pretty good house-painter. Then I went back and worked for the Boston Ballet, in the box office. And one summer I ended up in the South Bronx, putting security systems in supermarkets. The neighborhood was so dangerous that we'd arrive after the markets closed and get locked in for the night. When we were done, usually by three or four in the morning, we'd raid the deli and make these terrific sandwiches and wait for the morning crew to spring us.

The seminal experience for me came between my junior and senior year, when I took a summer off from theater and went to the University of California, at Berkeley. I had taken a lot of advanced placement classes in high school, and I got college credit, and at this point I just really wanted to get out of college. It didn't feel like the right place for me. I wasn't studying very hard, and I wasn't all that interested. But I couldn't do that to my parents. The only thing they had ever asked of me was to get an education. They were supportive in every way, but education had saved their lives, and they were determined that their children be educated. I couldn't deny them. But I thought I would try to get some extra credits and graduate early.

The other reason I went out to Berkeley was to visit my first girlfriend. I'd already met my future wife, but we were friends for seven years before we realized we belonged together, and at the time I was still curious about my girlfriend, who had left Tufts and returned to her home in Northern California. So I got on a plane for the first time in my life, and I felt like I was going to the moon, and when I got to Berkeley, the girl and I kept not connecting, and I tried to settle into my studies. I was studying Marxist economics and statistics and stuff like that, which wasn't very exciting, but they also had a series called *Shakespeare on Film.*

That was the summer I discovered that I had no interest and certainly no aptitude for economics, and that my real desire was up there on the screen. Watching those movies was a real turning point for me: Laurence Olivier in *Henry V* and *Hamlet;* Paul Scofield in *King Lear*, directed by Peter Brook; Orson Welles in *Macbeth;* yet another version of *Hamlet* directed by Tony Richardson. Those films, and that whole experience, pretty much laid out the future for me. I was torn between my obligation to my parents, and what I felt in my heart, and at the end of the day—with a very heavy heart— I decided I would give myself seven years to try to make a living as an actor.

I thought seven years was long enough so that it would be a real attempt, but not so long that I would throw away the rest of my life. I knew that it wouldn't happen overnight, just as I knew that there was a limit to how long I should pursue it. I knew that at some point it would be too costly and painful to go on, and seven years seemed to be about the right length of time.

But the funny thing is, I had very modest expectations. I wasn't imagining success or stardom and I certainly wasn't thinking of the movies. I was only thinking that if I could make enough money in the theater to pay for my rent and my food, I would be the happiest man in the world.

It was an amazing summer, except for the girlfriend and the weather. All I'd brought with me to Berkeley were shorts and T-shirts, and I finally understood what Mark Twain meant when he said, "The coldest winter I ever spent was a summer in San Francisco."

I went back to Tufts and graduated in December, a semester early, but I was doing a production of *Macbeth* and I stayed in Boston for a few more months. And in late May or early June—this was 1977—I moved to New York. I had a friend there, Henry Kelston, whose grandmother was subletting her apartment, and I took it, and then I went out and did what actors do in New York: I picked up the trades, *Backstage* and *Show Business*, and proceeded to go to open calls.

I knew absolutely no one in show business. I didn't even know anyone who knew anyone in show business. But I had heard that you looked through the trades and went to open calls, and that's what I did. And since I could sing a little, I figured my best chance was to try to get a part in a musical.

I found out they were casting for the bus-and-truck production of *Grease*, a version of the Broadway show they were going to take on the road. And before I went to audition, I decided to do my homework and actually see the show. I came away from that experience totally blown away. It was that good. I knew I couldn't do it. And I told my friend Henry Kelston that I wasn't even going to audition. And he said, "Wait a minute! You told me that you were going to audition for everything you could find, even if you weren't right for it, and you're already backing out?!"

And I said, "You know what? You're right. I'll go."

Now, unless you're an actor, you don't know about open calls. But you get there at 6:00 a.m. to find many pages of legal-sized yellow paper posted to the door, and you add your name at the bottom of the list. There are generally so many pages that you end up getting an outrageous number. I think I was number 2,862 or something. And then you get into an unbelievably long line that stretches around the entire block, and you begin to inch your way forward. And after about six hours you snake your way up the stairs and get closer and closer to the audition room.

So I was finally there. We were supposed to do a 1950s song, and I chose *Put Your Head on My Shoulder*. And I was thinking about all the crazy shtick I was going to do for the casting people to make it funny. And there was this guy in front of me, and he did *Jeremiah Was a Bullfrog*, and he did such a fantastic job that I felt like turning around and running away. But I didn't run. I went inside and decided I was going to sing that song like I meant every word of it. Maybe it was Tommy Thompson's influence; who knows? But that's what I did. I went in and started to sing. And there were two people in the room. Phyllis Grandy, playing the piano, and Vinnie Liff—one of the great casting directors on Broadway. We were in this tiny, little room in the Minskoff Building, at 1515 Broadway, and I got through a couple of verses, and Vinnie looked at me, full of admiration, and said, "Peter! That was beautiful!"

At that point, my knees buckled and my eyes filled with tears. I didn't fall to the ground or actually cry or anything—I managed to hold it back—but I was incredibly moved. I thought, *Those three little words will keep me going for seven years.* And I knew they would. That was all I needed.

Vinnie and Phyllis thanked me and I thanked them and I walked out, on Cloud Nine. And the next day I went to another open call, for *Hair*, and it was the same story: number 1,207. Everybody in creation was there. There were lines around the block. And I auditioned, and over the next two weeks, they called me back eight times. And I got my first job. It was a revival of *Hair*, on Broadway, with the original cast, including director Tom O'Horgan.

It was unbelievable. I had given myself six or seven years to make it as an actor, and less than two months after I'd arrived in New York, I was down at the Ukrainian Hall, in the East Village, rehearsing for a Broadway musical and getting whipped into shape.

They kept delaying the opening, though. And they kept replacing people. We kept previewing and previewing and they kept changing leads, and after doing a bunch of performances of *Hair*, I got a callback from the people at *Grease*. So on my lunch break, I walked over to see them, and auditioned for Vinnie Liff again, and he said something I didn't quite catch and I thanked him and left to go back to my job. And suddenly I heard this voice behind me, hollering: "PETER! PETER GALLAGHER! STOP!" It was Vinnie Liff. "YOU GOT THE JOB!" he shouted.

And of course, being a complete idiot, I said I had a job up the street. And Vinnie said, "Peter, are you crazy! This is the *lead*."

And I took a moment and thought about it, and I said, "You're right." I knew nothing about how the business worked. I didn't even have an agent. I went back and told Tom O'Horgan that I'd just been offered the lead in *Grease*, and would he mind very much if I left the show. I'd been doing the show for a while, in previews, and I told him that this other job presented a great opportunity for travel. I explained that I'd never really been west of Pennsylvania, except for that one trip to California, and that I wanted to see southern New Jersey and Florida and Indiana and the rest of the country.

And Tom said, "Are you serious? This is a *Broadway* show. We're in production. We're going to open in less than a month."

And I said, "I know, but I thought the bus-and-truck thing might be kind of great."

And he looked at me and shook his head, kind of in shock. "You *are* serious?"

"Yeah," I said.

"Okay," he said. "Let me talk to the guys."

I was so guileless in my request that it actually happened. They let me go. He even offered me the lead that night, but I said no, never having rehearsed the part. I didn't need that kind of pressure; I didn't want to have a heart attack on my last day on the show.

So off I went, to do the road production of *Grease*, which was just a great experience. And six months later I was invited to join the Broadway company. I did about 500 performances of that show. There were two guys on the show who are my friends to this day, David Paymer and Danny Jacobsen, and the three of us had a song we'd sing backstage:

Our careers have peaked and we will never work again!
We are making more money now than we will ever see again!

We honestly believed this was as good as it got. And we were all wrong, of course. Paymer went off to have a brilliant acting career in Hollywood, and Jacobsen segued into writing and created several hit shows, including *Roseanne* and *Mad About You*. As for me, I went on to do a production of *Caligula*, with the Robert Lewis Acting Company, and then I was offered a pilot and got flown out to L.A., first class. I remember sitting there with Laraine Newman and Christopher Lee and Mervyn LeRoy, of *Wizard of Oz* fame, feeling like I'd won the lotto.

The pilot was called *Just Us Kids*, and I kept wondering whether this was a mistake. I was a serious theater actor, and I believed this might affect my career. It didn't affect my career because the show didn't go anywhere, but I was later offered another series, *Skag*, with Karl Malden, Piper Laurie, and Craig Wasson. Karl played the foreman of a steel mill, and I was his son, and the show was written by Abby Mann.

We were shooting at MGM one day, and I was in the middle of a scene, a single, with the camera directly on me. I was playing a self-involved medical student who wouldn't come home to see his father—played by Karl—even though he'd just suffered a stroke. And I'm on the phone with Karl, explaining my position at great length, and suddenly I hear this strange sound—a sort of crackling, sizzling sound. But being a theater guy, I stayed on the phone: in theater, come hell or high water, you keep going. But then I noticed that everything was shaking. And I thought, *It must be the subway.* And I realized there was no subway in Los Angeles. And I was standing there, on the phone, still doing my enormous monologue, and I tried to look past the bright lights to see what was going on, and I was so determined to be the consummate actor that I even tried to make it look like part of the scene. And of course now I could see that everyone was gone; that I was alone on the set. The whole place was shaking, but I was still acting and there wasn't a soul left in the building! And finally it dawned one me: *This is an earthquake.* So I dropped the phone and ran to the door, having heard that that's what you were supposed to do—put yourself in a doorway. But these weren't real doors; it was a set, and the walls were bending and bowing. And finally I had the good sense to leave the building. And the crew and everyone was sitting around and they saw me coming, and one of them said, "First earthquake, huh?" And they all got a real kick out of that.

That was it. That's how I broke in. I did two features after that, almost back to back, *The Idolmaker,* directed by Taylor Hackford, and *Summer Lovers,* directed by Randal Kleiser. Neither of them did particularly well. Then I went back to New York and did *A Doll's Life* and it ended up being the biggest flop in the history of Broadway, at the time, anyway.

The next movie I did was *Dreamchild,* and, much later, in 1988, I did *Sex, Lies & Videotape,* and that movie seems to have put me on the map.

I'm on *The O.C.* now, and I'm considering a film or two, and I'm cutting an album this summer, my first, which I'm very excited about. But I'm still doing theater, and I think I always will. Sir John Gielgud used to say that you can't even begin to think of yourself as an actor until you've been doing it for ten years. Well, I've been doing it for a lot more than ten years, but I'm still learning, still studying, and I still feel like the luckiest guy in the world.

Advice? Well, I agree with that old saying: *90 percent of life is showing up.* So keep showing up.

For someone starting out, I would say that the most important thing is to stay passionate. And to study. I can't say enough about that. I owe a huge debt to all the great teachers and all the great actors I've worked with over the years, and I couldn't have stumbled through without their help.

So show up. Find the best teachers. And don't give up. You may not end up where you want to be, but wherever you end up is where you need to be. And it might be a pretty good place.

EVA GARDOS

EDITOR/DIRECTOR

"Don't wait for Hollywood to give you something, because it generally doesn't happen that way."

Eva Gardos began her professional life as an inner-city schoolteacher, but government cutbacks forced her into another line of work, and she ended up in the prop department of a zombie movie. When shooting ended, she was asked to help in the editing room, and that led, circuitously, to a job as a production assistant on *Apocalypse Now* in the Philippines, the experience of a lifetime.

When she returned to the United States, Gardos went back to editing, paying her dues on small, nonunion jobs until director Hal Ashby decided to take a chance on her. That job led to editing gigs with other respected directors, including Martha Coolidge, Peter Bogdanovich, and Barbet Schroeder, but she gave it all up to become a director herself.

Gardos knew that no one was likely to give her the reigns to a feature film, so she sat down and wrote her first screenplay. It was the story of a young girl whose parents escape the communist regime in Hungary, but in the process are forced to abandon their infant daughter. Eva Gardos was that infant daughter, and her true story, *An American Rhapsody*, was released in 2001. It starred Nastassja Kinski, Scarlet Johansson, and Tony Goldwyn.

Gardos was interviewed at her Hollywood home on June 13, 2005.

I was born in Budapest and was separated from my family when I was barely one. My parents were trying to escape from Hungary, and I was supposed to follow a day later, but there were complications and they were forced to leave the country without me. I didn't see them again for six years.

When I was seven, we were reunited in Canada. My father was an accountant, and my mother was a housewife, and I lived with them until I was fourteen, at which point I was sent away to a boarding school because I was a rebellious young lady.

I returned from boarding school in a miniskirt—this was the 1960s—and eventually ended up in New York City. I got a master's in Education from City University, and for the next five years, I was teaching in a ghetto school in Harlem. I was a proponent of open education and I was very involved in the politics of poverty, as well as active in the antiwar movement. In short, I was very much a child of the sixties.

I also think I was a pretty good teacher, but in the mid-1970s all the social funding dried up and hundreds of us were laid off. I found myself unemployed, without anything to do, and some friends asking me to help them on a low-budget movie. It was about Nazi zombies. I worked in the prop department.

After they finished shooting, they asked if I could help out in the editing room. It was 16-millimeter film, and this was a long time ago, before digital editing. Every time you cut a scene, or made a change, you would literally cut the film. And you would have to keep track of all the little pieces, because the editor would often change his mind and make you go back and find the parts you'd trimmed.

I was working with this guy, Norman Gay, and I became his apprentice. We were in a building on Broadway, in Manhattan, where a lot of editing was going on. Dede Allen was there. She was later nominated for two Academy Awards, for *Dog Day Afternoon* and *Reds*. Jerry Greenberg was also in the building. He edited most of Brian De Palma's movies, and people still talk about the amazing work he did on the helicopter sequences in *Apocalypse Now*.

We would hang out, and have lunch together, and I enjoyed their company. I also loved the editing, even though it was very detail oriented, and very labor intensive. You literally had to keep track of every single cut, and of each trim—the missing piece of film—making a note of each on a blank page and creating a log of each change, cut by cut. Imagine *one* scene where you have 600 cuts and you begin to get the idea.

Still, it was inspiring and very interesting. Norman liked to explain things as he went through the different versions, and it was a real education. The zombie film was later released as *Shockwave*. Brooke Adams played the ingénue. I'm sure she'll hate me for reminding everyone.

One day I found out that two of the editors in the complex, Barry Malkin and George Berendt, were about to go off to work on *Apocalypse Now*, for Francis Ford Coppola. I decided to try to get on that film, and I sought out Fred Roos, one of the producers, and told [him] I would do *anything* to work on the movie.

"Great," he said. "Pay your way over and you've got a job."

They were shooting in the Philippines, and I took my hard-earned cash and bought myself a ticket. As soon as I arrived, Fred Roos put me to work. He was in charge of all location casting, and I went out and found people to work as extras. I found a number of Vietnamese refugees, and I found quite a few Americans—guys who had never come home from Vietnam. They'd opened bars and decided to stay in Asia, and they had no intention of ever returning home. A lot of them played soldiers in the film, which wasn't too much of a stretch.

At one point, Francis heard about a tribe of people, the Ifugao, who were living up in the mountains. They were famous for the incredible rice terraces they built into the hills, but they did more than grow rice; they were said to be headhunters. Francis didn't care. He wanted an actual, living, functioning tribe in his movie, and the Ifugao were perfect, since they were ethnically very different from the mainland Filipinos. In fact, they were closer in appearance and lineage to the Montagnards, a fierce Vietnamese tribe that had fought on the side of the Americans during the war.

Francis asked me if I would go up into the mountains and try to talk these people into being in the film, and I agreed to do my best. I was young and very energetic and the idea appealed to me, even though I knew it was totally crazy. This was right after a typhoon had destroyed all of our sets, and everyone on the shoot was slowly going insane.

So I found this girl in Manila whose father, an American anthropologist, had run off and married an Ifugao princess, and she agreed to take me up into the mountains.

It was *way* up there. We took buses and hiked from one village to the next, and it took two days to get there. On the trip up, I had asked the girl about this head-hunting business, and she told me that the Ifugao didn't go out of their way to lop off people's heads, but if they killed someone in battle, they would sever the head and keep it under their hut as a trophy.

They were *definitely* very primitive. The men wore loincloths and the women were topless. With the girl functioning as my interpreter, I explained that we wanted them to come down to the valley, and to just go about their lives for a few months, and I said that we would pay them a few dollars a day, and give them pigs and chickens and whatever else they needed. We negotiated a little, and they seemed satisfied, but they said they would need a caribou, a water ox, to make a sacrifice when they arrived. This would bring the good spirits into the valley with them. I assured them that we would find them a water ox, and they said we should expect them in three or four weeks.

About a month later, a couple of hundred of them showed up. I had arranged for the delivery of a water ox, and it was waiting for them. Francis's wife, Eleanor, was there, making a documentary about the making of the movie, and as soon as the tribesmen arrived, they saw the water ox and got ready to make their sacrifice. Eleanor told me to hurry off and get Francis, and we returned in time to watch the sacrifice. Francis immediately decided that he had to re-create the scene for his movie. He was very impressed with the way they used the machetes to kill the water ox with only three or four well-placed blows.

That became a very famous scene in the film: Francis juxtaposed the killing of the water ox with the scene in which Martin Sheen kills Marlon Brando, also using a machete.

The whole experience on *Apocalypse Now* was really quite incredible. Everyone was putting everything they had into the film, literally to a point of madness. I was working with incredible people. Francis; Vittorio Storaro, the cinematographer; Dean Tavoularis, the production designer. Even the people in makeup and sound and art direction—everyone, down to the lowest production assistants—were completely committed to the film. It was a wonderful learning experience, to watch all of these incredibly creative people putting everything they had into their work. And it was so inspiring that one day, when one of the sound guys asked me what I eventually wanted to do, I didn't even have to think about it. "I want to direct," I said.

After the shoot, I moved back to Los Angeles and went through "The Boring Years." My first job was as an assistant editor on a commercial. Then I worked as a P.A. for Roger Corman, which was pretty horrible—the antithesis of working for Francis. With Francis, everyone wanted to make everything fabulous; with Corman, it was all about getting it done.

Then I got a job as an assistant editor on a string of TV movies and so-called After-School Specials. I thought I would have a better shot at getting into something creative through editing, and I didn't exactly love the jobs I was getting, but at least I was learning. I thought about going back to New York, but there was no way to become an editor in New York. The famous editors were all fairly young, and they would be around forever. Also, the union was almost impossible to break into. They had a limited number of editors, and they all worked, and the union liked it that way.

I started getting very depressed about my career. And one day I was in the parking lot of a studio, smoking a cigarette, and I ran into someone I knew who was working with Hal Ashby. Hal had been an editor, and he'd gone on to direct some wonderful films (*Harold and Maude*, *The Last Detail*, *Coming Home*) and at the time he was working on *Being There*. When Hal asked me what I was doing, I told him that I was working as an assistant editor, and that I was looking to move on, and he said he was about to start a new company, and that he was planning on hiring a number of young people to help them break into the business. Having been an editor himself, he knew how tough it was to get into the union. In fact, one of the few ways to break in was through a new company. When a new company becomes a union signatory, its employees automatically become members.

Six months later, I got a call from Hal Ashby. He was about to start work on *Looking to Get Out*, a film with Jon Voight, and he wanted me to work on it with another editor.

Hal had his own system for editing film: He would let the editor put together a first, rough edit, then come in and work with him. And he was very hands-on. He liked to be in control. This other guy had been working with Hal for a long time, and Hal had finally promoted him to editor. But two days into it, the guy quit. He'd been waiting for the promotion all this time, and when he finally got it, he decided he just couldn't take it.

I worked with Hal for the next year and a half. He became my mentor. He also fired me once and then hired me back, so there was a lot of drama. Those were the days when everyone was smoking pot and doing coke and working night and day and there was a lot of insanity to the process. But it paid off. After that, I got my first film as a solo editor, on *Valley Girl*, directed by Martha Coolidge. The film was released in 1983, and it was very successful, so those 150-hour work weeks really paid off. Martha and I got along very well, and ended up doing a number of films together, including *City Girl*.

I subsequently did *Mask*, for Peter Bogdanovich. I did Prince's film, *Under the Cherry Moon*. I edited *Barfly*, for Barbet Schroeder. I was suddenly in demand as an editor, and I was working with some wonderful directors, and I realized that I actually had stability and a career in what is generally a very unstable business. So what did I do? I decided I was ready to be a director. As an editor, I had learned so much about the process—what works, what doesn't work, and why—that it seemed like the natural next step. And it's what I wanted to do anyway.

By this time I had a young son, and, like a lot of parents, having a child brought back memories of my own childhood. And I kept thinking about what had happened to me when I was one, when I got separated from my parents, and about the people who cared for me for the next six years, and how traumatizing it had been to leave them to rejoin my family, a family I didn't even know. I began to write things down. I wrote between editing jobs; I wrote on weekends, after my son was asleep; and I wrote in the morning, before he woke up. Then I decided I needed more time to write, so I turned down jobs and worked less and less and wrote more and more. And I taught myself a little trick that I still use, which is that I always start my day by revising a few pages from the day before. That way, I don't have to sit down and immediately face the blank page, and that helps push me along.

I wrote and I just kept writing. I'd been an editor for a long time, so I had a good sense of story, and I'd read enough scripts over the years that I had a good sense of what you needed to make them work. After many drafts, I gave the script to my friend Colleen Camp, who'd been one of the

Playboy bunnies in *Apocalypse Now*, and who had decided to leave acting and get into producing. She was very taken with the story.

She had worked on *Basic Instinct 2* with Andy Vajna, a Hungarian-born producer, and she got the script to him. And I got a call from Andy and went to see him with the script in hand, but he wasn't really interested in the script; he wanted to see me about a movie he was making in Hungary. He desperately needed an editor who spoke Hungarian, and in the end Colleen convinced me to edit that movie for him, suggesting that it might lead to better things. The movie was called *The Minister*, and it starred the two most famous actors in Hungary, and it wasn't exactly the greatest experience of my life. But ultimately it worked out, because in the course of that job, I got to know many of the people who later ended up working on my movie, *An American Rhapsody*.

Oddly enough, while I was away in Hungary, two young producers who had read my script back in the States, submitted a copy to a screenwriting competition, and one morning I got a call and was told that I'd won the Hartley Merrill International Screenwriting Award. The award was worth a thousand dollars, but the best part was that I was automatically admitted to the Writer's Workshop in Sundance. I went shortly after I returned home, and with their help I made tremendous improvements to the script.

And Colleen never gave up. She was working with Peter Hoffman at the time, another producer, and every Friday morning, at the staff meeting, she would say the same thing: "You should make *American Rhapsody*." She also went to Bonnie Timmerman, the big casting agent, and asked for her help. Bonnie got the script to Nastassja Kinski, who felt an immediate connection to the story, and agreed to attach herself to the project.

Months and months went by. I kept working and waiting and waiting and working. Then one day, out of the blue, Peter Hoffman called and said, "I want you to go to Budapaest. If you can get the film started in three weeks, you have a deal."

Andy Vajna knew Peter from their days at Carolco, and he put some Hungarian money into the project. Then we got the script to Scarlet Johansson, to play the part of the troubled adolescent girl, me, and she loved it and committed. And I got the script to Tony Goldwyn because he was Colleen's brother-in-law, and he loved it and signed on. Then Bonnie Timmerman went to Budapest with me and we did a massive search for the little girl who was going to play the part of Scarlet as a child, or me as a little girl. And on the very last day, literally the very last girl we saw, that's who we got. She was a little too young, but she was sort of a genius, and she looked a lot like Scarlet, so we signed her on.

I still believe editing is probably the best education you can hope for if you want to direct, but it doesn't prepare you for the madness of that first day on the set. Within a few days, however, I found my footing, and all in all I must say it was a terrific experience. We made the film for $3.5 million and shot it in thirty days, and when we released it, in 2001, it launched my career as a director.

I think the best advice I can give anyone is to do it yourself. Don't wait for Hollywood to give you something, because it generally doesn't happen that way. After *An American Rhapsody*, I went down the road with several projects, and it's a real struggle to keep them on track. More recently, however, I found something I was really passionate about, so I sat down and wrote it, and at the moment it looks like that's going to become my next film. It's about a woman who went to Iraq to drive trucks for Halliburton, in the middle of a war zone, and it's a truly amazing story. I have been pushing this story along for a long time, but I'm passionate about it, and that passion is going to carry me until I get it made.

In Hollywood, things usually take a very long time to happen. It's a little like driving a truck through a war zone. If you're going to get through, you need to know exactly where you're going, and you have to drive as if your life depends on it. Your life may not depend on it, but your career certainly does.

ALAN GASMER

AGENT, WILLIAM MORRIS AGENCY

"Try to figure out what you're doing wrong, and stop doing it wrong."

When he was still in his teens, Alan Gasmer had visions of becoming a music mogul, but a downturn in the record industry, in the late 1970s, steered him toward movies. People really didn't need to buy records, he assumed. But they'd always need movies and television.

He did a little research and discovered that many of the power players in Hollywood had started as either accountants or lawyers, and the latter sounded more palatable. After he finished law school, he found himself working in a video store, the closest he could get to the business, but he soon learned that some of the top talent agencies had training programs, and that from time to time they deigned to hire complete unknowns. Gasmer applied at the William Morris Agency and became one of those lucky unknowns, eventually making a name for himself as one of the most prolific sellers of spec scripts in the business.

Gasmer was interviewed at the offices of the William Morris agency, in Beverly Hills, on June 8, 2005.

I was born in Philadelphia and was addicted to television as a kid. We only had three channels in our house, and I knew the TV schedules by heart. I remember asking my mother once whether the actors on *The Brady Bunch* heard the same music we heard, and she said, "Of course!" I wasn't sure she was right, and I remained curious about the way television worked, and about *who* made it work.

I was also interested in movies, but I was the oldest of four kids and my parents rarely had the time to take us out. I do remember standing in line with my father to see *Mary Poppins* and *The Sound of Music*, though, so it's not as if we were completely deprived.

By the time I was twelve, I had become interested in the *business* of movies. I read about all of the old moguls, and through my reading I became interested in the music business, too. By the time I was thirteen, I found out I could get a student rate on a subscription to *Billboard* magazine, and I ordered it. I would read it religiously, and when my subscription expired in the summer, at the end of the school year, I was very upset. I asked them if they could extend it, but it cost thirty-eight dollars for just nine months, which was a fortune in those days. My father could see how much I wanted it, however, and he gave me the money.

In high school, I found out that the library had a subscription to the weekly version of *Variety*, which had a compendium of movie, television, and music news. Apparently I was the only kid in my school that bothered to look at it, and I enjoyed it so much that I wanted my own subscription. When I called them and asked if they had a student rate, they laughed. But I later talked them into creating a lower rate for me.

I really loved *Variety*. I used to keep track of all the names of the people in the business, and I noticed that the successful ones kept showing up week after week.

I went to college at Penn State University, at the Delaware County campus, near Philadelphia, and majored in biology, and I immediately went to work for the school paper. I began writing music reviews, and the record companies would send me free albums. I also got friendly with the guys who ran the Spectrum, in Philadelphia, where all the big concerts were held, and I got to see most of the big acts that came through town.

In my junior year, I switched to Temple University, and I went from biology to political science. I became entertainment editor of the *Temple University News*, still focused on music, but in the late 1970s, when the record business took a nasty downturn, I began to wonder if that was such a good business to get into. A short time later, I got myself invited to a screening of *Looking for Mr. Goodbar*. After the movie we sat at a long table and ate and asked a few questions about the film. At that point, I began to feel that the movie business was a better bet than the record business. People didn't have to buy records, but they would always want to go out on Saturday night to see movies. I decided I needed to figure out how to get into the movie business.

I was still reading the trades, and I noticed that a lot of the powerful players had either started as lawyers or accountants. I knew I didn't want to be an accountant, so I went to see a guidance counselor at Temple and said I was thinking of going to law school. He came up with the idea of Southwestern University School of Law, in Los Angeles. I didn't think my parents would let me go—they had never been west of Philadelphia or north of Boston—but they surprised me. My father agreed to give me $200 a month to live. In his mind, that was plenty, and I didn't know any better.

So I went out to Los Angeles in August of 1980, without any idea of where I was going to live, and shortly after I arrived I hired a cab to take me around to look for apartments. But it was very confusing. We'd go down to the Mid-Wilshire area and I couldn't tell what kind of neighborhood it was. In Philadelphia, you'd see graffiti on the buildings, and you knew you didn't want to live there, but here you just didn't know. And I couldn't afford it, anyway. The rents alone were $400 to $500 a month.

At one point I saw a notice on a school bulletin board, a guy looking for roommates for only $200 a month, way out in San Pedro. My father didn't think this was a good idea, so he flew out to see what was going on, and with his help I found a place in West Hollywood. The landlady was from Philadelphia, and he liked that.

It was a period of adjustment, to understate the case. I had never lived away from home. I had never washed my own clothes. I had never gone shopping for food. I was twenty-one years old, and a very young twenty-one, and I hated it. I did laundry. I ate Chef Boyardee noodles out of cans. I didn't know anyone. I didn't like school.

I remember the very first final I had to take was a contracts exam on December 8, 1980. And just before leaving the house, I turned on the TV and found out that John Lennon had been killed. I flipped out. I took the exam and did very badly. By the end of the first year, I was on academic probation and came very close to getting kicked out, so I stayed around for the summer thinking I'd lighten next year's load by taking extra classes and working harder.

In the fall, I got to pick some of my own courses; I took entertainment law and copyright law, which I really liked. And for a while I had an internship at the music and legal department of Columbia Pictures, reading contracts, which was also pretty interesting. In a matter of months, I went from probation to the Dean's List, and they called me in and asked me how I'd done it. "It was easy," I said. "I'm finally taking some classes I'm interested in."

One night, I was at the UCLA Law Library, studying, and there was a girl there with a guy I knew from law school. And I said something silly, like I needed a drink or something, and she gave me a dirty look. And I asked her what she was doing, and she said she was working on a paper about the motion pictures antitrust laws and the consent decrees of the 1940s. And I said, "Oh, when they were forced to divest the theaters." She was very impressed with my knowledge, and three years later she married me. That was twenty-four years ago.

So I graduated from law school and went to work at Music Plus Video on Van Nuys Boulevard, in the San Fernando Valley, which was later bought out by Blockbuster. The only reason I was there was because I thought it was a way to keep my hand in the entertainment business. I still had the bar exam ahead of me, but I wasn't all that interested in pursuing law.

My wife, meanwhile, was going to Loyola Law. She ran into a girl she had known in high school, who was out with her boyfriend, and we started talking. I told them that I didn't want to be a lawyer, and he said, "You should be an agent." He told me that the big agencies had training programs, and that she knew the guy in charge of the program at William Morris.

So this friend of my wife's set it up and I went and interviewed at William Morris. And I knew someone who knew someone who knew someone who got me an interview at the Creative Artists Agency and at Triad. And the people at William Morris called me back and seemed interested in my music background, and I was reinterviewed five times before they gave me the job. That was in January, 1985. They put me in the mail room. I was the oldest guy there. And the only married one.

After two weeks in the mail room, I got promoted to Dispatch. Dispatch was where they would give you scripts and you would drive around to the various studios, delivering them. And I didn't know the city at all. I kind of knew Beverly Hills, and I had some vague understanding of the way Century City was laid out, but Hollywood and the Valley were terra incognita. So what happened was, they would send me out and I would never come back. This was in the pre-Map Quest days, of course. And cell phones weren't widely used then, either. And it became a running joke around the office. "Did Gasmer come back yet?"

One of the things you learn in the mail room and in Dispatch, or one of the things you *try* to learn, is who represents whom and who reports to whom, things like that. And you try to schmooze with the agents. But I was out on the road all the time, and nobody knew who I was. And I hated the job. Not only was I always getting lost, but I had to wear a tie and a nice shirt and penny loafers and I was always dying in the 100-degree heat. My wife used to go out and buy me cheap shirts and cheap shoes and cheap ties because we couldn't afford anything better, and the shoes fell apart and the shirts were scratchy and uncomfortable and I felt stupid in my cheap ties.

But I loved wandering around the studios. I think that's when I fell seriously in love with the idea of being part of the moviemaking machinery.

When lunch rolled around, I was usually at one of the studios, making a delivery, and I'd always try to eat at one of the commissaries. The food was pretty good and very reasonably priced. And I remember noticing how all the studios had their own little stores, with T-shirts and baseball caps and bags with the company logo, and the names of their hit shows and stuff. And I remember thinking, *Why doesn't William Morris have that?*

My wife had a cousin who had a small business making T-shirts and sweatshirts for sororities and fraternities, and I went to him and asked him to make some mock-ups for me. I wanted the stuff to look really classy, so I had him lift the logo right off the William Morris stationary, and I made sure he used the best quality T-shirts. Then I took the mock-ups over to William Morris and got permission to sell them, and I put together a memo and an order form and I began taking orders. There was a *huge* demand for these things. Our little apartment was so full of boxes we couldn't find our way around, and I'd go home at night to stuff envelopes, filling the orders. Shirts and T-shirts and sweatpants and baseball caps. The stuff was everywhere.

And that's how everyone got to know me.

While I was still in the mailroom, one of the first things I read was a script called *Diversion*. Michael Douglas was attached, and they were thinking of giving the female lead to Diana Ross. I was asked to do coverage on the script, which means you read it and write up a little synopsis and tell them what you think of the project. I couldn't put that script down. I told my wife, "This is a $100 million movie! This is a big fat hit! And if Diana Ross takes the role, it will change the nature of race relations in America!" I said the same thing to Carey Woods, who was the assistant to another agent, Stan Kamen. "This is unbelievable! You've never seen anything like this!"

He didn't pay any attention.

Finally one day I got to interview for an assistant's job, which is where you're basically a secretary to an agent, and you begin to learn the business of agenting, and they sent me to see Bruce Brown, who was head of the television literary department at the time. And he looked at me and said, "How come I don't know you?" And instead of explaining that he didn't know me because I was always on the road, delivering stuff, I said, "You know me. You bought my T-shirts."

And he said, "You're hired!"

I really wanted that job. I didn't care that I'd gone to law school and dissected Supreme Court decisions; this [was] what I wanted to do. Also, I had heard that the best motion picture agents had all started in TV, and I was pretty sure that that's what I wanted to be: a motion picture agent.

Almost two years later, while I was still working for Bruce Brown, my wife and I went to the movies. And as the movie opened, I realized I was watching *Diversion*. Only they'd given the Diana Ross role to Glenn Close and they had changed the name of the film to *Fatal Attraction*.

By this time, I'd been given a little freedom, and I chased a few projects and managed to sell a couple of TV movies. In December 1987, I got promoted. They just came in and said, "Congratulations. You're an agent." And I was sitting there and the phone rang and I was reaching for it, and they said, "Don't answer it! You're an agent now. You don't have to answer it."

Eventually, they sent me down the hall and gave me a little office, but they didn't give me a secretary because I wasn't worthy yet. And two months into my new career, in February 1988, there was a writers' strike. Nobody had anything to do. I was an agent and I had an expense account, and I would come in and read the trades and then go to lunch with someone else who had nothing to do.

And one day I was talking to this guy who had once worked in Dispatch, years earlier, and he told me that he had just done a cooking video with Wolfgang Puck. The only thing I knew about videos was renting them and putting them in my VCR and hitting the play button. But this guy was telling me that he wanted to do some exercise videos, and did we have anyone who might be interested? We had Heather Locklear, and we put together a deal and sold it to Universal Home Video.

Then I got a call from someone in the William Morris commercial department who was pretty impressed. "You seem to know about these deals," he said. I told him I didn't know that much about them, but that I knew how to read contracts, and that when I was in law school I'd spent some time reading contracts for Columbia.

We proceeded to put together an exercise video with Cathy Lee Crosby, and we made a deal on a Rita Moreno video that came out in both English and Spanish. Then I read some of Richard Simmons' old contracts and found out that he had made a deal on an exercise video called *Sweating to the Oldies*. I found a loophole in the contract that allowed us to make sequels, and we made a deal on that; one ended up selling 3 million units—with absolutely no marketing and no publicity.

By this time, the writers' strike was over. William Morris was very happy with me, because I had managed to bring in a lot of business at a time when the strike had pretty much shut down the town. So they said, "Do whatever you want, Alan. You've got carte blanche here."

I wanted to be a motion picture agent in the worst possible way, and I knew I'd have to earn that. So I would go home and read ten to twelve scripts every weekend, looking for something to sell. One day some writer called and asked if I was looking for new clients. "Yeah," I said. "If they're any good." The writer was from New Jersey, and he was in town working as a motorcycle messenger at Vendome Liquors, and trying to break into the business. And he sent me a script, and it was pretty good. It wasn't there yet, but there was something about it, so I agreed to work with him on it. I eventually sold his *third* draft to director Tony Bill, and it was released by MGM as *Baboon Heart*. The writer, Tom Sierchio, stopped delivering liquor for a living.

And the moment it sold, the trades treated it like it was big news. The story was in *Variety* and *The Hollywood Reporter*, and suddenly—just like that—I was in the business. And my phone hasn't stopped ringing since. That script put me on the map.

I can't even begin to tell you how many screenplays I've sold: *Rush Hour, Collateral Damage, First Kid, Mouse Hunt, Big Bully*, among many others. But I can tell you this: Very few scripts get made into movies. That's the reality of the business. It has very little to do with the quality of the script, and everything to do with the elements that become attached to it.

When somebody tells me they want to be an agent, I tell them that it's very competitive, like everything in Hollywood, and that they're going to have to start at the bottom, just like I did. There are a lot of lawyers and MBAs working in Hollywood mail rooms, and not all of them even get as far as a desk job.

In terms of writing, I always tell writers to write the best spec script they can. It should be original and, hopefully, it should be commercial, but more than that it should be something they are really passionate about. No one knows what's going to be selling two or three years from now, and no one can predict the marketplace, so I just tell them to write the best thing they can and to write from the heart.

The other thing I tell people is to hang in. In this town, the people that have the stamina to hang in are the ones who win. Most of the biggest names in Hollywood are people who have been fighting long and hard to get to where they got. If you have talent, in any area, and you stick with it, you'll make it.

I feel that way about my clients, which is why it's very rare for me to drop one of them. If I signed them, I must have seen something there. And if I saw something there, I know we'll find it again—and that we'll make the town see it, too. If you're a writer, you ought to be able to write your way out of anything. And if what you're writing isn't working, then ask yourself why and come at the material from another angle.

They used to call me the "Reanimator" around here because I could take a writer who had fallen on hard times and help him find his way back. But in the end, the writers really do it themselves; all I do is point them in the right direction. And that's my advice: Try to figure out what you're doing wrong, and stop doing it wrong. The rewards for getting it right are pretty spectacular.

GREG GERMANN

ACTOR

"Every time you step up to bat, you're starting over."

For Greg Germann, there was no breakthrough, no epiphany. His career crept up on him in modest increments, one small step at a time.

If you're a fan of Broadway, you may remember him from any number of shows, including Stephen Sondheim's *Assassins*, in 1991, where he created the role of John Hinckley. If you watch TV, you probably know him as Richard Fish, the money hungry senior partner at the Boston law firm that employed Ally McBeal. And if you like movies, you might have seen him in *Clear and Present Danger*, *Sweet November*, *So I Married an Axe Murderer*, *Jesus's Son*, *Joe Somebody*, and countless other feature films. He has also directed for television, and his short film, *Pete's Garden*, premiered in competition at the Sundance Film Festival.

At the time of the interview, Germann had just completed work on *Friends with Money*, with Jennifer Aniston, Joan Cusack, and Catherine Keener.

He was interviewed in Los Angeles on June 7, 2005.

I was born in Texas, and when I was still a little kid, my father wrote children's plays, a couple of which went on to win awards. Then when I was

nine, my parents separated, and my father went off to Baton Rouge to teach theater at Southern University. He wasn't around much.

I was drawn to theater as a kid because it was something I could do. It was a structured place for me to release the little talent I might have had.

The truth is, I don't know if I was a natural performer, or desperate for attention, or disturbed; maybe it was a combination of all three. But I loved it.

In high school, I did the typical high school plays. The first one I did was in seventh grade. It was called *The Life and Death of Sneaky Fitch*. I played Sneaky and I only have a vague memory of that. I enjoyed it, but it's not as if I did the play and walked off the stage and said, "Oh my God! I have to be an actor!" I do know, however, that facing the black void of the fourth wall from the stage was liberating.

After high school, I went to the University of Northern Colorado, in Greeley, on a scholarship. I went as a theater major, and it was there, as part of the theater department, that I decided this was really what I wanted to do. I did a lot of Shakespeare, and several musicals, and I realized I was going to have to move to New York to pursue it. At that point, it felt inevitable.

I wanted to get out of school and get on with my life, so I loaded up on classes and went to summer school. Another student and I worked with John Wilcoxson, the professor who ran the theater department, and with his help we created our own curriculum of "independent studies." As a result, I graduated in a little over two years.

I went to New York and tried to get into Juilliard. They took twenty-four students, and I narrowly missed the cut: I was as an alternate, the thirteenth of twelve. I decided I would create my own, four-year curriculum, and I signed up for classes with many of those same teachers, once again creating an independent program for myself. I worked with Robert Williams, who was just outstanding, with Edith Skinner and Tim Monich, and with Bill Esper and the great Clyde Vinson. It was a sort of self-imposed graduate program. I went to class and paid for the classes directly.

To make money, I went into business for myself. I didn't want to wait tables because I didn't want to be serving soup to the guy I would be trying to get a job from the next day. So I cleaned apartments instead. I was my own boss. I could blow through a place in the morning and go to class in the afternoon.

So there I was, cleaning apartments and taking classes. I also made time to become an intern at the Circle Repertory Company, a very well known Off-Broadway theater. It had been founded by Marshall Mason, a director, and by playwright Lanford Wilson, among others, and it was designed to bring all sorts of artists together—writers, actors, directors—to work in a collaborative environment.

In fact, my very first job in New York, other than cleaning apartments, was at Circle Rep, getting props for *Buried Child*, the Pulitzer Prize–winning play by Sam Shepard. In the play, one of the characters shucks thirty ears of corn every night, chops up four or five big bunches of carrots, and breaks about three-dozen liquor bottles. They had this big metal plate upstage, about the size of a door, and the actor would throw bottles at it from twenty feet away. It was very theatrical, but someone had to get those liquor bottles, the corn, and the carrots, and that was my job. Early in the morning, I'd be traipsing around bars in Greenwich Village, collecting liquor bottles. That was my introduction to life in the theater in New York City.

Before long, I actually did get up on stage. Circle Rep gave me my first professional acting role, albeit a nonpaying one. I was in *Hamlet*, and I got to play a page. William Hurt played Hamlet, Lindsay Crouse played Ophelia, and Beatrice Straight, who won an Oscar for *Network*, played Gertrude. It was an honor just to be in the company of these people, and the only reason I got the role is because I was the intern, the grunt who helped moved the scenery around.

Still, I was very excited about my role as a "page." I had actually researched the role, reading all about the life of a page in Elizabethan England. I put everything I had into it.

One night, after the performance, David Mamet, who was married to Lindsay Crouse at the time, came over to say hello. "I've been watching you," he said, "and I believed every moment you were on stage."

It was an incredibly impactful thing for Mamet to say to a young actor, and I'm sure he must have known it. It went well beyond encouragement. I was just a kid, playing a page, but he went out of his way to be generous.

Bill Hurt was the same way. I think everyone at Circle Rep was pulling for everyone else, which is what made it such an amazing place. It was a small, Off-Broadway theater, and everyone seemed to understand that they were there to encourage each other, and to pass on everything they knew about theater.

After Circle Rep, while I was still in the middle of my self-imposed studies, I started auditioning for plays—mostly outside New York. I got a job with the Yale Repertory doing *Night Is Mother to the Day*, a Swedish play. I did some regional theater in Atlanta. And I did *The Seagull* in New Jersey with Olympia Dukakis.

Then I tried my luck closer to home. I worked at the New York Shakespeare Festival, Playwrights Horizon, Second Stage, and a several Off-Broadway theaters. I became part of the New York theater scene in a small way. And one of the things I kept hearing was, *You can have a career in New York, but you can make a living in L.A.*

I didn't pay that much attention, though. I was single, without a family to support, and I was making enough money to get by.

That's not to say I didn't try to make money when I could. It was a struggle to get auditions, but I got a few, and I began to get cast in a few series and after-school specials. I did a little of everything, from playing a heavy in the final episode of *Miami Vice* to playing a flirtatious cross-dresser in an NBC series called *Tattinger's* who is trying to catch Jerry Stiller's eye.

Television was a completely new experience for me, and obviously not at all like theater. In theater, as an actor, you feel you have much more power and control. In film and TV, on the other hand, you're at the mercy of technology, and of the director—who can do several takes and choose the one he likes best. Initially, this was a big adjustment.

I later got a small role in a Roger Corman movie. It was called *Cookie*, but it was released in 1984 as *Streetwalkin'*, directed by Joan Freeman. It was about a hooker who takes revenge on a homicidal pimp. I was the pimp's sidekick, Creepy. That was my film debut: *Creepy*.

We shot the film in about twenty days, and I have great memories of it. Joan let me do a lot of improvisation, which I think is sort of essential when your name is Creepy. At one point, she let me take a small crew to Forty-second Street and we shot guerrilla-style, without permits. We were outside a porn theater, and the cameraman filmed from a hidden vantage point as I tried to sneak into the theater. The ticket-taker would have none of it. He argued with me, loudly, and Creepy got kicked out—all caught on film; my directorial debut.

After that, I started flying out to L.A. to audition for more parts. I was under the impression that being a stage actor gave me a little cachet. I don't know if people in Hollywood felt the same way, but I believed it, and it fueled my self-confidence.

I did several TV pilots, most of which were not terribly good, but everything in television happens so fast that you just get swept up in it. As a theater actor, that was very hard to get used to. In television, there is almost no process for an actor. You get the job and you show up and you do the job. In theater, you get the job and you show up and then you *develop* and rehearse the job.

After that, I did several episodes of *Tour of Duty*, a series about the war in Vietnam that first aired in 1987, and I ended up staying in L.A. for a couple of months. And that became my back-and-forth life for the next four years: I'd go to New York, do a few plays, find I was broke, then fly back to L.A. to make some money.

I didn't feel any need to move to L.A. I didn't want to give up my life in the theater. And in fact at one point I was out in New Haven, working on a terrific Richard Nelson play, *Principia Scriptoriae*, when I was asked to audition for the pilot of *Murphy Brown*. I was very conflicted about this. If I got the pilot, I would have to drop out of the play. So my agent told the producers about the play, and he said I'd fly out to audition, but that they only had forty-eight hours to say yes or no. I flew out and auditioned, and after forty-eight hours, not having heard back, I returned to New Haven.

A couple of days later, while I was in the middle of rehearsals, my agent called to tell me that they wanted me for the part. I didn't know what to do. When you audition for a pilot, you always negotiate the deal in advance, and that's what we'd done, but their option had expired. That put me in control, a rare position for an unknown actor.

It wasn't really about the money, though. I think, in those days, I was a bit of a snob about TV. I thought people would think less of me if I did television. I had been doing a lot of theater, and I thought theater was somehow "honorable." So I turned it down, and I felt good about myself, and Grant Shaud took the part and was terrific.

My agent didn't really understand, and I told him that I thought TV might turn me into a bad actor. And he said, "Material never determines how good you are; *you* do." I don't regret the choice I made, but I was afraid of doing a series for all the wrong reasons.

I stayed on the East Coast for a while, doing theater. At one point I got cast in *Assassins*, the Stephen Sondheim/John Weidman musical. It was directed by Jerry Zacks and featured some wonderful Broadway veterans, including Victor Garber, Lee Wilkoff, and Debra Monk. I played the part of John Hinckley. We were doing this play, and this was back in 1991, right at the beginning of the first Gulf War, and I was up there singing this beautiful and haunting love song, where John Hinckley is declaring his love for Jodie Foster. The audiences were very vocal about their feelings: They were either very angry and glowering from their seats, their arms crossed at their chests, or they were on their feet, pumping their fists and cheering. There was no middle ground. It's a play about assassins, not the presidents they targeted—about who they were, what they were about, and about the country that helped create them—and audiences were very passionate about what they were seeing on stage. That's what made it great theater.

For several years, I still traveled between Los Angeles and New York. In 1994 I was cast in the NBC series, *Sweet Justice*, with Melissa Gilbert and the great Cicely Tyson. I loved that show. John Romano, a terrific writer, was the executive producer.

I thought I might settle in L.A., but the show only lasted one season. Then, just as I was thinking about going back to New York, I was cast in *Ned and Stacey*, a sitcom with Thomas Hayden Church and Debra Messing. That lasted for two years. Again I thought about returning to New York, but I was cast as Richard Fish on *Ally McBeal*, which lasted five years, so I stayed.

I wish I had some advice, but I've always felt that if someone wants to get into show business, whether as an actor, a writer, or a director, advice can be pretty meaningless. If you really want to do it, you're going to do it regardless of all the obstacles that get thrown at you. And there are a lot of them, believe me. No one escapes. The business is ruthless.

But it's ruthless for good reason. The rewards—creatively, financially, and emotionally—are very, very high. And everyone who is attracted to the business wants to be part of that. That's why it's so competitive. It takes a lot of stamina, which is true of anything worth fighting for.

I remember early on, when I was just starting out in New York, somebody told me, "If you want this, you can have it. But you have to stay with it. It's all about longevity. It's all about the people who keep plugging away."

You need a little talent too, of course. It's true about cream rising to the top.

So that's my advice: Stay with it. Stay with what you love. Love will tell the tale. If you don't love it, you'll let it go. But if you love it, you will hold onto it with everything you have, because that's what it takes.

It still takes that kind of love and persistence. That part of it doesn't change. There are different levels of success, and the obstacles are always there—they just keep changing. In fact, as you make your way along, and more options become available to you, there are times when it feels more difficult than ever.

It's a little like baseball. Last time you were at bat, you hit a home run—but that has nothing to do with *this* time. Every time you step up to bat, you're starting over. You have to stay focused. You have to really want it. If your desire flags, even for a moment, you're going to strike out.

The secret may be this simple: Striking out is okay. The best hitters do. For me, the key is to allow myself to start over, to begin again.

LIZ GLOTZER

PRESIDENT, CASTLE ROCK ENTERTAINMENT

"Look for a job that appeals to you and get started."

Two decades ago, Liz Glotzer left a promising job at the Samuel Goldwyn Company and went to work for a bunch of guys who were known, collectively, as *These Guys*. One of them was Rob Reiner, the other four were less well-known. During her first month at work, the then-unnamed company lost its financing several times, but Ms. Glotzer and her five bosses soldiered on. The company survived, of course, and even managed to get itself a name: Castle Rock Entertainment.

Ms. Glotzer, now president of production, has worked on some classic films, including *Misery*, *The American President*, *In the Line of Fire*, *When Harry Met Sally*, and *The Shawshank Redemption*.

She was interviewed on June 30, 2005 in her Beverly Hills office.

I moved to Los Angeles from New York City when I was eleven years old, and it was the saddest day of my life. I didn't want to leave all my friends. My father was in the music business, however, and he needed to be in L.A., so I tried to make the best of it.

I adapted, made new friends, and grew to love the place. And when I was in my teens, I started babysitting for a number of people who would

play a role in my life in years to come. One of them was Larry Gordon, who went on to produce *Die Hard* and *48 Hours*, among other movies. He and his wife loved me because I could drive their kids to the mall and take them to movies.

When I was a senior at Beverly Hills High School, my parents decided they had had enough of L.A. and were moving back to New York. This was equally traumatizing, since I had made lots of new friends here, and I promised myself that one day I would come back to Los Angeles to live.

In the fall, I attended Bennington College, in Vermont. I knew I wanted to get into the film business, but I decided to play it safe and set my sights on law school. It never happened.

I came back to Los Angeles and went to work for a company that, in 1976, had produced *The Bicentennial Minute*, short, public-service segments [that] aired on TV and commemorated the American Bicentennial. The company subsequently began to make one-minute films about anything else that made sense to them. They did Easter, they did Kwanza—they did absolutely anything that lent itself to the sixty-second format.

Before I knew it, I was writing, producing, and directing some of the segments, and really enjoying the process of making those little films.

My other job was reading scripts for Larry Gordon and Joel Silver, a fellow producer. The two of them were incredibly charismatic, and I loved watching them in action. I would sit in the room and listen to their phone calls, the deal making, the arguing, the nudging, and before long I couldn't stand the thought of going back east to law school. I was sure I'd end up in some boring bank, where every day would be the same, and I decided I would stay in Los Angeles and try to find a place for myself in the film business.

I heard about this thing called the Peter Stark Program, at the University of Southern California School of Cinema-Television, and I applied and got accepted. This was 1983. The program was basically about the business of film, and most of the students were older than me—people who had been around Hollywood for a while and had other careers. They included lawyers and businessmen who were trying to learn how to make movie deals, or to get better at making movie deals. There were three or four of us, however, who had just gotten out of college, and we took it very seriously. We thought we would die if we didn't do our homework, and we were very committed to the program. One of my classmates was Neal Moritz, who went on to produce a string of big movies, including *The Fast and the Furious, Sweet Home Alabama, Cruel Intentions*, and *XXX*; another one was Stacy Sher, who later partnered up with Danny DeVito and Michael Shamberg and made such hits as *Get Shorty, Out of Sight*, and *Erin Brokovich*.

Through the program, I ended up with an internship at Universal Pictures. There were four possible jobs: distribution, marketing, physical production, and development. This last one was the best one, as far as I was concerned, because it involved working on scripts, and I actually got that job because Larry Gordon called and told the people at Universal that I was very good creatively. (The lesson here is that it helps to have someone pull strings for you.)

Oddly enough, I arrived at a time when everyone at Universal seemed to be quitting. The place was in disarray. Frank Price was in charge, and Sean Daniel was president, and Bruce Berman was also there, as vice president of production, but he was about to decamp for Warner Brothers. At times, it was so tense around the office that I began to wonder whether studio life was really right for me.

I worked with various executives, and one day I found myself on the phone with John Hughes. John had worked mostly with Bruce, on such films as *Home Alone* and *Ferris Bueller's Day Off*, and he was probably the hottest writer in Hollywood at the time. Anyway, one day Bruce's phone rang and his assistant was in the bathroom and I answered it. It was John, looking for Bruce, but Bruce wasn't in, so without much of an introduction John started reading his new script to me over the phone. He didn't know who I was, and I don't think it mattered: John just wanted a human being to hear it. He read me the entire script, which was a road picture called *Oil and Vinegar*. It was the most eagerly awaited script at Universal, and I was hearing it before anyone else. Before long, however, people found out that I was on the phone with John Hughes, and they began to crowd around, whispering and hissing: "What's it about?" "Is it great?" "Is it funny?"

The script never got made, but it gave me some cachet among the executives at Universal. If John Hughes would talk to me, they reasoned, maybe *they* should be talking to me.

On the day my internship ended, a Friday, the executives gave me a stack of scripts and told me to come back on Monday. I went home and read the scripts and made notes on each of them, and I was back Monday morning. I was never officially hired, but there was always something for me to do, so I didn't leave.

Eventually, I applied for a job as an assistant at the Samuel Goldwyn Company, and that's where I spent the next three and a half years of my life. It is also where I got my first big break. I was working for a guy named Jonathan Wachs, and I came across a script called *Mystic Pizza*, written by Amy Jones. The company ended up buying it, and Amy would come in for script meetings with Jonathan, Sam Goldwyn, and me. It was tough, because Sam's relationship with Amy became increasingly strained. After about twenty-five drafts, things were really bad between them. Amy liked me, though, and before she left she told me that I was never going to get promoted at that company unless I pushed and promoted myself. And that's what I did. I gave myself an office and a raise, and Jonathan shrugged and said, "See what you can get away with if you put your mind to it?" And I got away with it.

Not long after, I came across a group of very energetic producers who were starting a new company. Rob Reiner was one of the guys, and everyone had heard of him, and the other four were less visible but already part of the business: Glen Padnick, Alan Horn, Andy Scheinman, and Martin Shafer. They were known, collectively, as *These Guys*, and at the time they were trying to make a deal to get financing from the Coca-Cola people.

By this time, I was very unhappy at Goldwyn, and I was looking for a job. I was willing to do anything. I remember I went and interviewed with a producer who hadn't made a film in twenty-five years. There was an inch of dust on everything in his office—the scripts, the books, even the movie posters. It was hopeless, but I tried to convince myself that it was a very promising job. I remember telling myself, *I can revitalize this company! I can make it work!* But I didn't get the job. It seemed as if every job I applied for came down to two people, and I was always the other person. It was killing me.

Then I went off and interviewed with Martin Shafer, one of *These Guys*, and I thought the interview had gone terribly. He talked; I said nothing—

and maybe that's the reason he liked me, because I didn't say much. In any event, I got the job. That first month, the financing fell apart three times. Whenever I showed up for work, I never knew whether I'd be at a celebration or at a wake.

But I was working. And one of the first movies I got involved with was *Sibling Rivalry*, which was going to be directed by Rob's father, Carl Reiner. It was the first movie I had ever supervised, and it turned into a great experience. It was the beginning of my real career in the film business.

I have worked on many films over the years, and I am very proud of many of them—*The Shawshank Redemption* and *In the Line of Fire* come immediately to mind. But more important is the people I work with, and I've been very lucky in that regard. My bosses are not only talented, but *nice*, and we've been together so long that it's like a family. There are fights, of course, as in any family, but we get beyond them because we actually like each other. We also always make an effort to work with people we like. So far, we've been very lucky in that regard, too. And we must be doing something right, because the people we work with always keep coming back for more.

Cynics will tell you that there aren't that many nice people in Hollywood, and maybe that's true. But that's not the Hollywood I know. I think if you treat people with respect you get the same back, and that's what I've always done. I think being respectful is a good way to break into Hollywood. I also think people tend to overanalyze the hows and whys of breaking in. The truth is, you should just plunge in. You don't have to be all that calculating. Just look for a job that appeals to you and get started.

BRUCE GREEN

FILM EDITOR

"If you're not learning something new every day, you should get out of the business."

Bruce Green was raised near New York City and grew up with absolutely no interest in Hollywood or in the films it churned out. At the age of fifteen, however, everything changed: A friend took him to see a double bill in Manhattan, two foreign movies, back to back, and right away he knew what he wanted to do with his life. Movies went well beyond entertainment, he discovered. Movies could be more profound and more powerful than he had ever imagined.

Green ended up studying film at California Institute of the Arts, in Valencia, and spent a number of years working on small, socially meaningful projects before being sucked into the vortex of commercial Hollywood, which he grew to love. You might recognize some of his credits: *Cool Runnings*, *While You Were Sleeping*, *Phenomenon*, *The Other Sister*, *Runaway Bride*, *The Princess Diaries*, *Raising Helen*, and *Just Like Heaven*. In its review of this last film, the *New York Times* actually went out of its way to mention the "brilliant editor."

This interview took place in Los Angeles on May 13, 2005.

I was born in Eastchester, New York, about eighteen miles north of Manhattan, and I knew absolutely nothing about the motion picture industry. I didn't know how movies were made, or who made them, or how, and I didn't give it much thought.

When I was fifteen, my friend Peter Rainier—who went on to become an award-winning film critic—took me to the Bleecker Street Cinema, in Manhattan, to see a double bill. Peter was the only film buff I knew, and he couldn't say enough about *Grand Illusion*, one of the movies on the bill. "It is the greatest antiwar film ever made," he assured me.

I thought the film was a little boring, and I wasn't wild about being forced to read the subtitles, but the second film—the one Peter hadn't mentioned—absolutely blew me away. It was called *Un Chien Andalou*, and it opened with an eyeball being slit by a razor blade. The movie was written by Salvador Dali and Luis Bunuel, and it was only about fifteen minutes long, but I had never in my life seen anything like it. The images haunted me. I wasn't sure exactly what they meant, or if they meant anything at all, but that short film was responsible for making me think seriously about movies. I realized that movies could be about something other than the cool gun John Wayne was carrying.

Up until that time, I think I was a fairly normal kid. I was boiling over with pent-up frustration, and my hormones were running wild, and my head was always full of violent images. (Okay, maybe I wasn't *completely* normal.) And after I saw *Un Chien Andalou*, I felt connected to it in ways I didn't fully understand. I remember thinking, *My God, that's the most amazing thing I've ever seen! To have found someone who thinks like me!* I suddenly thought that making movies could be very cool. Movies could actually be *about* something. Most of the movies I had seen prior to that were Hollywood movies. I enjoyed them, and I found them entertaining, but I didn't connect with them on that visceral level. Watching a Hollywood movie was like going to an amusement park, and I assumed that making a Hollywood movie would be about as exciting as running a bumper car concession.

In the course of the next two years, I funneled my energy into social causes, and I turned into this precociously political high school kid. I protested the war in Vietnam and became very active in the Civil Rights movement, and at one point, I got arrested and expelled from high school.

A few weeks later, in the public library, I came across a 16-millimeter copy of *The Grapes of Wrath*. For the second time in my life, I found myself really connecting to something I was seeing on film. That movie seemed to validate all the energy I was funneling into the antiwar movement and into the Civil Rights movement, and it showed me that there was a historical basis for what I was doing—that there were people out there who were motivated to fight against injustice and for the things that really mattered. Once again, I realized the power of film. Film could reach deep inside of you. Film could *change* people.

I started thinking seriously about working in movies. I watched a lot of documentaries—*The Sorrow and the Pity, The Selling of the Pentagon, 16 in Webster Groves*—and I decided I should get into documentaries. I thought they would allow me to communicate a political and social agenda of my own.

I went to Bard College, in upstate New York, but quickly transferred to Cal Arts, in Valencia. I found myself working with Nam June Paik, the Korean video artist, helping out in any way I could, and, subsequently, for Pat O'Neil, an underground filmmaker. O'Neil was doing a lot of work with optical printers, linking two projectors together, one behind the other, and filming the projected images to create and fuse new images. This was an early version of digital special effects, the mechanical nuts-and-bolts precursors to CGI workstations.

I enjoyed working with experimental filmmakers. Most of my friends at Cal Arts were more interested in Hollywood, and in fact many of them went on to make mainstream careers for themselves, but I saw myself making small movies and socially relevant documentaries that were only shown in art galleries.

After I graduated, I went back to New York and tried to break into the documentary business, but I discovered that that world was controlled largely by trust fund kids. These people had Ivy League educations and independent means, and they didn't have to worry about money. I thought it was great that they were spending their money on movies instead of fancy cars, but I couldn't do that; I had to make a living. I wanted a family, and I already knew I wanted kids, and families and kids required upkeep.

In 1975, I ended up coming back to Los Angeles. I tried to get a regular

Hollywood job for a while, and I ran into an old guy who was a friend of a friend of a friend of my father, and who at one point had been president of 20th Century Fox. "Kid," he told me, "You have to have a mentor. You need someone who's going to take you by the hand and show you the ropes. If you don't have a mentor, you'll never get anywhere."

That was good advice, and I always kept it in the back of my mind, but I didn't immediately find a mentor. Instead, I went into business with Robbie Blalock, an old friend from Cal Arts. He had gotten hold of an optical printer from an outfit that was going out of business, and together we started an effects company called Praxis. We started doing special effects for low-budget features, commercials, and documentaries, and we ended up doing some optical printing for *Hearts and Minds*, the Academy Award–winning documentary about the Vietnam War.

After working on several others films, including *The Trial of Billy Jack*, I realized that I really wasn't interested in running a company and in being a businessman or a salesman. We spent 80 percent of our time knocking on doors and looking for work and not getting it, and I wanted to make better use of my time. I sold my share of the business to Robbie, who ended up doing the effects for *Star Wars* and winning the Academy Award. But that's another story.

I went to work for Haskell Wexler, the famous cinematographer. He was a real inspiration to me. He was on the left, politically, but he had found a way to work within the Hollywood system without betraying his ideals. For a while, I modeled myself on Haskell, and he became the mentor I'd been looking for. I realized it was possible to make a living in the business without sacrificing one's integrity.

One of the guys I met through Haskell was Elmo Williams, an editor and producer. He was also a big fan of Haskell's. He said Haskell was one of the few people he knew who was able to work in the belly of this monster we called *Hollywood* without compromising his morals or his politics. "Hollywood is a propaganda machine for our capitalist, imperialist culture," he said. "And Haskell makes it work for him without selling out. He's really something."

Haskell was a great inspiration to me, and for a time I thought I wanted to become a cameraman. Toward that end, I got a job as a production assistant on a low-budget film called *Cannonball*. It was directed by Paul Bartel and produced by Gene Corman, brother of the legendary B-movie producer. Part of my job was to take the cans of film to the editing room, and I met the film editor, who ended up offering me a job when shooting ended. I really enjoyed working in the editing room. There was something about the work, and about the types of people who were attracted to that work, that I connected with. I felt I was home.

I worked in editing for a while, then I got a call from my friend Robbie, who had just been hired to do effects on a little movie called *Star Wars*. They were looking for someone who had some knowledge of special effects, someone who could work as a liaison between the special effects people—then known as optical effects houses—and the director, George Lucas. And that's what I did.

I learned a number of things from that experience. One was that nobody had a clue as to how big the movie was going to be. I remember talking to Gary Kurtz one day, the producer, and he said, "If we're lucky, it's going to be as big as *Planet of the Apes*, and we'll get to make a couple of sequels."

As everyone now knows, the movie changed the course of cinematic history. When it came out, it was such a huge hit that I was automatically successful. If you were the janitor on *Star Wars*, you were considered the best janitor in the known universe. If you made coffee on the set, no one made coffee the way you made coffee.

By this point, I was in the Motion Picture Editors Guild, and I was suddenly very much in demand. People thought I must know everything about special effects, and it seemed like everyone was making special effects movies, so I was being offered jobs left and right.

But I fell in love with an English woman who was making documentary films, and instead of grabbing hold of the tail of the *Star Wars* comet, and riding it into the stratosphere, I moved to London and made small political movies with my new girlfriend. We spent a year-and-a-half doing that and had a wonderful time and I forgot all about Hollywood, but then we decided we were going to have children, and she wanted to have children in America. She didn't like the way the English raised and treated their children—she found it very oppressive—and we moved back to Los Angeles.

I got work as an assistant film editor in television movies. I worked on eight or nine of these, some good, some terrible, and I began to hone my skills as an editor. I really enjoyed the learning curve, because I could see that I was getting better and better, and I made up for my lack of skill and knowledge with my incredible enthusiasm. I could work twenty hours a day without complaining.

I think at that stage in your career, when you're just starting out, you have to be willing to work twenty hours a day, and you have to do it with enthusiasm, and when you get your paycheck you need to feel grateful that you're actually getting paid. If you can't do that, if you resent the long hours and the low pay, you should get out of the business. You have to have great passion for movies, and for the process of making movies, and for the kinds of people who make movies, and even for the atmosphere on a film set or in an editing room, because the chances of becoming successful are infinitesimally small. Ten years down the road, you might find yourself working on movies you don't want to be working on, or, worse, not working at all, and it's going to take all the passion you can muster to keep going. So, yes, you have to love making movies, because making movies is going to beat you up.

After working on a series of television movies, including several for Paul LaMastra, a very gifted editor, I was offered a job as the assistant editor on *Raiders of the Lost Ark*. LaMastra and I had just finished working on *Attica*, a television movie about the prison uprising, and he made the call that got me the job. He had worked with Michael Kahn, another editor, on *Hogan's Heroes*, and Michael had gone off to edit movies for Stephen Spielberg (and now has three Academy Awards to show for it: *Raiders of the Lost Ark*, *Schindler's List*, and *Saving Private Ryan*).

Anyway, Michael needed a new assistant, and LaMastra sent me over. I got the job, and Michael became my second mentor. In fact, it was Michael who made me a film editor. He took great interest in teaching me not so much how to edit a film but how to *think* like an editor.

And that's another thing: I meet young people nowadays who talk about how they know how to work this particular computer program or that program. That has nothing to do with becoming a film editor. That's about becoming a mechanic. It's easy to cut film together, especially with digital technology, but that's not editing. Michael taught me how to look at raw, uncut film and analyze it; he taught me how to feel it and look for the point of view and mold and bend that film into a coherent piece that tells a story that evokes emotion and laughter, or whatever else you want it to do. I spent more than six years working with Michael, learning my craft, before *he* felt I was ready to move on.

I had friends who were assistant editors when I was an assistant editor, and they went off to cut film long before I did. They kept telling me I was ready, wondering what I was waiting for, and I'd tell Michael about them. I'd say, "All my friends are editing. I want to get out there." And he would say, "You're not ready to edit. I'll tell you when you're ready."

People told me that Michael only said that because he didn't want to lose me, because I was too valuable to him. But my wife said, "No. Don't listen to them. Listen to Michael." And I listened to my wife.

When Michael finally told me I was ready, I went out and cut low-budget movies like *Friday the 13th*, parts four and five, and *April Fool's Day*. They may not be memorable movies, but I worked hard, did a good job, and learned a lot, and every director I've ever worked with has always asked me to come back and work for him again.

That was another great life lesson. Don't rush things. Don't make that leap in your career until you know you're ready to make it. I have seen people leave the nest too soon, and they've slipped, and nobody was there to give them a second chance. So be patient. Take your time. Hone your skills.

Hollywood likes young people, and Hollywood supports its young, but there's a limit to that support. If you go out and edit your first low-budget movie and it doesn't lose money, well, you'll get another job, and maybe another job after that, and you'll build a nice resume. But if you have too much hubris and you think you're the greatest editor around, people will actually want you to fail, and it will be tough to get a second chance. So don't hurry. This is for the rest of your life. Another two or three years is probably a good thing.

It's hard, but it's worth it. I worked such long hours as an editor that my wife used to say that she felt like I was having an affair with the director. The director was "the other woman" in our lives. I would come home and talk about the director; what he wanted and needed; how I had just found a clip that was going to save a difficult sequence; and on and on. Because the job doesn't begin and end with the editing. When I was an assistant, working for Michael, I learned that a big part of the job was to make the director and the editor as comfortable as possible. When Michael was working on *Raiders of the Lost Ark*, for example, I knew that Spielberg liked almond-flavored tea, and what kind of crackers he liked, and I made sure that the tea and crackers were always on hand. I learned to be ready for anything, no matter how small, and it didn't make me feel like less of a person. Tending to those details was simply part of my job. Another part of my job was to be a psychic.

One day, for example, Spielberg and Michael were editing the truck chase in *Raiders*, and Spielberg wasn't happy with the way one of the actors delivered his lines. So I went off and looked for all the other takes where the actor delivered the same lines, and I had them ready before they even asked for them.

That was something Michael had taught me: to put myself in the mind of the director so that I knew what he wanted before he knew what he wanted. That was what he meant when he said he was going to teach me to learn to think like an editor. And thank God he did.

For a while, after I went out on my own, I was cutting mostly low-budget films, but one day Michael was offered a film called *Punchline*. It had been written by David Seltzer, who had written *Table for Five*, on which I'd worked with Michael, and David was also on board to direct. David and I had met on *Table for Five*, and he knew me as an assistant, not as an editor, but Michael told him to hire me, and he did an amazing thing. He told David that if he wasn't happy with my work, he, Michael, would come in and finish editing the movie free. This was from an Academy Award winner; he had so much faith in me that he put himself on the line. David didn't know what to do. The studio wanted a more prominent editor, but in the end they hired me on Michael's unqualified recommendation. *Punchline* was a hit. The movie was well reviewed and even the editing was well reviewed, and it put me one step closer to becoming an A-list editor. I was being offered a lot of movies, but by this time I had two young daughters, and I told my agent that I only wanted to work on films my kids would enjoy.

I got a movie called *Cool Runnings*, about a team of Jamaican bobsledders. I loved the values espoused by that film. I did *Freaky Friday*, which I also thought was a wonderful film. And I've done five films for Gary Marshal, including *Runaway Bride*, which was a huge hit. I did another film for Gary that wasn't successful at all and wasn't particularly well reviewed. It was called *The Other Sister*, and it was about a retarded girl who falls in love with a young man who is also mentally challenged, and who is determined to prove that she is just as capable as her perfect sister. When that movie came out, I would sneak out and watch it with regular audiences, and I would see people laughing and weeping at all the right places. Sometimes, strangers would find out I had worked on that film, and they would go out of their way to tell me how much it meant to them, and how much it had moved them. And I have to tell you, the response I received on that one little movie, not a very successful little movie, has been worth more to me than anything else I've ever worked on—more than the great reviews, more than the box office. I am more proud of that film than of any other film I've ever done.

Today I'm in a position to pick and choose my films, and my first criteria is to avoid working with people I don't care for. I also look for films that connect with real life. You can become so obsessed with movies that you lose sight of everything else, and you end up simply regurgitating the same old stuff. I look for scripts that make me laugh and cry and make me happy to be part of the human race. I'm not interested in adding negative energy to the world. I also look for films from which I can learn. As one of my friends put it, "If you're not learning something new every day, you should get out of the business."

BONNIE GREENBERG

MUSIC SUPERVISOR

"Figure out how to live as cheaply as possible so that you can work free (or for next to nothing, anyway)."

Bonnie Greenberg loved music as a child, and later fell in love with movies, but it would be many years before she was able to fashion a career out of the two.

She attended college in Denver, Colorado, and spent most of her time on skis, then succumbed to family pressure and went on to study law. Fortunately, she attended law school in Los Angeles, and she made a point of taking any course that had anything to do with entertainment, no matter how remote.

She spent many years in the legal trenches before breaking out with a movie called *Hairspray*. Her credits are too numerous to list, but a few of them should be familiar: *The Mask*, *My Best Friend's Wedding*, *Pleasantville*, *The Best Man*, *What Women Want*, *How the Grinch Stole Christmas*, and *Peter Pan*.

She was interviewed in Los Angeles on May 18, 2005.

I was born in Roslyn Heights, Long Island, and had a typical, middle-class suburban childhood. My father was a little eccentric, though. He was a lawyer but he loved theater, and both he and my mother especially loved musicals. They would take my two older sisters to Broadway shows at least once

or twice a month, but not me—I was too young. "We'll take you when you're eight," they promised.

I had to settle for local theater, in Mineola. I remember seeing *The Music Man*, with Bert Parks, and *How to Succeed in Business Without Really Trying*, with Rudy Vallee. I loved them. Before the shows, and during intermission, I would walk over to the orchestra pit and just stare at the instruments. And after the shows, I didn't want to go home. Other kids were learning the alphabet, but I was more interested in the lyrics to "Trouble in River City." By the time *The Music Man* came out in movie theatres, I knew the entire score by heart—and I still do.

On my eighth birthday, I told my parents that I wanted to see a show on Broadway, as promised. They said I was still too young. I was traumatized. My parents had changed the rules on me.

I moped for a while, but when it was time for *Name That Tune*, I parked myself in front of the TV and forgot my troubles. That was my favorite show. To this day, I can identify almost any song based on a couple of notes.

At one point, early on, I thought I was going to make a career in music, but my father was a lawyer and kept telling me that I was going to be a lawyer. Still, both he and my mother encouraged me to participate in the school's music program. I took violin and flute and played piano. When I got to high school, I formed this little hippie-dippie trio. I played the harp and we performed contemporary pop music. I also loved movies, so I wrote reviews for the high school paper. I loved Charlie Chaplin and the Marx Brothers, and I especially loved musicals.

When it came time to go to college, I ended up at the University of Denver, in Colorado. I thought I'd go for a year or two, then transfer to a "smart person" school, but I ended up loving it. I found great teachers and at one point I decided I wanted to be a writer. I was particularly intrigued by some of the writing coming out of Africa, and even looked into joining the Peace Corps. I was interested in everything. My father kept pressuring me to study law, however, and I took the law boards and eventually enrolled at the Southwestern University School of Law, in Los Angeles, where my older sister was going.

Before long, I realized I was in the entertainment capital of the world, and I began to take courses in entertainment law. This led to an internship at a record company, now defunct. I'd been looking for something in movies, but those openings had already been filled, so I decided I would try to make the most of it. On my very first day, I was asked if I wanted concert tickets for a show that night, and I went. It was at the Pantages Theatre, and the featured acts were *The Dramatics* and *The Manhattans*. I couldn't believe it! Free concert tickets on my first day of work! What a great job! I thought that was the coolest thing that had ever happened to me.

I continued to work for the same record company all the way through law school, and by the end of the first year, I was actually getting paid a frugal sum. I learned to handle music licensing. If someone was making a small movie, or a documentary, or even a school play, and they wanted to use some of the label's music, they had to get the rights from us. It was my job to help take care of that. I enjoyed the work, but it wasn't all that inspiring. I wanted to be part of the creative end of show business, not sit at a desk poring over contracts.

One day, my boss approached to tell me that one of the lawyers would be leaving, and he said I could have his job if I graduated early. I decided to cram an entire year of law school into one semester, and I graduated, but the company was sold and I never got the job.

I thought about doing something socially significant with my life and again looked into the Peace Corps, and into teaching in Africa, at the University of Abidjan. But just before I committed to the teaching position, I had a car accident, hurting my back, and I knew I wouldn't be going anywhere for a few months. While I was recovering, I got a call from Bill Straw, at MCA Records, who wondered if I'd go to work for him. I had met him in law school, and at the time he was running the legal department at MCA, and I really hadn't planned on becoming a music lawyer. Then again, MCA was part of Universal, and I thought it might lead to work in the film business, so I took the job.

Unfortunately, back in those days, there really wasn't much synergy between music and movies, so it didn't look as if the job was going to be a bridge to much of anything. Still, I settled in. Sometimes, when someone called for the rights to a certain song, I'd ask them to hum a few bars, and I'd tell them, "If you can't hum a few bars, you don't deserve it." I was kidding, of course, just trying to add a little levity to the licensing business, but I'm not sure they were amused.

After a couple of years, there was a regime change at the company, and everyone I knew was fired. I thought it would be a good time to quit. The people at work had become this sort of extended family, and I didn't like the fact that everyone I knew was gone. Plus I was worried about staying. I knew I was about to get a big raise, and if I didn't leave then, I might never get out.

I went in to see my new boss to give him notice, and he thought I was quitting because of him. "No," I explained. "I never really wanted to do this for a living. I just fell into it."

He was disappointed, and he asked me to stay for a couple of months and train my successor, which I was happy to do. And the scary thing is, I began to enjoy myself, and I liked my new colleagues, and when the two months were up, I really didn't feel like leaving. But I couldn't back out, and I'm actually glad I had decided to quit, because I'm sure I'd still be there if I hadn't.

I didn't have any money, and I didn't have a job, so I did what any intelligent unemployed young woman would do: I rented out my apartment and spent four months traveling around Asia.

When I got back to L.A., with my funds dwindling, I ran around looking for an entry-level job in the movie business. I did a little freelance legal work for an attorney I knew, and one day he asked me if I wanted a full-time job with Paramount, in home video and television production. Once again, it was a legal job, and I didn't want it, but he had already set up the interview and I couldn't say no. I got the job, and I had mixed feelings about it, but it turned out to be fairly interesting. I learned how television shows got made. Just as I was getting into it, however, my boss quit, and I didn't get along with his replacement. I gave three months notice, even though I didn't have anywhere to go. The thing is, at that point in my career, I knew from experience that I would survive. That was an important lesson for me: The end of a job, even a job you love, is not the end of the world.

In the meantime, an actress I knew asked me to produce a play. I wasn't wild about the play but I liked the idea of learning something about production. I worked on it around the clock, and it opened at the Second Stage

Theater in Los Angeles. It didn't last long, and the experience taught me that if you want to be successful, you should only work on projects you believe in. Still, when all is said and done, and despite the failure, I learned a lot about producing a play. It was a great experience.

I was still gravitating toward movies, of course, and when I left my job, I took some classes at UCLA Extension: film, story analysis—things like that. I really wanted to learn everything about producing movies. But that didn't pay the bills, so I got an interview with Mike Rosenfeld, a founding partner of the Creative Artists Agency who was leaving to become a producer. He was looking for an assistant, and I told him I wanted the job, noting that I was willing to start at the bottom. He said he'd think about it, and I was ecstatic, but he called a few days later with bad news. "No one is going to hire you," he said. "You're an attorney. No one is going to feel comfortable sending you off to make them a cup of coffee or get their dry-cleaning."

"I don't care," I said. "I'll do it."

"It's not going to happen," he repeated. "You'll have to figure out another way to break in."

Then I heard that Stephen Haft was about to produce a movie with Robert Altman. I had met Stephen while I was producing that play, and I contacted him and told him I was looking for a job as an assistant. He said he'd hire me to do legal clearances for the music, which I didn't want to do—if I had, I never would have left my old job, where at least I was making real money—but I realized it might teach me something about making movies. I did learn a little something about movies, but I learned a lot more about what I needed to be doing with my life.

It happened one afternoon, while I was talking to Robert Altman, the director, about the musical arrangements. Everything in my past suddenly made sense. My love of music. My love of movies. My evolving knowledge of the business and legal ends of the business. Even the afternoons in front of the television, beating everyone at *Name That Tune*. I was a walking music library. I could take that gift and apply it to movies. It was as if a little lightbulb had gone off in my head.

As luck would have it, my friend Stanley Buchthal was in the process of trying to raise money for *Hairspray*. It had been written by John Waters, who also hoped to direct. Stanley asked me if I wanted to do the music for the film, both legal and creative, and he put together a package and made me the music supervisor.

The package got financed, and *Hairspray* became the first movie in my new career as a music supervisor. On the technical end, where I was a little out of my depth, I made a few mistakes. But my musical choices were solid, and this didn't go unnoticed. Beyond that, I learned something very valuable, which is that I seemed to have a real talent for combining the aural and the visual. I had a knack for putting music to movies in a way that furthered the story and serviced the film, to put the right music to the right image. A song or a piece of music is one thing on its own, but it becomes something else entirely when you combine it with images. And I seemed to know how to pick the right music for the right images.

I ended up doing a string of low-budget movies, learning my craft, but the movie that really turned things around for me was *Book of Love*, which was directed by Bob Shaye, the founder of New Line Cinema. It was a coming-of-age film, set in the 1950s, and I was very familiar with that era. So Bob asked me to supervise the music. I did all the legal work, too, but I didn't mind, because I was doing the music and loving it. And even though I wasn't making much money, I didn't care: I knew how to live very frugally. I was a familiar sight at the local thrift shop. And I was the Queen of the Early Bird Dinner.

Then one day I was having lunch with Jill Meyers, who was head of business affairs in the music department at Tri-Star, and she told me she was looking to make a move. I suggested she join me. She could do the business end of it, and I'd concentrate on the creative side, and we became partners. We did a string of independent movies together, including *Poison Ivy*, *Watch It*, *Nightmare on Elm Street*, *Suburban Commandos*, and *Menace II Society*. The *Menace* soundtrack did very well, and the exposure put us on the studio map. There's a lot of profit in soundtracks, and studios pay attention when they break out.

Eventually, Jill and I went our separate ways. I went on to do *The Mask*, with Jim Carrey, which was a breakthrough film for me. It encompassed everything I loved about the work: dancing, singing, music, and witty repartee. The film got a lot of attention, as did the music, and I realized I was in this for the long haul.

After that I hooked up with the Hughes brothers again, for *Dead Presidents*, and when it was released I found myself described, in print, as "the Jewish girl with soul." I was a consultant on *Sister Act* and on *The Santa Clause*, a pair of big studio movies. Then I got a call from my old friend Stanley Buchthal, who was doing a *tiny* movie: The budget was something like two hundred thousand dollars. I did that, too. It was called *Spanking the Monkey*. I loved it. I realized I could go back and forth between Hollywood and the Independents, and that I should consider any script at all, and always base my decision on the material. In quick succession I did *The Truth About Cats and Dogs*, *Flirting With Disaster*, *The Long Kiss Goodnight*, and *Kazaam*, with Shaquille O'Neal. The [last] movie was a box-office disappointment, but working with Shaq—as a rapping genie—was tons of fun.

Then I got a call from Patty Whitcher, who had been the unit production manager on *Book of Love*. She was line-producing *My Best Friend's Wedding*, with Julia Roberts, and asked if I wanted to do the music. That was another watershed moment in my career. It was a hugely successful studio movie, and the soundtrack was both a critical and commercial hit.

After that, I was gold. I felt incredibly lucky. I can be as insecure and neurotic as the next person, but the idea that I actually had a career was finally beginning to sink in.

One day, I got a call from Jerry Zucker, who had produced the *Airplane* movies and the *Naked Gun* franchise, as well as *My Best Friend's Wedding*, which is where we had first met. He asked me to commit to a movie he was going to direct, and I signed on. But a few days later I got a call from Ron Howard's office. He was in preproduction on *Edtv*, and he wanted to talk to me about the music.

On my way to the interview, I was a nervous wreck. To me, Ron Howard was Winthrop Paroo, the kid in *The Music Man*. That was still one of my all-time favorite movies, and here I was, about to meet one of the stars.

When I walked into his office, he stood up and shook my hand, and I couldn't get "Wells Fargo Wagon" out of my head. I'm sure I must have missed a lot of what he said—I kept seeing him as a kid, belting out the song—but when the interview was over, he was smiling, so I assumed it had gone well. When it was time to leave, I just couldn't help myself. "Listen," I said, "I'm sorry to do this, and I know everyone must ask you this, but I need to know: What was it like being that little kid in *The Music Man*?"

And he said, "No one ever asks me about *The Music Man*. They ask me about Opie and about Richie Cunningham." And he went on to tell me about being a child actor, and about working closely with his father, and about struggling to get the dancing right in those early roles.

A few days later, Ron's office called to offer me the job of music supervisor on *Edtv*. I was over the moon. But I had to talk to Jerry first. I'd committed to his movie, and I wasn't going to walk out on him. Jerry told me to take the job with Ron because things were looked iffy on his project, and in fact that movie never got made. So I did *Edtv*, with Ron, then worked with Jerry on *Rat Race*, and subsequently hooked up with Ron again on *Grinch*.

Eventually, I got so busy I actually had a small staff. I worked on *Pleasantville*, *40 Days and 40 Nights*, *Undercover Brother*, *Stuart Little 2*, *Peter Pan*, and many others.

Then life got in the way. My marriage ended, and both of my sisters passed away within ninety days of each other, and then I had an accident and reinjured my back. As I began to recover, I realized I wanted a baby and that I'd put that on hold for my career. I ended up getting rid of my whole staff, and I decided that from then on I was only going to work with filmmakers I already knew.

I could work and still have a life. And that's what I did. I met a terrific man and we adopted a little girl and I'm still working hard, but my life is my own.

More recently, I did the music for *Desperate Housewives*, on which I continue to work, and I just started supervising the music on *Take the Lead*, with Antonio Banderas.

I'm also teaching a course on music supervision at UCLA Extension, and I always have the same advice for my students: Figure out how to live as cheaply as possible so that you can work free (or for next to nothing, anyway). The important thing is to learn, to be like a sponge. I resented my father for pushing me to become a lawyer, but I did it and paid attention and my life went off in all sorts of interesting directions. So, Dad, I don't resent you anymore.

You can learn something from every job, no matter how miserable it might seem. And if you look at it that way, it'll be much less miserable.

The other thing I tell my students is that it's okay to be afraid. We're all afraid. None of us want to fail. But you've got to get out there and take your chances. If you don't, you'll never know who or what you might have been.

DAVID HAYTER

ACTOR/WRITER/DIRECTOR

"You have an idea, and you try to make it real. And you do anything you can to make it happen."

David Hayter got a taste for theater as a boy of nine, and a decade later moved to Hollywood to try to make it as an actor. In one of his first gigs, a nonunion commercial, he played the role of a disgruntled accident victim, and followed that up with the lead in a small movie that went straight to video. Later, Hayter did a lot of voice-over work, mostly in cartoons, but the only steady money came from tending bar, and he began to worry about the future.

Finally, Hayter decided to take control of his life. He and a friend agreed to produce a movie together, and he plunged in with all the energy and enthusiasm he could muster. The movie was well received at Slamdance, and even won a special jury award, but it never found a distributor.

Crushed, Hayter ended up answering phones for director Bryan Singer, and it turned out to be the best thing that ever happened to him. His acting career might be on hold, but he's on fire as a writer. His credits include *X-Men, The Scorpion King*, and *X2*, and at the time of the interview, he was juggling three high-profile projects for various studios, all of them based on comic book characters: *Iron Man, Watchmen,* and *Black Widow*. He hopes to make his directorial debut on *Black Widow*.

Hayter was interviewed in Los Angeles on June 16, 2005.

I was born in Santa Monica, California, to Canadian parents, but my father worked for Abbott Laboratories, a biotech company, and we moved around a lot. We lived in Arizona, and in Colorado, and at one point we moved back to Canada and shuttled between Montreal and Toronto before returning to California.

When I was nine, we were living in El Toro, and I auditioned for a part in *Pinocchio*, at the Costa Mesa Civic Playhouse, where my mother used to do community theater. We traveled a great deal, and it was a good way for her to get involved in each new community. One day, she was looking through the paper for open auditions and came across a play being performed exclusively by kids. She took me in, and I got the part, and I fell in love with performing.

When I was fifteen, we moved to Kobe, Japan. I went to the American school there, but in a city with barely a thousand foreigners, you are pretty much forced to pick up the language.

In 1989, we went back to Canada, and I attended the Ryerson Theatre School, in Toronto, but I had some conflicts with the teachers, and after a year we mutually decided that I should go my own way. So at the age of twenty, I moved to Hollywood, determined to break into the business.

I only had one friend there, a friend of the family, and I found a horrible studio apartment in Toluca Lake, overlooking the 134 Freeway, and settled in. Meanwhile, I got a job as a barback at a place on Ventura Boulevard—I was too young to serve liquor—and started making the rounds. I got my headshots, and I tried to get an agent or a manager, but nobody would even look at me. And one night, my only friend, the friend of the family, got drunk and began to yell at me: "How can you call yourself an actor when you don't even bother taking classes?!"

So I signed up for classes at the Beverly Hills Playhouse and spent the next three years studying acting, and that's where I made my closest friends in Hollywood, and where I started having a little interaction in the business.

The first job I got was a nonunion commercial. I played a motorcycle rider who had broken his hip and didn't have insurance. The camera cut to me and I said my line, "I broke my hip and the police blame me because I didn't have a license or insurance!" I delivered the line with a great deal of indignation, though I thought my character was an idiot, and that he deserved whatever he got.

After that, I got an episode on *Major Dad*, the television series. I played Yakov Smirnoff's son and used a Russian accent. I got my SAG card on that show and I was ecstatic. It was a huge moment for me. I was a member of the Screen Actors Guild! Surely I was headed for greatness!

I was wrong. Nothing happened for a year. I kept working at the bar on Ventura Boulevard, and I did some catering gigs. I'd go to big industry parties in Malibu, help set up tables, and tend bar all night.

In 1993, I auditioned for the lead in a little movie called *Guyver: Dark Hero*. It was based on a Japanese comic book, and they felt I looked like the comic book character, and that I had some of that *manga* quality they were looking for. I got the part. It paid five thousand dollars, which seemed pretty sweet at the time. We shot in a warehouse in Van Nuys, and on location in the Angeles Crest Mountains, which were doubling for Utah, and that's where I met my wife. She was an actress, playing the part of a hot archeologist with remarkable conviction. I didn't want to ask her out because I didn't want to be unprofessional, but I later found out that after meeting me she'd gone home and made a note to herself in her date-book; "Snag the Guyver!"

On her last day of shooting, I asked her out. She went home, opened her date-book, and checked off the entry. *Done.*

The film was never released theatrically—it was a small movie and that had never been the plan—but it soon became available at Blockbuster. I thought it was a pretty cool movie, and I was convinced it was going to change my whole career, but it didn't do a thing for me.

I kept studying and auditioning, and then I got into voice-overs. I did some voice-overs for Japanese anime, and I played the voice of Captain America on the *Spider-Man* cartoon series.

By that time, I was twenty-seven years old, still tending bar, and not getting any theatrical work whatsoever. And I had this friend I'd met at the Beverly Hills Playhouse, Randall Slavin, another actor, who came up to me one day and asked if I'd be interested in producing a movie with him.

Randall was just as unsatisfied with his career as I was with mine. He had played a small part in *Public Access*, which was directed by Bryan Singer, a mutual friend, and had subsequently got hold of a screenplay by Dylan

Kussman, another actor. Kussman played the redhead in *Dead Poets Society*, but he was also a writer, and when he first came to L.A., he had written a script about two writers who spend a week together in a Hollywood apartment. One of them is trying to sell his book, and the other one has writer's block and is losing his mind.

I thought the script was very good. I didn't pretend to be a writer, but I had studied writing, and I had written some short scripts and some short stories, mostly as exercises for myself, and I had read enough scripts to know that this one was pretty good. The whole story took place in one room, which was also appealing, because it wouldn't be too expensive to shoot. And, perhaps best of all, there were two great parts for two young leads: Randall, and me.

So I told Randall, "Sure. I'll help you make this."

Now, at one point, Bryan Singer had talked about wanting to direct that script himself, and he had talked about casting Robert Sean Leonard in the part I wanted, and Dylan, the writer, in the other. But Bryan was already well beyond that: He had directed *The Usual Suspects*, and he was getting ready to shoot *Apt Pupil*, and at this point it didn't seem like he'd really want to make such a small movie.

Still, I called Bryan to make sure he was okay with it, and, when I found out he was, I told him that I wanted to try to make the film with Randall, and that we were going to make an effort to raise the money ourselves. Bryan was very supportive. He said to let him know if there was anything he could do to help.

So I went out and started raising money for the film, figuring I needed a quarter of a million dollars. That was the day I began to take control of my own destiny. I was determined to create a project for myself, and I figured this was the way to do it. To this day, despite how that turned out, I still believe that that's the key to success: You have an idea, and you try to make it real. And you do anything you can to make it happen.

It struck me that, as an actor, I was uniquely qualified for nothing, except for pretending to be other people. But I did so much reading that it actually helped me prepare for other things in life. And one of the first things I did was to go out and read some books that told me the difference between a line-producer, a coproducer, and an executive producer.

Then I called my friend Adam Duritz, the lead singer for Counting Crows, and asked him if he would donate a song to our movie. (I was going to do anything I could to get the project off the ground.) And Adam said, "Maybe I could executive produce it?"

Then I called Bryan and told him that Adam was interested in executive producing, and Bryan became more involved. Suddenly, we were getting a little star-power, a little legitimacy, and I was able to set up a meeting with a potential investor. We made arrangements to meet him at the office of Adam's manager, and Adam and Bryan came to the meeting. I pitched the movie to this investor, beat by beat, with great passion. (At the time, it was called *Apartment 427*, but the name was later changed to *Burn*.) By the end of the meeting, the investor went on his way, but both Bryan and Adam were more on board than ever. Bryan ended up recommending a director, this guy Scott Storm, whom he'd known in film school, and we took a look at some of his student films and thought they were phenomenal.

Suddenly, we had a director. I felt really energized. I had direction, and I had a place into which I could pour my creative energies. Every waking moment went into getting the film made. I was so consumed by it that I stopped going to auditions and even stopped returning my manager's calls, and as a result I lost both my manager and my agent. I was no longer a viable commodity as an actor.

Then we got lucky. Bryan and Adam decided to give us half the budget out of their own pockets. But there was a caveat: We couldn't spend a penny of it until we had raised the other hundred and twenty-five thousand dollars ourselves. We had a start date, and we had half the budget, and we had three months to raise the rest of the money.

We went to everyone we knew, and slowly the financing began to come together. My investors were mostly stock market types. One man sent me ten thousand dollars with a note, "Sure, I'll play." Another asked how much it would cost to have a line in the movie, and I got him for twenty-five thousand. Later, on location, he told me he'd bet a friend a hundred thousand dollars that he'd get a speaking part in a film before the end of the year. And that's pretty much how I learned to become a producer: by dealing with that madness and that pressure and that intensity on a daily basis.

When the money was in place, we hired a line-producer, Anthony

Miller, who was invaluable. One afternoon, Anthony wandered onto the stage of *Mimic* and found out that the crew was about to toss one of the sets. It was an office set, but Anthony thought we might be able to make it work. For three hundred dollars, the cost of renting a truck, we hauled it away and began to convert it into a beautiful, one-bedroom apartment. Then we rented space on a stage in North Hollywood and shot our movie in seventeen very hot days in August.

We submitted the film to Sundance and Slamdance. Sundance turned us down, but Slamdance put us into competition. So in 1998 Randall and I went to Park City, Utah, for the film festival. We screened our movie, met with a ton of acquisition executives, and went to a lot of parties and acted like crazed young filmmakers. When it was all over, we had won a special jury award, but nobody wanted to distribute our movie.

Suddenly I was dead broke. And I didn't even have an agent anymore. And I was so desperately depressed over my inability to get the movie sold that I didn't know how I was going to survive. I thought to myself. *That was as hard as I've ever worked, and that was as much of myself as I've ever put into anything, and if that's not good enough, then I can't do this.*

So for the first time in my ten years in Hollywood, I decided to get a day job, a nine-to-five job—even if it kept me from auditioning for parts. But I wasn't even thinking about acting, to be honest. I just needed to make a living. Still, I wanted to do something film-related—I didn't want to feel that I was *completely* out of the business—and I called my friend Bryan Singer again. He was in the very early stages of preproduction on his next film, *X-Men*, and I asked him if I could have a job driving a truck or answering phones or anything at all. He said, "Sure," and he hired me to answer the phones.

It was still early in production, sort of *pre*-preproduction, so there weren't that many calls coming in. And one day Bryan suggested that maybe I could replace his assistant, John Palermo. "He's only nineteen and he doesn't care about movies or about the industry, and you're a filmmaker," he said. "Why don't you drive me around to some of the visual effects houses and other stuff, and you can take a look at the process and see how everything works?"

I was very excited about this. We started going around to visual effects houses and to various meetings, and no matter where we were or what the meeting was about, all Bryan ever talked about was the script. He is very script intensive. He was constantly discussing problems in the script, and thinking about ways to reshape the film, and I let him bounce his ideas off me. For two to three weeks, I just kept my mouth shut and listened to all of his concerns. And I'd been an *X-Men* fan since I was twelve years old, so I knew just about everything there was to know about these characters. One day, Bryan was complaining about the love triangle between Jean Grey and Cyclops and Wolverine, saying there was no scene in the movie between Cyclops and Wolverine. And he was also upset about the fact that they couldn't work the word *X-Men* into the dialogue without sounding grandiose and overblown and ridiculous.

And a few days later, I was driving him to the office, and I had an idea for a scene that addressed both those issues, so I shared it with him. I said, Cyclops could be playing basketball, and Wolverine shows up and they have a confrontation on the basketball court, and Wolverine ends it by saying, "I've got no interest in you, Xavier," then he taps the X on his chest and adds, "or your little X-Men."

And Bryan said, "Yeah, that's good. Write that scene for me."

I figured he was kidding. This was an $80 million movie. Why would he ask the guy who was driving him around to write a scene for him? The script had been written by Ed Solomon, who wrote *Men in Black*, and Chris McQuarrie, who wrote *The Usual Suspects*, and they were *actual* writers.

But Bryan called me at the end of the day and asked, "Where's my scene?"

And I said, "I'm not finished yet."

And I spent the next day writing a two-and-a-half-page scene, and rewriting it and honing it, trying to make it as good as I could possibly make it. I finally gave it to Bryan, but I didn't hear anything from him for the rest of the day. And the next morning, I asked him, "Did you read the scene?" And he said, "Yeah." And I said, "What did you think?" And Bryan said, "I put it in the movie."

From that from that day on, Bryan began taking me to story meetings with the studio. And he said, "Sit in the back, listen to everything we say, and take notes."

Unbeknownst to the studio, I'd go back and work till one o'clock in the morning, rewriting the script, and giving Bryan pages, and then I'd sit down with him to develop even more scenes. This went on for a couple of months, until one day one of the producers figured out what was going on. And he asked me to take a script and highlight everything I had written, and it added up to about 50 percent of the material.

So the producer went over to the studio, 20th Century Fox, and he told them what was going on, saying, "You have to make a deal with this guy. He could sue you. He could take back his stuff."

And I'm sure they were having a little trouble processing this. *The script was being rewritten by a guy who was making five hundred dollars a week answering phones?*

So I got called into the office of Peter Rice, the vice president of the studio, and he said to me, "David, we are going to give you $35,000. That's the Writers Guild minimum for a rewrite. That is what we're giving you for all of your work on this project, past, present, and future, and you are never to ask for another dime."

And I said, "That's very fair, and I appreciate it. Thank you."

And I walked out into the Fox parking lot, and I was absolutely thrilled: I was going to get $35,000!

We went to Canada to shoot the movie. I was there for eight months, constantly rewriting the script. Working and working and coming up with new scenes and rewriting all of those. And all this time the studio kept telling me that I shouldn't even think about getting credit on the movie. "It will never happen," they said.

I realized that if I didn't get credit on the movie, all the work would mean nothing. And I had met a producer on the set who was about to go off to do *Andromeda*, a cable series for Kevin Sorbo, and he said, "Once you're finished here, come over and I'll see about getting you on the show as a staff writer." That looked like my best opportunity.

Then it came time for the studio to submit the credits for the movie, as they do on every film, and Fox did not include my name. They only submitted the names of Ed Solomon and Chris McQuarrie. They were giants in the industry, and those were the names the studio wanted to see on the film.

Still, I had done so much work on the film, and I knew Chris, and I also knew he had a somewhat troubled relationship with Fox. So I called him and said, "Would you just take a look at the current shooting script and see if you think I deserve to share credit with you and Ed? It would be a huge honor and it would change my life."

And Chris said, "Have you spoken to Ed?"

"I don't know him very well," I said.

"Ed is a really nice guy," Chris told me. "I'll call him for you."

In the end, both Chris and Ed read my draft, and during the credit arbitration they wrote letters to the Writers Guild, which ultimately determines who gets the writing credit, and both of them said the same thing: "David Hayter is the architect of this material." I ended up getting sole writing credit on the movie, which was a huge financial sacrifice on both their parts, because of the bonuses that are pegged to the on-screen credit, and because of the residuals one can expect on a movie of that size.

People in this town tend to be greedy and selfish, but writers can be different. Not all of them, certainly, but I think many writers spend a great deal of time examining their own moral codes, so that they can apply them truthfully to their characters, and if they have any integrity, they try to live up to their beliefs.

At the *X-Men* premiere in New York, I ran into Peter Rice. Here was the guy who had done everything in his power to have me fired, and to keep me from getting credit, and he came strolling over with a big smile. "David!" he exulted, shaking my hand. "When I heard you got sole credit, I can't even begin to tell you how thrilled I was for you!" Later, he took Bryan aside and said, "Do you have any idea how much money this guy is going to make from this movie?"

I did pretty well, as did the studio. *X-Men* went on to gross more than $300 million worldwide.

And that's how I broke into Hollywood.

And by the way, remember John Palermo, Bryan's nineteen-year-old assistant? The one who wasn't interested in film? Well, he is currently running actor Hugh Jackman's company, and he'll be getting producing credit on both *X-Men 3* and *Wolverine*.

As for breaking in, I'll repeat what I said earlier. If you have a dream, only you can make it happen, and you're going to have to do everything in your power to get there. There's no one way to do it; no wrong way, no right way. Even dismal failures can lead to great success. If you want something badly enough, fight like hell. Eventually with a little luck, you'll find your way.

Gale Anne Hurd

GALE ANNE HURD

PRODUCER

"The people who are enthusiastic, who give it everything they've got, who work hard to solve problems and are 100 percent committed to the job—those are the people who will succeed."

Gale Anne Hurd was an avid reader as a child, mostly fantasy and science fiction, and she didn't consider a career in film until her junior year in college, when she quite literally fell into it by accident. She graduated from Stanford University with a double major in economics and communications, and immediately went to work for Roger Corman, the most prolific B-movie producer in cinema history.

While working her way up the ladder, she met James Cameron, and the two of them went off to make a little movie called *The Terminator*. Other movies followed, with and without Mr. Cameron: *Aliens*, *The Abyss*, *The Waterdance*, *The Ghost and the Darkness*, *Terminator 2*, *Dante's Peak*, *Hulk*, *Armageddon*, *The Punisher*, *Aeon Flux*, and many more, too numerous to list.

Ms. Hurd was interviewed on June 2, 2005, at her office on the Paramount lot.

I was born in Los Angeles, a fifth-generation Californian. My earliest and only connection to the film business was through my mother, who was a secretary to Jack Dawn, the head of the makeup department at Metro-Goldwyn-Mayer. She was one of five sisters, and all of them worked in jobs in the film business. Script supervisor. Day player. Extra. That type of thing.

When my mother married my father, she gave up her job and became a housewife, typical of women of her generation.

I attended Westlake School for Girls, with many kids whose families were in the film business. I was a very bookish girl, though, and not particularly social. I loved science fiction and fantasy. You could say I was the cerebral outsider.

When I was ten, we moved to Palm Springs. I initially attended a small private school there, and I remained a bibliophile, but I also embraced athletics. I competed in track-and-field events throughout Southern California.

In my senior year at Palm Springs High School, I applied to Stanford University, in Palo Alto, intending to major in marine biology. When I found myself competing with legions of pre-med students, I quickly changed my mind about a career in science, and decided that the humanities and the social sciences had just as much to offer. At that point, I really hadn't decided what I wanted to do with my life: I wasn't someone who at an early age had a burning desire to be a filmmaker. I really wasn't aware of any women in the film business who could serve as role models, so I never considered a career in film. In fact, I was being pushed in other directions. My father constantly reminded me that I was receiving a very expensive education, and he expected me to go to business school or law school. I was encouraged to look for a career that would lead to a substantial return on his investment.

I spent my junior year abroad, in Britain. Stanford had a program based at the former Astor estate, Cliveden House, in Berkshire, about an hour from London. At the time, the place was a magnificent ruin. I loved its history, and I loved the fact that it had once been the home of Nancy Astor, an American woman who was elected to Parliament. The estate was also the site of the Profumo Affair, which involved espionage, political treachery, the downfall of a cabinet member, and the resignation of the prime minister. It was very exciting stuff.

There were essentially two courses of study at Cliveden. One was economics, and the other was British film and broadcasting. It was impossible to pursue just economics and remain academically engaged, so I began to take film classes. The department was run by Julian Blaustein, who had been a Hollywood producer. His films included *Broken Arrow; The Day the Earth Stood Still; Storm Center; Bell, Book, and Candle*; and *Four Horsemen of the Apocalypse*. He loved the film business, and he had loved producing films, and he inspired many of his students to pursue careers in the entertainment industry. It was Julian Blaustein who instilled in me the belief that I could actually become a producer.

This was a critical time for me. I was studying economics, and I assumed I would go to law school, but this incredible man became my advisor and steered me in a completely new direction. I studied British film and British documentaries. One of the courses was taught by Basil Wright, who together with John Grierson had worked on the early documentaries for the National Film Board of Canada. I remember being struck by the fact that I was taking a documentary class from someone who was essentially one of the creators of the medium.

We watched three to four movies a day: documentaries, feature films, the Ealing Comedies. Michael Balcon once came to the school as a guest lecturer. He had been producing films since the 1920s, including two of the best known Ealing Comedies, *The Lavender Hill Mob* and *The Ladykillers*. We watched Carol Reed's *The Third Man*, starring Orson Welles, and we watched all the films Alfred Hitchcock made in England.

It was such an exciting time. Not only was I being exposed to wonderful movies, but [also] I was surrounded by students who had already decided on careers in film. It was a steady diet of movies and documentaries, and *discussions* about movies and documentaries, and I loved every minute of it.

I knew that my family would not be thrilled with my decision to pursue film, and I was right. My father insisted that I complete my degree in economics, so I decided to complete both majors.

Since I had declared my communications major so late into my junior year, however, I was forced to cram two to three years of courses into a year and a half. As luck would have it, I ended up taking three classes with Professor Stephen Kovacs: film aesthetics, film history, and a third course on American directors.

During my senior year, Kovacs was recruited by Roger Corman to run production at his Los Angeles–based company, New World Pictures. Early that summer, Corman told him that he was looking for an assistant. Kovacs wrote me a letter asking if I'd be interested in the job, and would I mind coming down from Palo Alto for an interview.

I didn't know who Roger Corman was—we certainly hadn't studied him in class—and there was no Internet in those days. But I was able to do a little research. I found out that he was known, primarily, as a producer and director of B-movies, which he'd been making since the 1950s: *Caged Heat, Big Bad Mama, Death Race 2000, Eat My Dust, Fighting Mad.* I prepared for the interview with all the zeal of someone preparing for an exam.

When I arrived at New World and was shown into Corman's office, I was all set to tell him how fast I could type, how quickly I could take notes, and that I could answer the phone in an efficient and professional manner. But he began the interview with a question for which I was entirely unprepared. "So, ultimately," he said, "what is it you want to do in the movie business?" He was basically asking me what I wanted to do when I grew up. And I decided to go for it. "Be a producer," I said. At that point I wasn't sure if it was a trick question, but Roger didn't seem fazed by my response, and I got the job.

One of the wonderful things about working with Roger was that he gave me incredible responsibilities. The second day I was there, I was asked to take a look at the rough cut of a film and give the director notes. I had never seen a rough cut, and some of my notes were inane. "When someone's walking, why don't we hear footsteps?" I didn't realize that most of the sound effects were added later.

By the end of the first week, I was asked to put together a cast list for Roger's next film. Roger didn't use casting directors, so I relied on the Academy Players Directory. I would flip through it and prepare lists of likely actors, and I'd call agents to check availability and ultimately even make cast deals.

Before the end of that first month, I was sent out to scout locations for a film called *Lady in Red*, then I went on to help out on *Saint Jack*, a Peter Bogdanovich picture.

One day, Roger called me into his office and told me I had to take over the marketing department. The two gentlemen who had been running it, and running it well, had had a family emergency, and they needed to leave. So in no time at all, I went from being Roger's assistant to running the marketing department. I had to learn how to commission key art, how to write synopses of films, how to write and direct narration for television spots, how to create trailer campaigns—and I had to do it all by myself. I didn't even have an assistant. I worked on countless David Cronenberg films, including *The Brood*; on *Rock 'n' Roll High School*, directed by Alan Arkush; and on Corey Allen's *Avalanche*. And I was also busy marketing foreign films, such as *The Green Room*, by Francois Truffaut, and Ingmar Bergman's *Autumn Sonata*.

Most people aren't aware that there was a flip side to Roger Corman. He was making exploitation movies, certainly, but he was also one of the few people releasing foreign art films in the United States.

After I had run the marketing department at New World Pictures for a while—and not very well, I might add—I made a deal with Roger. I really wanted experience on the set, and I assumed I'd start out as an associate producer. But Roger said no. "The skills you've learned in the office don't apply on the set," he explained. He offered me a job as a production assistant on *Humanoids from the Deep*, which was shooting in Mendocino. I took it. I went from running the marketing department to being a P.A.

The movie was directed by Barbara Peters, James Horner scored the film, and Rob Bottin created the special makeup effects. Years later, both James Horner and Rob Bottin went on to win Academy Awards.

From the very first day, I knew I had made the right move. I worked six days a week, eighteen and nineteen hours a day, in the rain mostly, and I had to do *everything*. I had to wrap cable. I had to load and unload the grip truck. I emptied the chemical toilets in the motor homes. I had to drive to the Oakland airport any time an actor arrived. And I even helped Rob apply slime to the monsters. For my efforts, I was making $180 a week, the same salary as when I was running the marketing department. My salary for Roger never changed.

I remember one day in particular. It had rained for days, and I was in mud up to my knees, wrapping cable. I'd been working all night with one other grip, and when the sun came up, I realized it was my birthday. For a moment, all I could think was, *Where had all that promise gone?* I was a

Stanford graduate with a great education, and I was wrapping cable, up to my knees in mud, in the pouring rain.

But the moment passed. The truth is, by this time I was totally hooked on movies. There was that one dark hour when I wondered, briefly, whether it was all worth it, but I got through it. And I just wanted to keep going. Roger was impressed with me because he could see that the experience hadn't broken my spirit, and he made me an assistant production manager on his next film, *Battle Beyond the Stars*.

It was a John Sayles script, being directed by Jimmy Murakami, who had come out of animation. I was back working in Roger's office, reading scripts and learning all about development. I was also involved in much of the company's physical production. One day, Roger sent me to check out the film's model shop. A tall, blond guy showed me around. I assumed he was the head of the model shop, but I was wrong. He was a model-maker. He showed me the models he'd been working on, mostly miniature spaceships, and he talked in great detail about the visual effects. I was quite impressed with him. He was very confident, and very much a leader, and he had a clear vision for the look of the film. As it happened, the original art director had come to us from the studio system, and he was used to having legions of people working under him, artists and draftsmen, pumping out designs and blueprints. But this tall guy seemed capable of doing everything himself.

About five weeks before we were set to start production, we still hadn't seen a single design for a set, and the production required *twenty-five* sets. I told Roger that I was nervous. I said there wasn't going to be time to build everything at the rate we were going, and I suggested that we delay the start date. Roger told me that was impossible. The actors were already locked in: Richard Thomas, Robert Vaughn, John Saxon, George Peppard, Darlanne Fluegel.

Then he asked me, "What do you suggest?"

And I said, "I know this sounds wild, but there's this guy in the model shop who is an incredible artist, designing and constructing the models, and he knows the sets, so why don't we give him a chance to art direct?"

And that's how, in the space of three months, Jim Cameron went from building model spaceships to becoming an art director. And he did an amazing job, by the way.

I was responsible for the art department, among other things, so Jim and I were working together practically twenty-four hours a day. I had to make sure we stayed on budget, and I had to beg, borrow, and steal to get the sets built, and to make sure the cast and crew pulled together to make the movie happen.

In the course of those very long days, Jim told me he was going to be a director. He had a lot of incredible stories, and he was already writing a treatment for one of them. In the course of that movie, we agreed that we would both go off, make one more movie on our own, then collaborate on the next one. If things went according to plan, Jim would write and direct and I would cowrite and produce.

I went off to produce *Smokey Bites the Dust*, once again for Roger. It was directed by Chuck Griffith, who had directed the original *Little Shop of Horrors*. Jim went off to work on *Piranha 2: The Spawning*. And while Jim was in postproduction, he called to tell me that he had a good idea for a movie. It was about a cyborg and time-travel.

"I think it's a great idea," I said, after hearing his pitch. "I think we can get this made." That became *The Terminator*.

I had so much naiveté and hubris that I was almost positive we could get the movie made just because it was such a good idea. I don't think that's a bad thing, though. I think everyone needs that kind of confidence when they're starting out.

Looking back, I realize I was very, very lucky. I worked for Roger Corman at a time when there were very few opportunities available to women. Roger was actually hiring women producers and directors. And Roger took me, a lowly assistant, and made me head of marketing. Less than a year later, when he felt I was ready, he gave me a chance to produce.

I learned a very valuable lesson from Roger: *It pays to start at the bottom.* I had been running the marketing department, but that didn't give me the skills to enter the business as a producer. As a P.A., I learned all about physical production. Later, I worked on screenplays and familiarized myself with the development process. And along the way I immersed myself in postproduction and distribution.

By the time I produced my first film, I had worked my way through every facet of filmmaking.

It's amazing, because I have people who come into my office today, looking for entry-level jobs, and they begin by telling me what they *won't* do. "I won't make coffee." "I won't send faxes." "I won't make photocopies."

And I tell them, "Then you won't be working here."

It's the people who are enthusiastic, who give it everything they've got, who work hard to solve problems and are 100 percent committed to the job—those are the people who will succeed. And believe me, if they give it their all, they will succeed much more quickly than they ever imagined. Hollywood is truly a meritocracy.

BARRY JOSSEN

PRODUCER/STUDIO EXECUTIVE

"Be patient and focus on getting that first 'yes.'"

At one point in his life, Barry Jossen thought he wanted to be an anthropologist, but a high school film class quickly changed his mind. He ended up in film school in Los Angeles, where he didn't know a soul, and for the next six months he drifted from one studio lot to the next, pretending to be a messenger so he could get closer to the action.

His strategy worked. His first job, for an established television producer, lasted six years, but the producer never gave Jossen a chance to become an actual producer. He told Jossen, point-blank, that he didn't think he had the talent for it.

Today, Jossen is executive vice president of production for Touchstone Television, where he oversees pilots, original movies, miniseries, and series, including *Lost*, *Grey's Anatomy*, *Alias*, *Scrubs*, *According to Jim*, and *Desperate Housewives*. Prior to that, he worked for Imagine Television, CBS Productions, DreamWorks, and LucasFilm, Ltd., where he had a hand in the success of shows like *Sex and the City*, *Spin City*, and *My So-Called Life*.

In 1997, Jossen won the Academy Award for Live-Action Short Film, having produced *Dear Diary*, starring Bebe Neuwirth and directed by David Frankel. His Oscar was a first for DreamWorks.

Jossen was interviewed at the Walt Disney/ABC studios, in Burbank, on June 24, 2005.

I was born in Yonkers, New York, and my family was in the gas station business. In fact, both sides of my family were in the business, and rumor has it that my parents were married off so that the two families could create some kind of dynasty. My father was a bit of a maverick, however, and he decided to get away from the family. He moved us as far away as possible, to Hawaii, which is where I went to high school.

In my senior year, I had fulfilled all of my electives, so I decided to take the one film class my school offered. It was called "Film as Art," and I loved it. I especially loved the process of shooting and editing Super 8 movies. I had loved movies as a kid, and when I lived in Yonkers, I would go to movies all the time, sometimes seeing the same movie forty times because there was nothing new around. In fact I remember watching *Diamonds Are Forever* over and over again, and finding myself overwhelmed by the size and scope of it, and by the glamorous lives those people led.

I always sat in the first twelve rows, and I do that to this day. I am determined to make sure that my field of vision only reaches as far as the edges of the screen. I don't want anything to distract me, and I like to feel as if I'm actually part of the film. That's probably because I used to fantasize about being James Bond.

TV was also important. I liked *Man from U.N.C.L.E.*, *Lost in Space*, *I Love Lucy*, and *Voyage to the Bottom of the Sea*.

But it was only when I took that film class in Hawaii, and found myself running around shooting a little action movie of my own, that I realized I wanted to be in the film business.

When I graduated from high school, I went to the University of Hawaii, in Honolulu, but after only a year I followed my girlfriend to North Carolina, where I began taking as many film classes as I could find. I ended up in Los Angeles, at Columbia College, one of those schools where you learn how to make movies. I was really into it, and I got a job as a film rejuvenator. I sat in a darkroom, cleaning film prints that had finished their first run and were now destined for smaller, second-run theaters. I remember cleaning 1,500 prints of *Star Wars* one time. It was terrible. Some times I would have to lop off bad pieces of film, and try to re-splice the print, not always successfully. I spent my days in that dark, airless little room, breathing all sorts of noxious chemicals, and I decided I had to get out of there. But I didn't know what to do. I had run out of money, and my parents had pretty much stopped helping me out financially, so my only hope was to get a real job.

Unfortunately, this particular film school didn't tell you how to go about doing that. I knew there were writers, directors, and actors, but I knew nothing about the rest of it—I was clueless. I knew all about the movie studios, of course, but I didn't know a single person who worked at one.

Finally, I came up with a plan of attack. I put a resume together, and I began to target the studios, one at a time. And because I had no car, I walked. For the next six months, I walked to 20th Century Fox, on Pico; and I walked to Paramount, in Hollywood; and I walked to MGM, in Culver City. I would arrive at the studio gate with my resume in a manila envelope, and I would tell the guard at the gate that I had a delivery. And once I got past the studio gate, I wouldn't leave. I would go from office to office, trying to look like I belonged, and trying to figure out how I could get a job.

One of my favorite experiences was at 20th Century Fox, where they were shooting $M*A*S*H*$ I would hang around and watch them shoot so often that the crew began to think I belonged there. People would come by and say hello to me, and I would smile and say hello back and sit there for hours, watching them put the show together. And every day, I would walk from one office to the next and ask if there were any jobs around. If anyone was especially nice to me, or they showed even a little interest, I kept going back to them, figuring that eventually they would find something for me to do.

At long last, I met a secretary who worked for Frank Konigsberg, a television producer, and I got my first big break. She wanted to know if I could start the following Monday, and whether I had a car. I said yes to both questions, but I was lying about the car. Fortunately, I was able to go to San Diego to borrow my sister's car, and I drove back and reported for work right on time on Monday morning.

Konigsberg was producing a four-hour miniseries on Jim Jones and the Guyana massacre, and I basically had three jobs: fetch, make copies, and take lunch orders. To this day, I always tell people who are just starting out that they shouldn't underestimate the importance of lunch orders. And to this day I pay close attention to the way an assistant processes the lunch information, and to his or her ability to get it right. If they get it right, they'll probably succeed.

I learned fast because Frank Konigsberg hated pickles. There couldn't be a pickle on his plate. Shortly after I started working for him, I hired an errand boy to help out. At one point, Frank asked the guy to go out and get a sandwich, and when he got back Frank called out to him three times, in a voice that was both angry and contained. When the guy went into his office, I heard Frank say, "What is this pickle doing on my plate?" The guy said, "What do you mean?' And Frank said, "I don't like pickles. Please take this pickle off my plate." The guy thought this was kind of rude, and he didn't handle it very well. I don't know exactly what happened, but suffice it to say that he no longer had a job. So once again: Pay attention to lunch orders.

I spent six years with Frank, eventually becoming an associate producer on some of his shows. I learned everything I could. I read through his old files at night, combing through deal memos and contracts—he had once done a deal with Bing Crosby—and I tried to process as much as I could about every facet of the business. Whenever I didn't have anything to do, which wasn't often, I still made myself useful. I would clean shelves, rearrange scripts, or reorganize the office files.

Toward the end of those six years, Frank's company was undergoing some changes, and it was about to go into business with Lorimar. I got a call from Phil Gersh, a respected agent, who told me that I should call him if Frank didn't take me with him to Lorimar. I didn't know what to do, but I worked up enough nerve to approach Frank. "I really want to produce one of your movies," I said. "It would be an honor and it would be great for my career."

Frank thought about it for a moment, but only for a moment, then said, "I don't think so."

"Why not?" I asked. "I would love to produce a movie for you."

"No," Frank said. "I don't think you have what it takes."

I was crushed. I had killed myself for this man for six years, and it was clear I had reached the end of the line. I called Phil Gersh, who put me in touch with Edgar Scherick, who had produced literally dozens of movies and miniseries, and had launched the careers of Scott Rudin and Brian

Grazer, to name just two. I had heard he could be quite tempermental, and that he had a reputation for throwing telephones at his assistants, but when I went in for my interview, he was very nice to me. We talked for a while, then he asked me if I knew how to budget a movie. I said I did, which wasn't entirely true, and he gave me two scripts and told me to call him when I was done looking them over.

One of the scripts he gave me was *Town of the Eighties*, a 232-page tome by Gil Dennis. Good as it was, there was no way it could ever be made at a reasonable budget. Plenty of other producers had already tried, but I didn't know that, so I disappeared for six weeks and found an accountant who helped me break the script down. I figured if I could go back to Scherick with a manageable budget, I'd be producing my first movie, so I worked incredibly hard. It was so important to me, in fact, that I went to the Directors Guild of America and to the Screen Actors Guild, and we worked out a formula so that a film could be made for pay television with an affordable residual schedule, scaled to network viewership. That formula revolutionized the way producers made modestly budgeted movies for pay television, which was still in its infancy, and it remains in use to this day. In fact, people call it *the HBO formula*.

When I went back to Scherick, with the budget, he couldn't believe it. He sat in his office, across from me, flipping through the pages one at a time, and I explained everything I had done, and how the formula provided that everyone receive an equitable share of the money. When he got to the page where I had budgeted his fee, he seemed a little taken aback. "This is wrong," he said, looking up at me. "I get $50,000 per hour. This is a four-hour project. My fee should be $200,000, not $100,000."

"Well, this is a system of ratios," I said. "As I explained earlier, the budget is designed to make things more balanced than usual. If you want to make this movie, that's all we can budget for you."

He looked at me in stony silence. "Do you know who you're talking to?" he said at last.

"Yes," I replied.

"No," he said, somewhat more forcefully. "Do you *really* know who you're talking to?"

"I do," I repeated.

"I'm Edgar Scherick," he reminded me, "and people don't just change my fee!"

"I apologize," I said, "but you asked me to do a budget, and this is the budget."

He tossed the budget at me and it landed on my lap. "Do you know what you're doing?" he asked.

"Yes sir," I said.

"No. I mean, do you *really* know what you're doing?"

"Yes," I repeated.

"Fine," he said. "You're the producer. Go make the movie." I was so stunned that I couldn't move, so he yelled at me: "What are you waiting for?! Get out of my office and go find a director and start producing!"

I went out and made the movie, which was released under the name *Home Fires*. It is about four days in the life of an American family, and I often call it the first art film made for television. It took a year to make, and we brought it in exactly on budget. Well, actually, we went $5,000 over budget. Scherick gave me a little bonus at the end of the shoot, over and above my fee, to show his appreciation.

And that was my first big break.

You only need one "yes" in this town. It took me six months to get that yes, but it was all I needed. My advice is to be patient and focus on getting that first "yes."

MARK JURINKO

CREATURE EFFECTS ARTIST/PUPPETEER

"That was the day it finally began to sink in. 'Hey! I'm in the movie business! I'm having breakfast with Arnold Schwarzenegger!'"

Mark Jurinko arrived in Los Angeles with thirteen cents in his pocket and a dream: to get a job with Hollywood's preeminent creature-maker, Stan Winston. He got off to a shaky start, living in his car for several weeks, but the dream actually came true within a scant five months.

Under Winston's watchful eye, Jurinko worked on such blockbusters as *Terminator II: Judgment Day*, *Batman Returns*, *Jurassic Park*, *Interview with a Vampire*, and *The Sixth Sense*.

At the time of the interview, Jurinko was working on M. Night Shyamalan's new film, which he wasn't at liberty to discuss, and on a Frank Miller film about the Persian-Greco war.

We met him in Los Angeles on September 7, 2005.

I was born in Phillipsburg, New Jersey, right cross the bridge from Easton, Pennsylvania, where I actually lived till I was thirteen. My dad was a bus driver and my mom was a dental assistant. I had a younger sister, and a younger brother, now deceased. We were very much a working-class family.

From as far back as I can remember, I spent as much time as I could in front of the television, watching horror movies. Saturdays were special days for me, because they often played two or three movies in a row. I idolized Lon Chaney.

When I was eight or nine, I found an old plastic fishing box, the kind used for tackle, and began filling it with makeup. My grandmother and mother would give me the stuff they were done with—lipstick, mascara, eye shadow, etc.—and before long I had a pretty extensive collection. I would sit in front of the mirror for hours, making myself look like Lon Chaney, and then I would run around trying to scare people. My friends and family thought I was a little strange, but they tolerated me because I did normal things, too, like play football, baseball, and basketball.

I was also into comic books as a kid, and I really enjoyed drawing, and I spent a lot of time copying stuff out of my comic books—mostly horror-related stuff (with the occasional superhero thrown in for good measure). My father kept pushing the sports thing, however, and I enjoyed it, and I even got into working out and getting buff, but by the time I was in grade school—where a couple of teachers went out of their way to tell me I had artistic talent—I pretty much knew I wanted to be a painter. I'm not saying I was thinking of it as a career, or even as a way to make money, but it's what I wanted to do. There was even a brief period when I managed to combine my love of sports with my love of art. I painted many of my heroes: Lawrence Taylor, Michael Jordan, John Elway, Troy Aikman, Randall Cunningham, Mike Schmidt, and others.

By the time I was five, my parents were divorced, and I lived with my mother, but shortly after I turned thirteen, I moved into my dad's house in Bethlehem. I went to high school there, and my routine didn't change much—I watched horror movies and played sports. The horror was more compelling than ever, though. On Friday nights, I would watch *Uncle Ted's Ghoul School*, and on Saturdays it was *Dr. Shock*. I didn't care if I'd seen the movies before—I was addicted to horror.

One of the movies I saw back then, *The House on Haunted Hill*, has stayed with me to this day. There is a scene where a witch comes floating out of a closet, and it scared the crap out of me and kept me awake for several nights. As for the classics—*Frankenstein, The Wolfman, Dracula*—I couldn't get enough of them. I don't think I'd be exaggerating if I told you I'd seen each of those movies a hundred times. And it went beyond story. I was especially intrigued by the makeup, and by some of the more complex effects.

I guess it goes without saying that Halloween was my favorite holiday. I had a big collection of latex masks as a kid, and I always made my own costumes, and I was usually the most outrageous monster on the block.

When it was time for college, I went to Kutztown University, in Kutztown, Pennsylvania, and majored in fine arts. It was fairly routine stuff— drawing, painting—but during my senior year I told one of my professors that I was interested in mask-making and special effects, and he let me create an independent course for myself.

During my last semester, I wrote a paper on Stan Winston, one of the greatest creature-makers of all time. He and his crew worked on *The Terminator, Jurassic Park*, and tons of other films, and I thought the man was a genius. They also created the creature in *Predator*, which was one of the greatest creatures I'd ever seen.

While I was in college, I had paid my tuition and my bills by managing a beer distribution company, and by working construction during the summer, which was more lucrative. But a couple of months after getting my diploma, I decided to pack up the old Mustang and drive across the country. I was heading for Hollywood, even though I knew no one there, and knew absolutely nothing about the town. The one thing I knew was that I wanted to go to work for Stan Winston.

I took off toward the end of 1989, and I spent about a week on the road. I slept in the car mostly, but a couple of times, when I felt I needed a shower, I'd check into a cheap motel for the night. By the time I got to Vegas, I only had three hundred dollars in my pocket, and I decided to stop and play a little blackjack. At one point, I had almost doubled my money. By the time I left, I was down to thirteen cents.

I was crushed. I had five hours to go before I reached Los Angeles, and I had no idea what I was going to do when I got there, or how I was going to survive.

When I got off the freeway, I found myself in Venice, near Gold's Gym, and I parked in a spot behind the building and went to sleep. In the

By the time we started working on *Jurassic Park*, I was on the inside, looking out. Stan would get hundreds of resumes a week, from all over the world, some of them from very talented people, and from time to time the *really* talented made it to the top of the pile and got hired. So, yeah—it happens.

If you were in, you were a lifer. Stan told me, "As long as I'm working, you've got a job here."

On *Jurassic Park*, I was part of the T-Rex sculpting team. As bad luck would have it, I was in charge of sculpting the right side of the head and neck. This was a forty-foot-tall dinosaur, and I had to climb way up into a scaffolding to get to him. But I couldn't do it. I was afraid of heights. I would take two steps and get dizzy.

Stan saw this and walked over and said, "What the hell is wrong with you?"

"I can't do this," I said. "I'm afraid of heights."

"You have no choice," he said. "You have to do it. It's your job."

But I couldn't do it. I just sat there, watching the other guys work, feeling like shit.

The next morning, Stan showed up and I was already at work, *not* working, still unable to climb into the scaffolding. And he said, "Come with me." I followed him outside and we got in his car and we pulled out and I asked him where we were going. "You'll see," he said.

He took me to Magic Mountain and made me ride the Colossus, this huge, wooden rollercoaster. It was the most terrifying experience of my life. I was crying. There were these two little girls in the unit behind us, laughing and throwing their hands up in the air with glee, and Stan was laughing his ass off too, but I was crying like a baby.

By the time we got back to the studio, however, I was cured. I climbed up on the scaffolding and got to work. No problema. I climbed up there like a monkey. From time to time Stan would walk by and shake the scaffolding to mess with my head. But I got through it. Stan Winston cured me of my fear of heights.

I worked for Stan for more than ten years, then I left to try my luck on my own. I worked on *Men in Black II*, *Blade II*, and *Reign of Fire*, and more recently I went back to work with Stan on *Jumanji II* and *War of the Worlds*.

I love what I'm doing, and the effects world has been very good to me, but I'm also out there pitching original, horror-based, creature-heavy stories. I'm still as much in love with creatures and horror as I was as a kid in Pennsylvania, maybe more so.

As for advice, all I can say is that you have to believe in yourself, and that you can never give up. It boils down to luck, timing, talent, and positive thinking, so just keep moving toward your goals till all the elements come together and make your dreams a reality.

JAY KANTER

AGENT/PRODUCER/STUDIO EXECUTIVE

"You need to work harder than the next man, trust your gut, and pick the right projects."

Jay Kanter began his career more than fifty years ago, in the MCA mail room, but his life changed in the space of one magical afternoon. Kanter was sent off to the train station to pick up an arriving stage actor, and over the next few days the two men—both in their early twenties—formed an almost immediate bond. That actor's name was Marlon Brando, and he became Kanter's client.

In the years ahead, Kanter established himself as a powerful agent, but it was his gentle personality that truly seduced people. By the early 1960s, he was head of production for MCA Europe, and ten years later he was named president of First Artists, a company formed by Paul Newman, Dustin Hoffman, Sidney Poitier, Barbra Streisand, and Steve McQueen.

In 1975, Kanter went to work for The Ladd Company, at 20th Century Fox, and a few years later he and his partner, Alan Ladd Jr., set up shop at Warner Brothers. In 1984, Kanter went over to MGM/UA as president of worldwide production, and by 1991 he was COO and chairman of production of MGM/PATHE Communications.

Kanter had a stellar client list, but he was also known for his impeccable taste in

Marlon Brando (*left***) and Jay Kanter**

movie stars than I've worked with in my entire career: Marlon Brando, Steve McQueen, the Cassavetes brothers, Warren Beatty—and every other dreamy actor you can think of. I'm sure there were a couple of famous actresses, too, but I don't remember any of them.

My career began one line at a time, in B-movies and B-television. My first "professional" play was *Enemy of the People*. I still remember the review: "Although her fresh beauty was a delight to the eye, her wooden portrayal of Stockman's daughter left so much to be desired that she should get out of the business." Up until that day, I figured I wasn't much of a looker, but I thought I had a little talent. My therapist got me through that low point, however, and later the same year I had the good fortune to meet Joe Stefano, who had written the screenplay for *Psycho*. He saw me in another play, *Call Me by My Rightful Name*, which had been directed by my friend, Tom Seldon, and he came looking for me after the performance. "I saw you in *Enemy of the People*," he told me. "I can't believe how much you've grown as an actress!" He said he was working on a television series, and asked if I'd consider one of the forthcoming episodes. I assumed I would never hear from him again, but six months later the script arrived. It was an episode of a new show called *The Outer Limits*, and a note was attached: "The part is Ingrid; the magic is yours."

I remember the day we started shooting, Joe turned to the director and said, "Does she understand her motivation?" The director nodded, and Joe turned to the cameraman and the operator. "Make her look like a movie star!" he said. I had a fat face and a brown, bubble hairdo, but luckily the cameraman and the operator were very talented. Conrad Hall was behind the camera, and he went on to do *Butch Cassidy and the Sundance Kid*, *American Beauty*, and *Road to Perdition*. William Fraker, the operator, made his name on *Jaws*, *Heaven Can Wait*, *The Freshman*, and *Honeymoon in Vegas*.

I played a nurse in the part, somewhat ironic for a girl raised on Christian Science, and my costars were Harry Guardino and Gary Merrill. When I saw the rough cut, I almost wept. I left the set, leapt into my car, and raced over to the MGM lot, where my friend Vic Morrow was shooting *Combat!* I rushed into Vic's dressing room in tears. "I'm not only ugly," I sobbed, "I'm untalented!"

When that episode of *The Outer Limits* finally aired, the last episode of the season, my career took off. I guest starred on *The Chrysler Hour*, playing Rod Steiger's drunk, hard-bitten daughter. I worked with David Niven, Charles Boyer, and Gig Young on *The Rogues*, a series. I did *Kraft Suspense Theatre*, *Ben Casey*, and *The Alfred Hitchcock Hour*. I was a corpse in *Hands of a Stranger*, and in 1966 I guest starred on *Star Trek: Where No Man Has Gone Before*, the pilot episode of what would become one of the most successful series in television history. I remember having to wear these powder blue stretch pants, and looking up at William Shatner, who didn't look too thrilled about *his* outfit, either.

My first real part in a movie—if you don't count my one line in *Reform School Girl*—was in *The Third Day*, which starred George Peppard and Elizabeth Ashley. I was thin and I thought I looked pretty good, dancing in front of the fireplace, but nobody saw the movie and I went back to guest roles in television. Then one day I got a call from my agent, Bud Moss, who told me I would be reading for the part of Lieutenant Dish in *M*A*S*H*, a feature that was being directed Robert Altman, whom I'd never heard of. On the appointed day, I walked into the audition wearing red lipstick, and Robert Altman saw me and said, "I'll give you the best part in the picture: 'Hotlips!'" I was thrilled, though I didn't let him know it, but then I went outside and did what all great artists do: I thumbed through the script to count my lines. It looked like I had a grand total of seven, so I drove home and called my agent and told him I didn't want the part. He asked me to reconsider, assuring me that Bob Altman was very talented, and I went back.

One of my big moments in the film was the shower scene, where I have this on-screen breakdown. I wasn't sure how I was going to play it, so—like all great artists—I decided to be *loud*. I worked myself into a veritable frenzy, yelling at the Colonel, and when I ran out of dialogue, I didn't hear anyone say "cut." The camera was still rolling, and I backed out of the tent, crying. I thought I had blown it. Then Altman hurried out, looking for me. "I had no idea you were going to do it like that!" he exclaimed. "You're *vulnerable*. You can stay in the film!" After that, Altman started adding wonderful things for me to play, as only he can do. The moral of the story is: Take the part (if the director has talent).

One of the highlights of the movie, and one of the happiest times of my life, was getting to play a cheerleader. I just loved it. I remember watching dailies with Bob at one point, and he turned to me and said, "Sally, you're going to be nominated for an Academy Award." I laughed it off, dismissing him, but inside I hoped he was right. As it turned out, he *was*. The role earned me an Oscar nomination and a Golden Globe for Best Supporting Actress. And you know the rest.

For me, the lesson is a simple one: When you have passion, there's no stopping you. Whatever happens as you make your way through Hollywood, don't let them take away your passion.

DEBORAH NADOOLMAN LANDIS

COSTUME DESIGNER

"A career is like climbing a steep cliff looking for toeholds and handholds."

Deborah Nadoolman Landis started at the very bottom—as a stock girl in the costume department at the NBC Studios, in Burbank, California—and broke into film with back-to-back, low-budget features, *The Kentucky Fried Movie* and *Animal House*. Her work on *Animal House* so impressed Steven Spielberg that he hired her to design the costumes for *1941*, then hired her again for *Raiders of the Lost Ark*.

Other projects followed—*Mad City, The Blues Brothers. An American Werewolf in London, Trading Places. Thriller* (Michael Jackson's eye-popping music video), and *Coming to America*, for which she received an Oscar nomination. In the early 1990s, she returned to the theater, designing costumes for the American Conservatory Theater in San Francisco, (*Dinner at Eight, Gaslight*), and for the Mark Taper Forum in Los Angeles (*The Waiting Room, Closer*).

Nadoolman, who has a Ph.D. in the History of Design from the Royal College of Art, in London, is currently a second-term president of the Costume Designers Guild, Local 892, the union that represents motion picture and television costume designers. She also teaches costume design to young film directors and producers at AFI and USC, and has written extensively about the field. Her second book, *Dressed: A Century of Hollywood Costume Design*, will be published later this year by ReganBooks/HarperCollins.

She was interviewed on October 17, 2005, at the Los Angeles home she shares with her husband, director John Landis.

I was born in the Bronx, New York, to a middle-class Jewish family, but grew up in Upper Manhattan, not far from the Cloisters. My father, Milton, was a pharmacist at Bellevue Hospital, and my mother, Laura, was a principal of the Hebrew Institute for the Deaf. In 1950, my pioneering parents opened the very first camp for deaf children in the United States, Camp Laughton, in the Catskill Mountains, and I spent every summer of my childhood at the camp. As the only hearing child there, I know that the experience profoundly affected the way I use my eyes, and heightened my innate sensitivity to color and silhouette. Deaf children rely heavily on their visual skills for information, and as a result I learned early to communicate in highly effective visual shorthand.

One of my favorite activities at camp was "Bunk Night." Once a week, each cabin had to write and perform a skit for the rest of the camp, and the costumes were created out of "found" materials and objects: bath towels, paper placemats, sheets—any treasures we could find. I discovered that I was pretty good at it, and, more importantly, I loved the hunt—the idea of creating something from nothing.

When summer ended each year, I would go back to public school in New York, but I remained interested in costumes, and was crazy about the theater. (I often went to Broadway shows after school and stood in back.) On weekends we would stay with my talented grandmother in the Catskills, and she taught me to knit, crochet, sew, and needlepoint.

My great passions at school were English literature and history, which in many ways are closely connected to theater and costume. History just seemed to come alive for me, and many kids my age found it boring, but I couldn't get enough of it. I loved the research, sitting in libraries, poring through books, and losing myself in the stories—the politics and people of the past. It was my "easy" subject, and for many years I believed that history would be my area of study.

But I also took drawing and painting classes from a very young age, at both the Museum of Modern Art, in Manhattan, and at the Ninety-second

Street YMHA, which is a well-known institution in New York. My family also made sure I was exposed to museums, theater, music, opera, and ballet, doing everything in their power to give me a well-rounded education, rich with culture.

When it was time for college, I really wanted to go to Bennington, an artsy school in Vermont, but my grades were too dramatically lopsided. I was terrible at math, and probably learning disabled. (My parents never acknowledged this, because they felt I was just "underachieving.")

I went to Goddard College instead, a kind and gentle school in Plainfield, Vermont, with no grades and very loose requirements. I went there thinking I might pursue my interest in history, but Peter Schumann's *Bread & Puppet Theater* took up residence in a farmhouse at Goddard, and I found the performance pieces incredibly compelling. It was a mix of radical politics and entertainment, based on the notion that art should be as basic to life as bread, and I reconsidered my future goals.

Toward the end of my freshman year, I was getting ready to take a summer train ride across Canada with a girlfriend who was originally from Los Angeles. She was part of a group of talented L.A. kids with whom I had become friendly at Goddard. They had all gone to high school with John Landis, who was still in L.A. When we arrived, I phoned John, who was a struggling writer/director. John took me to Disneyland for the first time.

During my junior year at Goddard, I became a theater major in Paul Vela's progressive theater department, with the emerging playwright David Mamet as my teaching assistant. My senior project—to create four iconic costumes for the *Commedia Del Arte*—perfectly blended my interest in history, performance, and costume. I had finally found a way to put my academic strengths and practical skills to good use. It was an epiphany: With that project, I discovered what I was meant to do with my life. Sitting in the college cafeteria with Paul Vela and David Mamet, brainstorming about my post-Goddard future, I decided on costume design—and the doors opened.

When I graduated, I returned to New York, thinking I'd get a job at one of the major costume rental houses that served the Broadway theaters, Brooks-Van Horn or Eaves, and I made a halfhearted effort to find work. I'd like to think that throughout my life I've made the right decisions, even when they were informed by anxiety: Maybe I was too intimidated to try to start a career in New York; or maybe I didn't think I would find work; or maybe I needed to get away from my parents. In any event, while I was thinking about all of these maybes, I decided to apply for an MFA. in Costume Design. It occurred to me, even then, that designers should go to school close to the work source, whether it was theater or film, exponentially expanding the possibilities of assisting and networking. I had been thinking about Los Angeles and about the movie industry, and about the challenge and opportunities of being in a new city—although the only person I knew in California was the very unemployed friend of friends, John Landis. Still, I could visualize myself designing costumes for films. So I applied and was accepted at UCLA, at the Department of Theater, Film, and Television.

Shortly after I arrived, I was disappointed to discover that UCLA's theater department had very little real connection to the entertainment industry. No Hollywood professionals ever came to visit the costume shop. At the beginning of my second year, determined to make my own way, I made two important strategic decisions: I took a course at L.A. Trade Tech to learn fabric draping and flat pattern cutting (because I wasn't getting the technical skills I needed at UCLA), and I became an assistant costume designer on *Visions*, a low-budget dramatic series on KCET, the local PBS station. I spent that whole second year finishing my MFA program, designing college shows, attending trade school at night, and assisting designers at KCET.

As the child of a union family, the moment I graduated with my master's degree, I called the Costume Designers Guild to get information about the local chapter, and about the professional requirements needed to join. I was put through to Sheila O'Brien, costume designer, founder and president of the Guild. To this day I will never forget that conversation. In response to my inquiry, Sheila said, flatly, "Young lady, I have Oscar-winners out of work. We don't need any more costume designers in Hollywood." Then she hung up on me.

There were many rules about getting into I.A.T.S.E. (the International Alliance of Theatrical Stage Employees), and in the early seventies it looked like the film industry roster was pretty much closed to young people. On the other hand, I learned that if you had a costume job in "live" television at a network, or at a costume rental house, and worked for a thirty consecutive days, you could get into Motion Picture Costumers, Local 795. This was *not* costume designing, this was working as a *costumer*—on the set, in stock, and dressing the actors—but it seemed to me that it would open doors, and that it was the perfect place for a costume designer to start.

With that in mind, I went to see Al Nichol, a veteran designer at Western Costume. He was warm and encouraging, but he said I was overqualified for the job, noting that someone with a master's degree shouldn't be helping out with rentals. I went away empty-handed.

My next meeting was one of the turning points of my life. I made a cold call to Human Resources at NBC Studios, in Burbank, and on a Friday morning I went in for an interview. As I waited to be seen, along with the receptionists and file clerks also looking for work, I realized how "unconnected" I was in this industry town. When I showed my fat UCLA design portfolio filled with costume sketches to the HR manager, he seemed to respond, amazingly enough. He asked if I had visited NBC's Costume Shop, and I told him I hadn't. He picked up the phone and called Angie Jones, the director of the department, and asked if he could bring me by.

Angie Jones wanted to know all about me: what I was interested in, and what I wanted to do with my life. From time to time, she would interrupt our conversation to ask one of her impressive stable of designers to stop by and look at my portfolio. After about three hours, Angie Jones turned to me and said, "Deborah, I'll see you on Monday. You'll start in wardrobe stock, and you're going to be doing a little bit of everything." When she told me my salary would be $325 a week, and that it included medical coverage and pension benefits, I went home in an absolute daze. I knew that after thirty days I would become a proud member of Motion Picture Costumers, Local 705.

As I was driving along the 134 Freeway, on my way home to Santa Monica, my head still spinning, I totaled my car—rear-ending a Lincoln Continental in dense traffic. I ended up in the hospital, with stitches in my chin, and I called my boyfriend to pick me up. When I couldn't find him, I called my friend John Landis, who took me home. I spent the weekend recovering, and, on Monday, I took a taxi to my new job.

At the time—this was back in 1975—NBC had the largest costume shop on the West Coast, bigger than the movie studio shops, which were already on their way out. NBC's Costume Shop was building costumes for all the big variety shows at the time: *Dean Martin and the Goldiggers*, *The Captain and Tenille*, *The Flip Wilson Show*, *The Sonny and Cher Show*, *The Carol Burnett Show*. They also shot soap operas, talk shows, and game shows (such as *Days of Our Lives*, *The Johnny Carson Show*, and *Jeopardy*), and each and every production needed a costume designer. I wasn't there as a designer, of course—I was there as a stock girl and an all-round assistant—but I couldn't be happier. This was a historically significant time. Many of the costume designers had worked in the Golden Age of Hollywood, and much of the workroom staff consisted of European artisans who had brought their gifts over from the old country. From the very start I had a strange feeling that we were approaching the end of an era.

Toward the end of that first week, Angie Jones saw me coming and going by taxi. When she asked me what had happened to my car, I told her about the accident. Angie didn't hesitate. "Deborah, go to the credit union and get a new car," she said. "I'm the president, and I will cosign your loan. If you aren't working here in three years, you will be working somewhere else." She had known me for five days, and somehow she had an unwavering belief in me and my abilities. I was stunned. Her unqualified support fueled my self-confidence and bolstered my self-assurance.

Angie was determined to train me as a professional designer. I was exposed to every step of the costume production process, and it was the most complete design apprenticeship one could imagine. I assisted many designers, all of whom had very different personalities and styles of working. I helped out in the millinery department, visited the ancient glove makers, and became acquainted with the Hollywood shoemakers. At NBC, there were experts who made foam rubber fat suits, applied feathers to gowns, and the best beaders, dyers, and embroiderers outside of Paris. My three-year NBC post-graduate education even included learning to make silk flowers. I did all the department drudgery, too: sending out the dry-cleaning, spraying plastic beads, polishing shoes, putting clothes in boxes, dressing extras, and going on errands. Angie taught me the job from the inside out: She was single-minded in her ambition to turn me into the most knowledgeable and resourceful person in any studio costume department. Her generosity and mentorship changed my life.

During my second year at NBC, my new boyfriend, John Landis, had finally managed to raise the money to finance *The Kentucky Fried Movie*, which he was about to direct. When Angie heard the good news, she was kind enough to give me time off to design the costumes. The following year, she granted me another leave of absence to design *Animal House*. Each time, I returned to work as a wardrobe stock girl, logging my union pension and health hours. Then I got a call from Steven Spielberg, who had seen *Animal House*. He asked me to come in to talk to him about his next film, and at the end of the meeting, he offered me the job as costume designer. "This is going to be a Spielberg-Nadoolman coproduction," he said with a smile. It was time to join the Costume Designers Guild.

As a result of those early experiences, I've come to believe that you really do need active mentorship to make it to the top in this business. A career is like climbing a steep cliff looking for toeholds and handholds. You prepare thoroughly for the climb, and your conditioning and education provide a strong determiner for success. Stamina and patience are underrated qualities, and are essential to those aspiring to a career in the motion picture business. Luck, opportunity, and the generosity of others will decide whether you reach the top. And there are many reasons that talented, creative people don't make it: lack of ambition, tenacity or social skills, or they're missing that DNA spark that makes people want to help them. Bad luck is also a grim reality.

At the end of the day, it really boils down to who you are. Professionals helped me get started in my early years, and I believe they helped me because of my passion for costume design, and my commitment to hard work . . . and maybe because they thought I had something of value to contribute. People have to *want* to help you. That process—finding a mentor, and eliciting a prized measure of generosity—is a talent in and of itself. It's up to you to convince the world, and that person, that you are worth the time and the effort. You must have the talent to make people believe in your value and in your ability to deliver on that promise.

There comes a point in any young career when a helping hand is needed to pull you over the top of the steep rock face. That will happen when someone in your own field, whom you deeply admire, recognizes your potential. Someday, with luck, someone much older and wiser will turn to you and say,

DEBORAH NADOOLMAN LANDIS | 213

"I pick you. You're the one." It is my sincerest hope that I have justified Angie Jones' faith in my abilities. Her active interest in the development of the next generation of costume designers has inspired me to pursue a second career of writing, teaching, and becoming the very *welcoming* president of the Costume Designers Guild, Local 892.

JOHN LANDIS

WRITER/DIRECTOR

"Learn from the masters: Watch as many old movies as you can."

At the age of twenty, John Landis—high school dropout, studio mail-boy, stuntman—wrote and raised the financing for what would become his directorial debut, *Schlock*. That small, independent film led to a string of studio features, including *Animal House* and *The Blues Brothers*, two of the highest grossing comedies of their day, and *An American Werewolf in London*, an entirely fresh take on the werewolf legend, which he had written more than a decade earlier.

In 1982, a tragic helicopter accident interrupted production on *Twilight Zone: The Movie*, produced by Steven Spielberg and John Landis. In the trial that followed, Landis and four others were acquitted and found innocent of any wrongdoing.

With the tragedy behind him, Landis went on to direct Michael Jackson's *Thriller*, a groundbreaking video that forever raised the bar on that end of the music business, then returned to features and television, carving out a career that defies easy categorization. His movies include *Trading Places*, *Into the Night*, *Spies Like Us*, *Three Amigos*, and *The Stupids*, his only children's film. His work in television includes *Dream On*, the Emmy Award-winning HBO series, *Weird Science*, *Sliders*, and *Sir Arthur Conan Doyle's The Lost World*.

At the time of the interview, which took place on October 20, 2005, in the book-lined library of his Beverly Hills home, Landis had just finished directing an original one-hour for *Masters of Horror*, a Showtime series. In addition, he was in pre-production on two features: *Bat Boy*, based on the musical about a half-boy/half-bat who is discovered in a cave in West Virginia, and *Epic Proportions*, a Depression-era comedy about two brothers who are extras in a movie about the Biblical plagues.

I was born in Chicago, Illinois, and my parents moved to Los Angeles when I was three or four months old. My father, Marshall Landis, was an interior decorator, and he came west to start a new business, but he died a few years later, when I was five. My mother, Shirley, was left to raise me and my two older sisters, Jean and Joan. She got a job at a bank in Beverly Hills, where she worked for the next thirty-five years.

We lived in Westwood, about a mile and a half from UCLA. The Veterans Cemetery was just beyond our backyard, and in those days it was a marvelous place: a lot of open ground, eucalyptus trees everywhere, plenty of space for my friends and me to play and ride our skateboards (two-by-fours with skates nailed to the bottom). Now the trees are gone and there are only graves there, including those of my stepfather and father-in-law.

The Veterans Home itself is on the other side of the freeway from the cemetery. In the old days, in good weather, you'd see all of these old guys sitting around or going for short strolls. Some of them had served in World War I, and I remember one guy from the Spanish-American War. When they died, we would ride our skateboards down to the cemetery to go to their funerals. Three veterans would line up and do a twenty-one gun salute, each of them firing his carbine seven times. Then they would give us the big, brass shells. I must have been to fifty or sixty funerals as a kid, just waiting for the gunfire so I could collect the shells.

When I was about seven, my mother remarried a man named Walter Levine and I gained a stepsister, Mimi, and a new half-brother, Mark.

I went to Bellagio Road Elementary School, in Bel Air, and then I went to Emerson Junior High, right behind the Mormon Temple.

My interest in film goes so far back that it's a little obnoxious. In 1958, at the age of eight, I went to the Crest Theater, on Westwood Boulevard, and saw a movie called *The 7th Voyage of Sinbad*. It was directed by Nathan

Juran and is perhaps better known for featuring the work of Ray Harry-hausen, the great stop-motion animator. It was a magical experience for me. I had the complete filmgoer's suspension of disbelief: That was me on the beach, fighting the Cyclops. I remember I came home and said to my mom, "Who makes the movie?" And she said, "The director," which in retrospect I realize was surprisingly sophisticated. So, from the time I was eight years old, whenever people asked what I wanted to be when I grew up, I'd say, "a director." And because I grew up in Los Angeles, I could take advantage of my proximity to the movie business and learn as much as possible about making movies.

I think that was a big advantage, knowing what I wanted to do with my life at such an early age. I bought every book I could find about the cinema, and I watched as many movies as I could. I watched movies on TV religiously. They used to have a program called "Million Dollar Movie" on channel 9, the local RKO station, where they would show the same movie every night at eight o'clock, and four times on the weekend. I would literally memorize the movies: *King Kong, Godzilla, Mighty Joe Young, The Day the Earth Stood Still, All About Eve, Citizen Kane, Them, Red River, His Girl Friday*. I liked every kind of movie.

When I was around twelve, I discovered that many of my favorite movies were directed by the same man: Michael Curtiz. He directed *Yankee Doodle Dandy, The Adventures of Robin Hood, Captain Blood*, and many others, but he is of course best remembered for *Casablanca*. I admired the fact that one man could work in so many different genres, and I began to pay closer attention to who directed the films. I became familiar with the work of Alfred Hitchcock, Cecil B. DeMille, Frank Capra, George Stevens, William Wyler, Howard Hawks, Leo McCarey, and others.

I know I paid much more attention to movies than I did to school. I'm sure I have learning disorders, though these weren't diagnosed as such back then—back then you were either a "wise-ass" or "stupid" or "lazy." I would get A's in English and History, but I always failed math, and I goofed off all of the time, so I was constantly in trouble. When I graduated from Emerson Junior High, my parents sent me to a very prestigious private school called Oakwood, which was really a hippie school founded by Hollywood lefties. My parents could not afford the tuition, but somehow they managed to get me a half-scholarship. I found myself going to school with the children of many famous people. The kids of Ernest Gold, Alex North, Elmer Bernstein, and Jerry Goldsmith—four of the leading Hollywood composers—went there, as did the kids of many writers and producers. I clearly remember the day Elmer Bernstein came to the school to give a talk on film music, illustrating his lecture by playing selections on the piano. I was only fifteen years old at the time, and the experience made an indelible impression on me.

I was at Oakwood when halfway through my second year they took away my scholarship. My parents could not afford the full tuition so I left, and for a while I was in a special program at UCLA for high school students, teaching reading to kids from Compton. Then Ronald Reagan was elected governor of California and cut all of the funding and the program vanished, so I basically became a high school dropout.

I decided to try to get a job in the film industry. I had a motor scooter, and I went all over town, from one studio to the next, from one production company to the next, trying to find work. I finally got a job in the mail room at 20th Century Fox Studios, on Pico Boulevard. I would get to work at seven in the morning and leave at seven at night. The pay was sixty dollars a week, and after taxes I took home forty-four dollars and change.

The head of the mail room was William Paparhristos. A couple of years ago, I spoke at the party honoring his fiftieth year of working on the lot—and he's still there! He let me ditch work to hang out on movie sets, because he saw how interested I was.

It was a very exciting time at the studio. They were building Century City on the old back lot, and they were very busy making movies and television. Some of the movies they shot while I was working there included: *Hello Dolly, Tora Tora Tora, Beneath the Planet of the Apes, Justine, The Only Game in Town,* and *M*A*S*H.* All the Irwin Allen shows were in production: *Lost in Space, Voyage to the Bottom of the Sea, Time Tunnel,* and *Land of the Giants.* They were shooting *Julia,* with Diahann Caroll, and *Peyton Place* with Ryan O'Neal. They were also working on *Batman* and on *The Green Hornet,* with Bruce Lee. I remember that no one really cared about Bruce Lee, but that every Thursday Steve McQueen and James Coburn would come to the lot for their martial arts class with him and everybody would go crazy. It was an incredible place. You know when you watch old movies about movie studios and the lot is teeming with monsters and showgirls and cowboys and lobster men or something equally silly? Well, it was just like that. When they were shooting *Justine*, which was being directed by George Cukor, there was a sequence with a transvestite ball. They had something like a hundred big burly guys, all in dresses and wigs. There were also about a hundred other guys in gorilla suits from *Beneath the Planet of the Apes*. They were all having lunch outside in a tent at these long tables. It was truly a great sight: a hundred men in drag eating lunch with a hundred gorillas.

While I was working in the mail room at Fox, my sister, Joan, was taking guitar lessons from a woman named Harriet Williams. There she met another guitar student named Tonda Marton. Tonda's father was Andrew "Bandi" Marton (Bandi is pronounced "Bundy"). All directors get typecast, just like actors, and Bandi had been typed as an action director. Billy Wilder used to joke that he'd do a scene where the boss was trying to seduce the secretary. But once the boss began to chase her around the desk he'd bring Bandi in to direct the second unit.

Bandi's most famous credit, as sole director, was *King Solomon's Mines*. He made other interesting movies, too, like *The Devil Makes Three*, with Gene Kelly; *A Crack in the World*, an excellent low-budget sci-fi movie; the first film version of *The Thin Red Line*; and *POW* with Ronald Reagan—the first Hollywood movie to show toilet paper! He directed many other features and lots of television, and, as a second-unit director, Bandi directed some truly memorable action sequences. In *Ben Hur*, he directed both the chariot race and the sea battle. He directed the battle scenes in *Cleopatra*, and he directed all of the flying sequences in *Catch-22*. He had a long and remarkable career, and he really fascinated me. He was a glamorous figure, married to Jarmila, a beautiful Czech silent film star. Bandi found it a little strange that I was so interested in him and his career, because being a director wasn't as cool back then as it is today. It was all about the movie star in those days— you were watching Clint Eastwood, not Sergio Leone—and the director was basically the audio-visual guy. Bandi and Jarmila were very helpful to me, and Bandi encouraged me to pursue directing.

I sought out other directors, too, and they found my interest in them as strange as Bandi had. I remember seeing George Stevens on the lot, and I went over to tell him what an admirer I was. "Oh?" he said. "Name seven of my pictures!" And I began rattling them off: *Diary of Anne Frank, Giant, Alice Adams, Shane, A Place in the Sun.* Stevens was so impressed that he bought me lunch.

Ironically, as exciting as things appeared on the lot, this was really the beginning of the end for the Hollywood studio system. The big names that came along at the tail end of that era, in the late 1960s and early 1970s—people like Steven Spielberg, George Lucas, and Martin Scorsese—that was basically the revenge of the nerds. That's when it started being groovy to be a director, but I had wanted to be a director since *Sinbad*. More recently, I had started writing screenplays, thinking that that was probably one of the better ways to become a director. Many directors started out as writers—Francis Ford Coppola, Paul Schrader, Peter Bogdanovich, Billy Wilder, to name just a few.

I had been in the mail room for about a year and half when Bandi was hired to do the second unit on a picture to be shot in Yugoslavia. It starred Clint Eastwood, Telly Savalas, Donald Sutherland, Caroll O'Connor, and Don Rickles, and was released in 1970 as *Kelly's Heroes*. Bandi said, "If you can get yourself to Yugoslavia, maybe I can get you a job." I knew my mother would never let me go without a guaranteed job, so I took all the money I had saved as a mail boy—about about eight hundred dollars—and bought a one-way TWA ticket to London. (I had no idea how far Belgrade was from London!) When I showed the ticket to my mother, she could see I was really determined to go. And she knew Bandi and trusted him, so she gave me her blessing. I was eighteen.

When I got to London, I found out just how far away Belgrade was! I hitchhiked and rode the rails and had all kinds of adventures on the way there. When I crossed into Yugolsavia, it was like going from color to black and white. Europe was pretty well destroyed in the war, but Western Europe had been rebuilt with American money. This was not the case behind the Iron Curtain. When you crossed that line, it was still just after World War II. These were bombed out cities, with portraits of Tito everywhere, along with big hammer-and-sickle symbols plastered on the buildings, and heavily armed men marching around in hobnail boots. It was both impressive and intimidating.

I got to the set and ended up as a gofer, which nowadays is called a production assistant. It was a completely international crew: an American director, Brian Hutton; a Mexican cameraman, the great Gabriel Figueroa; French and Austrian special effects people; Italian wardrobe; British grips, props, and sparks; and lots of Yugoslavs. I spent nine months working on that film. I had all of the pleasure, all of the pain, all of the joy, all of the hard work, and all of the very long days. In short, the complete experience of a major motion picture production. I turned nineteen on that location.

Brian Hutton was very kind to me, and I became friends with Donald Sutherland and Don Rickles. I vividly remember the first day of principal photography. Telly Savalas was drinking coffee from a paper cup and he turned to me and said, "Hey kid, hold this for me, would you?" I must have held that cup of coffee for forty-five minutes before I realized that he was never coming back for it.

One of the people I met on that set was James Cornelius Patrick O'Rourke. He was from Camarillo, California—very tall, and a few years older than me. He had just graduated from college, and he was bumming around Europe with a friend when he got hired to stand in for Clint Eastwood. "John, listen," he told me toward the end of the shoot, "there's a tremendous amount of production going on in Spain. When we're done here, we should go over there and try to get jobs."

When the movie wrapped, we drove to Almeria, Spain, where production was booming, and one of the first people we met was a British production manager. "Can you do horse falls?" he asked us. And Jim said, "Absolutely!" The next thing I knew, I was riding a horse through explosions! I spent about a year there, working as an extra, stuntman, dialogue coach, and gofer on American, Italian, French, German, and Spanish movies, mostly westerns.

When I returned L.A., I tried to get into the assistant director's program at the Directors Guild, but they turned me down because I didn't have a college degree. One night Jim O'Rourke and I went to see a movie on Hollywood Boulevard called *Trog*, Joan Crawford's last film. It was a silly monster movie, but it inspired me. I went home and wrote the screenplay for *Schlock*. My attitude was, "Fuck 'em. If I can't be an assistant director, I'll be a director."

Meanwhile, to make money, I did some work for Robert K. Weiss. He had a company called Video Systems, where they used to make industrials, and he hired me from time to time as a stuntman.

With the screenplay for *Schlock* in hand, I took all the money I had earned in Europe, which was about thirty thousand dollars, and Jim and I raised another thirty thousand from friends and relatives. Jim produced and I directed. We shot it in twelve days in Agoura, California, during a heat wave. I ended up playing the lead character, an ape-man! The most interesting thing about the movie is that it was Rick Baker's first big credit. I was twenty-one and Rick was twenty. Rick Baker went on to win seven Academy Awards, the first of which was for the extraordinary makeup in *An American Werewolf in London*.

Schlock was released by Jack H. Harris, and it made money, but we never saw a dime—which is traditional in the movie business. When *Schlock* came out, to promote it, I was on *The Tonight Show*, with Johnny Carson.

At the time, there was a comedy cabaret in West Los Angeles called *The Kentucky Fried Theater*, which had been created David Zucker and his brother, Jerry, and their friend Jim Abrahams. The three of them often played basketball with Bob Weiss, my producer, and the next time they played, David said, "I saw this kid John Landis on *The Tonight Show*. He made a movie." And Bob said, "I know that kid! He does stunts for me!"

That just goes to show how serendipitous it all is. Luck plays such a huge part in a career. I met with David, Jerry, and Jim and we went down a couple of blind alleys, but eventually we made *The Kentucky Fried Movie* together. The continuity person on *The Kentucky Fried Movie* was a beautiful young woman named Katherine "Boots" Wooten. And this is where even *more* luck comes into the equation: At the time, she was dating Sean Daniel, who was working for Thom Mount, at Universal Studios. Thom was the second in command to Ned Tanen, the president of production.

Boots would go home to Sean at night and tell him all these wild stories about *Kentucky Fried*. She had seen a draft of *National Lampoon's Animal House*, which had been written by Harold Ramis, Doug Kenney, and Chris Miller, and she kept urging Sean to hire me to direct the movie when the time came. Eventually, Sean came to the cutting room and watched a rough assembly of *The Kentucky Fried Movie*, and he subsequently hired me to supervise a rewrite of the script, and I went to New York and met with the writers, and we talked about the next pass.

When *Kentucky Fried* was finished, the suits at Universal liked it. Then the rewrite of *Animal House* came in, and they liked that, too, and I was told I could direct the movie!

After *Animal House*, I cowrote *The Blues Brothers* with Dan Ackroyd, and I got to direct that, too. Both films were financially successful, so I was allowed to make *An American Werewolf in London*, which I had written a dozen years earlier—while working as a gofer on *Kelly's Heroes*. It was basically the same screenplay, but now I had the clout to make it, and that's pretty much the way the system works. I have continued to write and direct movies and television since then.

In terms of advice: Watch as many old movies as you can. Look at the masters: Lubitsch, Wilder, Capra, Keaton, Hawks, Preston Sturgess, John Ford, Alfred Hitchcock, Stanley Kubrick, etc. Filmmaking has not really changed much in terms of how we tell a story. There have been fashions in editing and photography and there have been countless technological improvements, but if you look at a production still from 1909 and you look at a production still from 2005, you will see the exact same thing: a camera, performers in front of it, and the director and crew behind it.

I'm always baffled when a studio executive passes on a director, saying, "He can't direct that. It's too big for him." They don't seem to realize that the director's job is identical regardless of the budget.

Also, read as many novels as you can, including all the classics: Dickens, Twain, Tolstoy, etc.

The other major piece of advice I'd give you is to make a movie. I really believe that nowadays, with digital cameras and laptop computers, you can make a perfectly respectable little movie for almost no money. So get out there and make a movie. I also think film school is worthwhile, if you can afford it, though I'm unhappy that many film schools don't make students watch enough old movies.

So, first—learn from the past. Then take the technology that's available to you and go out and make a movie. That's the best advice I can give you.

MICHAEL LONDON

PRODUCER

"The key is not to be frightened off by the surprises life throws at you."

Michael London grew up in Minneapolis, and seemed destined for a career as a music critic. As a student at Stanford, he wrote music reviews for the college paper, and those reviews led to an internship at the *Los Angeles Times*. While there, he wrote about music, but he also found himself covering other aspects of the entertainment industry, notably the film business.

One of those assignments led him to brothers Joel and Ethan Coen, a pair of virtual unknowns who were just about to make a splash with their debut feature, *Blood Simple*. London's interview with the colorful duo led, eventually, to a meeting with the late Don Simpson, and that meeting changed the course of his life.

After several years as a studio executive, London went out on his own. His first project was a television movie for TNT, *Second String*, and he followed that up with five back-to-back features: *40 Days and 40 Nights*, *The Guru*, *Thirteen*, *House of Sand and Fog*, and, most recently, the runaway hit, *Sideways*.

At the time of the interview, London had just finished shooting two movies, *The Family Stone*, with Diane Keaton and Sarah Jessica Parker, and *The Illusionist*, starring Edward Norton and Paul Giamatti.

The interview took place on June 14, 2005, at London's Hollywood office.

I was born in New Haven, Connecticut, but moved to Minneapolis when I was thirteen, and that's where I went to high school. I was interested in the arts, in writing and theater, and I was also very, very engaged in music—pop music, and rock 'n' roll. I honestly never really thought that much about movies.

I went to college at Stanford University, in Palo Alto, where I was an English major, and where I wrote a lot of music reviews for *The Stanford Daily*. As a result of those reviews, I was offered an internship at the *Los Angeles Times*. When I was told that I'd be writing for the Calendar section, I jumped at the chance. My dream was to be a rock 'n' roll critic for a newspaper or a magazine, and this seemed like the perfect opportunity.

At first, I wrote primarily about music, but because the first priority of the Calendar section is film, and because I was a young, able-bodied reporter, they started asking me to do profiles of filmmakers, and stories about the movie business and the people who ran it.

Eventually, I got a little caught up in the daily grind of journalism. A newspaper is published every single day, seven days a week, so you have to focus more on quantity than on quality, and some of the joy just went out of the work for me. I was restless and bored, and my work began to feel a little uninspired to me.

One day, I was assigned to do a profile of Joel and Ethan Coen, and I remembered something that had happened a couple of years earlier. My father had called from Minneapolis. "You remember Joel and Ethan Coen?" he said. I said, "Yes; of course." I'd gone to high school with them and they lived down the street from us. Now they and a young producer were canvassing the neighborhood, trying to raise money for a movie. "They came into our living room," my father continued, "and they had a film projector, and they showed me some footage or a test reel or something, and I thought it was really very good. And I figured I'd call you, because you're in Los Angeles now."

I more or less cut him off. "Dad," I said. "Whatever you do, don't give Joel and Ethan money for this movie. *Do not invest in the movie business.* You don't know anything about the movie business."

I think my dad was a little disappointed, because he'd been sort of excited about the film, but he listened to me. "Okay," he said. "I'm sure you're right. I won't give them any money."

So here it was, almost two years later, and I'd been assigned to do a profile of Joel and Ethan Coen, who had just directed their very first movie, *Blood Simple*, a movie in which my father might have been a small investor (if he hadn't listened to me).

Today, everyone knows the Coen brothers as pretty colorful characters, but back then no one had really heard of them. So I went to meet them at Sam Raimi's house, in Silver Lake. They were friends of Sam's, a director, and the interview took place around midnight, on the large deck outside Sam's house, looking out over the lights of Los Angeles. It turned out to be the most interesting, colorful interview that a young journalist could hope for. They were very funny and irreverent and they kept finishing each other's sentences.

I also had a photographer with me, from the paper, and he took a fantastic picture of them, on the deck, high above the city.

I remember going home that night and thinking, *I haven't written anything really good in a long time, I'm going to write a story that will remind people that I'm a good writer.*

It was completely premeditated, plus I had seen their movie and really loved it, which gave me some real inspiration. And so I wrote a profile of the Coen brothers, and it got great play. A lot of times, the placement of an article depends on the art, and the photograph was really amazing: these two unusual brothers looking out over the twinkling lights of Los Angeles.

When I saw the story in the paper, and the play they'd given it, I reread it and felt really pleased. It had been a long time since I'd taken such pride in my work.

The next day, or maybe the day after that, I got a call from an agent by the name of Jim Berkus. "You know that story you wrote on the Coen brothers?" he said. "That was a really good story." He then went on to tell me that his friend Don Simpson, the producer, had read the story, and that he had called Jim Berkus to find out who I was. "He thinks you're talented," Berkus said. "And he wants to meet you."

What I didn't know at the time was that Don Simpson and his partner,

Jerry Bruckheimer, who had a deal at Paramount, had just lost their top executive, and they were looking for someone new to run their company.

I also didn't know that Don and Jerry prided themselves on not doing things the way other producers did them. My understanding is that Don said to himself that he could take a young journalist, like myself, and turn him into a better studio executive than any of the people who were then running around Hollywood at the time, trying to make their way up the ladder. "Don is interested in meeting with you about a job," Berkus said, getting more specific.

I told Berkus no; that I really wasn't interested in working in the film business. It felt like an alien world to me, one in which I would never fit in.

Jim Berkus called a couple more times, and I said no a couple more times. And apparently whenever I said no Jim Berkus would go back and tell Don Simpson, and Don would get more and more determined to lure me away from the paper.

Finally, I agreed to meet him, and one Friday night, after work, I went up to his house. And it was truly one of the great nights of my life. Don turned out to be this extraordinary, larger-than-life person, an amazing creative presence, and a wonderful raconteur. And of course I'd heard all the stories about him; that he was supposed to be some kind of out-of-control playboy, a rebel, a deeply troubled character. But what I saw was someone who was filled with imagination and filled with a love of working with talented people and of finding great stories and of sharing his love of movies with the world.

We spent about four hours together that night, talking about stories and movies and characters and music and books, and I walked out of there in a daze. All the things we had talked about, everything that had happened in that room with that guy, those were the things I had lost and wanted to feel again. And journalism just wasn't providing me with any of it anymore.

Still, I was very nervous about the business side of it. I didn't think I'd be able to talk like those people or dress like those people or act like those people. I knew a little about them because I had been covering the business for the newspaper, and I felt like they belonged to some secret club. They talked in code. I felt very much like an outsider.

When I finally changed my mind, and I decided to go to work for Don and Jerry, I think I must have been the only person in the history of the movie business who insisted on a one-year deal instead of a two-year deal. I was concerned that I might want to go back to journalism, and just as concerned that the film business might not work out for me.

Don had said, "It doesn't matter that you're not in the club. You don't want to be in that club. Come work for us and it will be fun and exciting, and all the things you love, all the things we talked about—stories and music and books and characters—that's what this job will be about."

And it was. Don was an outsider himself. And in fact he and Bruckheimer were having a little trouble with Paramount at the time. Don didn't want to be pigeonholed into making only those big movies that he and Jerry were known for, and he kept trying to pursue other projects, and it made things a little tense for everyone.

I worked for Don and Jerry for about three or four years—I was there during *Top Gun* and *Beverly Hills Cop II*—and then I left to take a job at Fox, as an executive. I spent four or five years working at the studio, and—while it was wonderful experience—I became more and more hungry to get closer to the creative process. In 1999, I decided to leave the studio and go out on my own as a producer.

The first thing I produced was a little TV movie for TNT, *Second String*, then I had some success with a number of features, and last year I did very well with *Sideways*. That movie was a huge turning point for me, and not just because it was so well received. That movie embodied everything I love about making movies.

My career was such an accident in so many ways that I'm not sure I'm the best person to go to for advice. I tend to subscribe to the theory that what you *think* you want out of life is not necessarily what you really want. I think it's good to have a sense of direction and purpose, certainly, but it's also important to let things happen to you. If you find yourself on a path that isn't the one you chose, don't be afraid to take that ride.

For me, the movie business didn't represent something that I consciously knew I wanted to do. But eventually I got to a place, especially with the movies I've been working on recently, where what I do has become everything I ever wanted to do. I like stories, I like the creative process, I like interesting characters, and I like tapping into the imagination—my own and that of others. I had never seen movies as a venue for any of that, and yet I now find myself working on movies that tell great stories and are full of life and energy and imagination.

If I'd been too focused on another path—a career as a music critic, say—I might never have been open to that strange Friday night with Don Simpson.

I think advice can be dangerous. I don't think a kid of eighteen, or even twenty-four, for that matter, really knows what inspires him. Life is so mysterious, and people are so complex, and I often find that the things you think you want are not the things that are ultimately going to make you feel the most fulfilled.

I think you have to go after them, of course; pursue the things you're really passionate about. But the key is not to be frightened off by the surprises life throws at you. The trick is to be open to the unexpected.

BERNIE MAC

ACTOR/COMEDIAN

"Failure is just life's way of preparing you for success."

You probably know Bernard McCullough from his hit television series, *The Bernie Mac Show*, and you might even know him from some of his movies: *Ocean's Eleven*, *Head of State*, *Charlie's Angels: Full Throttle*, *Bad Santa*, *Mr. 3000*, *Ocean's Twelve*, and *Guess Who*. But you probably don't know the Bernie Mac from the South Side of Chicago, the one who hauled furniture, fried fish, drove trucks, repaired refrigerators, and spent two decades in the trenches trying to make it as a standup comic.

Mac never really gave much thought to Hollywood. All he ever wanted was to make people laugh. He did that and a whole lot more, but success was a long time coming.

Bernie Mac was interviewed June 1, 2005, from his home in Chicago.

I grew up on the South Side of Chicago, in a family so poor I had to eat my cereal with a fork. That way you left plenty of milk in the bowl for the next guy.

I never really thought about Hollywood. I was a funny kid and my dream was to be a comedian. I used humor to make friends, to avoid fights, and to try to charm the ladies. And sometimes I just used it to get through the day.

I was fifteen when I got my first chance to show my stuff on stage. It was open-mike night at this place called The Regal, on the South Side, and I begged so hard for a shot that the man in charge couldn't say no. I got up there and did my Michael Jackson impression, and I bombed. The man said, "Come back when you're funny, kid."

I got home and told my mama, and she had wise words for me. "Sometimes when you lose, you win, son. Failure is just life's way of preparing you for success." My mama always said things like that; *Mac-isms* I call them. Those little pearls of wisdom helped me get through two decades worth of rough patches, and even now, with my mama long gone, they're still helping me: *Nobody's tying you down except your own self, Bernard. Ain't nobody gonna change your life but you.*

While I was still in high school, on weekends, I used to work my routines on the subway, riding it back and forth and making a dollar here and there. I also tried my luck downtown, by the museum entrance, entertaining tourists. It paid some, and it taught me a thing or two about comedy, but I needed a real stage if I was going to make progress, and I knocked on an awful lot of doors that didn't open.

Next thing I know, I'm married to Rhonda—the love of my life—and I got a kid on the way. So I had to buckle down and get me some direction. I got so much direction it's a wonder it didn't kill the comedy in me. I worked with my grandfather, cleaning office buildings, mopping floors. I worked for a moving company, hauling shit. I worked at the South Side Community Center, over on Eighty-third, running the athletic program.

At one point, I ended up on unemployment, which was about the most shameful day of my life. I remember this old lady at human resources, with these little half-moon glasses on the end of her nose—looked just like my poor granny. She said to me, "I'm going to give you four hundred dollars in cash and three hundred in food stamps. That ought to get you started." All it got me started was *crying*, and I hung my head so low that she reached out and squoze my hand. "Bernard McCullough," she said to me, "You hang on, boy. I know you're going to make it."

I'm glad she believed in me, but I wish she had told me how long it was going to take for me to make it. I got a job driving a truck for Sears, breaking down refrigerators and dryers and stuff. I got day work. I was out of my bed at the crack of dawn, looking through the classifieds and praying and knocking on more doors that didn't open.

Then a sad day came: My grandpa died. At his funeral, when it was my turn to talk, I got up and told all sorts of stories about him. The way he'd snort and huff at me at the dinner table. "I'll knock your eyeball out, boy! *Step* on it. You think I'm lyin'? I ain't lyin! Man's got to rederfrine hisself to succeed in this crazy world!" I'll tell you, people was rolling in the aisles. I chased sorrow out of that room.

Week later, I got a call from a woman who said she'd caught my "act" at grandpa's funeral. She told me her cousin had passed, and said would I come by and do the same for him. That was about the craziest thing I'd ever heard, but I went over and met her and she told some stories about her cousin, and I put on a show for his friends and family. I never even knew the guy, but people came by after to tell me I had the man down. "Brother, you made Jackson come alive!" "It was like he was in the room with us!"

That was sort of the beginning of my career, more or less. I'd go to funerals, parties, afternoon barbecues. You called old Bernie Mac, he was there. Nothing too small for Bernie, and all of it building my confidence. Before long, I started hitting the comedy circuit: Taste of Chicago, Chez Coco, The Dayton Gang. By this time, all the clubs had open-mike nights, and you'd have four, maybe five minutes to do your thing and bring down the house. I didn't bring down the house every time, but I was getting better all the time. And I was learning.

Here's one of the things I learned. I learned that there were four basic types of standup comics. There was the joke-teller, who just got up there and told bad jokes. There was the political comic, guys like Mort Sahl, who read the paper in the morning and could turn that serious shit into a funny show. There was the anthropologist, standups like George Carlin, who could dissect a person so deep you couldn't help but recognize your own self. And, finally, you had the comics that worked from pain. People like Richard Pryor and Carol Burnett, who milked the low points in their own life to make you laugh—and to make you *feel*. I used to think, *Man, that is sweet! That's the kind of comedy I want to do.* Trouble was, I didn't know *how*.

Meanwhile, I had a UPS truck to drive. Then a school bus for the handicapped. Then I fried fish for a living in a place so hot I lost ten pounds my first week there. I stuck it out, though. Sixty hours a week in front of that fryer, then I'd run off to hit an open-mike before the night was over.

At one point, I tried to get an agent, but nobody wanted me. "You're funny, but not funny enough." I went out and bought three hundred dollars-worth of records: Bill Cosby, Richard Pryor, George Carlin, Bob Newhart, Carol Burnett. I listened to them over and over. Timing, delivery, tone, inflection. "Pay attention," my mama used to say. "Some of it's bound to stick."

One day, a man who'd caught my show at a private party told me Arsenio Hall was coming to town, and that he might be able to get me up on stage to warm up the crowd before his act. "I'm there!" I said, and he set it up.

Night of the big show, with Rhonda and her whole family sitting in the audience, I'm two or three lines into my routine and people are literally booing me off the damn stage. Some woman even threw a bread roll at me. I kept trying to come up with something funny, anything—I'm not a quitter—but they were shouting so loud I couldn't even hear my own self. So I walked off the stage, and that's when I got my standing ovation: They were so happy to be done with me.

It took me a while to recover. I ain't lying. And the next time I went on stage, it happened by accident. Me and Rhonda was in Vegas, to see Redd Foxx, and we went in through the wrong door and ran into the man himself. "Mr. Foxx," I said. "I'm a big fan. And I'm a comedian myself."

"A comedian, are you?"

"Yes sir, from Chicago."

Next thing I know, he's got me going out on stage to warm up his crowd. Man, I was nervous. It was a *big* crowd. I'd never seen anything that big. I was shaking on the inside, maybe on the outside, too, but I launched in: "Black people, when they die, they want a good send-off. That's why they always have life insurance, so they can get themselves a nice casket and have a fancy, catered affair and impress their friends from beyond the grave. But Blue Cross/Blue Shield—no sir, ain't gonna waste their money on that shit. That's why they can never afford no medication. Anything wrong, they take aspirin. 'He got a fever.' 'Give him some aspirin.' 'He stepped on a nail.' 'Crush up some aspirin and rub it all over.' 'He got shot.' 'Put that whole jar of aspirin right in that there hole, make it stop bleeding.' "

When I got off the stage, Redd Foxx was waiting for me in the wings. And he said something that has stayed with to this day. "Mr. Mac, you're funny, but you have a little problem: You want to be liked more than anything else."

"Sir?"

"You're afraid to show people what you've got inside. And that's where the best stuff is, the stuff that's buried way deep down. You can't be afraid of that, Mr. Mac. That's what makes it real. Dig deep, son. Don't keep the good stuff locked away. That's the only stuff that really counts."

Then he marched out on stage and left me there, so shocked I could hardly breathe. But I couldn't stop thinking about it. The man made sense. The comedy he was talking about was the comedy of pain; Richard Pryor comedy. Carol Burnett comedy. *Honest* comedy. This was the type of comedy I'd always been attracted to, only I'd never had the guts to dig.

I went back to Chicago, to my old job frying fish, but the next time I got on stage, at the Dayton Gang, I got honest for the first time in my life. And for the first time in my life, I knew I'd really knocked them dead. I got three standing ovations. I said to myself, *If I can't do this full time, I'm gonna die.*

My big break came in 1990, at the Miller Lite Comedy Search. Damon Wayans was hosting. The final showdown took place at The Regal, in front of thirty-seven hundred people. I knocked it out of the park that night. I took first place. I went home thinking, *Bernie Mac is the funniest man in Chicago!*

Two weeks later, Bernie Mac was driving a bread truck in the baddest part of town. Gonna get his ass capped delivering bread! Finally, one miserably cold day, I up and quit. I went home and told Rhonda I was done delivering bread.

"Bernard—"

"Uh uh!" I said, cutting her off. "This time my mind's made up. We're not negotiating here. I'm a *comedian.*"

From that day on, I put everything I had into comedy. I worked every club. I took every gig, no matter how small. I auditioned for Def Comedy Jam and wowed them and that led to a small part in *Mo' Money*. I played a doorman in the film. Opened the door, closed the door. I opened and closed that door like nobody's business.

Next, I got a showcase of my own, but it didn't last. I worked with Rosie Perez on her HBO special, but that's didn't go anywhere neither. Then I got a little more film work. I worked on *Who's the Man?*, with Ed Lover and Dr. Dre. On *House Party 3*. On *Above the Rim*, with Tupac.

At that point, HBO gave me my own show, *Midnight Mac*, but it didn't exactly catch on. So it was back to bit parts in movies. *The Walking Dead. Friday. Get on the Bus.* I even got a few small parts on television, shows like *Moesha*, but it wasn't until we made *The Kings of Comedy* that I really broke out.

That comedy tour put me on the map. I had taken Redd Foxx's words to heart. I wasn't afraid to show people what I had inside. I was doing *honest* comedy, and it was working double-time.

Here's the thing: You live, you pay attention, maybe you learn a thing or two along the way.

And you get through it because you have no choice. I'll be honest, it was my mama, God rest her soul, who got me through the roughest patches. My mama and her Mac-isms:

"Self-pity is self brought on, and it don't do you any good anyway."

"Nobody owes you nothin."

"Rely on others and they will soon enough let you down."

"Life is about movement, Bernard. Forward movement. You just make sure your feet are pointed in the right direction."

"Suffering is a good teacher. It keeps you in its grip until you've learned your lesson."

I think the most valuable lesson she taught me was to listen to myself. "Don't be swayed by criticism and don't be swayed by praise," she used to say. "It's nothing but noise, and that noise is going to drown out your own true voice."

That's good advice. Listen to yourself. Respect yourself. And believe in yourself.

And when you're down, try to remember what my mama said: "Failure is just life's way of preparing you for success."

CARYN MANDABACH

PRODUCER

"That's key: an almost crazy amount of self-confidence. Without it, you're doomed."

Caryn Mandabach arrived in Los Angeles three decades ago, with no Hollywood connections whatsoever—not even the friend of a third cousin twice removed. So she started at the bottom, getting beer for the guys who ran a production truck.

Before long, she was working for Norman Lear, the legendary television producer (*All in the Family, Sanford and Son, Maude, One Day at a Time*, to name just a few), then went on to try her luck as an independent.

In 1980, she joined forces with Marcy Carsey and Tom Werner, eventually becoming part of Carsey-Werner-Mandabach, one of the last great independent suppliers of network shows. Together with her partners, Mandabach developed and produced some of the highest quality television in the medium's history, including *The Cosby Show, A Different World, Roseanne, Cybill, 3rd Third Rock from the Sun*, and *That 70s Show*.

Early in 2004, Mandabach left the partnership and started her own company, Caryn Mandabach Productions, which sold three shows in its first year. She also negotiated an unprecedented first-look deal with the BBC.

Mandabach has won the Emmy, the Humanitas Prize, The People's Choice Award, and the Peabody. She has two children, Marisa and Jonathan, who seem to enjoy making her anxious. She was interviewed on May 11, 2005, in her Pacific Palisades home.

I moved to Los Angeles when I was twenty, chasing a boyfriend who later became my husband. I'd studied theater and literature in college, and I'd tried teaching—which I found horribly debilitating—and I really needed a job. I wanted to be in show business, and I liked comedy, but I didn't know whether I wanted to write, produce, or direct. To be honest, I didn't really know the difference.

I did what everyone does. I knocked on a lot of doors, and didn't get anywhere, but then I was offered a job as a production assistant on a truck at the Olympic Auditorium. The truck was basically a rolling production unit, overflowing with cameras and video monitors and assorted technical equipment, and the guys were responsible for shooting the roller derby and professional wrestling, or anything else that happened to be going on in the auditorium that day. My job was to make sure everyone in the truck was happy, and that meant running to the store for beer two or three times a day.

I guess it was as good a place to start as any, plus the shows were occasionally entertaining. I still remember Killer Kowalski, a wrestler who made a name for himself by biting off the ear of his opponent. (He gave Mike Tyson something to aim for.)

Later, I got to watch the Los Angeles Lakers play basketball, and that was more fun, if slightly more sedate, but my job remained pretty much unchanged: Keep the guys happy. Go for beer.

Eventually, I had a falling out with the man who ran the truck. I won't go into a lot of detail, but let's say he really liked machetes, and that he also enjoyed driving on busy sidewalks while pedestrians were going about their business. I'll admit it: I was afraid of him. I'm sure I'm not the first person who was ever afraid of her boss, but I think my reasons were unique.

In any event, I had paid attention between beer runs, and I knew a little something about physical production, so I decided I could become a producer. It didn't seem like there was all that much to hiring cameramen and soundmen and writers, and I made the rounds with confidence.

In those days, there weren't many women in physical production, so people paid attention. But not too much attention. They hired me, yes, as a *secretary*, and I had a string of secretarial jobs. One of those was with KTLA, a local news station, where one afternoon my boss asked if I could help schedule the engineers. This meant making calls and telling people when to show up for work, which wasn't very demanding. I did it, and I hated it—it was a hopeless, dead-end job—and I spent most of my time calling around and looking for something else.

I ended up working for a woman who was producing a small public affairs show on KNBC. At the time, she seemed ancient to me, but I believe she was no more than thirty-five. She was a little insecure about her writing, and she liked the fact that I had been an English major, so she asked me to help her with the show's scripts, such as they were. A few months later, she was promoted to the station's news department—I'd like to think it was partly on account of the scripts—and I ended up getting her job.

This was the early 1970s, and there weren't very many women producers around, and I was lucky enough to be working for people who believed in women and in affirmative action. As a result, at the tender age of twenty-four, I became the young whippersnapper woman producer at KNBC.

It didn't last, of course. I got fired on Christmas Eve. Not for anything I'd done, but because they were cutting back. The Gay Guy got fired, too. So did the Mexican Guy. And even the Deeply Religious Lady got fired, so I knew they weren't playing favorites.

I wasn't all that upset, though. I left KNBC knowing that I could get a job as a producer, and I went to see Norman Lear, who was already well-established in television. He hired me as his first female associate producer. I was responsible for managing the physical side of the production—crews, equipment, staff, etc.—but I also managed the editorial side, the writers. I really responded to this. It was actually a very creative job, and lots of fun. I loved watching the scripts come together, and I kept my mouth shut (mostly) and learned. I was an associate producer on the pilot for *Mary Hartman, Mary Hartman*, and I followed that up by overseeing production on *One Day at a Time*. I learned a lot from both shows, but *One Day at a Time* was an experience in and of itself. In the space of thirteen shows, it had thirteen different executive producers and nine different directors. Norman kept firing people. I had a new boss every week, and every week I was determined to charm him with my energy and my intelligence.

I got fired, of course. Norman turned to me and said, "Caryn, as soon as you regain your mental health, I'll rehire you." I didn't know what he meant—I felt fine—but I didn't bother asking for an explanation.

At that point, I felt like a real producer. Those crazy last weeks, with all the firing and hiring and more firing, convinced me that I was truly in show business, and that I should behave as such, so I decided to start my own company. I ran around telling people that I was producing television pilots. Nobody had ever heard of a female pilot producer. They didn't know what to make of me. I was confident, and I seemed fairly knowledgeable, and I didn't wear a bra.

I got my first real break from Jeff Harris and Bernie Kukoff, a pair of writer-producers, and I worked on a couple of their shows. They'd done a show called *Joe and Sons* for CBS, and were developing *Detective School* for ABC. I met Marcy Carsey and Tom Werner through them, back in 1976, but it would be four years before our paths crossed again.

At around this same time, I was asked to produce commercials for the Miller Brewing Company. This was very cool, because I oversaw every facet of production, and I was allowed to take a few risks because the commercials aired on *Saturday Night Live*. I worked with Jay Leno, Howie Mandel, Gilbert Gottfried, and many others. I did five commercials, and I think they kept getting better and better. If there was a leitmotif in my life, I guess it was beer.

It was around this time that I met an unknown comic called Jerry Seinfeld. I got a call from his manager, George Shapiro, who asked me to produce a special for Showtime. I have the distinction of having put Jerry Seinfeld on national television. I was making contacts left and right.

In 1980, I joined forces with Marcy Carsey and Tom Werner, and we made television history. I am very proud of the work we did together, and I expect—and hope—that I'll be just as proud of the work to come.

Advice? Well, I think being ridiculously brave is mandatory. You need to believe that no one is really that much better or that much smarter than you are, if at all. That's key: an almost crazy amount of self-confidence. Without it, you're doomed. If you don't have faith in yourself, fake it—because you're not going to succeed without it.

DIANE NABATOFF

PRODUCER

"This business is about learning as much as you can about everything."

Diane Nabatoff had planned to become a professional singer, and in fact for a number of years, she did summer stock, Off-Broadway, and worked the clubs in and around Manhattan. But then she went to Harvard and fell in with members of the Hasty Pudding Club, and her career took a more theatrical turn.

After getting her master's in Business Administration, Nabatoff made her slow, steady way up the Hollywood ladder, learning the art of producing one small step at a time. To this day, she is very much a proponent of starting at the bottom. If you've lived the problems, she argues, you'll be better equipped to deal with the unexpected.

Nabatoff's feature credits include *Narc*, *Very Bad Things*, *Operation Dumbo Drop*, *The Proposition*, and the cult-classic *Near Dark*. Her cable and television credits include *Fear*, *Body Language*, the pilot for *Baseball Wives*, an HBO series, and *Knights of the South Bronx*, an A&E movie starring Ted Danson.

At the time of the interview, she was in postproduction on *Take the Lead*, a feature for New Line Cinema, starring Antonio Banderas.

She was interviewed in Los Angeles on July 5, 2005.

I was born in Manhattan and all I ever wanted to do was to become a singer. My father was a cardiovascular surgeon who specialized in varicose veins, and in fact invented the Nabatoff Vein Stripper, which is the method of choice for removing varicose veins. My mother was a kindergarten teacher, and she was among the very first educators to push reading in kindergarten. My parents were fairly conservative people, and relatively comfortable. I was the first of three children, the only daughter, and my father desperately wanted me to become a doctor.

I was painfully shy as a child, so my parents were amused when I told them I wanted to sing for a living. When I was fifteen, I was watching *The Dick Cavett Show* with my mother, and a girl my age got up and sang "Scarborough Fair." I asked my mother if I could take voice lessons. She thought this was laughable—"You can't even *talk* in front of people"—but my father said it was okay.

I signed up with the voice teacher who had taught Florence Henderson, and I was so nervous that I literally couldn't speak. But on the third class, my voice finally came booming out and he was shocked. "Look how fast you've learned!" he said.

I attended the Spence School, a private girls' school in Manhattan. I was still shy, but I managed to audition for a few shows, and I began to perform. I also did summer stock every summer.

I went to college at Harvard, as an English major—they didn't have a drama program for credit at the time—and early freshman year I auditioned for a part in *Fiorello*, the musical about the famous New York City mayor. I had just plunged into "Soon It's Going to Rain" when it started pouring. Needless to say, I got the part. We performed at the Agassiz Theater, in Cambridge, and I was immediately convinced that was what I wanted to do with my life: musical comedy—acting, singing, dancing, and making people laugh.

When I arrived at Harvard, the only singing group that existed was The Harvard Krokodillos, an all-male, a cappella singing group, and I decided we needed a female group. Although I was told this was impossible, I created The Radcliffe Pitches. We performed on campus, around town, and at other schools. I remember seeing more Harvard guys on a Saturday night, while

246 | HOW I BROKE INTO HOLLYWOOD

performing at Wellesley, than I ever saw at Harvard on the average weekend. Today the group is well-known and performs all over the world.

I also went to work for the Hasty Pudding Theatricals, which had been a staple at Harvard for over a hundred years, and is in fact the oldest theatrical organization in the country. The show was exclusively male, but women could work behind the scenes, and that's what I did. The first year, I was the props mistress (the only job available), and the second year I was made the tour manager, a first for a woman. My job was to organize the show's tours to New York, Washington, and Bermuda.

In my third year, I became the first female publicity manager, and in my final year I became the first female producer in the club's history. Because I had broken this final barrier, there was a tremendous amount of press, including articles in the *New York Times*, the *Wall Street Journal*, and *People* magazine.

During my four years at Harvard, I continued to perform in musicals and to sing with The Pitches, and I did summer stock every summer. I also kept threatening to quit school to pursue singing and acting full time, but each year my father would put my suitcases into the trunk of his car and drive me back to school. I think he still hoped I would become a doctor.

Toward the end of my senior year at Harvard, I was accepted by The Neighborhood Playhouse, the theater conservatory. I was thrilled, but my parents were horrified. They had hoped I would put my Harvard education to better use. In an act of desperation, my mother took all of the newspaper clippings she had collected about my days at Hasty Pudding and sent them to Joe Papp, the theater impresario who ran the New York Shakespeare Festival. A short time later, I got a letter from Papp asking me to come work for him.

I was really torn. The Neighborhood Playhouse was strictly about acting, whereas Joe Papp could teach me about producing. I loved singing and dancing, but I also loved producing, and I knew that this was a once-in-a-lifetime opportunity: Joe Papp was one of the true visionaries in American theater. It was clear I had to take this opportunity.

At the New York Shakespeare Festival, I learned about play development, audience development, and fund-raising, and in my limited spare time, I organized my own shows at nightclubs in and around Manhattan. I worked with an accompanist, on piano, doing blues, jazz, and musical comedy. I was a long way from my days of shyness.

I stayed with Joe Papp for a year, and from time to time we'd do these little showcases with stars to see if an act was worth taking to Broadway. One night, Meryl Streep came to sing for a small group of us. She was doing a workshop of *Alice in Wonderland*, and she was absolutely magnificent. It was one of the most magical nights of my life. When it was over, I couldn't believe that the rest of the world wasn't going to see what I had just seen. It was criminal. That was the night I decided I wanted to get into the film business. Film had the potential to reach a much broader audience, and it was there forever.

What's more, theater seemed so tenuous. The Shakespeare Festival would always be dependent on fund-raising and no one knew from one year to the next whether it was going to survive. I loved the theater but I decided I didn't want to be in a medium that was dependent on public funding. I figured I would return to the theater when I could find a way to finance a show.

So I left the New York Shakespeare Festival and got a job on the *No Nukes* film. There were a series of concerts at Madison Square Garden, featuring everyone from Jackson Brown and Bruce Springsteen to James Taylor and Carly Simon, and we went out and filmed them, then mixed the footage with documentary footage. It was a nonprofit venture, and we did not control which songs the artists allowed us to use in the film. I realized that if you want to control the creative side you have to control the financial side.

At that point, I had had enough experience with organizations that were totally dependent on other people for funding and survival, so I decided to learn the financial side of the business. I applied to the William Morris mail room and to Harvard Business School. There were no openings in the mail room so I went back to Harvard.

I remember my first day in business school. The professor said, "Look to your left, then look to your right. One of those people isn't going to make it."

I found a good study group to help me with the basics, and I helped them with the theatrical end of the business, things like public speaking and organizational behavior, where you needed people skills.

My father was of course ecstatic. He thought I had finally come to my senses and was going to become a businesswoman. What I didn't tell him was that my goal was to start my own company and stay in entertainment. In fact, while in school I was actually critiquing scripts for an independent producer who was adapting Off-Broadway shows for cable television. In Hollywood, this is called *doing coverage*. I didn't know the technical name for it then, but I enjoyed the work.

At the end of my first year, I got a summer internship at HBO. Although I was in the programming department, I was doing mostly financial analyses. At the time, HBO was primarily in the business of acquiring films, not of making them.

After my second year, when I was done with business school, I went back to HBO and found myself doing mostly research. Although I loved the people, I didn't see this as my future, and I asked them to send me to Los Angeles, where I'd be closer to the film industry. Unfortunately, they weren't set up for it at the time.

Then I got a job offer from the producer I had read scripts for while I was in business school, and I jumped. He had a deal with MTM Enterprises, the company that had been founded by Mary Tyler Moore and her husband, Grant Tinker, and he asked me if I'd move to Los Angeles to work for him full-time. The fact that I couldn't drive or that I didn't know a soul in L.A., other than my new boss, didn't seem to deter me. I flew out, took a driver's test, passed (miraculously), bought a car, and went to work. I had to drive over to Laurel Canyon every day. I would drive at the speed limit, trying not to listen to the honking and cursing of the frustrated drivers behind me, and I would arrive at work exhausted and stressed out by the experience. After doing the harrowing trip eight or nine times, though, I finally began to get the hang of it.

Three months later, my boss lost his deal with MTM and let me go. "What do you mean I'm laid off?" I said. I had just left a job at HBO and moved across the country for him! "What does that mean? I went to Harvard Business School. We don't get laid off!"

But I *did* get laid off. So I called everyone I knew, mostly back east, and started setting up interviews. Before long, I discovered that people tended to fixate on my Harvard MBA, but in a negative way—there were not a lot of MBAs in the movie business at the time. So I would bring a piece of masking tape to the interview, and, if they became overly focused on my business credentials, I would cover that part of my resume with my piece of tape. Then I would point to all the rest of it, the creative side of my history—the theater, the dancing, the singing.

Eventually, someone made a call on my behalf to Alan Landsburg, the producer, and I went to see him. He had a job for a segment producer on a show called *The World's Funniest Commercial Goofs*. This was not exactly the career I'd envisioned for myself, but I took the job. I found myself sitting in a room with three other segment producers, watching bad commercials, thinking, *What happened to my life?* though in fact we actually had a lot of fun.

When that ended, I was hired to do development for the company on TV movies and miniseries, a *real* job. I would look for new material, meet with writers, take pitches, and sell to the networks. I loved it and I stayed for three years.

Then I got a phone call from someone who wanted to introduce me to Ed Feldman, a feature producer. He had just produced *Witness*, the Harrison Ford movie, and the person who'd been working with him had left. I went to meet with him and he hired me, and suddenly I was at Paramount, working on features. The first movie I worked on was *The Golden Child*, with Eddie Murphy, where I was mostly an observer. Then I worked on *Near Dark*, director Kathryn Bigelow's cult classic. I went out to Arizona, without Ed, and was on set every day, learning how to produce a film. It was quite the experience. We were living in a disgusting dirty motel, so I slept with my clothes on and took showers in flip-flops. To compound matters, one of my leads decided to drive all the way from L.A. in character, as a vampire, and he stayed in character on and off the set. Imagine what anyone who saw him thought as he stopped for meals and gas. I felt like I was in an episode of *The Twilight Zone*.

Ed Feldman taught me how to produce a film. He was a veteran producer who knew the ins and outs of producing from beginning to end. He also knew that no matter how tough it got, it still had to be fun. I will always be grateful to him for the experience. In fact, I'd probably still be working for him, but he and his partner tried to go public and were forced to downsize, and I once again found myself out on the market.

My next job was at Vestron, where I was technically an executive but was very hands-on with the production. I worked on movies like *Hider in the House* and *Fear*, which were the kinds of movies that worked for the Vestron audience. They made their movies on lower budgets, so they were guaranteed a profit on video alone. They were trying to upgrade the quality of their films for theatrical release, but their success came mostly in video, and that was their first priority.

Hider in the House was actually the very first script I was handed when I got there, on my very first week. It was horrible. They had bought the title, and I don't think anyone had actually read the script. Still, they were ready to start shooting. I held everything up by making the writer rewrite it, which didn't make anyone happy, and I was given a strict deadline to get the script finished and in front of the cameras. From that experience, I learned a valuable lesson: If there are problems in the script, they don't go away when you start shooting; they just get bigger.

After three years at Vestron, the company went under—not unusual in this business—and again I had to find a new job. Luckily, I ended up going to work for Henry Winkler, running his feature division. We sold a significant numbers of films to the studios, as producers, but then Henry decided to focus on directing, so eventually I left and went to work at Interscope. That turned out to be my dream job. I loved every minute of it. I couldn't wait to get to work in the morning, and it was a pleasure to stay up till all hours reading scripts. I loved the people I worked with, and I learned something new every day from my boss, Robert Cort. We were hands-on producers. We would find material, develop it, sell it to a studio, then go out and make the movie.

Two years into that job, the company was bought by Polygram. Suddenly we were both producers and studio executives: We had the money to make our own movies. While there, I produced several films, including *Holy Matrimony*, *Operation Dumbo Drop*, *The Proposition*, and *Very Bad Things*. Seven years into it, however, Polygram was bought by Universal, and the corporate changes led me to make a change of my own. I had been working around-the-clock for so many years that I didn't have a personal life. I decided to shake things up, so I moved back to New York in 2000 and started my own company.

The company, Tiara Blu Films, was based in Manhattan. After being surrounded by coworkers and people at the studios, however, I found it much harder and much lonelier to work in New York, alone, so I called Ray Liotta, an old friend from *Dumbo Drop*, and asked if he wanted to be my partner. We made the rounds of the agencies, looking for films for him, and after sifting through mountains of material we came across *Narc*, a gritty, intelligent thriller. We got it financed through a company that no longer exists, and three days into the shoot I got a call saying that the money had fallen out and that we had to stop shooting temporarily. I had produced enough movies to know that if we shut down the production for even one day, it was over. So I told the financier to just make payroll, and that the rest of us would defer our salaries. Every week, I had to convince the crew to hang in while we waited for their checks to arrive. I really never knew from day to day if we were going to be shooting or shutting down.

When we finally finished shooting and I got into the editing room, I was handed a huge list of names of people I had never heard of but who were going to get producer credits on our movie. As it turned out, the financier had sold credits to raise money to finish the film.

Narc got into Sundance and was a big hit, but most of us hadn't been paid yet. At that point, things got even more complicated. Tom Cruise saw the film, called Paramount, and told them to buy it. He absolutely loved the movie. Paramount bought it, and our little movie was eventually released with *seventeen* producer credits and *two* distributor credits.

Unfortunately, Paramount decided to release the movie at Christmas, even though we argued against it. *Narc* got killed. That film was many things, but it was not a Christmas movie. It became apparent to me that you can have the greatest film but if it isn't released properly it will never find its audience.

Now it was time to get back to New York and start developing new material. I saw a small clip on CBS about Pierre Dulaine, an internationally acclaimed dancer who decided to go into the public schools of New York and teach ballroom dancing to inner-city kids. Despite endless obstacles—from teachers, parents, and even some of the kids—he managed to create a program called Dancing Classrooms, now part of the public school curriculum in New York. The kids learn self-esteem, respect, and partnership through dance. This was exactly the kind of story I wanted to tell—commercial but meaningful—and I tracked down Pierre, got his rights, and sold the story to MGM. Months later, the studio and I still couldn't agree on a writer, so I begged them to give it back to me. The following week, I sold it to New Line Cinema, and a mere four years later we were in Toronto, shooting, with Antonio Banderas in the starring role. The film is called *Take the Lead*, and we expect to release it this year.

At the moment, I have several features in various stages of development, and I am in postproduction on a cable movie for A&E, *Knights of the South Bronx*, inspired by a true story. It is about a successful corporate executive who came home one day and told his wife he didn't feel fulfilled. "I want to be a teacher," he said. He went off and became a substitute teacher in the South Bronx, and on his own time began teaching kids how to play chess. He ended up taking a ragtag team of black and Hispanic kids all the way to the national championships, which they won, and which led to a visit to the White House.

I am at a place in my career now where I have the luxury of going after material I love. I option it, develop it, package it, sell it, and make it happen. And that's key for me: to love the project. As a producer, you are the one who keeps things running, who keeps pushing the boulder up the hill, and it's never easy. If you don't honestly love the material, you're not going to find the strength to get to the top of the hill.

For me, this business is about learning as much as you can about everything. If you're looking to break into Hollywood, you shouldn't be afraid to start at the bottom—and in fact I would urge you to start at the bottom. Everything you learn augments your problem-solving skills later. Every person you meet becomes part of your world of relationships. In today's world of filmmaking, you have to be cognizant of both the creative and the financials aspects. Your knowledge of physical production helps you when you are shaping a story creatively, and your creative background helps when you run into difficulties in physical production. Of course, the best way to learn is from great mentors, and I had extraordinary mentors. They were hardworking, passionate, generous, inclusive, and they knew how to have fun during the process. What's more, they were real producers. Not many people know what a real producer does. My dad used to call me and ask, "What exactly is it you do again?" Well, a real producer is responsible for what you see on the screen, from beginning to end. He or she takes care of everything and every-one. I often describe myself as a shock absorber. You have to solve everyone's problems on the set (and sometimes off the set!), and anytime anything goes wrong it's up to you to fix it. And things go wrong every day, despite all the careful planning.

Given how many elements have to fit together, it is truly a small miracle when you actually produce a good movie. But when you do, it's an extraor-dinary experience. I have found that the best way to try to get close to that experience is to work with people you like, trust, and respect. This is a busi-ness of relationships. If you can build a family of people you want to work with, and can team up with them on each film, it will minimize the ups and downs of this roller-coaster business.

KEVIN O'CONNELL

SOUND MIXER

"Succeeding in Hollywood often comes down to your ability to work with people, and I think honesty is a good start."

Kevin O'Connell has been nominated for the Academy Award an astounding seventeen times, and he is still waiting to take an Oscar home with him. From a professional standpoint, however, his record-breaking nonwinning hasn't hurt him. He is booked two and a half years in advance, and he and his partner are currently committed to movies that don't even have a script yet.

Born in Long Island but raised in the San Fernando Valley, O'Connell was introduced to the business early, by his parents, and parlayed that entrée into quite the career. He has worked on close to 150 movies, including *Spider-Man* and *Spider-Man 2*, *The Passion of the Christ*, *Armageddon*, *Pearl Harbor*, *The Mask of Zorro*, *The Rock*, *A Few Good Men*, *Top Gun*, and *Terms of Endearment*. With the exception of *The Passion of the Christ*, all those films were nominated for Best Sound.

At the time of the interview, which took place on September 19, 2005, on the Sony lot, O'Connell was putting the finishing touches on *Memoirs of a Geisha*.

I was born in Beth Page, the town of Oyster Bay, Long Island, the fourth of five kids, but the family moved to California in 1961, when I was four, and we settled in the San Fernando Valley. My father went to work for 20th Century Fox as an accountant, and he was connected to all the big televisions shows of the day—*Batman, Voyage to the Bottom of the Sea, Lost in Space, Daniel Boone.*

While working there, he heard there was an opening for a secretary, in the studio's sound department, and he told my mother, Skippy, about it. She applied for the job and got it, and over the years Skippy became something of a legend herself. She was put in charge of hiring for the sound department at Fox, a position she held for more than twenty years, and everyone in the sound business knew her.

I found myself spending a lot of time on the lot, and I got to visit the sets of some of my favorite shows, like *Land of the Giants* and *Voyage to the Bottom a the Sea.*

At school, I was the poster child for Attention Deficit Disorder, though they didn't have a fancy name for it back then. I didn't pay attention, I never did homework, and I was always getting into trouble, so I became the proverbial black sheep of the family.

Movies and television, on the other hand, got my undivided attention at a very early age, and I remember becoming aware of the power of sound for the first time while watching *Planet of the Apes.* The sounds the apes made, and the sound of the snorting horses, seemed incredibly realistic to me, and they actually scared me half to death.

My second "sound experience" was even more memorable. My mother asked me to come to the studio for a family screening of a movie that sounded really dull. The characters had goofy names like Luke Skywalker and C-3PO and Darth Vader, and I couldn't imagine I'd enjoy it. But when the lights dimmed and that first battleship flew over the theater, I was hooked. From that day on, I really fell in love with movies, and I always found myself paying very close attention to the use of sound.

When I graduated from high school, I decided I wanted to be a fireman for the City of Los Angeles. One of the ways of doing that is to become a firefighter for the county, in the brush fire division, so I spent a year working with a camp crew, battling fires. We would go to the site of the fire and cut trails and dig ditches and try to get things under control, and it was brutal, backbreaking work, but very rewarding.

On one occasion, I was fighting a fire in Tujunga Canyon for three days, and when I got home my face was black, my skin was charred, my arms and legs had been scarred by the yucca plants, and I'd lost seventeen pounds. My mother couldn't believe it. "Why are you doing this to yourself?" she said. "Why don't you come down to the studio and look around and see if there's something you might be interested in?"

She suggested I try to get a job as a projectionist, which at the time was paying about $450 a week. I had been making only $700 a *month* as a firefighter, so it sounded pretty good. I was offered the job, on a trial basis, and I left firefighting and went to work at the studio, and after thirty days I had to take a test to determine whether I'd be admitted to the union. Unfortunately, I failed the test—it was fairly complicated, and I hadn't studied for it—so my mother suggested I try my luck in sound.

In those days, it was really hard to get into the union, but my mother pulled some strings and managed to get me hired at the sound department at the Samuel Goldwyn Studios, working for a man named Don Rogers. Nobody wanted to hire their own kids, because they didn't want to be accused of nepotism, so people hired each other's kids—Rogers hired me and my mother hired his son, Gary—and everyone was okay with that.

The first movie I worked on, back in January of 1978, was *The Magic of Lassie.* I was twenty years old, and I thought it was the most boring job on the planet. I had gone from riding around in a fire truck and rescuing people and animals from fast-moving fires, to sitting in a dimly lit room, watching the mixers stare at the same sections of the movie over and over again. I didn't know how they could bear it. To make matters worse, they were always shouting incomprehensible directions at us: "Guys—are we ready yet?!" "What's taking so long?!" "Faster faster faster!!!" "Let's go!" It was very stressful.

I was the machine room operator. My job was to load the 35-millimeter pieces of sound onto the reproducers, which in turn are fed to the stage, where the mixers actually mix the sound. I wasn't exactly wild about the job, and I wanted to get a better job, so I kept my eyes open and started asking a lot of questions: "What does that guy do? What's this guy's job? Who's he?" Eventually, they made me a recordist, which meant I was responsible for recording the sound and working closely with the mixers. Three of the guys

I worked with, Bill Varney, Steve Maslow, and Gregg Landaker, were great guys and great mixers, and they went on to win Academy Awards for *Raiders of the Lost Ark* and *The Empire Strikes Back*.

A sound mixer, by the way, has control over every single sound in the movie. He sits in front of a console that's about the size of a Greyhound bus, and, working with hundreds of tracks, blends the dialogue, the music, and the sound effects into a seamless, sonic landscape. The dialogue is broken down so that every character is on a separate fader, and all the sound effects are separated by groups. In an action movie, for example, the mixer controls all aspects of the track—car crashes, bullets flying, tires screeching, doors slamming, guns, explosions. He controls the music, too, of course, and each instrument is separated out for individual control. That way, he can deliver *exactly* the sound the director and the producers are looking for, and he can make all of them fit seamlessly into the picture.

After *Raiders*, when I was twenty-four, Don Rogers gave me the opportunity to become a sound mixer, and—with Bill Varney's blessing—I went to work on *Dead Men Don't Wear Plaid*. I was only working with about eleven or twelve tracks, which isn't a lot, but I had no idea what I was doing, and just getting through the day was a nightmare. I was so nervous that I stuffed paper towels into my armpits to keep the perspiration from showing. At the time, I didn't even understand that every sound has to be leveled out individually to play correctly in the scene, and my first stab at it was a complete train wreck: Everything was playing so loudly that I thought the mixing theater was about to explode.

In those days, the consoles weren't computerized. If I was doing a chase sequence, for example, I might spend a week making sure all the sounds were at the exact right level—the car engines, the skids, the gunshots, the police sirens, the whizzing bullets, the crashes, etc. Once I got everything just right, the producer would come in for a playback. After he heard it, he might say, "I like it, but let's make the siren a little bit louder." When that happened, you had to go back to the beginning and redo the whole thing. Nowadays, with everything automated, that would only take a couple of minutes, but back then it could take days.

Being a sound mixer is a real pressure-cooker job. You are always trying to make everyone happy—the director, the composer, the producer, the studio—and the number of high-profile personalities in the room can make it a real challenge.

My second film was *Poltergeist*, and it was pretty intimidating—I had Steven Spielberg leaning over my shoulder, day after day, telling me what to do. I was so nervous that sometimes I couldn't hear what he said, though I knew he was giving me directions because he was looking at me and his mouth was moving. I was so paranoid that every time I saw the picture editor whispering to his assistant I was sure I was about to get fired. Somehow, however, I survived, and the following year I worked on *Terms of Endearment*, which was nominated for an Oscar for Best Achievement in Sound. We didn't win, but it was pretty exciting getting that call at five o'clock in the morning, telling me that we were in the running.

In 1989, I won an Emmy for *Lonesome Dove*, and that was very exciting, and by that point my career was shifting into high gear. I think I've worked on about 150 movies, so I'm not going to name them all, but one of the big ones back then was *Top Gun*. I remember working with Tony Scott, the director, and Jerry Bruckheimer and Don Simpson, the producers. Tony would say, "Boys, I have to hear the sound of the jets more—they need to feel huge and powerful. *Kill!*" And then Simpson would say, "Guys, I'm not hearing the music. You've got to bring the music up a little." Then Bruckheimer would realize that we were drowning out the dialogue, so we had to crank that up, too. That goes a ways toward explaining why movies kept getting louder and louder.

People think sound mixing is a technical job, and, certainly, there are technical aspects to what we do. But it's more than mechanics. You have to understand what the filmmakers are trying to communicate, so you need to pay attention to absolutely everything that is happening in the room—and on the screen. If there are five conversations going on around me simultaneously, I'm listening to them all, actively looking for solutions—even before I'm asked for an opinion. Part of my job is to help find the right answers, and that means being as well informed as possible.

By 1990, I was mixing dialogue and sound effects with Rick Kline, my partner at the time, who was mixing music. We were one of the first mixing teams hired at Skywalker Sound, in Santa Monica, where we did *A Few Good Men* and *In the Line of Fire*, among many other movies. But by 1995, I was tired of doing both dialogue and sound effects, and Rick and I parted ways, amicably.

I ended up setting up shop at the Cary Grant Theater, on the Sony lot, with a new partner, Greg Russell, a terrific sound effects mixer. I had worked with him back in the 1980s, on such films as *Days of Thunder* and *Black Rain*, and we were a good fit. We are together to this day and, together, as a team, we've been nominated for nine Academy Awards.

In 1995, I got hired to work on *The Mirror Has Two Faces*, for Barbra Streisand. I had done some major movies by this time, but I was pretty nervous about meeting Ms. Streisand. Everyone had told me that she could be every difficult, and that I had to be very much on guard. She turned out to be one of the greatest directors I've ever worked with. She was polite, and professional, and—in a field where you don't get many pats on the back— she came closer than anyone I've ever worked with to letting me know she appreciated my commitment to her film. Also, from our many conversations, I got the impression that she really liked the fact that I didn't bullshit her. There is a lot of bullshit in this town, especially when you're dealing with powerful people, some of whom can be very intimidating, but I was never less than honest with her, and she made it clear that she appreciated it.

One day, she asked me what I was doing that weekend, and I told her I had no plans, so she invited me to dinner, and she asked me to bring my girlfriend along. We drove out to her place in Malibu, on a Sunday, at around 5:00 p.m. and I was kind of nervous about who was going to be there. But Barbra came to the door, alone, and she ordered in from a local restaurant, Tra di Noi, and it turned out to be just the three of us: me, Barbra, and Heather, who is now my wife. We just talked about movies and about life and ate and had some good wine, and then at around 9:00 she asked us if we wanted to go over to her friend Sandy Gallin's house and watch a movie.

Barbra didn't drive, and I had my Porsche Speedster outside, a two-seater, and she climbed in, put one arm around me and the other arm around Heather, and we raced over to Sandy Gallin's house to watch the Tom Hanks movie, *That Thing You Do*. If anyone had told me that one day I'd be cruising along Pacific Coast Highway in a Porsche, with Barbra Streisand next to me, I would have thought they were insane.

Oddly enough, when I was still a kid, my father had come home one day with an autographed Barbara Streisand album. My father let me know that I needed to take very good care of that album, since Barbra was a big star and the album was extremely valuable. I never told her that story, but I wish I had. Maybe she'll read it here.

I think the hardest I've ever worked was when I did *Godzilla* and *Armageddon*, back to back. We were working on *Godzilla* from 8:30 in the morning till 12:30 a.m., sixteen hours a day, straight, for eight weeks. We finished it on a Sunday night, or, more accurately, on Monday morning, at 1:00, and seven hours later we were working on *Armageddon*. For three weeks, we worked sixteen-hour days, but in the last two weeks, with the release date approaching, we worked on it for twenty-four hours a day. Greg and I slept in trailers that the company had brought in for us, and we would work in three- to four-hour shifts, independently, and then do a shift together before going off to our trailers to try to sleep for a few hours. Those last two weeks were like nothing I've ever experienced, and I couldn't do it again. I'm married now, with a three-year-old and another child on the way, and I want to spend time with my family. I have already put twenty-seven years of my life into this, and I love it, but I'm beginning to think about scaling back a little. It's not going to be easy, though. At the moment, I am booked for the next two-and-a-half years. Some of the movies I'm slated to work on are still in the development stage; some don't even have scripts yet.

I'm a currently finishing the sound on *Memoirs of a Geisha*, which I think is one of the most spectacular films I've ever worked on. Maybe it's partly me: After twenty-seven years of getting pounded by the speakers, I'm a little worn down by those big action movies, and I've learned to appreciate the gentler, character-driven films.

I have been nominated for the Academy Award seventeen times, and I have to say it would be really nice to win. I know most people in the sound community would like to see me win, too, so it's nice to have a cheering section out there. Still, it won't be the end of the world if I don't win. The truth is, every time I get nominated, it's the most incredible feeling in the world. Somebody calls before the alarm clock goes off and breaks the good news, and it's always exhilarating. If I don't get a lot of pats on the back during the course of the year, getting that morning phone call, with news of the nomination, is about as wonderful a pat on the back as one could possibly hope for.

It's hard for me to give advice. I was lucky because I had a mother in the business, and she pulled strings for me, but nowadays I'm not even sure that would work. The unions are very tough, and the people who get hired over and over again are the ones with the credits—guys like me, I guess.

But there are two things I would say. One, stay in school. To this day, I miss the fact that I didn't further my education before I began my career. I think it's important to get a well-rounded education, a real foundation, and I can't stress that enough.

The other thing I would say is to be honest. People think my work is technical, but in fact 90 percent of it is dealing with people. And I have always tried to be honest with people. I think my experience with Barbra Streisand really put the importance of honesty into perspective for me. Succeeding in Hollywood often comes down to your ability to work with people, and I think honesty is a good start. I also think it's important to treat everyone with equal respect. When I was starting out, I met a lot of assholes in the business, guys who were rude and enjoyed throwing their weight around, and I saw how it affected me, and how it affected everyone around me. I remember telling myself that if I was ever in a position of authority, I wouldn't become one of those guys, and I'd like to think I've succeeded.

My mother helped me get my first job, and I will always be grateful to her for that, but in Hollywood it goes beyond breaking in—you have to *stay* in. I think honesty and respect for others are a good start. Then there's hard work, of course, and determination. The people who make it in this town are the ones who never give up.

JEANNINE OPPEWALL

PRODUCTION DESIGNER

"A lot of people go to film school and only focus on the technical side of things, but I can't recommend that. That approach doesn't produce the type of person I want to hire."

Jeannine Oppewall always had a visual sense, but she never imagined she would put it to use creating sets for movies. She grew up in small-town Massachusetts, pursued a liberal arts education on the East Coast, and ended up in Santa Monica, California, working for Charles Eames, the world-class architect and designer. That experience led to a job with Paul Sylbert, the production designer, and that in turn launched her film career.

Oppewall's credits include *The Big Easy*, *Ironweed*, *Music Box*, *White Palace*, *Wonder Boys*, and *Catch Me If You Can*, as well as *Seabiscuit*, *Pleasantville*, and *L.A. Confidential*, all of which were nominated for Academy Awards.

She spoke to us on November 8, 2005, from New York, where she was working on Robert De Niro's film, *The Good Shepherd*.

I was born and raised in small-town Massachusetts, in what I guess you'd call a working middle-class family. We were New England Protestant types.

We understood that there was no salvation except what you created for your-self.

The town I grew up in had two kinds of people, really: the mill owners, and the people who worked for them, and we were the people who worked for them. So it was very clear to me as a kid that those people—the Wheelocks and the Rices and so forth—would never be interested in me. But it's funny because some years ago I got a letter from one of those guys: "Gee, of all the people I know, you're the only one that's become famous!" In reality, of course, I'm still "the people who work for them," since I'm a production designer, after all, not a producer or a studio head. *Plus ca change*, I guess.

I went to grade school and high school in the same small town, but I wasn't really drawn to the visual arts in those days. On the other hand, my mother was always incredibly aware of the physical environment, so she taught me to pay attention to the world around me, and to what things looked like, and what they meant.

Looking back at my family and its genetic history, I have to say that we all ended up in various aspects of design. My brother trained at the Rhode Island School of Design and for a while ran a program for the State of Massachusetts, designing equipment for handicapped people; my other brother went to work for Boeing, designing machinery used in the manufacture of airplanes; my father ran the tool-and-die department of a big New England textile company; and my mother designed and made one-of-a-kind doll costumes. So it seems that design is something that comes naturally to all of us, although personally I was not that interested in it. My father would come home at night and sit down and read the *Boston Gear* catalogue and I'd say, "How's the plot, Dad?! What's the *story*, Dad?!" And he'd growl at me, "Oh, you're more trouble than all my lack of money!"

Back then, and to this day—I liked stories. You might say I had *an addiction to fiction*. I was always reading under the covers at night, with a flashlight. So when it was time for college, I decided on a liberal arts degree, though I didn't have any specific thoughts about what I was going to do with my life. My interest was really in getting an education. I had no real plans. I think I assumed I'd be a journalist, because at that point in my life, I was very much attracted to books and to writing and to storytelling. I took a lot of art history courses, though—history of design, history of sculpture, history of architecture—but it was only because I found it interesting, not be-cause I thought I was going to make a career of it.

In my senior year, I had a friend in art history class whose father had been an executive at Herman Miller, the furniture company that manufac-tured and distributed some of Charles Eames' furniture, and my friend said, "If you go out to California, you should visit Charles Eames." And I said, "Wait a minute! We're studying him in school. He's got to be dead, right?" Wrong. He was still very much alive.

One day, out of curiosity, I went to visit the Herman Miller Company, in Zeeland, Michigan, to see what they were all about. When I stepped through the front door, I took one look around me and just *knew*. I had grown up in a Sears & Roebuck environment, and this was another world, and I wanted to be part of this world. I remember thinking, *This is for me!* I wanted to be living with the furniture they had on display. I wanted chairs like their chairs. I wanted to live among all those beautiful objects. I'm not sure I know how to describe it exactly. It was all about a visceral response to an environment, and in one fell swoop I understood that the environment in which you find yourself has a tremendous effect on who you are. Much later, I would discover that that's an intrinsic part of production design: Environ-ment and color tell you who the person is and, to some extent, how he got to be that way.

When I graduated, I went to visit Paul Schrader in Los Angeles. I had met him at school in Michigan—he'd gone to Columbia, I'd been to Bryn Mawr—and he was out there trying to write screenplays. And shortly after I arrived I went to see Charles Eames. He had a constant stream of guests, coming in and out of his office, and people were invited to visit and watch films and look around and chat. It was a little like a salon. I was quite im-pressed, and when I left I remember turning to the secretary and saying, half-joking: "You don't have any jobs here, do you?" And she looked at me, terribly seriously, and said, "As a matter of fact, yes, we do. We are desper-ately looking for someone to curate the slide library, the book library, the black-and-white picture library, and to help with postproduction on some of the films. Do you think you could so some of that?" And I said, "Yes, of course!"

A few days later I went back to talk to Charles, in a more serious, nonguest capacity, and he said, "You don't have a specific design background, so I'm sure a lot of people think you're probably not right for us. But that's not what matters: I can teach you how to draw. What I *cannot* teach you is how to think or how to see. If you can prove that you know how to think and how to see, you can stay."

I was living with Schrader at the time. He was trying to write screenplays, finding his screenwriting sea legs, as it were, (this was before *The Yakuza* and *Taxi Driver* put him on the map), and I would go off every day to work with one of the world's most famous designers.

I stayed with Charles Eames for eight years, and I learned everything I know about design at the feet of the master. Charles also made many movies—industrials, personal films, educational films—and I learned a great deal from those, too. Also, being in Los Angeles, I was exposed to the film industry, and I was naturally curious about it.

In 1982, Eames turned seventy-five and he began winding down. I was interested in ramping up, however, so I left his office and went to work with a friend at KPFK Radio, in Los Angeles, doing broadcasts for their cultural affairs department. I wasn't sure that that's what I wanted to do with my life, but I needed a change, and I wanted to be exposed to new things. I learned a lot about ear-to-hand coordination because I had to train myself to cut the programs while listening to them. And I learned a lot about storytelling, notably that you have to sacrifice good ideas if they don't keep the story moving forward.

While I was at KPFK, a friend in the film business introduced me to Paul Sylbert (the production designer, *Heaven Can Wait*, *Hardcore*, and *Kramer vs. Kramer*, etc.), thinking that we were somehow a good match. And I guess he saw something in me which I didn't see in myself—the same thing Charles Eames must have seen—because he was incredibly nice to me. "You know, you could be very successful in this business," he said. I laughed—I really didn't know what he was talking about—but he meant it. "No, no. I'm being serious," he added. "You have the personality for it. You could be very successful in production design."

I ended up going to work for him, and his art director told me that I needed to talk to the union about getting in. He kept calling them on my behalf, and eventually I went to see them. It was 9:00 on a weekday morning, and there was a guy sitting there in a brown-and-white, three-piece, pin-striped suit, and my immediate thought was, *This is the Mafia!* And the guy began talking, going on and on about the fact that this wasn't his only job, that he was connected to the "International," whatever that meant, and I finally said, "You know, I'm sorry—but I'm going to be late for work. I just want to get into the union." And he said, "Okay. But don't forget that I'm doing you a big favor by letting you in." Then he came out from behind his desk, grabbed my hand, and *licked* it. And I thought to myself, *I can do one of two things. I can either get angry and kick him, or I can laugh.* So I laughed and ran away. Of course, what I've figured out by now is that laughter is usually the healthiest and best approach to many problems in life. You can say something quite cutting to someone while you are laughing, and somehow it doesn't really seem to hurt.

I worked on several movies with Paul Sylbert, and then I got a call from a friend who made his living as both a designer and a theater director. Someone had asked him to design a little independent movie that was going to be shooting in Texas, and he was from Texas, so they thought he would do it for them—cheap. But he was mounting a play at the time and wasn't available, and he told them about me. "She'll be cheap," he said. "And I think she'll like Texas."

The producers called Paul Sylbert to ask about me, and Paul must have been quite complimentary: They gave me the job. They told me they would be sending me a plane ticket, and suddenly I was on my way. The movie was called *Tender Mercies*, and that was my first solo job as production designer, though the credit I took is actually for art direction. It was a little intimidating at first, of course, but I had learned much of what I needed from Paul Sylbert: how to manage the staff, how to talk to construction people, how to design sets, etc., and it went quite smoothly. I remember driving to the set early one morning, while it was still dark out, and feeling pretty good about things, and I remember thinking, *Well, okay—I've gotten this far. I guess I should trust in the future and see what happens.*

The movie ended up being nominated for an Academy Award, which was pretty shocking. It was a tiny film—the budget was maybe $4 million. Who knew?

Before it was even released, however, I went to work on *Love Letters*, for director Amy Jones (who went on to write *Mystic Pizza* and *Indecent Proposal*, among other films), and I guess that at that point I was officially in the business.

I have a good time at what I do, though I can't say I like the politics. The business has gotten much harder. I can't tell you whether that's because the movies I've worked on have gotten bigger and harder, or whether it's because the business has gotten meaner. But it is definitely harder.

My advice to people who want to get into the business is probably a little different from what you've heard. I personally think an informed, well-rounded education is the best foundation. It gives you a lot to draw on. A lot of people go to film school and only focus on the technical side of things, but I can't recommend that. That approach doesn't produce the type of person I want to hire. I want to be around people who have wide skills and wide interests because I think they bring a lot more to the project. I like to be able to have a conversation with them about something other than what molding we should be using on a particular set, because deep down I'm deeply *un*interested in molding. I'm interested in the characters in the film, I'm interested in the story, and I'm interested in the environment we're creating. I'm really not excited by moldings.

My feeling is, *Get the foundation first, worry about Hollywood later.* A person should have more than one dimension.

When I think back on it, maybe that's why Charles Eames and Paul Sylbert reached out to me—because they saw a little added dimension there. And that's what I look for: Someone who projects competence and interest. Or someone who's articulate. Or even someone I just think I'd have fun spending time with. Someone who knows how to laugh. People who are talented are thick on the ground in Hollywood. In my book, it isn't enough to be merely talented. You need to be a decent person as well.

JAMES ORR & JIM CRUICKSHANK

WRITERS/PRODUCERS

"Find someone on the inside who believes in you."

James Orr and Jim Cruickshank, a pair of Canadian imports, met in the mid-1970s, at York University, in Toronto, where both were studying film. After they graduated, Cruickshank took a job at a local film library, and Orr went off to the American Film Institute, in Los Angeles, to pursue the dream.

Years later, the two friends reconnected, and in 1978 they became writing partners. The partnership produced some of the biggest blockbusters of the 1980s, including *Tough Guys*, *Three Men and a Baby*, and *Father of the Bride*, and landed them a lucrative, long-term contract with Disney.

Orr and Cruickshank met us on May 2, 2005, at Fabrocini's, a restaurant at the Top of the Glen, in Los Angeles, and the interview was conducted at a neighboring Starbucks. Orr did most of the talking, but the laconic Cruickshank piped in from time to time to set his partner straight on a detail here and there. In fact, it was Cruickshank who pointed out that on that very day, twenty years earlier, Orr had reached him in Toronto to inform him that they had just made their first six-figure sale. That sale cemented the partnership and launched their joint career.

Jim Cruickshank (*left*) and James Orr

When I first arrived in Hollywood, I learned very quickly that the only thing that matters is the material, and that he who controls the material is king. I was a Director Fellow at the American Film Institute at the time, hoping to become a Hollywood director, but even then I knew that a director was nothing without good material. I had to find the right material, but the idea of writing alone didn't appeal to me. It was such a solitary business, and I wasn't interested in solitary pursuits. I needed to be around people. I needed a smart person around me who would brainstorm with me and make me laugh.

That was when I remembered this guy I went to college with in Toronto, Jim Cruickshank. I didn't know him well, but I remembered him as a funny guy, and a bit of an eccentric, and I knew he was trying to write.

That Christmas, I went back to Toronto to see my girlfriend, and I called York University to track Jim down. The only number they had was for his mother, so I called her and told her I was an old friend. "Well, he's married now, and working at a film lab," she said, and she gave me his number. I called him the next day and asked if he remembered me, which he did, and then I told him I'd been in Los Angeles for the past two years, at the AFI. "I've met a lot of successful people," I said, "and they're no smarter than we are. You want to try to work on something together?"

Jim liked the idea, but he pointed out that he was married and had a full-time job, so he could only work on the occasional long weekend, and after work. And that's what we did, believe it or not. I found a guy in Toronto who had a small business, and he owned an IBM Selectric, the one with the little self-correcting ball, and I asked him if we could use it. He was closed on weekends, so he gave me a key to his office and said we were welcome to the machine.

This was 1978. Shortly thereafter, Jim started coming to Los Angeles from time to time, and that is how we worked for several years. He would stay at the Holiday Inn, in Burbank, and we'd meet early in the day and write on a rented typewriter until we were too tired to go on.

When he went back to Toronto, I went about my business in L.A. I was living in a furnished apartment in Hollywood for three hundred dollars a month, driving a 1969 Dodge Dart, and earning a modest living doing documentaries. I was surviving. But I was twenty-eight years old, and I was beginning to worry.

So I did a very smart thing. I figured out that I needed to see how a film was shot, beginning to end, and I decided I should try to apprentice myself to a director—any director who would have me. I found out that a fellow Canadian, Ted Kotcheff, was about to go to Dallas to shoot a movie, so I called him up cold.

"Would you take me on as an apprentice director if I could get the Canadian government to pay my salary?" I asked him. How could he say no? I was basically telling him that I would work free. So I went to the National Arts Council in Canada, and begged. I said, "I'm Canadian and Ted's Canadian and this is a great opportunity for me to learn something, and all I need is two hundred bucks a week for eight weeks." The Canadians said no.

By this point, Ted was on location in Dallas, and I called him and told him what had happened. "Canada sucks," I said. "They don't support their artists."

Ted was busy with preproduction, and he didn't have time for this, and I could see he was eager to get off the phone. "Wait!" I said. "Don't hang up. You don't understand. I have to do this. I can't not do this. It's really important to me."

"Okay," he said. "Let me see what I can do. Call me tomorrow."

I thought he was just trying to get rid of me, and I was miserable. I thought I was finished. I thought, *Me and showbiz, it's over.* But when I called him the next day, he had good news. "I'll give you fifty dollars a day from my per diem, but I can't fly you here and I can't put you up," he said. "You get yourself to Dallas and figure out where you're going to stay, and you've got a job."

"Done," I said. "And Ted, thanks a lot."

I had no idea how I was going to manage it, but I scrounged the airfare together and arrived on the set and started working. I just ran around and got things for people and did what I was told to do. That first night, I crashed on the sofa in the production office, and that's where I slept for the next two months. And every day, at the end of the day, Ted gave me fifty dollars in cash, out of his pocket. The name of that movie, by the way, was *Split Image.* It starred Michael O'Keefe, Karen Allen, and Brian Dennehy.

When it was over, I went back to Los Angeles. I worked odd jobs, such as writing corporate training movies, but Jim and I never stopped working on our screenplays. I felt that we were learning the craft, and that we were getting better and better, which may have been my own ignorance talking. Not that there's anything wrong with ignorance. Ignorance is the best thing a young person has going for him when he starts out. The less you know about the business, the better. If you knew how things really worked here, you'd run for the hills.

I went back to Toronto in the summer of 1982, and Jim and I decided to get serious about writing. He quit his job at the photo lab and his wife agreed to pay the bills for a while. She was working as a bank teller, and they knew they could manage on her salary. We wrote a romantic comedy, called *Bandit*, but we didn't have an agent, so I contacted Ted Kotcheff's wife, Laifun, and asked if she would read the script. She read it and liked it and gave it to Ted, who called a few weeks later. "I like it," he said. "I'm going to help you rewrite it."

At the time, he was working on *Love at First Bite*, with Bob Kaufman, who had written the script, and he got Bob involved. Both Ted and Bob read and reread the script, and we made changes, and they kept asking for more changes. We were very happy. Jim and I were like a pair of puppies, panting for approval. When we were finally done, many drafts later, Ted gave the script to Stan Kamen at the William Morris Agency. Kamen's assistant at the time was Jim Crabbe, a kid, and he liked the script so much that he decided to represent us. Crabbe didn't have any clients at the time—we were his first real clients—but Jim and I didn't know this and we were elated. "Man! We have an agent!"

Not surprisingly, Crabbe had his own ideas about how to fix the script, and he asked us to make changes, and Jim came to Los Angeles to work on it. He had to borrow money to fly down, and I had to borrow money to rent an IBM Selectric, but before long we were up and running.

On the plus side, we found ourselves staying at a very nice place: Lionel Barrymore's old estate. A friend of ours had leased the house, and he let us crash in one of the rooms. It was huge. There was even a little railroad that took you from the main house to the pool. "This is the way to live!" Jim said.

We spent eight weeks fixing the script. In the meantime, Ted Kotcheff was getting a lot of heat. He had directed *First Blood* and *Uncommon Valor*.

In this business, it helps to have a friend with heat. I can't imagine where we'd be today if I hadn't badgered Ted to take me on as an apprentice. That's key. If you're looking to break in, you need to find someone in the business who really believes in you.

Anyway, we gave the finished script to Crabbe, our agent, and he introduced us to a producer. We went in to pitch an idea, and the producer had read our sample script and liked it. He didn't really respond to the pitch, but was producing a project in Canada at the time, and the project was in trouble. It had been greenlit, and the actors were standing by, but the script needed a little punching up. He decided to hire us, and since we weren't members of the Writers Guild, it was a good deal for him. He gave us a couple of grand, and we were thrilled.

For the next week, we were up every night, all night, working on the script. And we decided that instead of just punching it up we would completely rewrite it. We were determined to go back with a whole new script and really impress them. And that's what we did. We rewrote the entire script in one week! We gave it to the producer and his partners and everyone was very happy.

The problem now was the director. The script was a passion project for him, and it clearly wasn't the same script anymore. So the producer asked us to go to Montreal with him to discuss it with the director. The company offered us five grand for our trouble, which was a fucking fortune to us, and the next thing we know we're on our way to Montreal.

They had sent the script ahead, and the director had read it, and apparently he wasn't thrilled with the changes. We were told that we were basically there to listen to him, and to do more rewrites. We met the guy, and we were sitting in a room with him, and he started talking—and it soon became apparent that no one understood a word he was saying. He was Polish, and he had a very heavy accent. The little bits we did pick up were very confusing. He was trying to tell us that we didn't understand his vision. From his point of view, the movie was *A Midsummer Night's Dream* for children. It was Woody Allen meets Shakespeare. All of us were pretty confused. From the studio's point of view, the movie was supposed to be a teen comedy, and his version of the movie wasn't even close to the movie the producers wanted to make. In any event, the director went on for another half-hour, and no one really knew what to say. Finally, the producer said, "Well, that's a lot to digest. Let's take a breather and reconvene."

We walked back to the elevator in silence, and the producers excused themselves for a moment and went off to confer. They came back a few minutes later, and one of them flat out asked me, "Would you be willing to direct this movie?" And I said, "Lemme check my schedule. . . . You're damn right I would."

They told us to go back to our hotel room; they had to deal with the director. And on our way out I turned to Jim and said, "This is fucking insane. We started doing a little polish on a little movie, and I might end up directing it."

I *did* end up directing it. It was called *Breaking All the Rules*, and it was released the following year, in 1985.

Before it was released, Jim and I went to work on another script. We had made a few bucks, and we could finally afford to concentrate on the writing, and we thought we had a very good idea for a movie. The previous year, during the Academy Awards, both of us had watched Burt Lancaster and Kirk Douglas come out as copresenters, and one of us said, "Somebody should write a movie for those guys before it's too late." So that's what we did. We wrote a movie called *Tough Guys*, about two old gangsters who find that the world has changed a great deal since they went up river. The basic premise was simple: They might be old, but that didn't mean they weren't tough.

We wrote it, finished it in two months, and gave it to our agent, and Jim went back to his wife in Toronto.

When Crabbe read it, he flipped. He gave it to a bunch of people, and just about everyone responded very enthusiastically, including one producer who, ironically, thought it would be perfect for Burt Lancaster and Kirk Douglas. Crabbe was very optimistic, but I didn't want to say anything to Jim till I was sure this was going to happen. I didn't want to get his hopes up.

Finally, Touchstone stepped up to the plate. We weren't members of the Writers Guild, so Crabbe made a rock-bottom deal with them, but it was still more money than either of us had ever seen. At this point, I still hadn't told Jim anything. Then they got a director on board, Jeff Kanew, and they sent the script to Lancaster, who committed, and then a check arrived. I figured it was time to call Jim.

"Pack your bags and pack your wife and break the lease on your apartment," I told him. "You're moving to Los Angeles."

And he said, "I told you, James, I'm not moving to L.A. until there's money."

And I said, "There's money. I'm holding a check in my hand for a hundred and twenty-five thousand dollars."

Jim took a beat, then said, "I'll be there in a week."

He got a room at the Chateau Marmont—he wanted to arrive in style—and a few weeks later we met with Burt Lancaster in the office of the producer, Joe Wizan. Burt must have been feeling old, because he was having second thoughts about playing a tough guy in a movie. "Mr. Lancaster," I said, "we all want to believe that we will never be less than vital." And he looked at me and replied, "Spoken like a true young man." Then he shook his head and added, "I'm seventy-two years old. I don't know if I can do it."

And I said, "You have to do it. That's your legacy."

He held out for a long time, then he was in, then he was out again. Kirk Douglas had to call him. "One day one of us is going to be dead," he said. "This is our last chance to do a movie together."

Finally, he agreed to be in the movie, and suddenly we had the two stars we had envisioned in the roles from the very beginning.

The next time we met was at Kirk's house. It was Kirk and Burt and Jim and I, and it was pretty surreal. We went though the script line by line. They asked questions. We answered them.

Then it came time to do the movie and the insurance company balked. They read the script and weren't very happy. In the third act, there's a scene where the two tough guys are running across the top of a moving train, and the insurance company didn't think men their age should be running across the top of a moving train. Touchstone promised they'd get stunt guys, and they hired stunt guys, but on the day we shot that scene, Kirk and Burt said they wanted to do the scene themselves.

Sure enough, when the time came, they got on top of that moving train and did their parts. I looked at them and thought, *They really are those guys we wrote about. These two guys are seriously tough.*

We had written every role with an actor in mind. We wrote a role for Debbie Reynolds, and another one for Donald O'Connor, and the bad guy was written very specifically for Eli Wallach. But on the first day of shooting, we found out that the director had never offered the bad guy part to Eli Wallach; he had given it to Adolf Cesar. Before the end of that first day, something went very wrong. We got called to the production office and were told that Adolf Cesar had been taken away in an ambulance. He'd had a heart attack. Adolf Cesar was dead.

The next time we saw the director, Jeff Kanew, we teased him. "We told you we wrote it for Eli Wallach! You see what you did? Now poor Adolf Cesar is dead. You'll think twice before fucking with *us* again."

And when Eli Wallach showed up to replace him, I said, "A man had to die for you to get this part." That's showbiz.

Tough Guys was our big break. That movie turned us into studio writers. We became members of the Writers Guild, and then Crabbe negotiated a deal for us at Disney that ran from 1985 to 1996.

A couple of years later, we wrote *Three Men and a Baby*, which became the number one movie of the year. And a few years after that, in 1989, Jeffrey Katzenberg, the head of the studio, invited us to take a rafting trip down the Colorado River. It was just a couple of dozen of his close, personal friends, including Tom Cruise, John Badham, Don Simpson, David Hoberman, Bill Block, and John Ptak. It was pretty amazing. They had a raft coming up behind us, loaded with food, and every night on the shore of the river the chefs prepared a gourmet meal: sliced veal, barbecued ribs, fish, and of course there was plenty of beer and wine. You'd think I was saying to myself, *I've arrived. I've made it.* But actually I was saying, *My fucking arms hurt from paddling and everyone smells and I can't wait to go home to my nice soft bed.*

I think one way to break into the business is to find someone on the inside who believes in you. I started with Ted Kotcheff, and he led us to Jim Crabbe, who was just starting out. But at least Crabbe was already on the inside, and he believed in us, and that made all the difference.

The fact is, this is a very tough business, and it's run in a way that usually defies logic. For a young person, their best friend is their innocence. The one thing that will almost certainly kill his or her sense of possibility is knowing how this business works, and how little sense any of it makes.

I used to teach film classes from time to time, and I always had a little advice for my students. I'd tell them, "You're all going to suffer as you struggle to break in, but while you're waiting, whatever you do, *don't take a job you like*. Take a job you hate. If you hate your job, you'll keep pursuing the dream. If you like your job, you may end up doing it for the rest of your life."

And here's a piece of advice that Bob Kaufman shared with me many years ago, after Jim and I got our feet in the door. Bob was the writer-producer we met through Ted Kotcheff, while we were rewriting our first script, and he always made money, but he never seemed to have enough.

"Make sure your annual nut never goes over a hundred grand," he told us. "My nut is about *nine* hundred grand. I have an ex-wife, two kids, and a Rolls Royce. As a result, I've been forced to write a lot of shit."

That was good advice. If you keep your overhead low, you won't end up writing crap to pay the bills. Both Jim and I have been pretty good about the financial end of things. We've been offered enormous amounts of money to write really bad projects, and we never had to take them. And I think we're both pretty proud of that.

DAVID PAYMER

ACTOR/DIRECTOR

"A career boils down to climbing a ladder very, very slowly, and learning to grasp the rungs as they come along, one at a time."

David Paymer began his career with a traveling production of *Grease*, took the role to Broadway, then made the transition to Hollywood through a small role in *The In-Laws*. Not long afterward, Paymer moved to Los Angeles and made a name for himself in episodic television, and three years later he landed a regular spot on a new show—an actor's dream.

A few days into the shoot, however, the network decided it wasn't happy with the show, and it fired half the principals—including Paymer. Crushed, he began to explore other options, and for a time pursued a degree in family therapy. He also began to teach acting, however, and before long he found himself back in front of the cameras full time, in both TV and feature films.

Following a role in *City Slickers*, with Billy Crystal, Paymer again starred with Crystal in *Mr. Saturday Night*, a role that led to an Oscar nomination. More features followed in quick succession—*Quiz Show*, *Nixon*, *Amistad*, *Mumford*, *Get Shorty*, *The American President*—and Paymer is still going strong.

More recently, he has found himself on the other side of the camera, directing episodes of *Everwood*, for The WB, and a movie for Showtime, *Candor City Hospital*, which he cowrote with his brother, Steve. It is about a hospital where doctors actually speak the truth. ("I'll refer to it as 'minor discomfort,' but the pain will be excruciating.")

At the time of the interview, Paymer had just been hired to direct two other shows: *Jack & Bobby*, also for The WB, and *Medium*, the NBC series starring Patricia Arquette.

He met with us at his Santa Monica home on September 3, 2005.

I was born in New York City and grew up in Oceanside, Long Island. My dad was a classical pianist, but when I was a kid, he made his living as a scrap metal dealer, at the family-run Paymer Metal Company, in the Bronx. I could have been president of the Paymer Metal Company, but I decided to go a different way.

During the week, my father would be at work in the smelting factory, not the most glamorous setting, and on weekends he would play weddings and bar mitzvahs.

When I was eighteen, my parents got divorced and my dad remade his life. He already had his master's degree in music, but he went back to school, to the City University of New York, and got his Ph.D. He became a world renowned expert on Giovanni Battista Pergolesi, an obscure Italian composer who died at twenty-six, and he turned to teaching.

My mother was a travel agent, but mostly she raised me and my brother, Steve, who is a writer and also does some acting.

Before that, however, when we were still kids, my parents would occasionally break out of their assigned roles and do *Oklahoma*-style musicals at various local venues in and around Oceanside. My dad would write the music and my mother would act, and it was pretty amazing stuff. I remember being five years old and sitting in the front row of the Oceanside High School auditorium, seeing my parents on stage—my dad playing the piano and conducting his little orchestra, and my mother acting. It inspired me to want to pursue a career in acting, and when I told my parents, they both said the same thing: "Why? Please don't!"

They wanted me to become a doctor, and I always had this thing about making my parents happy, so I began to think about that, but in the eighth grade I played Oliver in a school production of *Oliver!* and I began to think about acting. I wasn't the most popular kid in school, nor the most athletic, but the theater kids became my friends, and we did a number of musicals together over the years—*Fiddler on the Roof*, *Pajama Game*, *Oklahoma*, *Once Upon a Mattress*. I felt I had found my niche on stage.

Our teacher, Barry Kaplan, whom I still talk to, always gave a big speech on the night of the opening—"Get out there and create the magic!"—and he was a great source of inspiration.

When I graduated from high school, I went to University of Rochester, in Rochester, New York, as a psychology major. I still hadn't made a decision to try acting as a profession, and at the time I was thinking I might become a therapist, but then my parents got divorced and I realized that people did what they had to do, and that maybe I should follow my dreams.

There was no theater department in Rochester, but they staged plays through the English department, and in my freshman and sophomore years, I began to get lead roles in many of the productions. I started to think that maybe I did have some talent, and I decided to transfer to the University of Michigan, in Ann Arbor, and to do a double-major, in theater and psychology, and I graduated in December of 1975, a semester early.

By this time, my father was remarried and was living in Woodmere, Long Island, and I went to live with him and his wife, Edye. I began commuting to New York for auditions. I would read through the trade papers, *Backstage* and *Showbiz*, and in June of 1976 I walked into an open call for The National Touring Company's production of *Grease*. I knew I would have to sing, and I decided to do that great old song, "Who Put the Bomp (in the Bomp Bomp Bomp)." I asked my dad to listen to the 45 record, and he wrote out the arrangement so that the accompanist could play it for me at the audition.

After I sang, I had to do a couple of scenes, and I had to dance—and I'm a terrible dancer. I felt bad for the girl who had to dance with me, because I'm so uncoordinated, and when it was all over, I went home and crawled under the covers because I realized I had blown it. Four days later, however, the phone rang and I was offered the part of Sonny Latierri. It was a one-year tour and rehearsals started in six weeks.

I couldn't believe it. To this day, I think that was the most important job I ever got, because I honestly don't think I could have lasted in this business without some positive reinforcement early on. I was only twenty-one years old, but I don't think I would have struggled endlessly, waiting for my big break. I'm one of those people who needs to know if he is on the right path, and if I hadn't got that job, I probably would have walked away from the profession.

I was on the road with *Grease* for ten months, and then the guy who was playing Sonny on Broadway quit, and they asked me to take his place. I was twenty-two years old and I was living the dream: I was an actor on Broadway. Treat Williams was playing Danny Zucco at the time, and during the course of my run, he was replaced by Peter Gallagher, and after Peter left he was replaced by Patrick Swayze.

I was on Broadway for two years, despite my limitations as a dancer. I was making $335 a week and I felt like a king. I found an apartment on the Upper West Side and found an agent and began doing commercials. I did a commercial for Subaru and another one for Ruffles. I did a car wax commercial, waxing a car. I was usually cast as the greaser, because casting directors knew me from *Grease* and knew I had that part down.

After about twelve hundred performances of *Grease*, just as I was beginning to get antsy, another very important thing happened to me. I went off to audition for the part of a New York cabbie in a movie that was shooting in New York, and I remember sticking a big wad of gum in my mouth and chewing throughout the entire reading. The movie was *The In-Laws*, with Peter Falk and Alan Arkin, and I got the part.

I had been taking an acting class at the time, with a guy named Bob McAndrew, and he would film a lot of our scenes in Super 8, with sound, and it was very helpful to see myself on film. That class really prepared me for my audition. A lot of acting teachers don't want you to see yourself on film, but I think McAndrew's approach makes more sense.

Just before the movie got under way, I noticed that my driver's license had expired, and on the first day of shooting, as I was negotiating the streets of Manhattan, and driving very erratically, I might add, one of the New York cops who'd been assigned to the location stopped me. Peter Falk and I watched as he came up to the window. "You got a driver's license?!" he barked. "Yes, I do," I replied meekly. Luckily, he didn't ask to see it.

I got through the driving part of the movie without further incident, and *The In-Laws* went on to become very successful. Peter Gallagher was then kind enough to introduce me to his agent, Susan Smith. She saw the movie and liked it, and she told me she would sign me if I moved to L.A. This was 1979, and I was definitely ready to leave *Grease*, so I made the move.

Susan was a great agent, and I am with her to this day. She sent me out on absolutely everything she felt I was right for, and I learned that if you get one in seven jobs it's the equivalent of batting a thousand in baseball. You're getting rejected 85 percent of the time, true, but if you're getting through the door, and you're prepared, you'll get work. I ended up doing a lot of episodic television. I was a guest star on just about every show of the period: *Happy Days, Barney Miller, Hill Street Blues, Cagney & Lacey, Moonlighting, Cheers*, to name a few. And I loved it. To me, acting in episodic television is like being in repertory theater. I got to play all sorts of characters—doctors, pimps, homeless people, lawyers, whatever—and I was learning how to act for the camera. When you're in the theater and you have to hit the last row in a 1,500-seat house, that's a performance. But when the camera is two feet away, and you're talking to a fellow actor, that's a personal experience, and you have to make the necessary adjustments.

After about three years of doing episodic television, I found myself auditioning for the pilot of *St. Elsewhere*, and I got the part. Three days into shooting, however, the network decided they hated the look of the show, and they fired the director, the cinematographer, and four of the lead actors. The executive producer called me in and said, "We're not sure what's going to happen. We may have to fire you, too." I suffered through a week of hell, in limbo, then someone from NBC called and invited me to the affiliates dinner, saying he'd send a limo for me. I was immensely relieved! This could only mean I wasn't going to get fired. The day after the dinner, I got fired.

I was absolutely devastated. I thought I had made it, that I no longer had to worry, but nothing could be further from the truth. Part of the business is breaking in; the other part is staying in. Maybe I was too "charactery" for Hollywood. I didn't think I'd work again.

I decided to enroll at Pepperdine University, where I explored becoming a licensed therapist, something I'd always been interested in, but I kept going to auditions and even took a job teaching acting at a workshop in North

Hollywood. In very short order, I started getting good parts again—in features, *No Way Out*, *Crazy People*, and in television—so I put my studies on the back burner.

In 1990, I went to audition for *City Slickers*. I was married by then, and my wife, Liz, took a couple of shoelaces and made me a stringy little tie for the audition. When I went in to meet Billy Crystal, he looked up and said, "Hey! I like that tie."

I got the part—my wife likes to think it was the tie—and we went off to shoot the movie in Durango, Colorado, and Santa Fe, New Mexico. While we were there, Billy was working on the script for *Mr. Saturday Night*, and a year later, with *City Slickers* behind us, Billy sent me the script, asking me to audition for the part of his character's older brother. I read it and told Liz I wasn't going to get the part. "He's going to give it Robin Williams or to Bruno Kirby or to someone well-known," I said. But I really wanted the part. It was a wonderful role—the actor went from age thirty to age seventy, an entire life, in the space of two hours.

I went in and auditioned, and I thought it went pretty well, and just before the July 4 weekend, I was called back to read for Castle Rock, the studio. I came away from that feeling like I had the first time I'd auditioned for *Grease*: I wanted to bury my head under the covers, convinced I'd blown it. As I left, however, Billy took me aside. "Good job," he said. "Very nice. But a long weekend's coming up, and I'm not going to decide before next week, so go home and don't think about it."

I went home and told Liz, "This is going to be a *really* long weekend. I blew it. And the guys from Castle Rock weren't going to give me the part anyway. They're going to want someone bigger."

Then the phone rang. "Hello, Dave? It's Billy Crystal. How'd you like to be my brother?"

I couldn't believe it. I thanked Billy and kept thanking him and then I got off the phone and hugged Liz and for the next twenty minutes I called everyone I could think of to tell them the good news.

Half an hour later, the phone rang again. "Hello, Dave? It's Billy again." There was a cautious tone in his voice that put me on edge. "Did someone call you a while ago pretending to be me?"

And my heart just stopped. I mean, I died. I couldn't breathe.

And then Billy said, "Ha ha! You see what I did? I made you think you didn't get the part, but you did."

The funny thing is, that was his first piece of direction for me. In the movie, Billy's character was always playing tricks on his brother, the character I would be playing, and Billy was already beginning to shape the relationship we would portray on film.

The film was a wonderful experience, and I was nominated for an Oscar in the Best Supporting Actor category. That was like getting my passport stamped. I felt as if I'd finally been invited to sit at the grown-up's table. My experience on *Grease* had been critically important to me, because it kept me going, but *Mr. Saturday Night* put me on the map. I had been working in movies and TV for fifteen years in relative anonymity, but now my name was out there.

And it's funny, because right after the nominations were announced, I ran into the producers from *St. Elsewhere*, the ones who'd fired me. And I couldn't help myself. I said, "Thank you for getting me out of television and into feature films." They grinned sheepishly, and I must admit that I felt a certain degree of satisfaction. That old saying is true: *Revenge is a dish best served cold.*

Going to the Academy Awards was pretty surreal, but not for the reasons you might imagine. My parents had been divorced for twenty years, and they hadn't spoken for fifteen of them, but there they were in a limousine with me and my wife, Liz, and with my brother, Steve, and it was absolutely wonderful to find myself surrounded by my family. I had decided to become an actor, and I was doing it, and it didn't matter that I wasn't going to win the Oscar, which I already knew. I was up against Jack Nicholson in *A Few Good Men*, Al Pacino in *Glengarry Glen Ross*, Jaye Davidson in *The Crying Game*, and Gene Hackman in *Unforgiven*. Hackman won, but I will tell you honestly that I never expected to win—even the trades were putting my chances at thirty-to-one—and that in no way did it diminish the experience. Even now, thinking back on it, it feels surreal, that I was in the same league with those wonderful actors.

I love acting, and I will always continue to act, but in recent years I've also turned some of my attention to directing. I'm doing mostly television at the moment, but a feature film is not out of the question. I'll probably start with a small, independent movie.

I think, you know, in this whole crazy business—whether it's acting, writing, directing, producing—you have to love what you do more than anything in the world. You have to fight incredibly hard, and you have to learn to stay committed in the face of continued, relentless rejection. It took me a long time to figure out that a career boils down to climbing a ladder very, very slowly, and learning to grasp the rungs as they come along, one at a time.

I also think you need a backup plan. Even before I returned to school, thinking about that counseling degree, I was always trying other things. I wrote two screenplays with my brother, one of which was optioned though never made, and then I got into teaching. The teaching not only helped pay the bills, but kept me creatively fulfilled while I waited for the telephone to ring. If you're just waiting for the telephone to ring, you are giving away all your power, and it will weaken you. You need to find something that fulfills you emotionally to survive because there will be long periods when the phone doesn't ring.

That's the best advice I can give anyone. Do something you love, even if it's your second or third choice. Find a way. And don't give away all your power. Find something that nourishes you creatively, because without that nourishment you won't survive.

MARC PLATT

PRODUCER

"You need to approach your career on the five-year plan. It's not what you're doing tomorrow; it's figuring out where you want to be in five years."

As a young man, Marc Platt decided he wanted to be a theater producer, and in fact he managed to produce an Off-Broadway show while he was still in college. But his inability to move the show to a larger, more commercial venue convinced Platt that he had to find a way to exercise greater control over his future projects. So he went to law school, got an internship with a pair of powerful Broadway producers, and subsequently went to work for Sam Cohn, the legendary, New York agent.

Platt was not interested in the business of agenting, but he saw opportunities there, and in fact the relationships he developed while working for Mr. Cohn eventually led to Hollywood, and to a string of top-level jobs at various studios.

When he decided to go out on his own, he produced several box-office hits, including *Legally Blonde* and its sequel, *Legally Blonde 2: Red, White & Blonde*, and the critically acclaimed HBO film, *Empire Falls*. More recently, he went back to his true love, the theater, and produced *Wicked*, one of most successful shows on Broadway.

Mr. Platt was interviewed on June 7, 2005, at his offices at Universal Studios.

I was born in Baltimore, Maryland, and ever since I was a kid, I was interested in storytelling. But as a kid it was mostly in the theater. I was always producing or directing plays: big productions—in my parents' backyard. I was always the producer and the director, always the guy in charge, and I'd get very pissed off when everybody had to go home for dinner because I thought they should spend more hours working and rehearsing.

I did more of the same when I went off to the University of Pennsylvania. I continued to be very involved in producing and directing plays, at a somewhat higher level, and in my senior year I managed to produce an Off-Broadway Equity showcase in New York City, a little musical called *Francis*. I went from door to door, talking to everyone I knew, and somehow I raised enough money to pay for a small theater and to put a good cast together. At that point, I thought that that's what I was going to do with my life—be a Broadway producer. I loved movies, too, but I didn't know anything about the technical side of filmmaking, and I certainly didn't know anything about the business end of it.

In any event, my little musical was very well received, and I had an opportunity to move it to a larger, more commercial venue. And I lost that opportunity because there were so many agents and lawyers and managers involved, all of whom understood the intricacies of the business better than I did.

That was a very uncomfortable position for me to be in, so I decided that from then on I was going to make sure I had a solid grasp of all aspects of the business. Creatively, I knew what I was doing and what I wanted to be doing, but I needed the tools to protect and facilitate that—I needed to figure out how to navigate the business.

So I went to law school at New York University.

At the end of the first year, having made the NYU Law Review, and feeling I had conquered the challenges of law school, I decided to look for an internship in the entertainment business. I sent off a hundred letters to every producer in New York City, in theater, film, and television, and only got one positive response: That was from Liz McCann and Nelle Nugent, two women who at the time were among the premiere producers on Broadway. They produced a string of hugely successful plays, including *Amadeus*, *Nicholas Nickleby*, and *The Elephant Man*.

For the next two years, I interned in their office. One day, Liz McCann found herself on the phone with one of the theater owners, discussing Peter Shaffer's contract for *Amadeus*, and realized she had a problem. "Where's that legal intern?!" she screamed.

I came into the office and helped her make sense of the contract, and she never let me out of her sight again.

For the next two years, I really learned the business of Broadway producing, and law school took a back seat. When I graduated, I told Liz McCann that I wanted to produce on Broadway, and that I thought I was ready. But she said that law school was a very theoretical education, and that I should seek out some practical applications. "You ought to become an entertainment attorney and learn the transactional side of the business," she said. "Then you can apply those combined skills and become a producer."

I thought that was good advice. I went to work for an entertainment firm, now known as Loeb and Loeb, and one day in 1985 I got a phone call from the most prominent and successful agent in the entire theater and film business. His name was Sam Cohn, and he operated out of the ICM office in New York. Sam represented so many actors and so many filmmakers that really, to my knowledge, nothing happened on Broadway without his participation. I didn't realize until later that very little in the film business happened without his participation, either.

I went to see Sam and he said, "I need to hire an attorney who will sit at my desk with me and basically negotiate on behalf of my clients. I have a lot of clients, and the volume of deal making is tremendous."

I had never thought of going into an agency, and that was not my goal; I just wanted to get on Broadway. But I knew that Sam represented some of the most talented entertainers in the business, and I thought that going to work for him would be a great opportunity, so I left Loeb and Loeb and became Sam's business affairs attorney.

Suddenly, at the age of twenty-six, I would find myself sitting in a room with Woody Allen, Meryl Streep, Bob Fosse, Robin Williams, Whoopi Goldberg, Arthur Penn, Mike Nichols, Jessica Tandy, Hume Cronyn, Cher, the songwriters Kander and Ebb, and just about everybody else. Needless to say, these were all hugely successful people, and I immediately got a sense of

Sam's reach and power. I was learning a great deal about Broadway, and at the same time I was being exposed to the ins and outs of the film business. I started developing relationships with writers and filmmakers that, unbeknownst to me, would carry me into Hollywood in the years ahead.

In fact, I was already beginning to get attention from the Hollywood law firms and studios with whom I was doing day-to-day business. They were offering me employment. "Come to Hollywood as an attorney! It's wonderful out here!" But that's not what I was interested in. I was still interested in theater.

There were, however, two companies that I had come to know particularly well. One of them was Orion, which was based in New York. We represented Woody Allen, whose films they distributed, back in Woody's heyday, and I used to go over to their New York headquarters all the time to negotiate Woody's deals. As a result, I got to know three of the principals very well. They were Arthur Krim, Eric Pleskow, and William Bernstein. The fourth partner, Mike Medavoy, was based in Los Angeles.

The other company I got to know quite well was RKO Pictures, an independent outfit headed by Mark Seiler. They were financing a number of independent movies, and I was very involved in the negotiations. For example, one of their films was *Plenty*, which was directed by Fred Schepisi and starred Meryl Streep. (Several years later, I would work with Meryl as a film executive, and twenty years later Fred directed *Empire Falls* for me, the recent HBO miniseries I produced with Paul Newman. But those are other stories.)

One day, Mark Seiler said to me, "You're a great lawyer, but you're also very creative and good with talent. You should become a production executive."

I didn't really know what that was, but Mark's idea was that I would come out to Los Angeles as business affairs attorney and then segue into production. I found out that there were actually jobs in Hollywood where I could combine my creative abilities and my business instincts, which pretty much defines the job of a production executive. I realized I could develop material, develop relationships with talent, and use my business acumen to navigate the corporate world—and that I would actually get paid for it.

So I thought to myself, *I really want to be in the theater, but the theater is a very tough business. Maybe I should try Los Angeles for a year.* By this point, I was married and had a child, and I discussed it with my wife, Julie, and we decided to try it for a year or so. If we didn't like it, I could always rejoin Sam in New York. Well, that was eighteen years ago, and we never went back.

While working with Mark Seiler at RKO, I fell in love with the job of being a production executive. I found myself very naturally suited to it. It combined everything I enjoyed doing, everything I felt I was good at. I worked with material, with writers, and with talent, and I got involved in deal making. And I learned the technical side of the business: how to prep a movie, how movies were shot and edited, how to use sound and music, and it all felt very natural to me.

About a year and a half later, while I was still at RKO, I got a call from Mike Medavoy, the other partner at Orion, the one I didn't know as well. He said he needed some help in production, and that his partners in New York had spoken very highly of me. He wondered whether I'd be interested.

In those days, Orion was regarded as a "mini-major," and I thought this could be a great opportunity. So I called Sam Cohn, back in New York, and I said, "I'm not coming back yet." And I left RKO and joined Orion as vice president of production.

Right at the start, I was given two projects to supervise as an executive, and I was with both of them from the inception. One was *Dances with Wolves*; the other was *The Silence of the Lambs*. Two years after joining Orion, I was named president of production, and for the next seven years, I held the same position at three different studios.

And that's how I broke into Hollywood. But the funny thing is, the whole time I was there, I kept wondering how I was going to get back to Broadway. And when I got tired of being an executive, and went out on my own as an independent producer in 1998, one of the first things I did was to look for theater projects.

I optioned *Wicked*, a book by Gregory Maguire, with the intention of developing it as a film. But at the suggestion of Stephen Schwartz, the composer/lyricist, I ended up turning it into a Broadway show instead. *Wicked* became one of the biggest successes of my career, both personally and professionally. I've had many successful movies, but in terms of personal goals, where I started out, and where I thought was going to spend my life, I must say that that experience was hugely satisfying. I felt I had come full circle.

Now, in terms of advice for people who want to break in, I always tell them a couple of things.

First of all, get a good liberal arts education. I think undergraduate school gives you a wide spectrum of opportunities, a chance to learn so much in so many different areas. You become socialized. You mature. You absorb. I don't think it's good to get too focused, too early, on being a director or a writer or an actor. I think to become a great filmmaker or a great actor or a great producer you have to take the time to experience life and to draw on those experiences. It's not all about holding a camera or cutting a film; those are things you can learn later. It's about taking the time to develop your personality and your soul and your values. When you're young, life should be about experiences. I'm a big proponent of that. It will make you a much more interesting filmmaker. The other elements—moving a camera, cutting a film, acting, writing—you can learn later, if you find you have the instincts for it. But learning about life and humanity, well—that should come first.

The second thing I would say is: Don't be daunted by the size and scope of Hollywood. When you're starting out, it often seems impenetrable. It's all about staying with it, and making informed decisions.

In my career, I have found that one makes two basic kinds of decisions. One is intellectual, and the other emotional. And I've been the most successful and certainly the most satisfied when I made decisions with my heart, not my mind. So I always tell kids, "If you have a dream, follow it. Even if it seems impossible."

You have to believe in yourself. And you have to take the time to get some life experience. And as you move toward your goal—and this is very, very important—you need to approach your career on the five-year plan. It's not what you're doing tomorrow; it's figuring out where you want to be in five years. Once you have that figured out, you can go backward and plan the steps that will get you there. That way, you'll see things clearly: *Okay, this job I'm working on today, it's not what I want to be doing with my life, but it's going to get me to where I want to go, so I will do it as if my entire future depended on it.*

If you think like that, in terms of your first step into Hollywood, a lot of doors will open. But if you aim too high too soon, you'll be disappointed, or worse. Whether you want to be an executive, a writer, a producer, an actor, or a director, you need to remember that those first few jobs are just stepping stones. That's the way it is for most people. And that's certainly the way it was for me.

SYDNEY POLLACK

DIRECTOR/PRODUCER/ACTOR

"Sometimes people are so monomaniacal that they don't see what's around them; they're too focused on the goal."

Sydney Pollack has been directing movies for more than four decades, and his credits have made him a true American icon: *They Shoot Horses, Don't They?*, *Jeremiah Johnson*, *The Way We Were*, *Three Days of the Condor*, *Absence of Malice*, *Tootsie*, *Out of Africa*, *The Firm*, and, most recently, *The Interpreter*.

Ironically, Pollack set out to be an actor, but he was disappointed with how he was doing. When he finally fell into directing, it was immediately clear to those around him that he had a way with actors. Twelve of the actors he has worked with over the years have been nominated for Oscars, including Jane Fonda, Barbra Streisand, Paul Newman, Dustin Hoffman, Teri Garr, Meryl Streep, Klaus Maria Brandauer, and Holly Hunter, and two of them actually went home with Academy Awards: Gig Young, for *They Shoot Horses. Don't They?* and Jessica Lange, for *Tootsie*.

Pollack himself won two Oscars in 1985, for the unforgettable *Out of Africa*: one was for Best Picture, the other for Best Director.

As for the acting career, Pollack thought he had left that behind, but while filming *Tootsie* he was literally forced to take the role of Dustin Hoffman's befuddled agent. The scene between Pollack and Hoffman in the Russian Tea Room turned out rather brilliantly, and Pollack's acting career got an unexpected boost.

The interview took place on June 3, 2005, in the Beverly Hills offices of Pollack's production company, Mirage Enterprises.

I was born in Indiana and had no predilection to movies at all. I just went to see movies like any other kid. But when I was in high school, in South Bend, I started acting in school plays, and by the time I graduated I found myself fantasizing about becoming a professional actor.

My parents were middle- to lower-class, income-wise, and we didn't have enough money for me to go to a good college. Still, my father made a living, and I worked, too. I was a paper boy for most of my early life, and when I got my driver's license, I spent summers working for the Highway Department, cleaning out weeds and painting guardrails and shit like that.

My father had always insisted that I save half of what I earned, and by the end of that last summer after high school, I had saved $800. This was the late 1950s, and that was a lot of money, and I talked my father into letting me go to this acting school I'd heard about in New York City. I think I was just trying to avoid getting a real job, but it worked: He let me go.

At the time, I had no idea how great a school this was. It was called The Neighborhood Playhouse, and I can say unequivocally that it was the best acting school in the world. My dance teacher was Martha Graham, *personally*. My acting teacher was Sanford Meisner, a genius. The school offered the best of everything, and I had simply lucked into it.

At the end of that first year, I was invited back for a second year on a full scholarship, and shortly after I returned Meisner asked me to be his assistant. I didn't have any wish to teach, but he was such a hero to me that I went ahead and took the job. I still had time to pursue my acting, though. In 1954, I made my Off-Broadway debut in *A Stone for Danny Fisher*, with Zero Mostel and Sylvia Miles, and I subsequently made it to Broadway in *Dark Is Light Enough*, with Tyrone Power, Katharine Cornell, and Christopher Plummer. Neither of those performances led to much of anything else.

Shortly thereafter, however, I met John Frankenheimer, who at the time was one of the hottest directors in television. He was directing all the big Playhouse 90s, and I went over to audition for a small part. He wasn't too interested in me as an actor, but when he heard that I was Sanford Meisner's assistant, he was extremely impressed. He told me that Meisner had taught a master acting class at 20th Century Fox the previous summer, and that he, Frankenheimer, had been allowed to audit the class. He said he had learned a lot from the experience.

Frankenheimer gave me a small part in a television show, but it was only because he wanted to talk me into working with him as an acting coach. He was getting ready to direct the Henry James piece, *The Turn of the Screw*, and Ingrid Bergman had agreed to star in it. She had never before done television, and this was a huge event.

The thing was, there were two little kids in the piece, and Frankenheimer wanted some help with the kids. He offered me the job of coaching them, and I took it. It worked out pretty well. After that, Frankenheimer got his first big movie, *The Young Savages*, with Burt Lancaster, Telly Savalas, and Shelley Winters. There were also a couple of kids in that picture, and he asked if I'd go back to Hollywood with him to help out.

I decided to go because the project seemed interesting and because I wasn't exactly setting the world on fire as an actor (though once in a while I'd get to play a friend of a friend of the soda jerk). By this time I was married and with a kid, so I needed to make a living, and the job with Frankenheimer paid pretty well.

It turned out to be a strange job. I spent a lot of time on the set hiding from Burt Lancaster. Everybody was afraid of him because he was a huge star and very intimidating and liked teasing people, and he seemed to enjoy teasing me in particular. "Hey kid, come here!" he'd say—he called me *kid* all the time. "Everybody, pay attention! I want you to listen to the *New York Acting Coach*. Now what did you just tell those kids to do, kid? Could you repeat it for the rest of us?" I would turn beet-red. I didn't know what to say. I'd mumble something and try to get away, but he just kept at it, needling me.

Then, gradually, things changed. He started asking me questions about his own part in the movie, and we had a few brief conversations, and he stopped needling me. I could see that all along he was actually very interested in hearing what I thought.

A few days after the picture ended, I was packing up and getting ready to fly home when I heard from his secretary. "Mr. Lancaster wants to see you," he said. I was in a rush to get to the plane, but it was Burt Lancaster, so I went. I met him at his office at the old Columbia Pictures lot, over on Gower Street, and he said, "You know, kid, you should be a director."

I was insulted. I thought he was saying, *Just look at yourself. The way you look you're never going to make it as an actor.* Then he said, "I'm going to call Lew Wasserman." I didn't know who Lew Wasserman was. I was repped by MCA as an actor, but I didn't talk to anyone that high up—Wasserman ran the whole Universal operation—so I had no idea what he was talking about.

Anyway, Burt picked up the phone and called. "Lew," he said, "it's Burt. I'm sitting here with a young man named Sydney Pollack, and I think he can direct. He hasn't directed anything, but I want you to talk to him anyway. He can't be any worse than those bums you've got doing television for you now."

So I went to see Lew Wasserman, feeling humiliated and a little silly because I knew that he was only seeing me because Burt had told him to see me. And I had nothing to put on the table. I'd never directed anything.

"Burt says you should be a director," he said.

I didn't know what to say.

"Well," Wasserman continued. "Do you want to be a director?"

"I don't know," I said, feeling even more humiliated. "I never thought about it."

"Where do you live?" he asked.

"New York."

"Can you move out here?"

"I guess," I said. "I'll have to talk to my wife."

"Well," he said. "How much do you need a week to live?"

And, like an asshole, not wanting to ask for too much, I said, "Seventy-five dollars."

And Wasserman said, "All right. I'm going to pay you seventy-five dollars a week for six months. You move yourself and your family out here and I will put you under the wing of some people at Universal Television. You'll observe, and we'll see what happens."

I signed a contract, and only found out later that it was for *seven years*.

Everything was at their option, and at the absolute minimum. The six months at seventy-five dollars a week was a given, but beyond that they had the right to exercise their options at any time. They more or less owned me.

So I came out to Los Angeles and just started watching these guys work, and I made friends with two men in particular. One of them was Dick Irving, who was producing a bunch of shows for Universal. The other was Frank Price, who went on to run Universal and later became head of Columbia.

They didn't really know what to do with me, and I didn't know what to do with them. I was this kid that Wasserman had foisted on them, and I basically just hung around. I didn't have an office or anything, so I spent a lot of time on their couches, just watching, listening, and waiting.

Anyway, they had a kind of silly television show called *Shotgun Slade*, a half-hour western with Scott Brady, where the gimmick was that this guy's got a sawed-off shotgun in a holster on his horse. They used to shoot it in two days. And they used contemporary jazz music as a background, another gimmick.

The show had just been cancelled, but there were four episodes left to shoot, and they decided to give me one of them. I had no idea what I was doing and I screwed it up royally, but the acting turned out pretty well, and that saved me.

More importantly, however, the experience taught me that I had learned absolutely nothing as an observer, and that in two days of actually directing an episode, I immediately began to figure things out. I remember sitting in the editing room and watching the guy putting the show together and asking him, "Why doesn't that work?" and "Why doesn't this work?" and "How come that works?" And he didn't even have to tell me, because I could see what I'd screwed up. I could see why the shots didn't work and I could see the shots I'd missed entirely, and suddenly everything sort of snapped into focus.

I don't know why they didn't fire me. I think the acting was good enough so they decided to give me another chance. And I did well on the next one.

I ended up doing four-and-a-half years of television at Universal, starting in 1961.

In those days, all the new blood was coming out of television. It wasn't coming out of film schools, the way much of it is today, because there were only a handful of film schools, and they weren't making any noise. The way to graduate from TV to film was to get some Emmy nominations, so the studios paid a lot of attention to the Emmys.

During my last three years in television, I was nominated each year. Once for *Something About Lee Wiley*, an episode of Bob Hope Presents the Chrysler Theatre, the studio's big anthology series, and then for a *Ben Casey* two-parter starring Kim Stanley, who won an Emmy for her performance. I won in 1965, for *The Game*, another episode in the anthology. Cliff Robertson also went home with an Emmy.

After that, people were sending me movie scripts, and it turned out that Universal didn't have a clause in my contract covering movies. So as soon as I got my first movie, I busted the contract. They couldn't hold me. They could stop me from doing television for other studios, but not movies. Still, sometimes it was difficult to get permission when I got offers for other television shows. I'd have to go see Lew Wasserman. I'd tell him about the other offer and why it was important to me, and he'd listen and pick up the phone and say, "Do you have a show we need Pollack for next week? No?" Then he'd hang up and look at me and say, "Okay. Go ahead."

My very first movie was at Paramount. It was called *The Slender Thread* and starred Sidney Poitier and Anne Bancroft. After that I directed *This Property Is Condemned*, with Robert Redford, whom I already knew. We had met a few years earlier, on the set of a little movie called *War Hunt*. We had both made our film acting debuts on that movie.

I guess the short answer to your question—how did I break into Hollywood—is that I got pushed into it. I never set out to do it. I wasn't a film buff. I didn't have any real knowledge of film lore until after I got into the industry. That's what's weird about it. And I still have the hardest time talking to people who believe that it's all volitional; that you have to know exactly what you want to do when you're eleven years old.

In my case, it didn't work that way at all. For me, it was a series of accidents.

Back in the 1960s, there was a huge catch-22. If you wanted to direct a film, the studio would ask to see your work. And you'd say, "Well, I don't have any work to show you because nobody's giving me a job." And they'd say, "Well, we can't take a chance without first seeing what you can do."

You literally couldn't get into the business that way. The film business was totally populated by the people who were there from the beginning, or got into it in the 1940s. There was no new blood coming in.

Occasionally, you'd get someone like Elia Kazan, who made his mark on Broadway. Or Josh Logan, who also started as a stage director. But mostly there wasn't a way in.

When television came along, in the 1950s, they drafted most of the guys from live TV—people like Sidney Lumet and John Frankenheimer and Arthur Penn. All those great guys came from live television. None of them had ever done film in their lives. And there wasn't another big wave of newcomers until television switched to film. I was part of that second wave, along with people like Robert Altman, Mark Rydell, and Dick Donner. We were all television workhorses. We ran from one television show to the next. We directed everything.

The acting career, that came later—and, again, it was an accident. It happened on *Tootsie*. I hadn't acted in twenty years, since my debut with Redford, and Dustin made me do that role. He kept saying to me, "Where are the machine guns?" He didn't believe there were any machine guns, like in *Some Like it Hot*. He was looking for that *thing* that really drove the action, and he kept saying to me, "Where are the fucking machine guns? Why do I put the dress on? Tell me why Dorothy puts on a dress."

I had already cast Dabney Coleman in the part of Dorothy's agent, the part I ended up doing, but Dustin kept fighting with me. He kept saying, "There's nothing to make me to put on a dress!"

I said, "If your agent tells you that you're never going to work again, you put on a dress."

And he said, "If Dabney Coleman tells me I will never work again, I won't put on a dress. But if *you* tell me I'll never work again, I'll do it."

And I said, "Dustin, you're getting paid a fortune for this! You're an actor! *Act!*"

And he said, "Acting is hard enough. Why do I have to make it up? Why make it harder if we can use the truth? I want *you* to play the agent."

He felt I'd be more convincing as the guy delivering the ultimatum, and that that would help his performance, but I dismissed him out of hand. Then I got a call from Mike Ovitz, who was his agent and my agent, and he said, "Sydney, you're going to have to play that part."

And I said, "Mike, I've got my hands full. I've got a script that doesn't work and I've got an actor playing a woman who doesn't look *anything* like a woman. I haven't seen a test shot yet that worked. Plus I don't have time to learn lines and get into makeup and put on a suit. And I don't want to be directing myself. I'm not doing it."

Then I started getting flowers. Every day, two dozen red roses would arrive, with notes. "Please be my agent. Love, Dorothy." This went on and on, and Dustin began to drive me crazy. I finally switched Dabney's role and did the part, and that started my belated acting career.

I began getting acting offers, even though I wasn't much interested in acting anymore. But some parts came along that were hard to resist: I took a role in *Husbands & Wives*, the Woody Allen film. I did an uncredited cameo in *Death Becomes Her*. I took a small role in *The Player*, for Robert Altman, an old television buddy. I was in *Eyes Wide Shut*, the Stanley Kubrick film, curious to see what Stanley did on the set. And I even did a small, recurring role in *Will & Grace*, the NBC series, because David Kohan, one of the show's creators, is my old assistant and a friend.

The real reason I take any role is to spy on the director. A director never gets to see how another director works. But as an actor, you can learn a little something from every director.

Acting is not that interesting to me, personally. It's a wonderful profession, and I love working with actors, but it's not the same as directing.

I think, in terms of advice, I believe you have to leave room for accidents in life. Sometimes people are so monomaniacal that they don't see what's around them; they're too focused on the goal. You've got to loosen up a little. Keep your eyes open. See what happens.

The other thing, and this isn't something I could have said until five or six years ago, is that today anyone can make their own movie. Get out there and take advantage of the technology. You can literally shoot and edit a little film on DVD for a few thousand dollars. I'm not talking about a feature; I'm talking about a fifteen-minute movie that really shows what you've got.

Someone, somewhere in Hollywood is going to take the time to pop that DVD into his computer and take a look. So make something that's really going to grab them, something unlike anything they've ever seen before.

Fifteen minutes. That's all you need. You shoot after work, you shoot on weekends, you put it together on your computer. If you do it right, you're going to get somebody's attention, and it might just be someone who can open doors.

GAVIN POLONE

PRODUCER

"That's how I came into my own: as an angry, aggressive guy."

Gavin Polone started out as a literary agent, but for a time considered becoming a different type of agent altogether: a government agent. When that didn't pan out, for reasons the Central Intelligence Agency wouldn't share with him, he became more focused on his work at International Creative Management, and steadfastly made his way up the corporate ladder.

He eventually left ICM, joined United Talent Agency, became a partner there, then was eased out, as they say, and went off to launch a management and production company of his own. As a manager, he represented many of the industry's heavy hitters, both in television and in feature films, but he eventually got out of the management business, too. He decided that he really wanted to produce, and he didn't think he'd be taken seriously as a producer if he continued to handle talent. Too many managers use their clients to finagle producing credits on films and television series, and they don't do any of the actual producing work, and Polone didn't want to go that route. He wanted to be in the thick of it.

Some of his television credits include *Curb Your Enthusiasm*, *Gilmore Girls*, *Hack*, and the recent miniseries, *Revelations*. At the time of the interview, he'd received orders on two new series, *Thief* and *Emily's Reasons Why Not*, and had just begun pro-

duction on *The Showbiz Show with David Spade*, a satire of Hollywood celebrity and the black hole of self-absorption that defines so much of the entertainment community. His features include *8 mm*, *Panic Room*, *Secret Window*, *Seeing Other People*, and *Little Manhattan*. His next movie, *Population 436*, is already filming and another feature, *Super Ex*, starring Uma Thurman and Luke Wilson, is slated to begin shooting before the end of the year.

Polone was interviewed in his Los Angeles office on June 13, 2005.

I was born in Los Angeles and lived in the San Fernando Valley until my parents were divorced, when I was fifteen, then I moved to Beverly Hills with my father. I had a sister, two years younger than me, and she stayed with my mother. My father was a lawyer, active in real estate; my mother made and still makes television movies.

I watched a lot of TV as a kid, and in high school I still watched TV, but I read a lot, too. And when I went off to the University of California, in Berkeley, I decided to study film. I didn't really intend to go into the film business—I was actually thinking of getting into real estate—but I thought film would be an easy and fun way to breeze through college. We watched a lot of old movies and foreign films, but we were also required to do a lot of papers, and it turned out to be much more demanding than I'd expected.

I graduated with a degree in film, then came back to L.A. and got my real estate broker's license. The idea was that I'd start out as a broker and eventually develop real estate, so—with that in mind—I set up meetings at several brokerage companies.

Before I went to my first meeting, however, a girl I knew took me to a party at the home of her uncle and his wife. The uncle was a producer; the wife was an agent. I was talking to the wife, telling her that I didn't really know what I should do with myself, and she suggested I get into the business. She said she thought I might be a good agent. Oddly enough, my mother had been pushing for the same thing, and she had already set up a meeting for me at the William Morris Agency, to see about entering their training program.

When I finally had my meeting at William Morris, I found the guy in charge of the program to be very pompous. He began by trying to dissuade me from applying, noting that it was a very difficult program, then said it would be at least six weeks before the company would even let me know if I'd been accepted. I thanked him and went home and thought about this, and about the fact that I'd be working fifteen hours a day for $250 a week, and I never called him back.

A couple of weeks later, I got a phone call at ten in the morning. I was still in bed, in my father's house, which should give you some idea of what my life was like. I didn't have a job and I didn't have anything to do because I had graduated a year early and all my friends were still in college. Anyway, I answered the phone and it was this woman, Marci Glenn, who was a friend of my mother's. She was working at a small agency, and she was about to join ICM, and she had been told that she could bring an assistant with her. "Do you want to come work for me?" she asked.

"I can't type," I said.

"Don't worry," she said. "You can learn."

I didn't really have any other prospects, and I was sick of living with my father, so I said yes. I had a couple of real estate–related interviews set up, but they were easy to cancel.

This was a Thursday, and Marci was starting at ICM the following Monday. So that weekend I enrolled in a two-day typing class, because I'd done some hunting-and-pecking in college and it was just too damn slow, and on Monday I showed up at ICM in a tie. I figured that that's what I was supposed to do.

Right away, I realized that Marci would have been a lot better off if the company had assigned an assistant to her. I didn't know the place, or the politics, and in retrospect she could have used someone on the inside. But I think Marci felt better working with someone she knew a little, rather than a complete stranger.

Marci was a talent agent, representing actors. Her big actor at the time was Stephanie Zimbalist, who was the star of *Remington Steele*. My job was to answer the phone and to book deals and to make appointments, and slowly I began to familiarize myself with the place.

I soon learned that majority of the assistants at ICM were professional secretaries. At the time, the company didn't really have a formalized training program, so most of the assistants weren't thinking about becoming agents.

Even the mail room guys at ICM acted like they would never do anything but sort mail.

After a few months, I realized I wasn't doing a very good job—I screwed up some appointments, stuff like that—and I decided to get more organized. I began reading a lot of scripts, and doing coverage, basically providing a brief synopsis of the stories for Marci, so that she wouldn't have to suffer through the whole script herself. I also did a lot of internal breakdowns, where I would describe the individual characters so that Marci could figure out which of her clients might be right for which parts.

I remember reading the pilot for *L.A. Law* and thinking it was fantastic. Then I read the script for *Raising Arizona* and felt the same way. I was suddenly more interested in the business, although I still didn't think I wanted to be an agent.

One thing I did notice, however, is that the assistants who at least *acted* like they wanted to be agents were better treated than the ones who were happy to be secretaries. In fact, people seemed to look down on the secretaries. So in order to get treated better, I began to let people know I wanted to be an agent.

I also tried my hand at writing. During my lunch breaks, another assistant and I tried to write a few spec TV episodes. We thought we could break out of the drudgery of being assistants by becoming writers on TV shows. We wrote an episode of the new *Gidget*, which was a syndicated show, and we wrote an episode of *Nine to Five*, the TV series based on the movie. We also wrote an episode of *Hunter*. We did all of this on our lunch breaks, and nothing came of any of the scripts, although we thought our stuff was much better than anything we were seeing on TV.

I eventually moved out of my father's house and got my own apartment, but it sucked. Just imagine the kind of shitty apartment a guy making $350 a week would have, and that was my apartment, only worse. Also, because my friends were still in college, I didn't have anyone to spend time with. Marci would go home early, to be with her kid, and I used to stay late at the office. At one point, I got friendly with Howie Klein, an agent in the TV literary department. His assistant was a married woman, and a professional secretary, and she used to leave early. So I found myself weaseling my way into Howie's office, helping him make calls or whatever he needed, and within two months Howie asked Marci if she would trade assistants with him. That's how I went from the talent side of the business to the TV lit department, and I found it much more interesting than the whole actor thing.

At that point, I started thinking that I might try to become a junior executive at a studio or at one of the networks. I got an interview at Warner Brothers, to become the manager of development in the TV movie department, and I came close, but I didn't get the job. Then I came close to a job at ABC, as manager of current programming in the comedy department. I didn't get that, either. I was only twenty-one, and I think that may have been an issue.

I started becoming discouraged and decided I wanted to leave the entertainment business, so I applied for a job with the Central Intelligence Agency. I felt I wasn't enjoying life. I was bored, and unchallenged, and being an assistant was a grind, and ICM wasn't exactly the friendliest place in the world.

I called the agency and got an application, and they invited me to visit them in their offices in South Del Monte, a bit of a drive from L.A. On the morning of my appointment, I showed up in the office in a suit and I told Howie I had an appointment to go to. He had the decency not to ask where I was going, which I would have had to lie about, anyway, given the clandestine nature of the operation, and he sent me on my way.

I got to the CIA's offices and had a meeting with a woman who was maybe four feet tall. I'm not kidding. She asked me a few questions, just basic conversation, then asked if I'd be willing to submit to a written test. Two weeks later, I showed up at the UCLA campus, for the test, and I found myself being herded into a room with a couple of dozen other people. They all looked like they were from another country, or in the military, and I felt very out of place but still hopeful. The test went well. It was your basic aptitude test, with some geography and politics. Nothing too demanding.

A month later, I got this packet from the CIA. They said I had scored very well on the test, and would I please fill out this detailed application so they could better assess whether I was the type of person they might want to hire. They also asked me not to tell anyone about the application, which I thought was great.

I filled in the application, some stuff about my background, my education, and my interests, then put my name and address on the top of every single page, per their instructions, and mailed it back to them. I was sure I was in. I imagined myself flying off to Langley, Virginia, where they would train me before sending me off to Afghanistan or some place equally dangerous and exotic. I was excited and happy about life.

A month later, a letter showed up at my father's house, addressed to *Gary* Polone. I had my own apartment, and that's the address I had put on every page, right under my name, per their instructions, and they sent the letter to my father's house. And they couldn't even get my name right! The letter said something like, "We've reviewed your file and you don't possess *any* of the requirements we're looking for in an applicant and your file will be destroyed within thirty days." I was devastated.

I went back to work and stayed later than ever. I went to staff meetings and subjected myself to the drudgery of taking notes and typing them up on my IBM Selectric. There were no computers then, so you had to retype the entire document if you made mistakes, or if the status of a project changed at the last minute. I worked really hard, not because I cared about the work but because I had no life.

The hard work drew the notice of several agents in the company. They wondered about the guy who stayed in the office long after everyone else had gone home. Then, by sheer chance, ICM decided to implement a training program, similar to the ones they had at several other agencies. They decided to start with four trainees, and they asked me to be one of them. This was in 1986.

They hadn't really thought it through, though. We weren't agents and we weren't assistants, either. We were somewhere in the middle—some kind of agent purgatory. I was taken off Howie's desk and put in an office with one of the other trainees, this girl, Carol, and right away we both realized that we'd been given nonjobs. Still, I decided I would start looking around for clients. That's what agents did, after all. I would talk to some of the assistants, to see if they had heard of anyone who sounded promising, but had no representation, and I also started to read some of the unsolicited scripts that were floating around the office.

Carol was more on the talent side, and she began doing the same thing—looking for actors who could become hip-pocket clients. The idea was, if we booked jobs for any of these people, a real long shot, we might actually be allowed to sign them.

To make ourselves sound more professional, I would answer Carol's phone and she would answer mine. It sounded like we were real agents, with assistants. I tried to get jobs for my nobody clients, and in time I made a few small deals that didn't really impress anyone of note. This went on for a few months, and in January, 1987, they decided they needed a new agent in the TV lit department. I told them that if they didn't promote me, I was quitting, so they did the intelligent thing and promoted me.

People always ask you about your first big sale, but it doesn't really work that way. You sell a little TV movie here, or you get a client an option on a script, or another client gets a staff job on a series. Also, in the beginning, you don't really have any of your own clients, so you're basically helping other people out. Of course, they respected you more if you had your own clients, so you went out and tried to find people worth signing. Internally, you'd find out about clients who weren't happy with their representation, and maybe you'd take them off the hands of that agent, and you'd also talk to the studios and try to find promising writers.

Before long, I actually had a few clients of my own. Then Howie left to become a manager. Since I'd been his assistant, and since I knew most of his clients, I was able to talk some of them into signing with me. I shared those clients with Howie—he managed them, and I became their new agent—and that's how, six months into the job, I found myself with eight clients. I had been making $400 a week, and I managed to get that bumped to $550, at which point I realized I had some value to the company. I started hinting that I wasn't making enough money, and I made them think that I was interviewing with other agencies—which I wasn't. Finally they came to me with a two-year contract: $50,000 the first year, and $60,000 the second year.

That was huge for me. I felt I would never need to make any more than that in my life. I didn't love being an agent—I would much rather have gone to work for the CIA—but I was getting a little traction. Within the hierarchy of the world I inhabited, I was no longer a member of the lowest class. And I even had an expense account.

In a matter months, I went from a person who cleans his own bathroom to someone who was able to hire a housekeeper once a week. I was only twenty-two years old, but I began to feel like an adult. And one of the first things I did was to buy a condo. I even brought in a roommate who paid rent and helped me make my mortgage payments.

I felt good about my life, but I still wasn't passionate about the job. The only clients I was able to sign were the ones no one else wanted. And it was hard for me because I was very shy back then. I had to take people to lunch and I'd have nothing to say, so eventually I stopped taking people to lunch. One time I turned in my expenses for the month and they only came to $140, and I got called in. "Why aren't you using your expense account?" I was asked.

"I don't like going to lunch with people."

"That's your job."

So I would try to go out more. I would always begin by flagging down the waiter and ordering right away, and then I would go to the bathroom and stand around for a few minutes to kill time. People must have thought I had a bowel problem or a cocaine habit.

Eventually, I grew into the job. When you have eight clients, and they're all working, it's easy to get that ninth client. I did a lot of work in series television, and I represented most of the guys on *The Simpsons*, and they would tell other writers about me, and I'd take these new writers to lunch and sign the ones I liked.

The thing I enjoyed most, however, was stealing clients from other agents. It was very visceral. And I think it played into my anger problem. What was my anger problem? I don't know. I was just an angry person. But that's how I came into my own: as an angry, aggressive guy. And I had good taste in material, which gave me the confidence I needed to keep signing the right people.

Toward the end of my two-year contract, I was bringing in a lot of money for the agency—relative to what I was costing them in salary and expenses—but I was eager to break out of TV and get into features. They were resistant to the idea, however. The guy who was running the feature department, Bill Block, wanted me in his department, but the guy running TV, Jack Dytman, didn't want to lose me.

Still, I began to sign some feature guys. I signed David Koepp, who went on to have a huge career (*Bad Influence, Death Becomes Her, Mission: Impossible, Spider-Man*), and I signed David Goyer, who also went on to a huge career (*The Crow, Blade, Batman Begins*).

I thought I'd really scored with Koepp. I was under the impression that I was battling CAA and Triad to sign him, but it turned out that neither of them wanted him. As for Goyer, he was just a guy delivering Pepsi on the studio lot, and he'd been easy to sign. And I got him his first sale pretty quickly: *Death Warrant*, for Jean-Claude Van Damme.

At the end of my two-year contract, I still wasn't happy. In fact, I was *less* happy. Some of the more senior agents were pimping my clients. I would bring a writer in, and I would ask Jack Dytman for help signing him or her, and Jack would come to the meeting to impress the potential client. But the next thing I knew he had taken my client for himself. So I left and went to a smaller agency, Bauer-Benedek, which subsequently merged with Leading Artists to become the United Talent Agency, where I eventually became a partner. Before long, however, we all decided that I would be much happier on my own.

For a while, I became a manager/producer, but I soon realized that I wasn't going to be taken seriously as a producer if I was still managing clients. A lot of managers will use their A-list stars to get producing credits on the film. They don't actually do the job. I didn't want to be one of those managers, so one day I told all of my clients that I was getting out of the management business, and I went off to produce. The only client I kept was Conan O'Brien, and that's because he's so far out of the mainstream of film-making that I knew there wouldn't be a conflict. Plus he happens to be the greatest guy on the planet.

And it's not as if I was abandoning my clients. I continue to give help and advice to any of the ones who need it, and I'm still working with most of them, developing series and features.

Looking back, I guess things could have been worse.

SARA RISHER

PRODUCER

"One, take that assistant job and work hard and don't complain. And two, don't ever think you're too good for a job."

Sara Risher's first job in the film industry was seductive in the extreme: She was the personal assistant to director Peter Yates during the making of *The Hot Rock*. One of the perks of the job was having lunch with Yates, and Robert Redford, on an almost daily basis. The other perk, perhaps somewhat more valuable, was the experience: She was a young woman, just out of college, and she'd been offered a front-row seat to the nuts-and-bolts of filmmaking.

Risher did two more films with Yates, then took a job with New Line Cinema, a small, New York–based company that was in the business of buying films for distribution.

New Line eventually got into the business of making movies, and Risher went on to produce of a string of successful films, from *A Nightmare on Elm Street* (and its many sequels) to *Pump up the Volume, Last Man Standing*, and *In Love and War*.

After twenty-five years with New Line, Risher formed her own company, Chick-Flicks, and in 2004 released her first film, *Raise Your Voice*, starring Hilary Duff. She expects to release two more films within the next year.

She was interviewed in Los Angeles on May 16, 2005.

I was born in South Carolina, and grew up in Virginia, and as soon as I graduated from high school, I went off to Marymount College, in Tarrytown, New York, and never looked back. I majored in drama and history, and at one point I thought I could change the world through socially relevant theater, but that didn't happen.

Instead, a few weeks after finishing college, I found myself interviewing for a job with Peter Yates, a British director. He had just finished *Bullitt*, with Steve McQueen, and was about to start production on *The Hot Rock*, and he was looking for a full-time assistant. The movie starred Robert Redford, hot off *Butch Cassidy and the Sundance Kid*, and had been written by William Goldman, who'd also done the script for *Butch*. My job would be to follow Peter around and take notes and deal with the writer and the actors and just be basically on-call twenty-four hours a day. Was I interested? I thought for about half a second—*Well, duh!*—and said yes.

It was heaven. At the time, I didn't realize that this was the ultimate fantasy job. The film had a huge budget, for those days, anyway, and somehow the studio had finagled permission to film anywhere in New York City. We went around Manhattan like we owned it.

In the middle of the day, when we broke for lunch, I'd run off and find something suitably extravagant and deliver it to the trailer, and the guys always insisted that I join them. So there I was, with Peter Yates, this handsome, blue-eyed Brit, and Robert Redford, who was even more handsome, and the two other leads, George Segal and Zero Mostel. They were always competing with one another to see who could make me laugh, and Zero always won. He wasn't the best-looking guy in the room, but he was certainly the funniest.

When I think back on it, it's still hard to believe. I was a young woman, just out of college, and I was sitting in the director's chair, next to Robert Redford, and we were making a movie. Did somebody say something about socially relevant theater? I don't think so.

I also enjoyed being one of the few women on the set. In those days, there were absolutely no women on the crew, and this was a male heist movie, and the only female actresses were Tope Swope and Charlotte Rae, who were there only very briefly. The rest of the time it was Peter, Robert, George, Zero, Ron Leibman, Paul Sand, Moses Gunn, William Redfield, the all-male crew, and me. I guess you could say I was completely seduced by it. Okay, I was spoiled rotten—but I worked hard. And I loved the hard work. I'd get out of bed every morning looking forward to the day ahead.

After the shoot, Peter asked me if I'd continue working with him, and for the next couple of years, he was my boss. I worked with him on *The Friends of Eddie Coyle*, starring Robert Mitchum, which we shot in Boston, and on *For Pete's Sake*, with Barbra Streisand, which we shot in L.A.

I became very close to Peter and his family, whom I am friendly with to this day. They had a big, rambling apartment in New York, on Park Avenue, and whenever they left town they asked to me to stay there. I felt like a princess. They also had a very posh rental in East Hampton, on Lilly Pond Road, and one summer they went off to Europe and told me it was mine. I was in heaven. I felt like the luckiest girl in the world. I had a great boss, a great job, and I loved my life.

After that summer in the Hamptons, things changed. Peter was supposed to direct *Three Days of the Condor*, but for reasons that remain unclear, he was replaced by Sydney Pollack. Peter was suddenly without a movie, and he had to let me go. I started thinking about theater again, and about changing the world, and one afternoon I came across a small ad in *Variety* about New Line Cinema, an up-and-coming distribution company. They mentioned the hip young owner, Bob Shaye, and they named some of the cutting edge directors he was introducing to American audiences, people like Werner Herzog and Lina Wertmüller.

I called for an interview, and I went in and met with Bob and told him about my experience with Peter Yates. When Bob said he was interested in getting into production, I made it sound like I knew absolutely everything there was to know about production. I was lying through my teeth, of course; I knew a little something about making movies, but nowhere near as much as I pretended to know. I also tossed around the names of Redford and Mitchum and Streisand, my close personal friends, and I ended up getting the job.

At that time, 1975, New Line consisted of about ten people. They had only been in business for a few years and their focus was on acquisitions. My main job was to scout the world for films for the company to acquire, and to organize publicity for the films we actually managed to acquire. I was supposed to handle everything from the trailers and the radio spots—we couldn't afford television in those days—to the posters and the press releases.

Before I even acquired my first film, however, during my very first month on the job, Bob called me into the office and handed me a 16-millimeter film. "Here," he said. "Take a look at this. I need you to handle all the advertising and publicity for me."

I looked at the movie and couldn't believe my eyes. It starred a 300-pound transvestite named Divine, and it had a somewhat difficult title: *Female Trouble*. At that moment, I realized that everything I had learned from Peter Yates—big budgets, the union, Hollywood—was completely useless to me. This was a new world. This was a nonunion, nonbudget world, a world without trailers or nice lunches or expense accounts. If Peter Yates represented the Hollywood Establishment, Bob Shaye was the rebellious outsider who lived on the distant fringes.

Right after watching *Female Trouble*, I met the director, John Waters. We clicked immediately and have been friends ever since.

I ran around for several weeks, prepping the movie for release, and I thought it would be nice to have Divine arrive at the theater in a limousine. I remembered that Peter Yates' agent, the legendary Sam Cohn, had his own personal limo, and that his driver was a very nice guy. I took a chance and called him, and asked if I could hire him for a few hours on the night of the premiere. He checked his date book and said it sounded fine; it didn't look like Sam would be needing him that night.

On the appointed evening, there was a terrible snowstorm. But we got through it in the limo, in high style. The premiere was a huge success, and when it was over we filed out to make the trip to the party. To my horror, the limo was gone. It turned out that Sam Cohn had needed his driver after all, and he'd been called away in the middle of the screening. I had to run out into the street, in a blinding snowstorm, to find cabs for my director and my stars. I was a long way from *The Hot Rock*.

I spent that first year at New Line focusing on acquisitions. We were buying pretty interesting movies in those days, films like *Get Out Your Handkerchiefs*, and I really enjoyed working with these assorted *auteurs*. But then Bob decided we should try to make a movie of our own, and we raised enough money to produce *Stunts*. It was about a stuntman who dies while making a movie, and we made it for less than a million dollars. It had a limited theatrical release, but it was subsequently purchased by NBC—so we made a decent profit. I was credited as associate producer. It was my first credit.

Suddenly, we were filmmakers.

We produced a string of John Waters movies—*Polyester, Desperate Living*, and, later, *Hairspray*—and we got into the low-budget horror business. Then in 1982, Bob found a script that was destined to change the company's fortunes. It was called *A Nightmare on Elm Street*, and it was written by Wes Craven. We knew it was something special. Wes was very smart and clearly very talented, and he was also the consummate professional. We knew he was going to make a name for himself as a director, and we wanted to be part of it.

We spent a year developing the script, and trying to get financing, but it was harder than we'd imagined. Finally, Bob put himself and the company on the line, and in a matter of weeks, we had the budget covered. I thought Bob had behaved with incredible courage, but he said he believed in the script and he believed in Wes and that he knew it was worth the gamble.

Things were going along perfectly, but a few days before we were to start shooting, on location in Los Angeles, some of the money fell out. Bob sent me to L.A. to break the news to the crew. I was six months pregnant at the time, and I showed up at the read-through, and I had to tell the entire cast and crew that we weren't going to be able to pay them at the end of the first week. I asked them to please stick with us, to have faith, and I promised them that we would make good on the money.

How could they turn me down—a very pregnant woman? We didn't lose a single member of the crew.

The second week, we still couldn't pay them, and John Burrows, the production manager, pledged his own salary to keep the film going.

The film got made and spawned half-a-dozen sequels (and, yes, everyone eventually got paid). New Line still wasn't part of the Hollywood Establishment, but it was no longer on the fringes. Shortly after *Nightmare* was released, we signed a deal with RCA Columbia Home Video. We made a film called *Critters*, with Stephen Herek, another gifted director, and it also did very well. And then we made *A Nightmare on Elm Street, Part 2: Freddy's Revenge*, with director Jack Sholder.

At this point, having spent so much time in Los Angeles, I managed to convince Bob that we needed a presence there. I moved out in 1987, with my son, Nic, who was three at the time, and I have been in L.A. ever since.

New Line Cinema went on to make film history. It was bought by Turner Pictures, and suddenly we had a huge influx of money. As president of production, I worked on about forty films, including the *House Party* series, *Pump up the Volume*, *Book of Love*, *Wide Sargasso Sea*, *Surf Ninjas*, *Menance II Society*, *Blink*, the *Teenage Mutant Ninja Turtles* franchise, and, of course, three *Nightmare* sequels.

In 1994, the company was bought out by Time Warner, which later merged with AOL. Sweeping changes followed. I was given a production deal and went on to launch a company of my own, ChickFlicks. Last year, we released *Raise Your Voice*, with Hilary Duff, and *Murder Without Conviction*, a Hallmark television movie. We have two features in the pipeline. *The Harder They Come*, and *Bad Hair Day*, along with half a dozen other film and television projects in various stages of development.

I love movies, and I think there are two ways to break into the business. One, take that assistant job and work hard and don't complain. And two, don't ever think you're too good for a job.

When I became Peter Yates' assistant, I thought I was very lucky, and I believed I was truly on my way. But when that job fell apart, I didn't think twice about taking a much less glamorous job with a company that was just finding its way. Keep your eyes open. Look for opportunities. Take intelligent risks.

And another thing: Be nice. It's true what they say about meeting the same people on the way down as you did on the way up. I know this from experience. One of the financiers on *Raise Your Voice* used to hang pictures in my office. That's how he got his start. I'm glad I was nice to him.

TODD ROBINSON

WRITER/DIRECTOR

"The one component that connects all successful people, here and elsewhere, in any endeavor, is that none of them ever quit."

Todd Robinson has been an actor, a documentary filmmaker, and a writer, and recently landed his first major directing project, *Lonely Hearts*, starring John Travolta, James Gandolfini, Jared Leto, and Salma Hayek. The film is slated for release this year.

His writing credits include *White Squall*, directed by Ridley Scott, two TV movies—*The Four Diamonds*, with Christine Lahti, and *Mermaid*, with Ellen Burstyn—and dozens of episodes of series television, as well as several pilots. His documentaries include *The Legend of Billy the Kid*, for which he won an Emmy, as well as two Academy Award finalists: *Wild Bill: Hollywood Maverick*, about filmmaker William Wellman, which made its debut at Sundance, and *Amargosa*, about a Death Valley artist and recluse.

At the time of the interview, which took place in Los Angeles on June 14, 2005, Robinson was in postproduction on *Lonely Hearts*.

I was born in Philadelphia and raised in Media, Pennsylvania, a suburb. My father was and still is an architect, very prolific, and he studied with some of the great men in his field; my mother studied music in college, then went on to get a master's in counseling and became the dean of a local college. We had a pretty traditional upbringing. My mother would turn to my younger sister and me and say, "Go out and play and be back for dinner by six." And that's what we did. We'd go to the woods or to the creek or ride our bikes all day. It was a very Beaver Cleaver childhood.

I was never a great student—I was dyslexic, and probably had ADD—and early on I turned my attention to music. I hoped to go to the Berkeley School of Music, in Boston, but I met a girl in the theater department at my high school and took a drama class that changed my life. I became completely absorbed in theater, and I went on to get a fine arts degree in drama from the theater conservatory at Adelphi University in New York. I was on my way to becoming a classically trained repertory actor.

In the summer of 1981, a friend asked me to drive with her from Chicago to Los Angeles, and I jumped at the chance because I knew we'd be going through Denver. I had been there once before, and had visited the Denver Center Theater Company, and the facility was so beautiful that I told myself I would go back and work there some day. So I cold-called about auditioning, figured out the dates, and off we went.

When we arrived in Denver, I went to my audition, and to my surprise was cast in a big production of *How to Succeed in Business Without Really Trying*. It was my first professional job, and I got my equity card.

The following summer I went to work at The Troupe Repertory Theater, in Colorado Springs. They worked us like dogs for a couple of hundred dollars a week: three months, six shows a week. And on the seventh day we rehearsed for the next show.

When we finally got a day off, I went to this little college movie theater in town and sat down to watch a double bill. I had never heard of either of the films. One was called *The Duelist*; the other was *Days of Heaven*. I went in and watched these two movies, back to back, and I walked out in a daze. That was an absolutely seminal moment in my life: I hadn't realized that movies could be so deeply moving and so stunningly beautiful, and I said to myself, "That's what I want to do with my life. I want to make movies." I didn't know exactly how or what I wanted to do in movies, I just knew I belonged there.

For a time, I continued to support myself as an actor. Over the years, I did plays wherever I could get work, mostly in regional summer stock and Off-Broadway. I was a pretty good dancer, too, and I auditioned for a zillion Broadway musicals. It was tough, but I managed to make a living.

Finally, in 1984, I decided to move to Los Angeles. I thought I would try my luck in movies and television. I managed to get a little work, as a day-player on the occasional soap, and in a commercial from time to time, but it was never enough to pay the bills, so I had regular jobs, too. I worked as a waiter at lots of different restaurants, and I was fired from every one of them. I was incapable of being a waiter. If you ever had me as a waiter, you'd remember.

I was still acting, of course, and I found myself working on the Pulitzer Prize–winning play *Streamers*, by David Rabe, which was being produced by Elizabeth Ramsland, the woman who would later become my wife. At the time, she was an assistant to Jim Crabbe, a literary agent at the William Morris Agency. I didn't even know what a literary agent was, but I told her I had an idea for a movie, and I guess I pitched it to her, not really knowing I was pitching, and she said, "That's pretty good. You should write that down." That got me started on what would eventually become *The Legend of Billy the Kid*.

Then one day I scored a great day job. I had a buddy from an acting class who was working as a glamorized janitor at a building in Santa Monica, part of the UCLA Extension program. He helped instructors collect projects from the students at the end of the day, and when that was done he'd pick up a mop and clean the place and lock up. He got a part in a movie—an awful movie, by the way—but he was convinced he was on the verge of breaking out, so he let me have his job. It only paid six bucks an hour, but it was perfect. While I was waiting for the students to get done, I'd sit there and teach myself to write. It was my own little UCLA scholarship program. Still, given my dyslexia, I suppose it's sort of ironic that I became a writer. But I instinctively knew that the way you use words was far more important than how you spelled them, and my limitations never got in my way.

So I began to write, and I realized that while I was writing I was completely at the cause of my life, by which I mean I was in control of it. I'm compulsive, and as driven as anyone you'll ever meet, and every day I would get up and make it happen for myself. I could do what I was doing and no-body could stop me, and at the end of the day, I could look at something I'd written and say, "I did something today." It gave me a sense of accomplish-ment and empowerment.

Acting, on the other hand, had always been elusive for me. I was always waiting for permission to do what I wanted to do. I needed someone to give me the opportunity to act, and, when the opportunity came along, I was looking for their approval. But with writing you are actually building some-thing. You have control. The moment I became aware of that, I fell in love with it and never thought much about acting again.

The other thing that struck me about writing is that no one has a job without a good script. And I thought, *If I can learn how to create a script, and if I can get really good at it, I will control my own destiny.*

The very first thing I wanted to write was a story about the Lincoln County War, which is essentially the story of William H. Bonney, better known as Billy the Kid—the very story I had pitched to Liz, my wife. I had become obsessed with the story as an actor, because it is truly operatic, and Liz thought that as part of my research we should visit Lincoln, New Mex-ico, scene of the Lincoln County War.

So we went. And you have to understand: There's really not much there; the town has a population of about forty people. And we're walking down the street and I see a good-looking guy with long hair walking the other way and my wife sees him and says, "John?"

It turned out it was John Fusco, a screenwriter. And she introduced me and asked him what he was doing there, and John said: "I'm writing a movie for Tri-Star about Billy the Kid and the Lincoln County War."

And of course I'm dying inside. I thought I *owned* the subject. But here's John, an established and hugely talented writer, working on the exact same project. I was very upset. I figured my project was finished. I couldn't believe this was happening to me. But after we parted company, Liz said: "Don't worry. I have an idea."

When we got home, she put me in touch with Frank Q. Dobbs, this big, honking Burl Ives of a guy who had been a combat photographer in Viet-nam and who was working as a cameraman and director. I told Frank what had happened—basically, that someone had beaten me to the idea—and he suggested we make a documentary about the subject, and that we consider using Fusco's movie as a component of our documentary. So we began. Frank became a true mentor to me and really showed me how to make a film. But I still had to make a living.

Then I remembered this story I'd been carrying around inside me, a story my friend Stacia Millard had once told me about her older brother, Chris Millard, who had struggled with childhood cancer. He had gone back to school one fall after a very traumatizing summer of chemotherapy, and the very first class assignment was a familiar essay: *What I Did on My Summer Vacation.* And Chris went to his teacher and said, "I can't write that. I was sick all summer." So the teacher said, "Okay, then. Write whatever you want."

And he wrote a short story called "The Four Diamonds," about a young squire who goes out to become a knight and is captured by the subject of his quest, an evil sorceress. And his teacher came across the story only much later, months after Chris had passed away, and she took it to his parents and urged them to read it. And she said, "This story is the story of Chris's battle with cancer. Charles the Mysterious is you, his father. The Evil Sorceress represents his disease. And facing the Black Knight is facing death." And she was right. When you read the story, you realize that Chris was preparing his family for his death, which at that point he knew was inevitable.

In any event, it was a gut-wrenching story. And through my wife I set up a couple of meetings and went out and pitched the story at a bunch of places. Disney bought it for television, and I sat down and wrote the script. The movie aired in 1995 and starred Christine Lahti, Kevin Dunn, and Tom Guiry. It was pretty amazing. Within a year of committing myself to becoming a writer, I was actually making a living at it.

After that, I got several jobs in television. I wrote for a series called *The Outsiders*, based on the S. E. Hinton novel, and for another one called *The Young Riders*. And with the money I was making, I was able to keep working on my Billy the Kid documentary.

The idea had been that I was going to write and produce the documentary, but by the time we were finished Frank turned to me and said, "Hey, you directed this. All I did was point the camera." I couldn't believe he was being so gracious. But I was delighted, and we finished the film and actually sold it on spec, which is next to impossible—though I didn't know that at the time. I ended up winning an Emmy for it, but the Emmy belongs as much to Frank as it does to me.

I now realized I wanted to be a director, which is pretty tough, especially if all you have to show for yourself is a documentary. So I kept writing, looking for an opportunity, and then I got a job directing for *America's Most Wanted*. The way it worked was that they gave you a hundred thousand dollars and told you to make a story in twenty minutes. And it was very exciting: You had a camera in your hand, and you figured it out as you went along.

My work was well received but it didn't immediately lead to any other directing assignments. So I kept writing and sold a few scripts that never got made. And I kept making documentaries, because I'd had such good luck with the first one, and because I loved them. I made one about William Wellman, the maverick Hollywood filmmaker, which premiered at Sundance. Robert Redford actually introduced that film himself. He had known Wellman in his youth, so I guess he felt a personal connection to it.

Then I sold a script called *White Squall*, and Ridley Scott became attached as the director. He knew I was interested in directing, and he told me that it was crucial I continue to learn about the camera. A director should know how to operate, compose, and move the camera himself, he told me. Ridley had started in art school, drawing, and had made his way into commercials through the art department. And while he was making commercials, he learned all about the camera. Ridley was another real mentor to me.

I did another documentary, *Amargosa*, about Marta Becket, a reclusive woman in Death Valley who was a dancer and a painter. And that and *Wild Bill: Hollywood Maverick* both ended up on the short list for Academy Awards. I only bring that up because a lot of people think awards ceremonies are purely self-serving. They aren't. For a young filmmaker, that kind of recognition gives you the confidence to keep going. You realize, *I'm not crazy. I really should be doing this. I'll keep going.*

And of course I kept writing, honing my craft. Story is very much about structure. And I had learned a great deal about structure by working on documentaries. They forced me to examine the narrative from a subconscious, intuitive place, without a script. At the same time, I was learning to make the stories fit into the three-act structure I'd been learning as a writer.

I ended up writing *Lonely Hearts*, the feature film I just finished directing. It is based on a true story about the so-called "Lonely Hearts Killers," who lured their victims through the personals, and it focuses on the two detectives who eventually tracked them down. The script had a personal component in that my grandfather, a detective in Nassau County, New York, at the time of the murders, actually helped the two principal detectives track the killers.

In any event, I had written the script with the intention of directing it myself, but I didn't have a real track record as a Hollywood director, and the script pretty much languished for four years. Then I was introduced to Holly Wiersma, a producer who is a genuine force of nature. She read the script and became instantly committed. And she actually had a plan. I've been in hundreds of meetings with hundreds of producers and executives over the years, and most of the time no one has a plan. But Holly had a strategy, and it was this: She was going to introduce me to all of the covering agents at the big agencies, and they in turn would introduce me to their "newer" clients, and these clients were going to feel as if their agents were really working for them. I love actors, so sitting with them was always a pleasure, and this in turn was good for the agents, who got positive feedback about me, then went on to introduce me to some of their bigger clients—the ones who might actually help me get the movie made.

Another thing Holly did was to tell me to have my meetings at the Chateau Marmont. "It's a very incestuous business," she said. "You have to be out in the open, where people will see you and talk about you and who they saw you with."

I didn't even know where the Chateau Marmont was, but it definitely was *not* my style. Still, I took her advice and started meeting people up at the Chateau, a very trendy Hollywood hotel. And she was right. Before long, people I had never met were calling their agents saying they wanted to meet me. And suddenly I was having meetings with guys like Ray Liotta, Matt Dillon, and Ed Burns. And while I was sitting there, at the Chateau, other actors would come by and say, "Hey, Todd, what's going on with the project?" It seemed like the whole town suddenly knew about me and my movie, and it was all because Holly knew what she was doing.

In the course of a year, I met with more than 400 actors. It wasn't about coming in and reading a line, but about listening to their stories. They would sit down and tell me about themselves, and I would listen, because I'm a fairly social guy and I was genuinely interested. And these people became fans.

Eventually, the agencies heard good things about me, and they realized that they could put me in a room with their best clients, and that I wouldn't embarrass them. And one day, a William Morris agent called Cassian Elwes convinced another William Morris agent, Fred Westheimer, to put me in a room with one of his star clients, John Travolta. And the funny thing was, Westheimer had heard about me through James Gandolfini, who was one of the 400 actors I had met with, and who had really responded to the material. Westheimer read the script and got it to John's producers, who read it and recommended it to John, who agreed to meet with me.

Finally, in September, 2004, I flew to Maine to meet with John. I had to drive to this hotel that was about seventy miles south of Bangor, in the middle of the night, in this incredible fog, and I thought I was going to die on that road. The thing about John is, he's a night owl, and he had scheduled the meeting for midnight. He liked to work out of this hotel because he has a home nearby, on one of the islands. And while I tend *not* to get nervous around people, this was different. I knew that if John committed to the film, I was going to be directing a pretty big movie, so I was a little anxious. And the harrowing drive hadn't helped. I'd also seen John's Boeing 707 sitting on the ramp at the airport, and that reinforced the idea that this was The Big Time, one of those moments that could change the course of my life.

Anyway, I got to the hotel and I met John in the bar. He was very nice, but intense and clearly very serious about his choices—and he wanted to make sure I was serious, too. He said he dug the script, and he seemed to like me, but then he had a question. "How are you on the set?" he asked. "Are you a yeller? Are you passive-aggressive? How do you deal with people on the set?"

I thought that was a great question, and it just so happened I had an answer—in a manner of speaking. "Let me ask you something," I said. "Can you guarantee that a film will be a success?"

"No," he said.

"Well, neither can I," I said. "So once you get past the money, what's left?"

"I don't know," he said. "Why don't you tell me?"

"The experience of doing it," I said. "You can make a great movie, and it can still fail. So you better have a remarkable experience making it. For me, there are only three reasons for doing anything. The money, the material, and the people. And it's never been about the money for me. I am passionate about this movie because it's a powerful, personal story. When you get past that, making a movie, any movie, is like going to war, and when I go to war, I want to come out like a band of brothers: initiated by the experience, stronger for it, and forever connected by it. After all, a year after you make a film, it's a little plastic disc sitting on a shelf, so it's got to be about more than the result. It's about the process. If the process isn't positive and fun, with great people, what's the point?"

And John looked at me, nodded, and took a beat. "I can't give you an answer at this very moment," he said finally. "But I won't keep you waiting."

As I left, I knew it hadn't been the best meeting of my life, and I didn't know what to think. But two weeks later he was attached, and in March, 2005, we began shooting.

My approach to anything has always been pretty simple: I just keeping butting the door with my head until the door opens.

The other thing is: Don't listen to anyone who is negative.

If you believe in something, don't let anyone take that away from you. After all, when you look at a mustard seed, you can't tell whether it's going to sprout into a dandelion or a redwood. Ideas need to be watered and cared for and nurtured. Most people come from a place of fear because they can't see what you see. So you must learn to communicate your ideas clearly, and visually, so that others are swept up in your passion. In the beginning, however, when the idea is just a germ, it's very fragile. You mustn't listen to anyone: You have to live in denial until it takes root and is strong enough to stand up to criticism.

There is a chronic shortage of good material in Hollywood, today more than ever. If you don't believe me, go to your local multiplex and try to find a movie worth watching. So what I'm saying is: If you do good work, if you refuse to take no for an answer, your dreams will be realized, recognized, and celebrated.

Still, Hollywood isn't for sissies. It's a very tough town. It's a rough business. If you want to make a lot of money, I'm sure there are easier ways to do it. But the one component that connects all successful people, here and elsewhere, in any endeavor, is that none of them ever quit. That doesn't guarantee success, of course, but quitting always guarantees failure. So that's the first thing: You can never quit.

The second thing is: You shouldn't have a parachute. If you have a backup plan, you'll use it. So it's better not to have one—you have to keep swimming to keep from drowning. I deliberately didn't have a backup plan, which basically forced me to keep going.

When I sit down to write a script, it never occurs to me that it won't get made. If I thought it wouldn't get made, I probably wouldn't be able to write it. So you have to believe, even if—as I said earlier—that means living in denial for a time. And you have to keep at it. If you're serious about writing, you have to get up and write every day. Even if nothing comes, you have to sit in front of that blank screen and focus, because something is happening, even if it doesn't seem like it is. It is a mysterious, often unconscious process. Also, remember to give yourself a break from time to time. Deadlines are imperative but ultimatums are death. A career isn't one script or one movie. It's a lifetime of work. That is how you will be judged.

Nothing is going to stop you from succeeding except yourself. I really believe that. And remember: It's your failures that make you stronger, not your successes.

So go do it. Be true to your sensibilities and to your point of view. That's what makes you unique. That's what will separate you from the pack. And *never* give up.

MARK ROSMAN

WRITER/DIRECTOR

"In Hollywood, you can be loved to death. Try not to let it get you down."

Mark Rosman broke into the business in 1982, and over the course of the next two decades had to break back in *four more times*. The son of a Beverly Hills dermatologist, Rosman lived in the center of the action, but he didn't know a soul in the business. He ended up going to film school in New York City, then came home, wrote a script, and actually raised the money to make the movie himself.

That low-budget movie, *The House on Sorority Row*, actually launched his career, but it wasn't exactly the career he'd envisioned. The only thing that got him through the low points was his self-described addiction to the crazy business of making movies.

Rosman's credits run the gamut from low-budget genre movies (*The Invader*, *Evolver*), to television series (*Even Stevens*, *Lizzie McGuire*), and television movies (*The Blue Yonder*, *Life-Size*), to mainstream features (*A Cinderella Story*, *The Perfect Man*).

He was interviewed in Los Angeles on May 19, 2005.

I was born and raised in Beverly Hills, and I've wanted to be part of the film industry ever since I can remember. Kids used to dream about running away with the circus; I used to fantasize about stowing away on a grip truck, riding

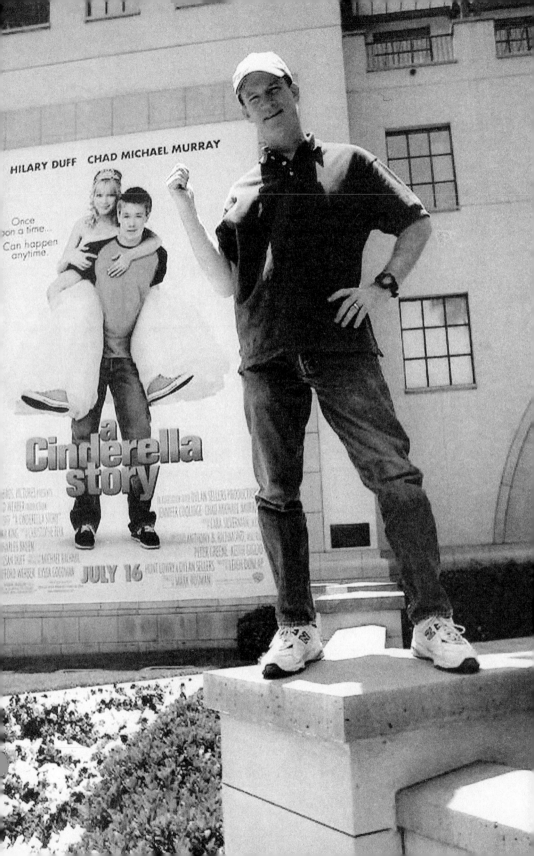

it back to the studio, and only emerging after hours, when everyone had gone home for the night. I figured I could live in the studio for the rest of my life.

The odd thing is that nobody in my family was in the film business. My father is a dermatologist, my brother is a lawyer, and my sister married a lawyer. But I loved the whole idea of movies right from the start. If there was a crew filming a movie down the street, I was the kid who would stand there and watch them all day long and forget to eat.

By the time I got to Beverly Hills High School, I knew I was going to make movies. I had already managed to get through my junior high years without turning in any written reports. Instead, I prepared slide-shows and progressed to Super 8. By the time I was in high school, I was churning out little 16-millimeter movies with sound. I realize I'm dating myself here, but this was in the pre-Handycam days.

I also made use of the school's rudimentary, two-camera, black-and-white television studio. I would book time and bring in some students from the theater department and run my own version of Playhouse 90. I remember taping *The Zoo Story*, the Edward Albee play, and screening it for the class. I later got my hands on the school's 16-millimeter camera and filmed a Ray Bradbury short story. I actually sent it to Mr. Bradbury, who wrote back to let me know how much he'd enjoyed it.

After high school, I went to UCLA, but you couldn't major in film until your junior year, so I spent my first two years fulfilling my liberal arts requirements, and at the end of my sophomore year excitedly applied to be a film major. To my shock and amazement, the film school turned me down. It was my first big rejection in the film business, and I was devastated. They told me that the criteria had changed: They were looking for people who weren't quite so focused on film, and they weren't actually watching the submitted films because that gave an unfair advantage to those students who could afford to make them. None of it made any sense to me.

I could have gone to USC, but I didn't want to live downtown and I didn't feel like commuting, so I applied to New York University. I sent them my opus—an original, 16-millimeter, thirty-minute, black-and-white, *Twilight Zone*–style thriller—and in short order they wrote back to tell me I'd been accepted in the film program.

My parents were very supportive, but they were also very worried. I was the youngest of three kids, and they knew how much I wanted this, but they thought I might be going about it the wrong way. At one point, my father had suggested that I become a lawyer, go to work for a studio, take over the studio, then hire myself to direct a movie. I wasn't sure I liked that idea. I thought it would take about thirty years to get there, and I didn't want to wait that long. And who knew if I'd even hire myself at that point?

Going to New York was a real eye-opener for me. I'd lived in Beverly Hills my whole life, in this safe, suburban cocoon, and New York was the epitome of urban living. I loved it. For the next two years, my whole existence was about film, big city life, and genuine Italian cannolis, and—for reasons I can't really explain—I felt very much in my element.

During my senior year, I was dating a girl from Sarah Lawrence College, in Bronxville, New York. She told me that director Brian De Palma was going to make a feature film with students from their film department, and she urged me to sit in on the class. On that very first day, as De Palma started handing out crew positions, I quickly volunteered to be his first assistant director. We ended up making *Home Movies* for about $350,000 and it had some real stars in it: Kirk Douglas, Nancy Allen, Vincent Gardenia, and Keith Gordon (now a director himself). I remember walking down the corridor with Kirk Douglas one day, and he was talking to me, and my walkie-talkie squawked. And just as I reached for it, he snapped, "Never look away from the star!" I've taken those wise words to heart.

Anyway, I learned a lot from that movie. It was like going to the best graduate school in the world. One day, during the shoot, waiting for the trucks to show up, I asked Brian for advice on getting my first feature off the ground, and he said, "Don't tell people you're going to make a movie. Just start doing it. Finish the script. Raise the money. Pick a start date. Get going. Tell them you're *making* a movie."

When I came back to L.A., I had to move in with my parents, due to lack of funds, but I took De Palma's advice to heart. I sat down and wrote a script, which was no easy feat. I never thought of myself as a writer. I'd grown up watching television, and I wasn't much of a reader. Plus in film school I hadn't taken any of the writing classes. But now I was forced to write something, and I went out and bought two books I thought might be helpful. The first was *Screenplay*, by Syd Field. It was a step-by-step guide to screenwriting. It explained everything you needed to know about structure and plot points and character development and even screenplay format. It was very useful. The other book was by Lajos Egri. It was called *The Art of Dramatic Writing*, and it was extremely helpful in terms of getting into the heads of my characters.

The result was a script called *The House on Sorority Row*. It was a horror movie, more or less. There had been a resurgence of films like *Halloween* and *Friday the 13th* and I thought I should try to break into that market, although I was actually more interested in suspense and Hitchcock-style thrillers. The thing is, I was convinced I could make this movie. I'd been making movies ever since I was a kid, and I had film school behind me, not to mention those months with De Palma, so I was feeling pretty confident. Film school had been particularly valuable, since everything I did was critiqued by the teachers and my fellow students. If there's a better way to learn, I'm not aware of it. I still remember my favorite teacher, who was also my toughest. He taught me never to be satisfied. My best pal and I would come in with a cut that we thought was an absolute masterpiece, and he'd take one look and say, "That's a good first cut, guys. Now go back and make it work."

In my heart, I knew that shooting the film wasn't going to be a problem. It was the script I was worried about. I wanted feedback, so I showed the first draft to a number of people to get their reaction, and I listened without letting my personal feelings get in the way. "It's boring." "I know who the killer is right away." "It's not scary enough." I took their comments to heart and went back and did several more drafts, doing my best to get it right.

That was a very valuable early experience for me, by the way. If you're a writer, try to get your script to people you admire, people who have experience reading scripts, and people whose opinions you respect. (In other words, *not* your family!) Even if you don't like what they have to say, it will make your script a better script.

Four drafts later, I went out and knocked on doors and raised the money to make it. "I'm *making* a movie," I told people. "Would you like to invest?"

In the meantime, I also tried to get an agent. I called the Writers Guild and they were kind enough to give me a list of agents, but most of them didn't accept unsolicited material, and none of them were really interested anyway. When I told them I was in the process of raising money to make my movie, they were very supportive, in their own way. "Come back when you've got it financed," they said.

It was dispiriting, but in fact it was also helpful. It forced me to go out there and really fight. I went to everyone I knew and to everyone those people knew. I told them I was making a low-budget movie, and I gave them a "package" that included a copy of the script, the proposed budget, articles about the success of recent horror films, and even a letter from legendary director Jack Arnold, who assured them that he'd step in and take over if I messed up. And guess what? I didn't raise a dime. The only money I raised came from family members, and that was only $75,000.

Luckily, however, I had sent the package to a guy I'd known in high school. He was working for a small company in Washington, D.C., making industrial films, but they were eager to get into the film business. They read the script and liked it and almost immediately gave me $50,000, with a promise to complete the movie if it went over budget.

I began casting right away. I put ads in the trades and hundreds of sorority-type girls turned out to audition. It was a dirty job, but somebody had to do it. I signed Harley Jane Kozak and Kate McNeil and Eileen Davidson, and we went off to shoot the movie in a small town just outside Baltimore.

The shoot went fairly well, but when I got back to L.A. and looked at the first cut, I realized I'd made a horror movie that wasn't particularly bloody. All of the killings took place in the shadows, or off-camera, sort of like a Hitchcock film, and I knew audiences would be screaming for blood and gore.

I ended up doing reshoots in my parents' backyard. In one night, I staged six grisly killings that I later inserted into the film. The day after the shoot, I was sitting in my room, working on the film, when I heard a *genuine* scream from the backyard. My mother had her charity ladies over for tea, and one of them had found a finger in the grass. I had to run out and explain that it was a rubber finger, a prop I'd used in my movie. My mother's friends never again looked at me in quite the same way.

Anyway, I ran out of money before I finished the film, so I packed up the picture and the sound reels and got into my car and made the rounds of every distribution company in town, from the largest to the smallest. MGM was interested for about two seconds, long enough to give me false hope, but after their interest waned I found myself in discussions with a small company called Film Ventures. The company was famous for a movie called *Great White*, which never got released. It was a complete rip-off of *Jaws* and Universal got an injunction against the company and managed to halt its release. I still remember sitting in the office of the president, which was full of little shark-shaped balloons—part of an advertising campaign that never happened.

But they liked my movie, and that's all that mattered, and they scraped together the money I needed to finish it. *The House on Sorority Row* was the last film they ever released. It opened at the El Capitan theater, on Hollywood Boulevard, and at The Crest, in Westwood. I rented a limousine and took a group of friends from one theater to the other, listening to audience reaction and eavesdropping on conversations in the men's room. It was the greatest night of my life. Seriously, it was a dream come true. And the film was actually a success. The final budget had come in at around $450,000, and it went on to gross $7 million dollars in U.S. theaters alone.

I never saw a penny. I made nothing and the investors made nothing. It was quite the comedown, but it didn't dampen my enthusiasm for film. As far as I was concerned, the film was a huge success. I even got good reviews in the *Hollywood Reporter* and the *Los Angeles Times*. I got my share of bad reviews, too. I remember one from Baltimore in particular. The reviewer wrote something like, "The ad claims it was shot in Baltimore. That's not the problem. The problem is that it's *playing* in Baltimore."

I didn't have time to think about the bad reviews, though. Film Ventures was so happy with the film that they immediately hired me to direct another movie. It was one of those terrible, low-budget, toxic-waste-turns-people-into-mutants movies, and the experience practically turned *me* into a mutant. I got fired. In the space of six months, I went from the best day of my life to the worst.

On the other hand, I got a lot of high-level meetings as a result of *Sorority Row*. I had fans at Columbia and at Universal and at several other places, and they all said nice things to me and listened to some of my other ideas, but nothing happened. I've since discovered that that is often the case. In Hollywood, you can be loved to death. Try not to let it get you down.

A year later, I got a call from my friend Alan Shapiro, whom I'd met at NYU. He had a producing deal at the Disney Channel and wondered if I had something I could pitch. I thought this was a little bizarre. I had just shot a horror movie, and I was supposed to find something for Disney. At first I couldn't come up with anything, but then I started thinking about my own, personal list of wishes, and I found myself thinking of my grandfather. He was a great amateur photographer, the only person in my entire family with a creative streak, but he died when I was five years old and I never got to know him. All my life I wished I'd had a chance to know him, and I came up with a story that captured that feeling. It was about a ten-year-old boy whose grandfather, an aviator, dies while trying to beat Charles Lindbergh across the Atlantic, and about how the boy goes back in time to get to know his grandfather—and to try to save his life. It was called *The Blue Yonder*. I pitched the idea, the studio bought it, and it actually got made. It starred Peter Coyote, Huckleberry Fox, and Art Carney, and it aired on the Disney Channel in 1985. To this day it is the most heartfelt movie I've ever done.

Michael Eisner and Jeff Katzenberg had just taken over Disney, and they liked the movie so much that they immediately offered me another movie, *Spot Marks the X*. It was about a dog that knows where some criminal's money is buried. They gave me an overall deal at Disney. I couldn't believe it. I was twenty-eight years old, I had an assistant, and I had my own office on Dopey Drive. I had finally made it, right?

Then the Writers Guild went on strike and everything came to a screeching halt. I didn't work again for more than three years. Actually, I should say I didn't get *paid* for more than three years; a real writer always works. I spent the time writing spec scripts, and it wasn't until 1992 that a company bit. It became a thriller called *Evolver*. I then got a directing deal on a no-budget cop movie called *The Force*. It starred Kim Delaney and Jason Gedrick. I thought I was on a roll again, but it wasn't until 1996 that I got another low-budget film, *The Invader*, with Sean Young. Then I found myself back where I had started: trying to break into Hollywood.

By this time, I had a wife, a child, and monthly mortgage payments, so I was looking for financial stability. I decided I'd had enough of features and threw myself into TV.

In 1998, I cowrote a script that became a TV movie for The Wonderful World of Disney. It was called *Life-Size*, and it was about a girl who accidentally brings her doll to life. The girl was played by Lindsay Lohan; Tyra Banks played the doll. I directed the movie, which did well, and that led to another TV movie, *Model Behavior*. But interest in TV movies was rapidly waning, so I got into series work. I was hired on a few shows—*Even Stevens*, *Lizzie McGuire, State of Grace*—but all of them were eventually cancelled and I once again found myself unemployed.

For almost a full year, I couldn't get anything going, but I found myself intrigued by a script someone had sent me, and I started developing it with the writer, Leigh Dunlap. The script had already been turned down by every studio, but we rewrote it and sent it off to Hilary Duff, who had starred in *Lizzy McGuire*. Her mother read it and loved it and suddenly everything clicked. Hilary had just finished shooting *The Lizzie McGuire Movie*, and the buzz was good, and everyone was looking for the next Hilary Duff project. So a script that had been passed on by absolutely everyone in town was suddenly the focus of an intense, three-day bidding war.

When the dust settled, Warner Brothers bought it, promising to make it a "go" picture. It was budgeted at $19 million, and initially there was some resistance to having me direct it. But Hilary and her mom, Susan, went to bat for me, and I got the job.

The movie was called *A Cinderella Story*, and, yes—it features a wicked stepmother. It was released in 2004. Almost as soon as I finished it, I went on to direct *The Perfect Man*, for Universal. That movie also stars Hilary Duff, along with Heather Locklear and Chris Noth. Heather plays a single mother who makes a lot of bad choices, and Hilary plays the daughter who is determined to change everything.

Those movies changed everything for me. I am now a feature director. And, like most feature directors, I am always looking for my next film.

This is real roller-coaster business, and it's not just about breaking in, but about surviving. Breaking in is hard, granted, but staying in equally tough. In most businesses, you work hard and you get something in return.

Well, that's not the way Hollywood operates. Here, you've got to want it every day, fight for it every day, and never lose faith in yourself.

Somebody once said, "Talent plus perseverance equals luck." I would add one short phrase to that equation. "Talent plus perseverance plus *personality* equals luck." In other words, don't be a jerk. I guess if you're supremely talented or your movies gross tons of money, you can afford to be a jerk, and—as if to prove the point—there are many jerks in this business. But if you want to work, it really pays to be a good person. You are not going to do this alone, so first and foremost learn to be a team player, and learn to acknowledge the help of those around you. In Hollywood, it really *does* take a village.

Also, try to remember that passion isn't enough. Passion is important, even critical, but if you're not addicted to movies, you should get out of the business. The movie business is a little like an illness. You keep going and going and going because you really desperately want that next fix. That's a terrible thing if you're a junkie, but in the film business it's almost a prerequisite.

Finally, be open to change. I started out as a thriller writer/director, then found myself writing a heartfelt movie about a young boy and the grandfather he never knew. When I wrote and directed that movie, I learned things about myself that surprised me, and those things changed the course of my career. So be open to new things. You might discover that you're not at all who you think you are, and the result might come as a pleasant surprise you.

In closing, I'll leave you with a favorite Japanese saying: "It's not how many times you fall, it's how many times you get back up."

That's the secret: Just keep getting back up. If you're still standing, you're still in the game.

ROBIN SCHIFF

WRITER/PRODUCER

"Tune in to what you're passionate about and focus on that."

Robin Schiff has been a member of the Writers Guild of America since 1980, and she's not about to quit anytime soon. The child of upper-middle-class professionals, Schiff recalls that her parents made every effort to dissuade her from pursuing a career in the entertainment industry. Luckily, she didn't listen. One failed novel and several screenplays later, she found a niche for herself in television, where she managed to make a nice living without getting much of anything produced.

It was only many years later, when she turned her hand to comedy, that she found her true voice, writing a play that changed the course of her career, and of her life.

Schiff has written feature films and television movies, but her biggest success has been in series television. Her credits include *Working Girl*, *Delta*, *Party of Five*, *Almost Perfect*, *Grosse Pointe*, *Miss Match*, *All About Us*, *The Bad Girls Guide*, and *Romy and Michele: In the Beginning*. At the time of the interview, she was awaiting the debut of yet another series, *Emily's Reasons Why Not*, which she executive produced.

Ms. Schiff was interviewed in Los Angeles on August 24, 2005.

I was born and raised in Brentwood, about three miles from where I live today. My father was an orthodontist and my mom was a mom, and I had a younger brother. My parents were upper-middle-class Jewish professionals, and all of their friends were pretty much like them. We lived in L.A., but we didn't know anyone in the entertainment business.

I was a pretty unhappy child, which was partly my nature and partly the family dynamic. I was a very sensitive kid and I thought my parents were highly critical of me. Nobody was an alcoholic, or physically abusive, but emotionally it was really tough. I didn't feel it was okay to be myself.

I started spending a lot of time reading and writing, and by the time I was eight, I was fantasizing about being a famous author and seeing my first novel prominently displayed in bookstore windows. I also fantasized about being on *The Today Show*, where much was being made of the fact that I was the youngest author in history (or at least in the history of *The Today Show*).

There was a rule in our house that we could only watch one hour of television on weeknights, and that we had to be in our rooms by 8:00 p.m. But there was no rule about what time the lights went out, so I could read all night if I wanted to, and I read absolutely everything. I liked fantasy—*A Wrinkle in Time*; *The Phantom Tollbooth*; *Half Magic*. I went through a Gothic phase, too: *Jane Eyre, Wuthering Heights, Rebecca*.

By the time I was about eight or nine, I began writing stories of my own. I had a little typewriter, and I would always write stories that were a version of whatever I happened to be reading at the time. So if, for example, I was in the middle of *Gone With the Wind*, my story would be set in the South and my characters would sound like the characters I was reading about, only they did and said exactly what *I* wanted them to do and say. Unfortunately, if I didn't finish my story by the time I finished my book, I abandoned it, so I abandoned a lot of stories.

I went to Brentwood Elementary, and I had a teacher there, Joyce Sussman, who loved me and loved my writing, and she kept encouraging me to work on my stories. And later, at Paul Revere Junior High School, I had a drama teacher, Mrs. Klenes, who encouraged me to get into acting, and for a while I focused on acting. I always felt transported by acting, and I acted all through junior high and high school. Acting was an escape for me; acting made me feel as if I actually had some control over my life.

After high school, I went to the University of California, Santa Barbara, but I only lasted two quarters, and I eventually returned to Los Angeles and enrolled at UCLA. By that time, I had lost confidence in my acting abilities, and I had pretty much stopped writing, so I decided to study American history. I was actually very interested in literature, but I really didn't like the few English classes I took because I was bored by all of the analysis and symbolism. *The Great Gatsby* is a wonderful book, but they ruin it by tearing it apart. Conversely, I read *Abasolm Absalom!* by William Faulkner, which is *supposed* to be a great book, and all I could think was, "How about some punctuation, pal!"

I also studied French in college. I had taken years of private French classes as a kid, and I had really loved my French teacher, Madame Furino. Compared to the adults I knew, she was a little strange—or at least *exotic*. She introduced me to the idea of astrology long before astrology was fashionable. She also had some black powder on her armoire, and from time to time she would take a pinch from the bottle and spread it all around us. She made the whole world seem a little magical. She was another one of those people who over the years made me feel it was okay to be myself, and maybe even pretty wonderful.

But history is where I ended up, once again because of a great teacher, Dan Howe. He taught intellectual history. We would read a smattering of politics, economics, religious thought, fiction, philosophy and try to understand what it felt like to live in that time and to think like those people. It was interesting, but I didn't know what I was going to do with it: I knew I wasn't going to teach. Meanwhile, my parents kept bugging me to go to law school or business school, but I didn't even want to think about either of those possibilities. I wasn't thinking about show business, either. In my family, show business wasn't a career; it was a hobby.

One of my friends from Pali High, and also from my two quarters at UCSB, was David Hoberman, who went on to become a studio executive and then a very successful producer. When I got out of UCLA, David's father, Ben, who'd run KABC Radio in L.A. for many years, helped me get a job at a media buying service. The job boiled down to buying time from radio and television stations. I hated it. The money was shitty and it was all about numbers and I hated going to an office every day. I would think, *If this is my life, I'll kill myself.*

As I drove to work every day, winding my way through all the wealthy neighborhoods, into Hollywood, I began to wonder how I might work for myself, make lots of money, meet interesting people, be creative and stimulated, and all sorts of other things that were probably pretty naïve (though they eventually came true). And as I started to inventory my abilities, I began to think about writing again. But that's all I did: *think* about it. Then I took one of those EST training courses, the Werner Erhard self-realization thing that was fashionable in those days, and I discovered that, for me, the course could basically be boiled down to what later became the Nike slogan: Just do it. That turned out to be a fairly valuable lesson. People would say, "I can't dance because I don't have the right shoes and the right leotard," but what it boiled down to was whether you were a dancer or not, and—if you were—figuring out how you were going to get out there and make it happen.

As a result, I decided to write a novel. It was based on a member of the staff at Pali High, with whom I'd had an affair. (He was later fired; I wasn't the only student he'd been sleeping with, just his choice that particular year.) I would set my alarm clock for 6:00 a.m. and I would write from six to eight, and then I would go to my horrible job for my measly $200 a week. And every Friday, the guys would send me to the bank to withdraw $1,200 in cash for the weekly cocaine buy. I thought that was kind of rude.

As I was finishing the novel, I went to my parents and said, "I've been working on this book for a year, and I need you to subsidize me for a year so that I can finish it. Think of it as graduate school." My parents were not impressed. I argued that this seemed unfair, since my younger brother was at Harvard Law School and they were paying for that, but they still said no. I was outraged. I thought I had made a good argument, but they didn't see it that way. Neither of my parents thought I could make a living as a writer, and both of them were still hoping I would go back to an actual graduate school. By now, however, I realized that I was not equipped for the "straight world," like working in an office, and I became highly motivated to prove them wrong. My anger at my parents fueled me for many years.

I became obsessed with finding a way to quit my miserable job. One day

I was watching a game show on TV—I've always loved game shows—and I decided to try to get on as a contestant. I waited for the show to end and took down the necessary information, then called for an audition. A few months later, I was actually on the show, and I won $7,500. At the time, my rent was so low that the money felt like it would last me forever, so I quit my job and tried to concentrate on my novel.

By the time I finished, about six months later, my mother was working as a landscape designer, and one of her clients was Lee Rosenberg, a well-known agent. Although she never read the novel, she arranged for me to meet Lee. He read the novel and was sufficiently impressed to take me on as a "pocket client," which meant he'd represent me without officially signing me to the agency.

Rosenberg didn't sell the novel, and he lost interest very quickly, but it took me a long time to figure that out.

At around this time, David Hoberman got me work as a reader for Bobby Roth, a director. People would submit books and screenplays, and I would read them and prepare a written report with my opinions, what the business calls "doing coverage." Through that job, I got some additional work at the Kohner-Levy Agency, also reading scripts. The work wasn't bad, but I was slow and I got paid by the script, so it wasn't very lucrative. On the other hand, the books and scripts were generally so horrible that I began to develop confidence in my own abilities.

After I finished the novel, I gave it to a friend of mine, the daughter of Keenan Wynn, the actor. She read it and thought the dialogue was very good. That encouragement, combined with my belief that I could at the very least write a better script than the scripts I was covering, made me wonder whether I was a screenwriter, not a novelist. At around the same time, I heard from a girl I'd gone to high school with, Carol. She wanted to write, too, and we decided to write a screenplay together. We came up with a terrible idea, something about an old woman in an old-age home and a little boy who helps her break out and God knows what else. It was horrible, but Carol knew a few people in the business and began to send the script around to various studios and agencies. She couldn't deal with rejection, however, so she put my return address on the envelopes, and I'm the one who got all the rejections. The script went nowhere.

Then I got an idea for a screenplay and decided I should try to write it on my own. I got to work on a story about a woman who always finds herself in bad relationships, and whose best friend is a guy she only sees platonically. Then one day she meets a man who seems like he might be the one, and they get engaged, straining the platonic relationship—and forcing the guy to declare his love or lose her forever. I wrote it very quickly, with no outline, and I gave it to Lee Rosenberg, my agent, but I honestly don't know if he ever read it because by this time he had stopped returning my phone calls.

One day, I came home to find yet another rejection on that first script. It was from the Creative Artists Agency, and it was accompanied by a cover letter: "We're not interested in the script, but are you the Robin Schiff I went to Pali High with?" The letter was signed by Cheryl Peterson, whom I'd grown up with and gone to school with, but who had never been a close friend.

I called Cheryl and told her that, yes, I was the same Robin, and she told me that she was working as a reader at CAA, which was a new agency at the time. We chatted briefly and I said I had written a novel about my affair with one of our teachers at Pali High, whom she of course remembered, and I said I was working on a new, *better* script. She asked me to send her the book and the script, which I did, and she showed them to a full-fledged agent there and he liked them enough to sign me. Not long afterwards, Cheryl herself became an agent, and I became one of her first clients.

I remember trying to call Lee Rosenberg, to tell him I was leaving him. He didn't return my call, so I sent him a note, which was probably unnecessary. I don't think we'd spoken in a year.

That platonic-friend romantic comedy—called *A Portrait of Friends*, an awful title—became my first sale. It was optioned by Henry Jaglom for $2,500, and that fee included several rewrites. Jaglom had just finished directing two movies, *Sitting Ducks* and *A Safe Place*, and I was warned by his own agents that he could be extremely difficult. He was. I had no idea what I had signed on for. He was really all about improvisation and had only been interested in the bare bones of my story. I wrote a draft, per his instructions, and gave it to him, and he rewrote it and gave it back to me with his name on the cover—and my name nowhere in sight. So I took another pass at the script and removed his name and put my name back on the cover. He then wrote me a threatening letter, but we got through it. I must say that now, these many years later, we are on good terms and I admire his work, especially the movie *Deja Vu*.

When that was over, I still wasn't a member of the Writers Guild—that measly option didn't qualify me for membership—so I decided to write another script on spec. It was called *Little White Lies*, and it was about a shampoo girl at a hair salon. The place had lots of wealthy customers and the girl would hear about society parties and crash them, searching for a rich husband. Then she met a runaway boy and that relationship changed her values. It wasn't as bad as it sounds, really. In any case, the script found its way into the hands of Len Hill, an established movie-of-the-week producer, who paid me $10,000 to option it. Suddenly I was a real writer, making the rounds and pitching ideas.

That script got made many years later, on German TV—it had an unpronounceable title: *Friseuse und der Millionäre*—and to this day I haven't seen it. But for the next eight years, I was out there getting jobs and making a living, though nothing ever got produced.

I was so frustrated at working and never getting anything made that I felt like blowing my brains out. Instead, I got involved with The Groundlings, the comedy improv group, and after a while I realized I was a *comedy* writer. During my years there, I wrote a sketch called *The Ladies' Room*, about women in a restroom in a pick-up bar, which I later turned it into a full-length play and sold to HBO. I had hoped to see it produced on *Showcase 86*, one of their series at the time, but it never happened.

Meanwhile, Len Hill took me to NBC to write a TV pilot called *Sorority*, which also didn't get produced, but it led to a job on *Rags to Riches*, a series that starred Joe Bologna as the father of five adopted orphan girls. The network licensed a bunch of classic songs and changed the lyrics to make them relevant to the escapades of the five little scamps. It was a little bizarre.

I was on staff for a year, but it was a very tough time for me. My father was dying, and I went to Cedar's Sinai every day after work to visit him.

I kept working on the show, though, and I continued to obsess about *The Ladies' Room*. I thought my play was really good. I was tired of middle-aged men in story meetings telling me how women thought and felt and talked. I *knew* how they thought and felt and talked, and that's what I had tried to capture in the play, allowing myself to be as honest and as vulgar as I needed to be. I also had come to believe that I was personally more entertaining than anything I had ever written, and in writing the play that's what I'd been attempting to harness.

Finally, after many unsuccessful attempts to raise money for *The Ladies' Room*, Aaron Spelling decided to mount the play himself, thinking he would later try to turn it into a TV series. When the play was produced, it sort of put me on the map, and Romy and Michele, two of the supporting characters, really took off.

After the L.A. production, Spelling took the idea to NBC, as he had planned, and urged them to try to turn Romy and Michele into a sitcom. I wanted to retain the rights to the characters, so I changed their names to Torie and Nicole. The network shot a pilot, starring Lisa Kudrow, whom I had known from The Groundlings, and Christie Mellor, who'd played Romy in my play. The pilot didn't get on the air, and the rights eventually reverted back to me.

After a few more twists and turns—and six more years!—the play was read by two female executives at Touchstone Pictures, which at the time was being run by my old friend, David Hoberman. They wanted to make it as a feature, thinking it could be a female *Wayne's World*, and I came up with the idea of turning it into a high school reunion about two girls who were not all that popular in high school, and who went to their ten-year reunion and lied about all the wonderful things they had accomplished in the decade since. The script was in development forever, and over the years Lisa Kudrow became a huge star on *Friends*. We got the script to her and she committed to the movie, and her star-power got it greenlit. It was released in 1997 as *Romy and Michele's High School Reunion*. The tagline was "The Blonde Leading the Blonde."

I've had one thing or another in production since 1988, and the best advice I can give anyone is to tune in to what you're passionate about and focus on that. There were times in my professional life when I tried to be a people-pleaser and focused on what I thought was best for my career, and those efforts seldom ended well.

I think you should be passionate and honest about whatever you do. You might get your heart broken, but you will rarely regret your role in whatever went on.

LALO SCHIFRIN

COMPOSER

"Study everything. Get to know everything. . . . And practice practice practice."

Born seventy-three years ago in Buenos Aires, Argentina, Lalo Schifrin is a classically trained composer, arranger, and conductor who began playing piano at age five—and hasn't stopped since. When he was nineteen, Mr. Schifrin was offered a scholarship to the prestigious Paris Conservatoire, where he continued to hone his classical skills but found himself falling hopelessly in love with jazz. As soon as he returned to Buenos Aires, he formed a sixteen-piece jazz orchestra, taking the city by storm. One night, Dizzy Gillespie was in the audience, and he was so impressed with Mr. Schifrin that he invited him to join his quintet in New York City.

Schifrin spent five years with Gillespie, as the quintet's musical director, before Hollywood called. In the decades since, he has scored more than a hundred movies, including *The Cincinnati Kid*, *Bullitt*, *Cool Hand Luke*, *Dirty Harry*, and *Enter the Dragon*, as well as the universally recognized theme to *Mission: Impossible*.

Mr. Schifrin is a fan of Latin jazz and bossa nova, and is particularly fond of orchestral jazz. His interest in classical music has never waned, however, and a few years back he was the principal arranger for The Three Tenors.

Still, Mr. Schifrin remains a huge fan of Hollywood, and Hollywood seems to feel the same way about him. Some of his recent films include *Rush Hour*, *Shrek 2*, *The Bridge of San Luis Rey*, *Bringing Down the House*, and of course, the theatrical versions of *Mission: Impossible*.

Mr. Schifrin was interviewed on April 7, 2005, at his Beverly Hills home, in an office he shares with his piano, his innumerable awards, and a vast collection of handmade pipes. His hair is long and white and combed straight back, and he wears large, tinted, aviator-style glasses. He speaks with a slight, Spanish accent.

The man who brought me to this country was Dizzy Gillespie, the famous trumpet player. It was 1956, and he was in Buenos Aires with a U.S. State Department band. One night, Dizzy heard me playing, and after the show he came backstage and asked if I'd be interested in going to the United States and joining his band. I thought he was joking, but he wasn't joking, so I went to the U.S. Embassy and applied for a visa. Two years later, I had my green card.

When I got to New York, Dizzy was waiting for me. I played with him for the next five years.

One day, early on, he said, "Lalo, write something for me." So I wrote something for him—the very first thing I had written in America. When I was done, I went over to his house and played it for him on the piano. He asked me how I was going to orchestrate the work, and I told him that I saw it as a combination of elements: part jazz quintet, part brass, and part Latin percussion.

We recorded it for Verve Records. The album was called *Gillespiana*, and it sold a million records.

The recording company was very pleased, of course. They started giving me more work, and eventually signed me as an artist, composer, and arranger. I worked on many different projects, with many different artists.

At the time, Verve Records was a subsidiary of MGM Records, and in those days MGM was one of the biggest movie studios in Hollywood. Back then, a man named Arnold Maxim was president of MGM Records, and he seemed to like me. Once a month, Arnold went to Hollywood to meet with MGM's Board of Directors, and he suggested they hire me to score a movie.

They finally did, on a movie called *Rhino*. Robert Culp and Harry

Guardino played two adventurers in the heart of Africa, searching for the rare white rhinoceros, which they were hoping to save from extinction. It was a low-budget movie, and—from an ecological point of view—well ahead of its time.

I had to move to Los Angeles to score the film, but I didn't know what the future held so I kept my apartment in New York. I went out and met everyone and watched the rough cut of the film, and then I sat down and wrote the score. It went well. I made a good impression on both the studio and the musicians who worked on the film with me. I think they were surprised I had managed it. I was a composer from South America and I lived in New York, but somehow I had done my first movie score without any major mishaps. And that's how it started for me in Hollywood.

Immediately after *Rhino*, the studio asked me to do another movie, so I stayed for a while in a hotel in Los Angeles and my late wife came out to join me. This next film was a French film, *Les Felins*, starring Jane Fonda, Alain Delon, and Lola Albright. In English, it had a terrible title, *Joyhouse*. They might as well have called it *Whorehouse*.

Before long, I went to France to work on the film. I used a little bit of jazz, some electronics, and a touch of the symphonic. That beat—that mix of styles—became my signature sound; that was the Lalo Schifrin sound.

When I returned home, it looked like I had a new career in Hollywood. So I left my apartment in New York and rented a house in Coldwater Canyon, in Beverly Hills. I knew Stanley Wilson, in the music department at Universal, and he introduced me to Jennings Lang, who was in charge of Universal Television at the time. I did a Movie of the Week for Jennings, and it went well, so he introduced me to Clint Eastwood. Clint had just come back from Italy, where he had done several spaghetti westerns for Sergio Leone, and Jennings was trying to make a feature called *Coogan's Bluff*. He hired Don Siegel to direct the film, and everything clicked: Don, Clint Eastwood, and me. The movie was released in 1968, and I went on to do several more movies with Don, including *Dirty Harry*, which again starred Clint Eastwood.

I had my own musical style, which I guess helped set me apart from other composers. Maybe that was part of the reason I did well. But a lot of it was luck: I was in the right place at the right time.

I also had the benefit of a classical education. I come from a very musical family, and they made sure I got the classical foundations. Then I discovered jazz as a teenager and it was like a religious conversion for me.

When I first went to Paris as a young man, to study at the music conservatory, I dutifully attended all of my classes. But at night I went to the clubs and played jazz with the best jazz musicians around, including many American expatriates. It was an incredible experience, and it was a real luxury. I'd like to stay I was a struggling bohemian, but that wasn't the case. I had a small scholarship, and it was more than enough—more than most of my friends had. And I loved music. It's good to love what you do.

When I first arrived in Hollywood, I had no agent, but I worked hard and met people who gave me good advice. I will never forget what composer Henry Mancini told me. "Don't turn anything down," he said. "Stay late. Work hard. Do your best."

I took his advice to heart. Sometimes I'd be working till three in the morning, to make sure I got the music exactly right, and I had to be back at work before seven that same morning. But I didn't mind. I felt that everything was coming together. The classical training in Buenos Aires, coupled with my love of jazz, was inspiring a whole new sound for me. I felt my compositions were really going somewhere. I should say here that I owe a special debt of gratitude to Dizzy Gillespie. It was Dizzy more than anyone who helped me develop my musical personality. Dizzy was absolutely ruthless when it came to music. He had an incredible ear, and he wouldn't stop working on a composition until he had every note just right.

The movie that really put me on the map? That would have to be *The Cincinnati Kid*, with Steve McQueen. That was another MGM movie. Ray Charles sang the title song, which was a real honor for me.

I can tell you a story about that movie. It was directed by Norman Jewison, edited by Hal Ashby, and produced by Martin Ransohoff. I was in the spotting room—in those days it was all mechanical, film and sprockets, not digital, the way it is today—when the phone rang. It was Marty Ransohoff. He wanted me in his office right away. I went to see him and it turned out that he and Norman Jewison weren't even speaking anymore. Unfortunately, that often happens in the film business. I would have to say that by the time the composer comes on board there's a better than even chance that the marriage between the producer and the director—which usually begins with a nice glass of champagne and lots of friendly toasts—is heading for divorce.

"Kid," Marty said to me, "don't listen to Jewison. I'm in charge here."

It turned out they didn't see eye-to-eye on *anything*. They couldn't even agree on the ending of the movie. So I decided to try to please them both, and I wrote two separate scores. In the end, they used parts of each score, more or less splitting the difference, but I had to do six versions of the final sequence before they were both happy.

Some weeks later, I ran into Henry Mancini and told him about the two scores, and he said, "Lalo, never do that again. You'll spoil them." But when the movie premiered, I was very proud of the result.

Another early movie I remember well was *Charley Varrick*, with Walter Mathau. It was also directed by my friend Don Siegel. The movie opens in a little town in Nevada. It's very peaceful and pleasant, with little children going to school and such, and Don wanted the music to match: He wanted something pastoral, with lots of strings, a bit of Americana—something Aaron Copland might compose. And he had good reason for this approach: As soon as the main titles ended, one of the most violent bank robberies ever put on film was going to explode across the screen. Don said he wanted the violence to be as sudden and as shocking as possible.

I knew Don very well by this time. We had done several movies together, and we had become close friends. One day, when we were recording the opening sequence, Don was in a booth behind me, and I knew he couldn't hear me. I knew exactly when Don's credit appeared on the screen, of course, and I wanted to shock him and surprise him, in much the same way he wanted to shock and surprise his audience. So I told the musicians, "When we get to that third beat, I want you to play the noisiest, craziest, shrillest, loudest music you can manage."

When we got to the third beat, and Don's credit appeared on the screen, they went crazy. Trumpets blared and cymbals crashed and strings cried out. It was complete pandemonium. I have never in my life heard anything so horrible. And Don came running out of the booth, just white, and then saw me and the musicians laughing and realized it was a joke.

"Lalo," he said when he recovered. "You almost gave me a heart attack."

A week later he took me aside and asked me to take the next morning off. He said the engineer was having a little trouble with the third reel, and he wanted the problem solved before I came in.

So I arrived a little after lunch, and as I made my way up the stairs to the dubbing stage, I could hear the main title music, *my* music. I thought something was very wrong. I didn't understand why they were going back to the first reel. And when I walked in, my God! They were playing one of the most horrible porn movies I have ever seen, set to *my* music! I will tell you, I am not a Puritan, but this was really shocking—it even had donkeys—and Don and everyone saw the look of horror on my face and started laughing. That was his revenge. He was paying me back for my little joke.

I love music. And I love movies. I remember when I was a little boy, maybe five years old, I would go the movie theater on Saturdays to watch serials—one film after another, back to back. I especially loved horror movies, but my parents didn't approve, so my grandmother would take me. She didn't approve of horror movies either, but she enjoyed spending the afternoon with me and spoiling me and buying me chocolate.

I got to see all of those wonderful old movies, *Dracula*, *The Mummy*, *Frankenstein*, with all of those great actors, Boris Karloff, Bela Lugosi, Lon Chaney. And I remember paying particularly close attention to the music. And one Monday, at school, I remember bragging to my friends, as usual, that I had seen two horror movies over the weekend. But this time I had something to add: "I bet you anything that without the music it wouldn't have been frightening at all."

I think that that was an important moment for me. I had discovered the power of music at an early age. And from that day on I became a student of film. I would see a movie ten, twelve times, just to study the music. In those days, the composer didn't mean much. You couldn't go to the store and buy a soundtrack the way you can now, unless of course it was a musical or *The Wizard of Oz* or something. If it was a thriller or a suspense film or an action movie, the soundtrack was just background. But I was curious to see how it worked, so I kept seeing the same movies over and over again.

And that's how I learned. I studied. And that's my advice to anyone try-

LALO SCHIFRIN | 361

ing to break into the movie business. Study everything. Get to know every-thing. Watch movies and read scores and pay attention to form.

And practice practice practice. Never stop practicing. That's the only way. Practice hard and find your own way. And develop your own style. Style, *genuine* style, is what sets you apart from the competition.

ROBERT M. SCHWARTZ

ATTORNEY

"Many lawyers use the profession as a stepping stone to something else in the business—they end up running studios or large agencies or producing movies."

Robert Schwartz grew up in Los Angeles, the son of a successful movie producer, but he was urged to explore a career outside of Hollywood. He considered Wall Street, briefly, then opted for law school, and today he is a litigator at O'Melveny & Myers, one of the top law firms in the country.

Schwartz describes Hollywood as a "breeding ground for litigation," and that, of course, is what keeps him busy. Whether it's the big television star holding out for a massive pay increase, studios suing and countersuing for the rights to produce *Spider-Man*, or angry adults battling over the stratospheric profits generated by mega hit films and TV shows (*Batman*, *Friends*, *Lord of the Rings*, to name a few), Schwartz often sees people at their worst. Still, he finds his job as a litigator intellectually rewarding and endlessly challenging.

Schwartz was interviewed on May 26, 2005, in his office overlooking Century City.

I was born in Los Angeles, and I grew up around a lot of kids whose parents were in the entertainment industry. My father was a film producer. His credits included *Coal Miner's Daughter*, *Sweet Dreams*, and *St. Elmo's Fire*. Prior to that, he was a television executive in New York City, but he moved to Los Angeles in the 1950s at the behest of Howard Hughes, who wanted him to run his film company.

While I was growing up, my dad maintained a solid wall between his professional life and our family life. He felt the movie business was not necessarily the best influence, and he didn't want to glamorize it. He wanted to make sure we knew there were plenty of interesting, intellectual things going on in the world that had nothing to do with the entertainment community. It's not that he disapproved of the business, or of the people in it, but he made a concerted effort to downplay its attractiveness to his two sons.

I was intrigued by Hollywood, certainly, but I was also interested in politics, architecture, and medicine. All three of those seemed like potential careers.

I went to Beverly Hills High School. There were plenty of kids there whose parents were in the entertainment business, but the cliques weren't really divided along those lines. They were based on interests, just as they are elsewhere: Drama. Surfing. Being stoned. Being stoned and surfing. Sports. Student government.

I was a drawn to the debate team. I really liked public speaking and got intensely involved in debating. I loved standing up in front of people and trying to persuade them that I was right. I loved going to tournaments and watching how other people handled themselves during the debate rounds and how the judges reacted to what my adversaries said. Most of all, I loved winning.

When it was time for college, I went to Williams, in Massachusetts. It was a fantastic school, but it felt too isolated. So, after my freshman year, I transferred to UCLA and found myself back in California. I graduated after my junior year, then moved to Mammoth, a resort area in the Sierras, and worked on the mountain and skied. To this day, skiing is one of my passions.

After that extended vacation, I attended law school at the University of Southern California. By the time I graduated, I still didn't know quite what kind of law I wanted to practice, or even whether I really wanted to be a lawyer. I did know that it could be a stepping stone to another pursuit, but I was unclear on what that might be. I can't say I was leaning toward entertainment law, but I wasn't disinterested, either. Now that I look back on it, I'm a little surprised at my lack of focus, but I was ambitious and wanted to succeed at whatever I did.

Still undecided during my third year of law school, I went to New York to interview with various law firms, and I came very close to working on Wall Street. In the end, however, the desire to stay in California was overwhelming.

I'd done well in law school and had a lot of choices among law firms. I figured I could dabble in different areas before making a decision about the type of law I'd practice. One of the firms I interviewed with was O'Melveny & Myers. I felt a positive connection to the people there, and I thought they would give me the opportunity to find my field. So I accepted their offer to start in the fall of 1984.

After taking the bar exam, I became more interested in the possibilities of entertainment law, and I realized that I had probably been avoiding it because my father was still actively working in the film industry. I didn't want people to feel that he had pulled any strings for me, but now that I had a job at a firm that was involved in entertainment, I realized I had earned the right to pursue it, if, indeed, that's what interested me.

I started at O'Melveny's main office, in downtown L.A. Since I wanted to work in the Century City office, however, where the entertainment practice was centered, the firm let me make the move. There were about thirty-five lawyers in the Century City office, about half of whom were involved in entertainment work, and four of those were involved primarily in entertainment related litigation. By that time, I was definitely interested in exploring entertainment, but I was also interested in corporate law and in real estate. Ironically, the only area that held no appeal for me was litigation.

During the rotation, however, I was exposed to litigation, and the attraction was instant. I immediately knew that this was what I wanted to do with my career. I guess in many ways it harkened back to my days in debate, and to my desire to stand up, make myself heard, and *win*. There were two big differences, however: One, I was there to solve real problems. And two, I was getting paid. That seemed like a pretty good deal.

One of the elements I really enjoyed was the fact that the studios would often call the litigator, not the deal lawyer, before the problem became a serious problem. They were looking for a way to dissuade people from filing a lawsuit, and it was my job to help them do that.

And that's how I got into the film industry: I did well in law school, I got a job at a top-tier law firm, and I became exposed to a part of Hollywood that the average moviegoer doesn't even know exists.

Now, more than twenty years later, I am a partner at the firm, and have a terrific practice. Hollywood is a breeding ground for litigation. A lot of people manage to end up feeling that they've been unfairly treated on a project or on a deal, whether it's the studio or the talent.

A typical example is the pitch that wasn't going anywhere. You didn't think much of the idea yourself, when you first heard it, but years down the road that pitch, or what you decide must be some *version* of that pitch, turns into a huge, box-office success. Now you change your tune: "That was *my* idea. I brought that to the studio. Without me, they had nothing. This picture never would have happened if I hadn't pushed it along." The fact that you didn't have a deal, or that over the years ten other people pitched that same idea to executives around town, or that similar elements can be found in plenty of other books and movies—well, so what? You maintain that there was a verbal agreement in place to hire you if the project went forward. And of course you remember being assured that you would be taken care of, and so on and so forth. So you're mad as hell and you're going to fight this thing.

Every time a movie succeeds, dozens of people come out of the woodwork. There's an old saying, *While success has many fathers, failure is an orphan.* No one wants to be associated with a bomb, certainly, but when a movie is a hit a lot of people line up, each claiming to be the biological father. Most of them you can dismiss, since they have no real connection to the movie. But even those who have legitimate contracts, and who have already been taken care of, tend to think they deserve more. They look at the contract and ask their lawyers if there is some way to change its interpretation. "If I hold it up to the light like this, or if I look at the small print at this angle, can I get more out of the studio?" Let's be fair, though. It's not just the talent side that creates these disputes. The studios can take strong positions, too. And sometimes they're actually doing it against their better interests, pushed along by an angry A-list actor or a powerful director.

One frequent source of disputes concerns television performers. Each summer—I can set my calendar by this—a number of stars will refuse to honor their contracts. They want better deals for themselves, so they simply refuse to show up for work and use that as a bargaining chip. These disputes arise on all the top shows, *Everybody Loves Raymond*, *Friends*, *Seinfeld*, and even on some shows that are failures out of the gate, and every summer I know I'm going to be dealing with an agent or an attorney who has told his client that he or she has an almost a constitutional right to hold out for more money. It is always the same story: "Without me, the show wouldn't be a hit. And, yes, I know I agreed to perform, and that I have a contract, but the fair-minded thing to do in view of the success of the show is to give me a big raise—or at least a bigger raise than the one you gave me the last time I held out."

If a show stays on the air for any length of time, they'll take it even further. They'll invoke the so-called Seven Year Rule. This is a provision of the labor code that says a contract for personal services can't be enforced beyond seven years.

I handled a case a few years ago, involving an A-list star and his ex-girlfriend. When they broke up, he asked a studio to give her a producing deal. When no projects came of it, she sued both the studio and her ex-boyfriend, claiming that they had breached the contract and ruined her career. It just goes to show: In Hollywood, no good deed goes unpunished—if there's potential for a lawsuit there.

While being in the public eye is a big part of being on the front lines of the entertainment industry, neither A-list actors nor the studios like being in court. That explains, in part, why a lot of cases, even those with little merit, are settled. Unfortunately, that can bring even more people out of the woodwork, and they're not always going to be on their best behavior.

Thankfully, the work is seldom uninteresting. I defended a case brought by the National Cathedral Foundation, in Washington, D.C., for example, over the movie *The Devil's Advocate*. You might remember the stone relief in Al Pacino's apartment—those sculpted figures that came to life toward the end of film. Well, we were sued by the National Cathedral because they felt that the film's art director had been inspired by those figures, which they said debased the original art through depictions of nudity and through its association to the devil.

To respond, we hired art historians who had worked at museums around the country—the Metropolitan Museum in New York City, the National Gallery in Washington, and the Getty Museum in Los Angeles—and put on a presentation that became something of an art history lesson. We traced sculpture to its very roots, and argued that even the original artist had borrowed from 3,000-year-old traditions and designs, and from the work of a number of well-known artists from the sixteenth and seventeenth centuries. I learned a lot of history in two weeks!

I was also involved in Sony Pictures' battle over the rights to produce *Spider-Man*. The parties' deals and claims were so entangled, and so much was at stake, that it took *six years* to resolve the disputes. As the trail was coming to an end, my wife went into labor with our son, Benjamin. I was up all night, and went to court in the morning to deliver the closing argument for Sony. (We won, and Sony went forward to create what has become a very successful franchise.)

Sometimes the battles are about neither art nor money. I was one of the attorneys who represented Oliver Stone and the makers of *Natural Born Killers* after a pair of misguided kids shot and paralyzed a convenience store clerk in Ponchatoula, Louisiana. As part of their defense, they told the court that they'd been inspired by "Mickey" and "Mallory," the characters portrayed in the film by Woody Harrelson and Juliette Lewis. In the wake of those statements, the victim's family went to a Louisiana court and sued Stone, the producers, and the studio. Based on legal liability standards that flow from the First Amendment, we convinced the judge that there was no evidence to impose liability on the filmmakers. He agreed, but the case went to the Louisiana Supreme Court and to the United States Supreme Court, *twice*, before it was finally over.

Many lawyers use the profession as a stepping stone to something else in the business—they end up running studios or large agencies or producing movies—but I'm very happy right where I am. I love what I do. The work is always different and interesting and intellectually challenging.

Whatever you choose to do, the legal profession is a terrific way to get into the entertainment industry. Unfortunately, I'm not the only one who thinks so: Every year there are many hundreds of law school graduates looking to break in. But don't despair if you don't immediately get that dream job. Take the best job you're offered, even if it's not connected to the enter-tainment industry, and make a point of distinguishing yourself within that firm. A year or two down the road, you can make the move to a company with a higher profile in the industry.

There isn't any one way to break in. But hard work is always involved. That can't be overstated. No one accomplishes anything in this business, or any other, without hard work, no matter how lucky they might appear to be. (As my father used to tell me, many of those so-called overnight sensations had been at it for twenty years.) Still, if you work hard and actively look for opportunities, at some point you'll find yourself at the right place at the right time. It may not happen as quickly as you'd like, so keep plugging away. If it looks like luck, that's no accident, either. People who succeed create their own opportunities.

WILLIAM A. SCHWARTZ

WRITER/PRODUCER

"You have to want this—writing, acting, directing—more than anything else in the world, because there really is no rhyme or reason for success in this business. The more you know, the less you know."

For almost three decades now, starting with an episode of *Kojak* in 1977, Bill Schwartz has been a Hollywood rarity: a writer who almost never stops working.

Although he got into the business hoping to become a director, Schwartz's early success as a writer convinced him that he was better off at home, in front of his IBM Selectric, so he settled in for the long haul.

Schwartz has worked on a dozens of shows, from *The Incredible Hulk*, *Heartbeat*, *Baywatch*, *Flipper*, and *Touched by an Angel*, to *Promised Land* and, more recently, *Wild Card*. He also wrote and produced several critically acclaimed television movies, including *License to Kill* and *To My Daughter*.

He was interviewed on June 12, 2005, at his home in Agoura Hills.

I was born in Montclair, New Jersey, and after getting kicked out of Montclair Academy for being the kid who always got caught with his hand in the cookie jar, I was shipped off to Schuyler Prep, a private school in

Schuylerville, New York. It turned out that being away from home was the best thing that ever happened to me. I graduated early and convinced my parents to send me to the American School in Lugano, Switzerland. It was one of the most beautiful spots in the world, but somehow I managed to spend most of my time indoors, watching movies.

There was one theater in town, and we had a teacher who really loved film, and he would bring movies in to show us. But they weren't the kinds of movies I would have been likely to see back home. I saw *The Bicycle Thief* and *The Garden of the Finzi-Continis*, by Vittorio De Sica. I saw Fellini's *Amarcord* and *8½*. I saw *Wild Strawberries* by Ingmar Bergman. The list goes on and on—the best of European filmmaking. The funny thing is, it wasn't even a real class. It was just a group of people who loved films, and after we watched them we'd eat great food and drink wine and stay up well into the night, talking about them. I found the small, personal stories very moving. They were so culturally removed from my life in New Jersey, but the values and ideas had no boundaries, and that struck a nerve.

Still, I needed a career, and a life, and upon returning to the States, I attended Lake Forest College, near Chicago, without a clue as to what I'd be majoring in.

One day, I was listening to Simon & Garfunkel's song, "At the Zoo," and I decided to make a little film based on that song. I invited a bunch of friends to the zoo, and I shot all this bizarre and wacky footage of their antics, and of the animals, and then I went back to the dorm and sat down with some borrowed editing equipment. For the next few days, instead of going to class, I cut the film to the music. It was all trial-and-error, and frustrating as hell, but it was also really exciting to see it come together. There was something magical about the way I could make the right animal pop into the frame on cue, precisely where I wanted it.

Then, completely by accident, I heard about this religious organization that was putting up money for student documentaries. I applied for one of the grants and got it. The documentary was supposed to focus on elements of religion on college campuses, and this was the early 1970s, when religion was getting bashed by free love, sex, and rock 'n' roll. I rented a 16-millimeter camera and found a guy at school who knew how to use it, and I got him to shoot it for me. We went out to the Bahai Temple in nearby Wilmette and interviewed people, and we also did interviews on campus. I didn't go in with any preconceived story, just a list of questions. "How often do you pray? Does prayer mean anything to you? Do you have sex on Saturday night and go to church Sunday morning to confess? Do you believe God can absolve you of your sins?" Etc. etc.

I found that most kids were either very religious or not religious at all—there seemed to be no middle ground—and this was the story that unfolded in my documentary.

That Christmas, when I went home, my mother told me she had met Jan Kadar at a party in New York. Kadar, a film director, had won the Academy Award for Best Foreign Film in 1965, for *The Shop on Main Street*, and he was part of that whole new wave of directors that included Milos Foreman and Ivan Passer.

I went to New York to meet him and we really hit it off. I was like a sponge. No matter what he said, I thought it was remarkable. If he'd been a cult leader, I would've joined. Luckily for me, he was both a great person and a great director, and he became my mentor, my second father, and a dear friend. It was Kadar who got me into the business, and who gave me a passion for film that I carry with me to this day.

He was working on a movie called *Adrift*, a psychological drama about a widower who begins to have an affair with a young woman with a past. It was being cofinanced by a European company and an American company called MPO Productions. I ended up going to work for Kadar the following summer, as his personal assistant. They were shooting part of *Adrift* in Puerto Rico, and on my first day I was sent to the airport to pick up the lead actress. She arrived with her boyfriend, and she was gorgeous. On the way back to the set, she kept staring at the ocean and begging me to stop the car. I told her that my job was to get her to the set as soon as possible, but she kept pleading. "Can't we please stop for a minute? The water is so beautiful!" So I stopped, and she and her boyfriend got out, took off all their clothes, jumped into the water, dried themselves off, and got back into the car. I was twenty-one years old and I was thinking, *I love movies!*

For the next week, my job was to stand off to one side of the camera holding a towel for the actress as she came out of the water, nude, and climbed into my arms. She played some sort of water nymph, and she was in the water all the time. I remember calling my father, a doctor, and telling him about my job. He knew right away that medical school was not in my future. I'd been given a taste of show business, and there was no turning back.

After the shoot was over, Kadar took me to Vienna, where they cut the movie. The producer spoke Hungarian, Kadar's native language, and the editor spoke a little Czech and a little German, but no Hungarian. So I was in the editing room listening to these fractured conversations in Hungarian, Czech, and German, with a little English thrown in to further complicate matters, and I found myself learning the language of film. By the time the editing phase was over, I had a pretty good idea of how a movie was put together. This was especially valuable, since the core of European filmmaking is about telling a story through images, not dialogue.

When I got back to the States, I made arrangement to transfer to the NYU Film School. And the following summer, I went back to MPO for another job. One of the people on staff was Michael Cimino, who was making commercials at the time but later went on to direct a number of movies, including *Heaven's Gate*, for which he is famous, or infamous, depending on your point of view. He was making a fortune. I couldn't believe people made that kind of money in this business, for doing something they loved, and I was thrilled to be pursuing it.

This new job involved an army training movie, on which I was made the assistant to the assistant director; in other words, a glorified gofer. I had long hair, which I wasn't asked to cut, thank God, and for the entire summer, we'd go from army base to army base, traveling through Georgia and Alabama and Florida.

I remember one time I was in Columbus, Georgia, working on a base there, and I was sent off to the airport to pick up some electricians who were coming to join the crew. En route, I had to stop at the bank to pick up some cash to take care of the per diems, so I had $5,000 in my pocket, mostly in hundreds. And I was sitting at the airport in a rented Camaro, waiting for these guys, when a cop came up to the window and rapped on it and told me I was in a red zone and that I would have to move. The plane was just landing—I could see it—so I went around once and pulled up to the same spot, and of course the same cop came up to the car. Only this time he and his partner decided to arrest me, and they put me in the back of the squad car and called for someone to tow the Camaro.

I assumed we were on our way to the precinct, but at one point we stopped at this really bizarre trailer park, and I thought, *I'm dead!* I had visions of me and my long hair disappearing into a swamp. But then we kept going and arrived at the Muscogee County Jail, and they made me empty my pockets. When they saw that huge wad of money, they immediately knew what I was: a long-haired, hippie drug-dealer. As they counted the cash, one bill at a time, I tried to explain, but they didn't believe me and tossed me in a cell. I kept asking them, "What happened to my phone call? Don't I get a phone call?"

After about three hours, they let me use the phone, and I got through to the base. The crew contacted our army liaison, who called the police and told them that, yes, I was a long-haired hippie from New York, but I was *his* long-haired hippie, and that they should release me immediately.

After I graduated from NYU, Kadar went off to Montreal to shoot *Lies My Father Told Me*, and he made me his first assistant director. It was a fabulous experience. I worked closely with Kadar, and with the writer, Ted Allan. During preproduction, Ted rewrote the script per Jan's notes, and I had a chance to watch him work, a remarkable, educational experience. When the shoot was over, Kadar could see that I was seriously hooked on movies. And he said, "If you really want to be in this business, and you're determined to become a director, you should write."

I'd learned a little something in that editing room in Vienna, and I'd learned a lot more from watching Kadar, and I'd picked up so much about structure from watching Ted tear the script apart and put it back together again, so I was only *slightly* terrified at the prospect of sitting down and writing my first script. It was called *Monkey Life*, and it was about a Jewish family with two sons; one of them wanted to be a doctor and the other a photographer. It featured an evil, Jewish mother and a downtrodden doctor father, but by the end of the film, the roles of the parents had been reversed and the young man's eyes had been opened to some valuable truths, etc. The script had a few autobiographical elements, as you can imagine, and with great trepidation I sent it off to the American Film Institute, in Los Angeles, and applied for a fellowship. I got in.

I drove out to Los Angeles, found a place to stay, and went off to my first day of school. Shortly after I arrived, I found myself talking to God. Okay, not God; Charlton Heston. He was an honorary member of AFI and took an active part in the lives of its fellows. He asked me what I wanted to do, and I told him I was there as a writing fellow but that I actually wanted to be a director. And he said, "Write what you know. As you get more experience, you'll have more to write about. But until that day, my advice is to stick to what you know."

In the spring of that first year, I applied for a grant with *The Mary Tyler Moore Show*, and I went in and met with Grant Tinker, who was the top guy at MTM Enterprises. I repeated what I had told Heston: I was a writing fellow, but I wanted to direct. He asked me what I was working on and I said I was writing a comedy about the night they killed Rasputin. He must have liked that, because I got the job. It paid seventy-five dollars a week, and it wasn't really a job. I was told to just hang around and observe and try to learn a little something.

And that's what I did. I was on the set every day, for weeks on end, watching Jay Sandrich direct. Nobody even talked to me. Then one day Ed Asner came over and said, "Who the hell are you? And why are you always writing things in that little notebook of yours?" I told him, and he said, "Come down and join us." And suddenly I was sitting at a table with Ed Asner and Mary Tyler Moore and Valerie Harper and Cloris Leachman and Gavin MacLeod and Ted Knight and Nancy Walker, along with the producers—Jim Brooks, Stan Daniels, Ed Weinberger, and David Davis. This was the cream of the crop, and I couldn't have found a better place to learn. MTM Enterprises had *Bob Newhart* and *Texas Wheelers* on the air, and they had just sold *Rhoda*. The next thing I know, thanks to Ed Asner, I was hired as Ed Weinberger's assistant.

Ed [Weinberger] was a great guy, but as odd as they come. He never said hello and he never said goodbye. If you ever watch *Taxi* and stick around for the credits, you'll hear a guy sort of groaning right at the very end. Well, that's Ed.

They sold two more pilots that season: *Phyllis*, for Cloris Leachman, and *Doc*, for Barnard Hughes. I was made an associate producer on *Doc*, which lasted one season. I was reading scripts and watching them shoot and sitting in the editing room and learning everything I could about postproduction. But the most fun was sitting in on rewrite night, when they went though the scripts trying to make them better and faster and funnier. There was one writer there, David Lloyd, who was kind enough to read several drafts of my Rasputin script. I was writing it for AFI, and that was keeping me busy, so I never even considered trying my luck on any of the MTM shows. Also, for some strange reason, I still thought I was destined to write and direct features, not television.

Then *Doc* got cancelled and I was out of a job. It had been a very valuable experience, not the least of which were Jim Brooks's parting words of wisdom: "If you want to be a writer, write."

I went home, started collecting unemployment, and went to work on a screenplay. In the weeks and months ahead, I found myself commiserating with my friend Mark Kupher, who was a year ahead of me at AFI and who was the hot guy at school because he had done a short film with Jack Lemmon. He had just met one of the story editors on *Kojak*, and he was trying to come up with a sellable story for them, and he would call to bounce ideas off me. We would talk every day, for hours at a time, and this went on for several weeks.

Finally, feeling a little guilty about stealing my time, he called the story editor on *Kojak* and told him he'd been working with me on an idea and could we please come in and pitch it to him. And we went in and pitched a story about a beautiful model who suffered from split-personality disorder, and they bought it in the room. This was 1977, and I had my first writing assignment.

At the time, Universal was a great place for writers and producers. All the offices were connected. Everybody hung out. It was like a big club. Stephen Bochco was right next to the *Kojak* office. He and Stephen Cannell were doing a show called *Richie Brockelman, Private Eye*, with Dennis Dugan in the lead. Bochco was already a wunderkind, even way back then. I told my mother about him, and once again she played a role in my career, reminding me that as a boy of thirteen I had worked for Bochco's mother, selling her costume jewelry door-to-door. I immediately arranged to run into Bochco in the elevator, whereupon I promptly shared this tidbit, hoping the connection would lead to something wonderful.

"That's nice," he said, visibly underwhelmed. "What are you doing here?"

"An episode of *Kojak*."

From that day forward, he called me "Bunky." I thought we were developing a nice relationship. Then I discovered that everyone whose name he couldn't remember became "Bunky." Anyway, Bochco said he couldn't give me an assignment on *Richie Brockelman*, but that he'd be glad listen to any of my ideas. I took him at his word. I wrote a thirty-page treatment for an episode, and I gave it to him. He read it and found it too serious, and too long. So I came back with ten pages and he found that one too comedic. I told him I'd go off and write something else, and he said, "Don't write anything! Just call me with a one-liner."

A few days later, I was at the beach, watching the jets making their way toward the Santa Monica Airport, and I had a brainstorm. I called Bochco and said, "Richie Brockelman takes flying lessons."

"Great!" he said. "You have a deal."

Before I could even write that script, Bochco introduced me to the guy who was running *The Bionic Woman*, with Lindsay Wagner as Jaime Summers. They were desperate for scripts, and I didn't have anything, but a few nights later I was home watching a rerun of *The African Queen*, with Humphrey Bogart and Katharine Hepburn, going downriver on that old, leaky boat, and I called up and got the producer on the line. "Jaime Summers on The African Queen!" I said.

And he said, "Great! Sold!"

That was the first script I ended up writing, and I became a member of the Writers Guild. It's amazing what happens in this town when you're actually writing a script for money. I got an agent and he immediately got me a meeting to pitch a TV movie at NBC. It was about a woman who was trapped in a dull marriage and turned to prostitution. I'd learned to keep it short and simple, so I summed it up with a one-liner: "The American version of *Belle du Jour*."

While they were thinking about it, I turned in my *Bionic Woman* script and was offered a seven-year deal. But then NBC called to say they were buying my movie idea, and I decided not to get locked into a long-term deal. The NBC movie led to yet another movie, *Zuma Beach*, which was produced by Brian Grazer, and I realized that a wonderful thing had happened: I had a career.

As for advice, I would give everyone the same advice I give my son: You have to want this—writing, acting, directing—more than anything else in the world, because there really is no rhyme or reason for success in this business. The more you know, the less you know.

It takes talent, of course. And it takes luck. And part of the talent is being ready for the luck when it finally shows up. You can't survive without either of those. Talent and luck. So you hope and pray for both.

As for becoming a writer, I will give you the same advice Charlton Heston gave me: *Write what you know.* When you're young and just starting out, you may not have the life experience to create new worlds. Stories are different than term papers. Interpreting life isn't as easy or as simple as researching the facts. You have to have enough experience to evaluate and synthesize life. And until you get that experience, work with what you know, even if it doesn't feel like much. You'll have more to write down the road.

I'm still learning. And one of the things I've learned is that Hollywood is the only business in the world where experience and wisdom are tossed aside to make way for the young, the hip, and the inexperienced. It's called ageism, and it makes no sense. But at the end of the day, they always come back to the established writers to help them put some heart and soul into the stories. The trick is to last long enough so you become one of the writers they're always going back to.

KEVIN RODNEY SULLIVAN

WRITER/DIRECTOR

"I think that's what it's all about: **The willingness to do it.** *I had made a decision to achieve my goals by any means necessary, and that's what it takes."*

Kevin Rodney Sullivan started life as an actor, but he found freedom and true success when he turned to writing. He spent the better part a year working on a spec script that didn't sell, but it did the next best thing: It got Sullivan his first writing assignment.

Writing for shows such as *Fame*, *Cagney & Lacey*, *Knots Landing*, and *Knightwatch* led to work behind the camera, too, and in 1998—having proved himself time and again in television—Sullivan made his feature directorial debut on *How Stella Got Her Groove Back*, starring Angela Bassett, Taye Diggs, and Whoopi Goldberg. His most recent feature was *Guess Who*, the hit comedy with Bernie Mac and Ashton Kutcher.

Sullivan was interviewed on June 27, 2005, at his offices in Venice, California.

I grew up in the Fillmore District of San Francisco, the youngest of three children. My dad drove a bus for the municipal railway, my mom worked as a secretary at St. Mary's Hospital, and we lived in a place called St. Francis Square, which was one step up from a housing project. Just a block away, beyond the playground, you'd find the really funky, hardcore projects. It was a tough neighborhood, and as a little boy, growing up there in the 1960s, I saw everything.

Members of the Black Panthers would come over to the playground and interrupt our games to give us lessons in self-defense. They told us we had to be ready for the revolution. I was five when JFK got killed. I remember listening to Martin Luther King over loudspeakers, outside the overcrowded Macedonia Church, unable to get in. A year later, he was dead. I remember the tanks and trucks and the troops moving into the neighborhood, rolling literally outside my bedroom window, into the Mayfair Market, because the whole country was expecting riots.

There was other stuff going on, too; regular stuff. By the time I was five, I thought I wanted to do something in theater. My kindergarten class put on *The Farmer in the Dell*, and I was the farmer. I remember being in dress rehearsal, and seeing my friends out in the yard, playing ball, and for a moment I thought I should be out there, with them. But then I took another look at that little stage, and I said, "Nah! I like this."

In retrospect, I feel blessed. Already at that age I knew what I wanted to do with my life. Part of the reason I am where I am today is because I found my way so early. By the time I was eight, I was in a summer workshop of *Oliver*, the musical, and I was absolutely hooked.

At home, my parents didn't know quite what to make of my interest in theater. I'm sure my dad thought I was gay, but both he and my mom were very supportive. She was more hands-on, more of a nurturer, and she pushed us to explore. My brother was a great guitar player, and my sister could paint and sing, and I stayed interested in acting.

But I was interested in other things, too. I was a straight-A student. I played football, basketball, and baseball. I ran track and played soccer. And I was president of my class every year through eighth grade. I don't know how I fit all of that into my days, but I managed.

As time went by, I decided I should try to get some real acting jobs. I started looking in the *San Francisco Chronicle* to see if I could find something that might be right for me. I didn't find anything, but I came across the name of a talent agency, The Brebner Agency, and I started sending in Polaroid snapshots of myself. I would enclose little notes: "I want to be an actor!" And every three or four weeks, I'd actually call the agency to follow up.

It got so the receptionist recognized my voice. If she wasn't busy, she'd humor me. If she had too much to do, she was short and would tell me to stop calling and sending pictures. I knew I was bugging the shit out of her, but I didn't know what else to do.

When I was in sixth grade, I played Puck in *A Midsummer Night's Dream*. Some people from the San Francisco Shakespeare Company saw the performance, and through sheer coincidence invited Ann Brebner to see it. After the performance, she called me in for a meeting. The receptionist immediately recognized me from my picture. "You're the little son of a bitch that's been calling me for the past year!" she said, but she was smiling.

Ann Brebner ended up putting my entire sixth grade class in *They Call Me Mr. Tibbs*, the Sydney Poitier movie. We played a group of kids walking down the street as Poitier chased a bad guy. That was my first taste of movie making, and I liked it.

After that, Brebner kept getting me auditions. In 1970, I got a job in an alphabet cereal commercial, a national spot; me and two white kids flying though San Francisco in a psychedelic, magical boat. I had a big-ass afro and I'm sure that's half the reason I got the gig. We floated along on invisible wires, singing along with the pop soundtrack, "I love you, Alphabits, wherever I go!" Aldo Ray was also in the spot. He played a construction worker who looked up and saw us flying through the air.

The commercial was pretty big. I made $7,000 that year, and that got everyone's attention at home. Suddenly I was in the game.

Not long afterward, I had a strange dream, a melodramatic, *West Side Story*–type love story, and I wrote it up for an English class at school. My teacher gave me an A-plus and took me aside. "Kevin," she said, "you have a gift." Thanks to her, I began to think about writing. I wrote now and then, mostly for myself, and meanwhile I kept getting small parts in theater productions and doing commercials. This was back when *Sesame Street* was just starting out—they'd had a good year on PBS—and they were doing a live show at Golden Gate Park. I auditioned for the part of the Master of Ceremonies, and I got it. I had to sit on this big garbage can with a microphone and introduce the various skits, and there was this dude with a beard behind me, doing the voices of the puppets that were interacting with me. It was Jim Henson. I had no idea at the time that he would become an empire-maker with his Muppets. The telecast bombed, but for some reason I got good reviews.

I went on to get a part in a move called *Thumb Tripping*, with Meg Foster, who struck me as the most gorgeous creature on the planet, then I got a series called *Wee Pals on the Go*. It was based on a comic strip by Morrie Turner, an African American, and it was this sort of integrated neighborhood comic strip. Morrie was in it, along with me and four other kids. I played Randy, the kid with the big afro who loved sports. The series lasted for a season and a half, and when it was over my producer gave me an 8-millimeter camera for Christmas, along with a Moviola. That summer, I shot my first film. It sucked, but I was hooked.

All the money that I made went into a trust fund. I still took the bus to school, and still went to football practice, and the only thing that changed was that everywhere I went people would sing the theme song from *Wee Pals*. My status as a minor, local celebrity didn't keep me from getting my ass kicked on the playground, though. I was small but I was tough—I'd fight anyone. My limited fame didn't get me girls, either, but I was okay with that, for the time being, anyway: In acting, I had found my passion.

When it was time for high school, I got a scholarship to St. Ignatius College Prep, a Jesuit all-boys high school in the Sunset District of San Francisco, an hour from my home. The school had 1,200 boys, only forty of them black. Academically, it was very challenging: It was the first time I had ever struggled with classes, and it wasn't pleasant. The fact that I wasn't welcome in the theater program didn't help, either. I was a black man in a white school. I felt out of place and no one tried to make me feel otherwise.

Meanwhile, I was still getting acting jobs, and at one point I was asked to join the Young Conservatory of the American Theater, in downtown San Francisco. Denzel Washington and Annette Bening would later get their start there, too, and I was thrilled to be part of it.

I was also writing more, and I became interested in directing. As a senior, I convinced the theater department at St. Ignatius to let me direct *Ceremonies in Dark Old Men*, by Lonne Elder, and it went over very well. In addition, they asked me to play the lead in *Tea House of the August Moon*. That was a pretty big deal. St. Ignatius had never had a black man play the lead in one of their productions. The geisha was played by a white girl from Mercy High. I had to kiss a white girl in Asian makeup, and that was a big deal, too.

Toward the end of high school, I found myself being recruited by several schools in California. One was the California Institute of the Arts, in Valencia; another was the University of California, at Davis; and another still was UCLA. I decided to try to get into Juilliard instead.

When I went for my audition, I found myself facing John Houseman, who had just won an Oscar for his role in *The Paper Chase*, and I almost shit my pants. I did a couple of scenes, and he watched politely, then said: "You have talent, but you're only seventeen years old. Most of our students come here after four years of college. I don't think you're ready for New York City just yet."

I ended up going to Willamette University, in Salem, Oregon, because they offered me a scholarship through their theater program. It was funny: They recruited me as if I'd been an athlete. I told them I was definitely interested in theater, but that I thought I'd like to major in English because I was increasingly interested in writing. They were cool with that.

Unfortunately, I was bored to tears at Willamette. I was a whale in a fishbowl. The very first year, I went to audition for one of the supporting roles in *Two Gentlemen of Verona* and they ended up giving me the part of Proteus, the lead. I did a number of other plays, and even directed *Slow Dance on the Killing Ground*, by William Hanley. Then I decided I would try to produce a play I had written, but I was so bored that I asked the school if I could go off and do it as an independent study program. They had no problem with that. I went home to produce my play, and I never went back. Part of it was that I didn't want to go back. The other part was that my parents had divorced, and that my mother had been diagnosed with cancer. I stayed around and helped her out, and I made a few dollars here and there through small acting jobs and commercials.

By the summer of 1978, my mother was in complete remission, and I went to Los Angeles to try to get work as an actor. Not an atypical story: a twenty-year-old kid trying to break into Hollywood.

I had one friend in L.A., a fellow actor a few years older than me, and I had the SAG card I'd been given at age eleven. And almost right away I booked a small part in *More American Graffiti*. I worked on the Vietnam section of the movie, and spent two weeks on location, back in Northern California.

When I returned from the shoot, I found this funky apartment behind Grauman's Chinese Theater, right across the parking lot. Just as I was settling in, my one friend died of a heart attack while shooting a TV commercial. He was twenty-five years old, a big, strapping, athletic guy, but he had a heart condition. With him gone, I felt completely alone in L.A.

I couldn't seem to get another acting job, so I went to work for an alarm company, Morse Signal Alarm. I worked from ten at night till six in the morning, monitoring the systems via computer. I did that for six months. Then I got a job at a law office, as a file clerk. When I wasn't filing, I'd make photocopies and run errands and shit.

I was disillusioned, scared, and depressed. I didn't even love acting anymore. I felt I had burned out my passion for acting too soon. It suddenly seemed less interesting to me. I wanted to write, but I was so down I was having trouble focusing. Then one morning I sat down and started working on a feature screenplay, and seventeen days later it was finished. I just wrote and wrote. I had read enough plays and screenplays to know what I was doing, more or less, so I did it. And after seventeen days, I looked at the hundred and twenty pages in my hand and I felt like the most powerful man in the world. I was charged. I felt I could fly. I was literally roaring inside my little apartment, acting as if I'd just scored a touchdown in the Super Bowl. I was immediately addicted to that feeling: of finishing something; of doing it on my own; that kind of power.

The screenplay was not great.

But I knew a guy who was working as a gofer at Fox and he gave it David Madden, a young story editor who went on to became a respected producer. Madden read it and called me in and told me, "You know what? You have talent." He sent it off to some agents and I went and met with them, and they felt I had talent, too, but I needed to work at it.

I started reading about screenwriting. I took a class at UCLA Extension. I pored over several books on the subject, including Syd Field's great primer, *Screenplay*. I learned that research was important, and that it was essential to have an outline, and that I needed to have a solid handle on where I was going and what I was trying to say.

In the first script, I had just looked at the whole thing as a giant improvisation, with me playing all the parts. My goal then had been to get to know all my characters so intimately that I could play each of them, and when I sat down I simply tried to make them come alive on the page. In the process, I turned into Sybill, that woman with sixteen personalities. All of those characters were living in my head at the same time.

Now, however, I was learning that a movie is really about architecture. It's the math that counts, the structure, and you need that to make it work. Movies are also about theme, so you have to keep asking yourself: *What is this movie about? What is driving me to tell this story?*

When I felt I was ready to write a second script, I decided to write a political thriller. Thematically, I wanted to deal with the dark side of ambition—how ambition affects your life and how it affects the choices you make. (My own personal ambition had led to this crappy apartment in Hollywood, where I was eating beans and rice four times a week.) But I also wanted my second screenplay to be sexy. I called it *Power Play.*

As I started exploring my themes, it became a story about a female senator from the great state of Kansas, the daughter of a senator, who decides she wants to run for the presidency. It had been partly inspired by Nancy Landon-Kassebaum, who was the only female senator at the time, back in 1980, and whose father, Alfred M. Landon, a governor of Kansas in the early 1930s, had once made his own unsuccessful bid for the presidency. The other important character in the story was a news photographer.

I liked the theme, and I thought it was solid, but I realized I didn't have enough story. I felt I didn't know Washington well enough to set a script there. So I borrowed $600 from Jonathan Estrin, a new friend, and bought a ticket on the Trailways bus. They had a deal: $99 one way, and $1 for the return.

I called a Best Western in D.C., and got a deal on a room for two weeks, and then I called Senator Kassebaum's office, but not the one in D.C., where they were savvy; I called the one in Kansas. I told them I was writing a movie for Francis Ford Coppola, and that I was going to D.C. to do some research, and that I wanted to meet with the senator. The elderly, Midwestern secretary who answered the phone was very impressed: "Oh my God! You're from Hollywood!" Precisely the reaction I was hoping for. She bought my line of bullshit and said she'd make things happen for me in D.C.

I then called United Press International, in Los Angeles, and I told them the same lie. They bought it, too, and promised to hook me up when I got into D.C. After I got off the phone, I began to wonder whether they might actually call Coppola.

When it was time to go down to Union Station to get on the bus, I couldn't believe I was doing this. It was crazy. How was I going to survive on that bus for four days? I had a duffel bag, with my one white shirt and my two ties, and a few changes of underwear. And that was it. And I told myself, *Get off the fucking bus!* I was pacing up and down the aisle, and I'm pretty sure I was on the verge of getting off, when this older black woman, who looked like hell warmed over, said to me: "I'm running away." I was thinking: *Good for you lady! I'm on a bus to Washington having told the biggest lie of all time! They're probably gonna throw my black ass in the federal penitentiary for the rest of my ridiculous life! I got my own problems!* But I couldn't take my eyes off her—she seemed to be coming from a deep and profound pain. And there was truth there. She repeated: "I'm running away from my own son." So I stopped pacing and sat down in the seat across from her. I listened as she unburdened herself. And before I knew it, I looked up and we were half way to Vegas.

The entire journey became an amazing blessing, because for some reason, almost every passenger that got on that bus seemed to gravitate toward me to tell their story. Soldiers, young couples, older people, blacks, whites, whatever. They all wanted to talk to me. And I felt that the universe was giving me all this information, this gift, because I was taking a risk. And to this day I still feel that many of my characters and ideas were born in the course of those four days, on that bus, as I made my way across America, with the real America all around me.

When the bus finally got to Washington, they had lost my bag. I don't know how they managed it, but apparently they accidentally transferred it onto another bus. They promised to track it down, but meanwhile I had to go meet the UPI guys—and I'm pretty funky from four days without a shower. When I got there, I could see the looks on their faces: *Working for Francis Ford Coppola? This kid? Right!* But they humored me and let me tag along to what turned out to be Ronald Reagan's first day in office. And over the course of the next week, I met all sorts of well-known journalists, had dinner with David Hume Kennerly, the Pulitzer Prize–winner photographer, and sat down with members of Senator Kassebaum's staff—all of whom were either buying my story or *saying* they were buying my story. On my very last day in Washington, Senator Kassebaum herself gave me an hour of her time. I experienced a woman in power. I could feel her ambition, and I got a sense of the price she'd paid to get there. A week later, I felt I was ready to go home and write my political thriller. I had a genuine feel for D.C. And I had a deeper understanding of the characters. I was also much clearer on the themes.

When it came time for me to get on that bus, however, the thought of spending another four days on the road just about killed me. Then my girlfriend reached me at the motel: A residual check had arrived from my acting days. It was enough to cover a flight home. So I flew home—forfeiting the one-dollar, one-way bus fare back—and started writing.

Looking back, I think that's what it's all about: *the willingness to do it.* I had made a decision to achieve my goals by any means necessary, and that's what it takes.

It took me three months to finish the first draft, and I supported myself with acting jobs. I even had a recurring role on *Happy Days.*

When the script was done, I was able to get it to an agent at William Morris—through Jonathan Estrin, the same friend who had loaned me the $600—and they signed me right away. The script went out, and nobody bought it, but in a matter of months, I got an assignment to write an episode of *Fame.* After that, I was asked to adapt a book called *The Planet of Junior Brown,* by Virginia Hamilton. Once again, *Power Play* got me the job: The script hadn't sold, but it had convinced Hollywood that I could write.

For the next four or five years, all I did was write. I kept learning about structure, which helped me tell my stories the way I wanted to tell them. Whenever I ran into a problem, it was usually connected to the architecture of the script.

At one point, I was offered a pilot by CBS. I wrote it, but it didn't get made. Then ABC gave me a blind commitment to write another pilot. When I finished writing it, every studio in town wanted to be in business on that pilot. I used the leverage to insist that I would commit to the first studio that would let me direct an episode of television. MGM won the bidding because they had a series I knew and loved: *Fame*. And that's how I made the transition to directing. I parlayed the little power I had into a small directing gig, muscling my way in.

A short time later, my pilot actually got made and became a series called *Knightwatch*. I couldn't believe it. At the age of twenty-nine, I was the sole creator and executive producer of a prime time network series. We lasted ten episodes, struggling in the same time slot as *The Cosby Show*, over on NBC, but we got our shot and I loved every minute of it. Writing, producing, directing, and editing the series became film school for me.

After we got cancelled, I spent a year writing a feature for George Lucas about the Tuskegee Airmen, called *Red Tails*. Another amazing experience: to learn from one of the masters of our industry. When I returned to L.A., I kept directing TV, working on *Frank's Place*, *I'll Fly Away*, and *The West Wing*. Then HBO hired me to direct *Soul of the Game*, the amazing story about Satchel Paige, Josh Gibson, and Jackie Robinson when Jackie broke the color barrier in major league baseball. It was not lost on me that I, too, was breaking a barrier as the first African American to direct an original picture for HBO. *Soul* led to my first feature, *How Stella Got Her Groove Back*. More recently, I did *Barbershop 2: Back in Business*, and *Guess Who*, with Bernie Mac.

At the moment, I'm working on two feature films at opposite ends of the spectrum. One is a fifteenth-century comedy for Sony Pictures, based on my original story, which is easily twice the budget of anything I've done. The other is a small independent feature for Lions Gate, which I'm writing, producing, and directing. This is the beginning of what I hope to be the shape of my career. I've survived three big studio movies, and I like studio movies, but I also like the little ones. If you look at directors like Steven Soderbergh and Robert Rodriguez, who straddle both worlds, those are the guys who seem to be having the most fun.

For anyone trying to break into Hollywood today, I have one word of advice: write. It's the one thing that everyone can do, but very few people can do it well. And it's also the one thing Hollywood always needs: great material.

Many people can learn the technical aspects of directing, but few can compose a solid story. And if you can't tell a story, you won't make it as a director. I know this from experience. When I go to work on a movie, my primary tool is my pen. If a scene isn't working, and I'm standing on a set with 150 people looking to me for answers, I can always go to my laptop to find the solution.

We go to movies to see and hear stories. A film is nothing without a compelling narrative. That's why writing is where it all begins. If you can develop the skills to execute stories, and to execute them well, doors will open.

DIANE WARREN

SONGWRITER

"The teacher told him not to bring me back. 'She is tone deaf,' he said. 'She has no ear for music.'"

Diane Warren is arguably the best-known songwriter of this generation. Her songs have been recorded by some of the most successful performers of the day, including Celine Dion, Whitney Houston, Michael Bolton, Aerosmith, Brandy, Ricky Martin, Aretha Franklin, Gloria Estefan, LeAnn Rimes, Trisha Yearwood, Rod Stewart, Cher, Christina Aguilera, Faith Hill, Mariah Carey, Mary J. Blige, Toni Braxton, and Eric Clapton. They have also been featured in more than a hundred movies (*Con Air*, *Ghostbusters*, *Pearl Harbor*, *Coyote Ugly*, *License to Kill*, *Notting Hill*, *Runaway Bride*, *Legally Blonde*, *Message in a Bottle*, etc.), garnering five Oscar nominations, four nods from the Golden Globes, and a Critics' Choice Award.

In 1996, Warren won a Grammy for "Because You Loved Me," which was featured in the Robert Redford/Michelle Pfeiffer film, *Up Close & Personal*.

As if that weren't enough, she has been named Writer of the Year by ASCAP (The American Society of Composers, Authors, and Publishers) *six times*, the only female songwriter in history with that distinction.

Warren was interviewed on September 8, 2005, at Realsongs, the Hollywood-based company she founded almost two decades ago.

I was born in Van Nuys, California, which is not that far from Hollywood but really a million miles away. My mom was a housewife and my dad was in insurance. I had two older sisters—one was fourteen years older, the other eleven years older—so in some ways I felt like an only child.

Music was a big part of my life from very early on. There was always music playing in our house. Even as a baby, I can remember the radio playing day and night. My parents liked Top-40 stuff, popular, commercial music, and I remember responding to Motown and The Beatles.

By the time I was seven, both of my sisters were off in college, and they left a large collection of albums behind. That became part of my ongoing musical education. I would sift though the collection, more curious about the people who'd written the songs than about those singing them, already knowing—even at that age—that I wanted to write.

As the years passed, I became a regular at used record stores in and around Van Nuys. I would search through the twenty-five-cent bins for names I recognized and buy albums by the armful. I was like a sponge. My goal was to learn everything I could from the songwriters I admired, then try to build on that. I would listen to a song over and over again, not to imitate it but to get a sense of the hooks and melodies I responded to, and to try to figure out why.

To this day, people still ask me why I don't perform, but from the very start my goal was write, never to perform. Even as child, I wanted to be the one behind the curtain, hidden away. I never saw myself as a singer. I didn't like the idea of being up on stage, in front of people. I knew, intuitively, maybe even psychically, that I wanted to be a songwriter—although I hadn't written a song yet so I'm not sure *why* I knew this.

When I was about ten or eleven, my father went on a trip to Tijuana, and he brought back a little guitar for me. I went to take lessons, not far from the house, and when my father came to pick me up the teacher told him not to bring me back. "She is tone deaf," he said. "She has no ear for music." I think the teacher was upset with me because I didn't want to learn the scales. I just wanted to make up my own songs and my own rules. I was already writing by then, two and three songs a day at times, though most of them probably sucked.

When I was fourteen, I asked my father to get me a subscription to *Bill-*

board magazine. I wanted to know everything about the music business—who wrote what, who produced what, who sang what. My friends would go out with boys and get high and I did a little of that, too, especially the "get high" part, but I was very focused on my writing. *Think of a song, write the song, finish the song.*

As a result of my obsession, I wasn't doing well in school. I was getting Cs and Ds. Then one day my dad made a deal with me: "I will get you a twelve-string guitar if you get nothing less than a B this semester." He really believed in my songwriting talents, but he also wanted me to do well in school.

I applied myself, got As and Bs, and got my twelve-string guitar, but the next semester—sad to say—I was back to Cs and Ds. Still, for a brief, shining moment I was almost an A-student.

My first break came while I was still in high school. My dad used to play bridge with Dave Cavanaugh, who worked at Capitol Records, and he kept telling him how talented I was. "My daughter's a great songwriter!" he'd say. "You should really listen to her sometime."

Through Cavanaugh, my dad learned that Capitol Records had this thing called the Los Angeles Songwriters Showcase. He made some calls and before long I found myself in a small room, auditioning for two guys. They didn't like any of my songs, but they were okay about it. "You're going to be really, really great," one of them said, "but you're not there yet."

I smiled and left, but I was actually pretty pissed off. I had a lot of anger in me, and when I think back on it, I know that in some ways my anger kept me going. I remember telling myself, "What do they know?! I'll show them. I'll come up with something next time that will really blow them away."

I kept going back to the showcase, with new songs each time, because that's the way I am: You shut a door in my face and I will find ten new ways to get back in. But I guess they still didn't think I was ready.

I kept trying, though, and my approach to writing was the same then as it is now. I don't wait around for inspiration. I sit down and come up with an idea and I work on it until I get it right. Back then, I only played guitar, though later I taught myself a little piano, but I'm not a trained musician. I think that kind of worked for me, though, because it left me open to try things that I probably wouldn't have tried if I'd known better. When you're trained, you're taught all sorts of rules—you can't do this or that chord, you can't follow this with that—but not knowing the rules turned out to be kind of liberating for me. I didn't know the correct way of doing things, so it allowed me to be spontaneous. I often do things that seem weird and crazy but they end up working and making sense. I guess I still don't know what I'm doing, but I know what I'm not doing better than when I was younger.

Between the auditions and going to school, I went to see every music publisher in Los Angeles. They all told me I had potential, and I came to hate that word. It was the same as being told I wasn't ready, and I didn't want to hear it or believe it. I was absolutely determined to become a songwriter.

Finally, in my junior year, I found out that the father of one of the girls at school was in music publishing, and I went over to the house and played a few songs for him. He ended up publishing one of them, which doesn't mean the same thing it means in the book world—getting a song published doesn't guarantee that anyone will actually ever hear it. So no one ever heard that song, but just the fact that it got published was kind of cool, especially for a kid, and it gave me a little confidence.

The song had a strange title. It was called "Don Quixote Had His Windmills." It was about dreamer. I guess it was about me, because I was a dreamer and still am a dreamer.

I kept trying other publishers, and I kept getting rejected, but I didn't give up. And my father was really wonderful: He drove me from one place to the next and continued to believe in me.

Later, when I finally got my driver's license, I got a job making deliveries and pick-ups for Music Express, a messenger service. I used to take tapes of my songs and drop them off with every delivery I made, and my boss caught wind of it and fired me on my birthday. I had only lasted two weeks.

Then one day I met Jack White, who was producing songs for Laura Branigan, and through him I got signed by Arista Publishing. Laura recorded a number of my songs, and one of them, "Solitaire," made the top ten in 1983.

My first really big hit, however, came a couple of years later. Motown was producing a martial arts movie called *The Last Dragon*, and they needed a song for DeBarge, the group that was doing most of the music for the movie. I got a call from Linda Blum, whom I'd met at Arista Publishing, and she told me about it. So I sat down and wrote "Rhythm of the Night." Motown and the producers listened to my song and loved it, and they put it in the movie.

I still remember driving along Sunset Boulevard one day and hearing the song on the radio, *my* song. It was kind of freaky, but in a good way. I had loved listening to the radio as a kid, and here I was listening to one of my own songs on the radio. I imagined that thousands of people were listening to my song at that very moment, and it was a great feeling.

There was another moment like that a few years later, in 1988, when I went to Russia. I was talking to a songwriter there who spoke no English, and through an interpreter he asked me what songs I had written. And when I mentioned "Rhythm of the Night," he goes, "Ah! DeBarge!" And he started singing my song to me. It really showed the power of music. He didn't speak English but he knew the song. Russia was still a communist country at the time, but somehow my song had gotten through. I was really touched. I remember I had tears in my eyes.

I had some other hits early on, including "Nothing's Gonna Stop Us Now," by Starship; "Look Away" by Chicago; "Blame it on the Rain" by Milli Vanilli; and "If I Could Turn Back Time," which became Cher's comeback song in 1989.

People often ask me if I write with an artist in mind, but I really don't. I just try to write a great song, and when I'm finished I usually know who the song is right for. The song tells me who should be singing it.

I went through a lot of years of rejection, too. I'm a hustler, though. I think I'm a mix of confidence and insecurity, and the insecurity isn't bad because it keeps you hungry. You always want more, but in a good way.

And it's not as if people came knocking back then. I had to fight for it. That was certainly the case with mainstream Hollywood. I had to keep banging away at the door, and it was a very big door. I kept thinking, *I've been here long enough! When are you going to let me in?*

I generally like writing songs for movies, but I don't like the fact that everything is done by committee. Everyone in Hollywood has an opinion, and they seldom agree on anything. For me, it's largely about intuition, so I'm not a big fan of the committee approach.

I have a lot of fun stories about Hollywood, and about the movie industry, but I have one from about ten years ago that's not so much fun, and I know people generally prefer those types of stories—so that's the one I'll tell you.

There was an actress/singer who will remain unnamed. She had asked for a song for one of her movies, something she was going to sing herself. So I sent her a song and she called me and said, "Diane, I don't want the crumbs off the table. I want the good stuff." Now, I'm cool with someone not liking something I've written, but there are better ways to express it—gentler, more respectful, more professional—so I was kind of taken aback. And having recently started therapy, I decided to speak my mind. "Hey," I told her, "you could have said that in a nicer way." And she said, "Hey, if I suck in a movie, you can tell me I suck." And I said, "I wouldn't do that. My mother taught me that if I had nothing nice to say, I shouldn't say anything." But I was still a little annoyed, so I asked her if she had looked at the music charts lately. "No, I haven't," she said. "Why?" "Because I have three songs in the top ten," I said. And she said, "Well, why didn't I get those?" And I guess I was still pretty pissed off, because I replied, "Look, you opened the door to honesty, so I think I need to walk through that door. I didn't give them to you because you're too old. Those other artists are young; they're still in the game; they're still making hits." There was total silence for a moment, then she said, "You really go for the jugular, don't you, Diane?" And I said, "Well, you wanted honesty. You were honest with me and I felt I had to return the favor." Then I cut her off, telling her I had to go to therapy. And she said, "How long do you think you and your therapist are going to talk about our little exchange?" And I said, "I probably won't talk about it at all. I only talk about things that matter to me." And that was the end of that.

I have been working in this same building for twenty years, and I still write in the same small room that was my first office. Some years ago, the music critic Robert Hillburn came over to interview me, and he called my room "The Cave." I haven't cleaned it in twenty years. I don't want to clean it, because I'm lazy, and I don't want anyone in there moving stuff around, because I'm kind of superstitious.

Back then, there were times when I couldn't make the rent, and the landlord came close to evicting me. But as I started doing better, I began needing more space, and I rented more and more offices. Now I have the whole floor, and I even have recording studios here. It's pretty slick, but it's not really me. I'm a little grungier than this. I don't care about these types of things; I care about the work.

One of my friends once said that I had the hunger of someone who still needs to pay the rent, and in some ways he was right. I don't ever want to get too comfortable. I don't think comfort leads to creativity, though maybe that's just another one of my superstitions.

My shrink says I don't have a personal life, that my life is my work, and I agree with her. I don't think everyone has to have a typical life. I don't want to be married and have kids. I'm happy waking up next to my cat, and I'm happy working. I have always been a serious workaholic. I'm here six and seven days a week, and I work twelve to fourteen hours a day.

I'm still hungry. I'd like to think that I haven't written my best songs yet. I like to look ahead, to what's coming, not to the things that are behind me. On the other hand, I once saw something about myself on TV and was kind of amazed: I couldn't believe I had written all those songs. Still, the past isn't that interesting to me. I don't believe in resting on your laurels. I'm all about the next song.

Advice? I think you need to be great at whatever you do. Get as good as you can at your craft, whatever it might be. It also helps to develop pretty thick skin because you're going to need it. And you have to work really, really hard—harder than you can imagine. Luck might open the door, but it won't keep you in the room. Hard work will keep you in the room.

And don't wait for inspiration. Show up, do the work. I believe you need to work your muscles every day. The harder you work them, the stronger they get.

There are moments now and then when I feel like I've arrived, but not often. From time to time I'll hear something I wrote on the radio, and I'll think, *Wow! That's not bad.* And I felt pretty good when I got my star on Hollywood Boulevard, which was kind of surreal and weird. They actually shut down part of the street, and I remember thinking, *I got arrested around here once.*

But you know, for me, there's still so much to do. I am always reaching for the next level. I don't ever want to feel like I'm there. I want to feel like I'm always on the journey, that the next great song is just around the corner.

JERRY ZUCKER

WRITER/DIRECTOR/PRODUCER

"People would much rather watch a ten-minute DVD than read a 120-page screenplay."

Growing up in Shorewood, Wisconsin, Jerry Zucker never imagined he would someday find his way to Hollywood. He loved making people laugh, but never really thought he would entertain anyone beyond his family and his circle of friends.

His first film, *The Kentucky Fried Movie*, which he made for $650,000 with his brother, David; their longtime partner, Jim Abrahams; and director John Landis, grossed more than $20 million at the box office. Other comedies followed—*Airplane!*, *Top Secret*, the *Naked Gun* series, *Ruthless People*—but Zucker explored drama and romance, too, as both a writer and producer. *Ghost*, which he directed, was one of the highest grossing films of its day, and *My Best Friend's Wedding*, which he produced, was also a huge, international hit.

At the time of the interview, which took place on September 1, 2005, at his home in Los Angeles, Zucker was in preproduction on *Friends With Benefits*, a romantic comedy.

I was born in Shorewood, Wisconsin, a middle-class suburb of Milwaukee, the youngest of three kids. My sister, Susan, now lives in Connecticut, and my brother, David, lives here, in L.A. My parents, who are still in Milwaukee, have been married for sixty-four years.

We had a pretty traditional upbringing, with good midwestern values. It was a relatively innocent time. We walked a mile to school in the snow, which didn't seem like a big deal at the time, especially when our parents told us that they walked *ten* miles through blizzards. But to my kids, who were born in Los Angeles, it was like I was from the Gulag.

My father was in real estate. He built and managed office buildings, and I am still fascinated by the construction process. At one time, I actually thought I might go into business with him, but I never got the chance. My brother, on the other hand, spent a few years working for him as a construction expediter, and that came in very handy later.

I was always a bit of a goof-off, or maybe a lot of a goof-off, and I was always interested in entertaining people and making them laugh. I was short, so I think part of it was to get attention, but the other part of it was that my brother and I inherited a good sense of humor from our father. He was a very funny guy, good with puns, and everyone in our family valued a good joke. At the dinner table, David and I would feed off each other to try to get everyone laughing. Getting a spontaneous laugh at our house was a badge of honor. We also inherited some theatrical genes from our mother, who was an actress when she was younger, but gave it up to raise us. Once we got into the business, we tried to repay her by putting her in all of our movies.

I was in a few plays in high school, but always smaller parts, and I watched movies, but I wasn't really interested in film. A lot of directors have these stories about the first time they watched some classic like *Lawrence of Arabia*, and how they knew right away that that's what they wanted to do with their lives. "I want to be the guy who makes those things happen! I want to be a director!" Well, I *wasn't* one of those guys. I never had that moment. I went to see movies and enjoyed them, but I never really fell in love with film as an art form. I think that for me, and for my brother, and for Jim Abrahams, whom we began to work with very early on, it was really more about a desire to entertain and to make people laugh.

One thing I remember from those early years was all the time we spent watching TV, which turned out to be a big influence in our lives. We watched a lot of B-movies on TV, along with shows like *Mission: Impossible*,

Dragnet, Highway Patrol, and *M Squad,* with Lee Marvin—some of which were sort of noir in style. We had a lot of affection for those shows, but we also laughed at them. My brother and I would watch them together and supply punch lines or make up dialogue for laughs. On Sundays, the whole family would watch together. We'd be in the den, in front of our one TV—which seems sort of primitive now (once again, the Gulag to my kids)—and we'd eat on snack tables, kind of like dinner theater. I remember watching old movies, too, like *Creature from the Black Lagoon,* and making fun of them and talking back to the characters on the screen.

At one point, David and I took our father's Super 8 camera and began to make little movies of our own. One was a spoof of *Mission: Impossible.* Another time we filmed a party at our house, and we created a primitive soundtrack with the reel-to-reel tapedeck. We'd layer in funny voices, or one of us might pretend to be a TV announcer, and we'd try to get people to say stupid things.

The other big influence in my youth was *Mad* magazine. We loved the way it made fun of itself. A cartoon character would say, "I'm stuck in this stupid magazine." Or, "I know you're stupid because you're reading this dopey magazine." We liked the way it was able to jump out of its own frame, as it were. It was our first exposure to pure satire, and we loved it.

I was also influenced by growing up in Milwaukee, where people have this sort of self-deprecating sense of humor. We're not big city people, and we know it, and that helps keep us grounded. Most of the people in the world are not from L.A. or New York or Paris or London, and I think we have always understood that underdog sensibility.

When it was time for college, I didn't stray far—I joined my brother at the University of Wisconsin. He was a junior by that time, studying communication arts, and I thought I would go into journalism because I had worked on the high school newspaper. Neither of us thought about the movie business. When you grow up in Milwaukee, you don't think about it. Maybe that's changed since I was a kid—with shows like *Project Greenlight* and all the cable channels—but for us it just wasn't a realistic option. We didn't know anyone in the movie business, unlike L.A., where every garage mechanic is working on a spec script and has twenty-five friends in the industry. In Milwaukee, you might have a connection at a brewing company, or maybe you know the guy who makes bratwurst at Usinger's, but nobody was making feature films.

Still, David had brought one of Dad's cameras to school with him, and he took a film course junior year. One of the requirements was to make an 8-millimeter movie, and he asked me to be in it. It was called *The Best Things in Life Are Free*. I played this guy who takes psychedelic drugs (something David and I never actually did) and everything looks dreamy and trippy, but then I have to go to the bathroom, and for the rest of the whole ten-minute movie, I'm running around desperately looking for a place to pee. When my character was finally able to relieve myself, that gave him more pleasure than the drug, so in a sense maybe we had made an early antidrug movie.

We showed the movie to the class, and people laughed at all the right parts, and we thought that was really great. *We're making people laugh! Wow. Let's do it again.*

We made a bunch of movies, and in those days we had to play the sound (music, basically) separately, so one of us controlled the projector and the other one ran the reel-to-reel deck. It was hard to get them synchronized, though, so from time to time we'd have to slow down the projector to let the sound catch up, and inevitably someone would come by after the screening and say, "Man, those slow-motion parts were so cool! What made you think of that?"

When David graduated, he tried to get a job at an ad agency or in local television, but he couldn't find anything, so he went to work for my dad, in the construction business. One of my dad's friends had some video equipment, and at one point he told David that he should make industrial videos, but David wasn't interested. Then one day he went to Chicago to visit a girlfriend and they saw this show called *The Groove Tube*, produced by Ken Shapiro. A movie by the same name, based on the show, was released years later, but this was way before that. The show consisted largely of a series of black-and-white videos that spoofed film and television, and they had several monitors running simultaneously. The stuff was sometimes pretty scatological, and almost always funny, and it was unlike anything on television in those days. I remember one bit with a puppet, "Safety Sam" I think his name was, who was talking about safety as if he were addressing a group of children. But when the camera moved in, very slowly, you realized that the puppet was actually a penis with a little hat.

David was so inspired by the show that he drove all the way from Chicago to my apartment in Madison, and when he got there he was talking so fast he could hardly catch his breath. "I just saw this amazing thing! They had this video tape—and all these monitors—and they played all these funny bits—and charged admission! We could do something like that!"

And he called my father's friend, the one who had offered David the use of his video equipment, and the man agreed to loan it to us. I still wasn't convinced—I hadn't seen the show—but it sounded like a lot of fun, plus David was very enthusiastic and I had always trusted him.

That Easter, before I got home, David went to pick up the very bulky equipment, which consisted of one of those huge reel-to-reel Sony videotape machines, a tripod, a camera, and a monitor. On his way home, he ran into Jim Abrahams, and he invited him to come over to the house to play with the stuff. Jim was a few years older than us, and had always been on the periphery of our lives. His father and our father were business partners at one time, and our sisters were best friends and roomed together in college. I always thought he was a very cool and very funny guy, but I was too young and too nerdy to actually hang out with him.

A couple of nights later, my brother and Jim and I and a good friend of Jim's, Dick Chudnow, were in the basement of my parents' house, fooling around with the video equipment. And it was a lot of fun because—unlike film—you could play it back right away. And you could erase it. And those two things alone made it a fantastic comic play tool. You could see what you'd done wrong and what didn't work and you could do it over. It was fast and it was cheap. And that immediacy—that instant gratification—made it a real blast. Of course, nowadays that's nothing. But back in 1970 it seemed revolutionary.

So we started fooling around with some ideas, really just goofing around in front of the camera. We would do take-offs on commercials, or we'd tape a basketball game and dub our voices over the voices of the announcers, going for laughs. Nothing brilliant, but funny, and it worked. So we began to show the tapes to people, to family and friends, and they would laugh. Sometimes we'd get ten or fifteen people in a room: We loved to hear a crowd laughing. And no matter how many times we had seen it, when the audience laughed we laughed right along with them, as if we were seeing it for the first time. I think more than anything else we are driven by the sound of laughter.

We liked it so much that we decided to start a live comedy troupe. One night, the four of us were having dinner at a Big Boy's restaurant, and we started throwing names around for our new venture. There was a Kentucky Fried Chicken across the street, and one of us said, as a joke, "Why don't we call it 'Colonel Sanders' Kentucky Fried Theater?'" And it stuck. We became "Kentucky Fried Theater."

We did our very first show at the university, at the student union, and it was kind of a disaster, mostly because we ran out of material. We simply didn't have enough stuff for a real show. But people laughed at what we had—some of it, anyway. Then we found a bookstore in Madison with a room in back that was large enough for about seventy people. It was in terrible shape, and we basically had to rebuild the place, which is where David's experience in construction came in very handy. It took us about a month to finish, and we didn't have the same kind of budget that David was used to, so it was mostly held together with cardboard and masking tape. When the building inspector came by to check it out, we were amazed that he actually approved the permit.

That summer, the summer of 1970, we hired a couple of actors and put a piano on the stage and opened the show. We did comedy skits and a little improv, and we had two monitors on the stage, running the video bits. We got a couple of bad reviews—the campus paper complained, saying our show was silly and had no political message—but most of the responses were positive and we were a big hit with the students. I think the *absence* of a political message actually made it refreshing. People had spent so much time being serious and heavy and political that at that point they were as sick of the antiwar movement as they were of war. They seemed to welcome this type of escape, so maybe we were in the right place at the right time.

We ran the show for about a year, and we were making ends meet, more or less, but we weren't making a living, and eventually we decided to move to Los Angeles. We were looking for a bigger venue and we didn't really know where to take the show, but we decided it would be easier to starve in Los

Angeles than in New York. It was warmer in L.A. and we figured we could sleep in a park if it came to that. And that's where the entertainment industry was. And by that point we were beginning to see ourselves as wanting to be in show business.

We went to Los Angeles and had dinner with a cousin of ours, Jack Brody, who owned a building on Pico Boulevard, near 20th Century Fox. He and his partners had planned to build a convalescent hospital there, but the market was soft and they'd put the plans on hold, and he said we could use the space. It was perfect. It was huge, and there was an apartment upstairs where we could live, and there was a parking lot across the street that could handle the cars, if we ever got successful enough to have to worry about that.

It took us three months to build the place—David oversaw construction, I did most of the electrical wiring and plumbing, and Jim would cook these great dinners every night. We all worked like dogs, but we had a really fun time doing it.

A week before opening night, we walked around the UCLA campus giving away free tickets. We started out with just two shows, on weekends, but before long we were doing six shows a week—and selling out. It was great. We were four guys not long out of college, and we were making enough money for food and gas and clothes. Best of all, we were having fun.

The show ran for five years, and we were even on *The Tonight Show* a couple of times. By this time, we really didn't know what we wanted to be. We weren't prolific enough for television, and we weren't really performers at heart: We performed because it was cheaper than hiring real actors. But eventually we began hiring people to replace ourselves on stage so we could focus on the writing. For us it was all about developing a really fast pace, and moving from joke to joke, and keeping the audience laughing. Then *The Groove Tube* came out, as a movie, and once again that inspired us to try to turn our own show into a movie. We were always aware that we owed a lot to Ken Shapiro, a true innovator.

One night, we saw John Landis on *The Tonight Show*. He was on the show because he was a twenty-one-year-old kid who had just directed his first film, a low-budget movie called *Schlock*. He was so young that David thought he might actually talk to us, and he called the distributor of his film and got his home number. John was shocked that the distributor would give his number to complete strangers, but after he calmed down he accepted David's invitation to come to our show. He came, and he loved it, and a few days later we took him to lunch and asked him a lot of very naïve questions about the movie business. We knew nothing about how movies got made or what screenplays looked like, and John sent us a screenplay he had just written as a sample. The title was *An American Werewolf in London*. John had written it long before it got made.

After that, we got in touch with Robert K. Weiss, a producer who had seen our show so many times that we had become friends. We got together with him and John and talked about making a movie based on our show, and David and Jim and I went off and wrote the screenplay, about a third of which was taken directly from the show.

When we were done, we took the screenplay to all the studios, and they all turned it down. Then we started looking into alternative sources of financing, from a number of mini-studios and from various production companies, and they all turned it down, too. Finally, we went to people who had tons of money and were thinking of getting into the movie business, and we met a real estate guy who read the script and liked it and said he was interested in financing it. He wasn't willing to finance it entirely on his own, but he said he might foot the bill for ten-minutes worth of film, then take those ten minutes and show them to his friends and try to help us raise the rest of the budget.

This seemed like a great idea, so we put together a budget for the ten minutes—$30,000. But this guy kept hemming and hawing, refusing to commit.

One day, we were sitting in his office, and John Landis was in a chair just in front of me, with his leg perched on his right knee so that I could see the bottom of his shoe. He took a pen and wrote on the sole of his shoe, "This guy is a schmuck."

The real estate guy looked over at him, suddenly concerned. "What are you writing on your shoe?" he asked. " 'This guy's a schmuck'?!"

John was more savvy about the business—Jim and David and I had really wanted to believe it was going to happen—but before long the deal went away. We were crushed, but we still knew it was a good idea, so we pulled together and decided to believe in ourselves. We put up all the money we had, and went to our families for the rest, and we raised the $30,000 we needed for the ten-minute film. We then picked four bits from the script, and—with John Landis directing and Bob Weiss producing—made our sample film.

When we were done, we took it to all the studios in town, and they all turned it down, so we went to Kim Jorgensen, a guy we had known back in Shorewood who had become a very successful theater owner. He seemed kind of vague and flaky and unfocused, but he was very smart, and he invited us to come in and show him our ten-minute film. He loved it—he thought it was hysterical—and he decided to show the film in front of a live audience. He invited us to attend, and even made a little announcement before showing it. "Tonight, ladies and gentlemen, you are going to see a few minutes from a new film, *The Kentucky Fried Movie*. You are the first audience to see the film."

It was a night I will never forget. It was the first time we had seen our jokes on film in front of a live audience, in a real movie theater, and they all laughed. The film *worked*. It was a great feeling; just an amazing high.

Afterwards, Kim said, "Give me a week and I'll get you the money." We signed a deal with him, making him executive producer, and he took the film to his friends at United Artists Theater Circuit, who actually played our film before the scheduled shows. The audience laughed, so the Theater Circuit people decided to finance the rest of the film. If it turned out well, they knew there would be a huge upside for a movie with such a low budget, and even in the worst-case scenario, they could play it in their own theaters and probably recoup their investment.

We made *The Kentucky Fried Movie* for $650,000 and it went onto gross more than $20 million at the box office. We had broken in.

I think one of the reasons we succeeded is that we were persistent, and that seems like good advice—but you can persist and persist and never make it.

I think for anyone trying to break in, it's worth thinking about trying to make a sample of your work with whatever resources you have. Nowadays, with all the equipment out there, you can probably put a short film or video together for a couple of thousand dollars. Not long ago, I read about these guys who made a little film of a plane landing on a freeway. They did the special effects themselves, on their computer. It looked good and it was funny, and it raced around the Internet—so lots of people saw it. That was pretty resourceful, and it got them noticed, and they actually ended up with a film deal.

In the movie business, people would much rather watch a ten-minute DVD than read a 120-page screenplay. And the truth is, most people can't tell from reading a script whether it's good or smart or funny. I mean, every studio that read *Airplane!* turned it down, until we got it to Paramount.

The other thing is to try to get the thing seen and heard, no matter what it takes. I think one of the things that really helped us was performing in front of a live audience. The audience will tell you whether it's working. None of the executives that read our screenplay for *The Kentucky Fried Movie* thought it worked, but it worked in front of an audience. So that's important: Try to get your work in front of an audience. Film is all about communication. If you paint a picture and six people like it, that's fine. But you need a larger audience for a movie. Film is not a medium for a handful of people. It is not about private self-expression. It helps to keep that in mind.

Finally, don't think about what your film will do for you career; think instead about what you are giving the audience, and about how you hope they will respond.

ACKNOWLEDGMENTS

We would like to thank the team at ReganBooks—Judith Regan, Cal Morgan, and Elizabeth Yarborough—for believing in this project from the start, and for their commitment to making it happen. And we would like to thank all of the battle-scarred Hollywood veterans who were generous enough to share their experiences with us: Your stories are the heart and soul of this book.

INDEX OF NAMES